WHO'S WHO IN
AMERICAN
HISTORY

WHO'S WHO IN AMERICAN HISTORY

LEADERS, VISIONARIES, AND ICONS
WHO SHAPED OUR NATION

NATIONAL GEOGRAPHIC

WASHINGTON, D.C.

Contents

(previous pages) Meriwether Lewis and William Clark lead their legendary expedition into new western territories, 1804 to 1806.
(opposite) Future First Couple John and Jackie Kennedy celebrate their engagement, Cape Cod, 1953.

The Citizens of America . . . are, from this period, to be considered as the Actors on a most conspicuous Theatre, which seems to be peculiarly designated by Providence for the display of human greatness and felicity . . . it is in their choice, and depends upon their conduct, whether they will be respectable and prosperous, or contemptable and miserable as a Nation.

GEORGE WASHINGTON, 1783

THE NATION OF MANY NATIONS

AMERICA'S PAST IS PEOPLED WITH DAUNTLESS INDIVIDUALS WHO VENTURED INTO unfamiliar worlds, beginning with the hunter-gatherers who made their way to North America from Asia thousands of years ago. Scant pieces of their lives have been unearthed and they will always be nameless, as will most of the Native Americans who populated the continent when the first Europeans began to filter in during the 16th and 17th centuries. The names of some of the Europeans, though—the conquistadores and colonizers and spiritual seekers—have survived through the centuries to become players in the unfolding American drama.

That drama now spans more than 400 years, during which settlers and politicians, religious leaders and rebels, artists and activists, inventors and entrepreneurs, showmen, scalawags, and sports greats have perpetually redefined the character of American life and propelled the nation in new directions. This book highlights the achievements, life trajectories, and failings of those individuals who have become an iconic part of American history. Owing to space limitations, only a sampling of people who played a key role in that history could be included in the volume.

George Washington, commander in chief of the Continental Army, on Dorchester Heights during the 1776 Siege of Boston—a turning point in America's fight for independence from Britain

A ring excavated at Jamestown, Virginia, the first successful English settlement in America

A New World

The first Europeans to arrive on the continent, mostly English and Spanish, encountered long-established cultures with well-defined traditions, lifestyles, and alliances with or animosities toward one another. Some 500 distinct tribes speaking 300 languages spread across North America at that time, but their people were quickly decimated by European diseases and dislocated by the ever increasing flood of new colonial arrivals, particularly along the eastern seaboard. By the mid-1700s, Britain had established 13 colonies stretching from Georgia to Maine (then part of Massachusetts); Spain claimed Florida, the Southwest, and some of the Pacific coast, while the French had a presence along the Mississippi corridor.

Britain's colonies were disparate in character, but a number of them had been established by religious seekers who saw the New World as a promised land where they could exercise their faith with impunity. All of the colonies, one way or the other, were meant to be profitable ventures for wealthy backers in the Old World. Yet as they became fully established and began to truly prosper, the colonies also began to resent the Old World yoke. In the 1760s, when the British Parliament voted to levy new taxes on the colonies to pay for their governance and protection, the colonists grew ever more resentful of their lack of say in the matter. A few determined men had the audacity to speak out against king and Parliament, and they were gradually echoed by others. By 1776, the 13 colonies of British America had announced their independence from the mother country, fomenting an unprecedented rebellion against the world's mightiest empire. The men who led that rebellion—politically, diplomatically, and militarily—would become celebrated as the nation's Founding Fathers. And when independence was finally—and miraculously—achieved, they went on to fight with one another about how to create a more perfect union, with freedom and justice for all.

An Indian encampment on Lake Huron about 1845, when white encroachment threatened native lifestyles

The promise of freedom and justice was long in coming for the some 700,000 enslaved African Americans who lived in the new republic and were treated as commodities. It was also a promise that did not extend to Native Americans, who found that as the 19th century progressed, they could expect little accommodation from most whites, who believed it was their Manifest Destiny to take control of the continent. Though they attempted to fight off the encroaching white presence, over and over native peoples were forced off their lands and pushed deeper into the continental interior, despite the efforts of implacable native leaders who led courageous but in the end futile wars of resistance.

A drum used by the Gray Reserves, Pennsylvania's First Regiment Infantry, a unit of the Union Army

Disunity and Its Aftermath

By the mid-1800s, the white population itself was far from united. North and South were pulling apart over what was both a deeply human and an economic issue—slavery. Increasingly industrialized and antislavery, the northern states produced politicians and abolitionists who attempted to stop the spread of the vile and "peculiar" institution west, where gold rushes and new agricultural technologies were enticing a flood of new settlers and seekers. Southern politicians responded in kind to the North's seemingly overbearing, anti-southern stance. To the agrarian South, slavery was considered a sacred reality—important to the culture and at the heart of its economic lifeblood, even though only a small percentage of families owned slaves. Despite attempts by cooler-headed politicians at compromise, the conflicted halves of the country grew irretrievably entrenched, and by 1861, 11 southern states had declared their right to leave the United States of America and form their own country—the Confederate States of America.

As with the Revolutionary War, the Civil War produced a remarkable crop of warriors and civilian leaders who would go down in history, but whose abilities and ultimate effectiveness continue to be debated by scholars. But the war also took somewhere between 752,000 and 851,000 lives on the battlefield—the most in American history, as brother fought brother. It also destroyed the lives of others who survived but would never recover from the war's after-effects. The end of the fighting only brought new regional strife, as the South attempted to rebuild itself while still insisting on a kind of residual slavery in the form of Black Codes and sharecropping, and the re-formed nation suffered under inept politicians. The new rulers that emerged were not politicians but captains of industry and finance—railroad barons, bankers, inventors, and steel magnates who ultimately swept America from a largely rural, agrarian world into a more urban age, where electricity, automobiles, and a host of new ways of communicating knit the fabric of the country into a closer weave and at the same time empowered populist journalists, novelists, politicians, labor leaders, and activists to expose and upend the injustices perpetrated on the working classes by the robber barons of the gilded class. And once again, the nation embraced its Manifest Destiny—this time a destiny of empire that reached beyond its own continental shores. Ready for a bigger place at the international table, America began annexing various territories and fighting to take others.

President Abraham Lincoln poses with Gen. George McClellan at his headquarters on the Antietam battlefield in Maryland.

Modern Masters

The coming of the modern age and its innovations made the globe more interconnected, with more intricately intertwined national interests. When Europe became embroiled in the conflagration of a world war, America was eventually pulled into the maelstrom, and new thinkers, commanders, and propagandists emerged to deal with the consequences. Although many European countries joined the League of Nations in the war's aftermath, America hunkered down into isolationism, though it did at last respond to the countless voices of women's rights advocates who for decades had lobbied for suffrage. The 1920 election saw the first time in American history that all women were allowed the vote. Nine years later, the Great Depression struck with a force that defied previous financial panics. Escaping the hard times, at least momentarily, people turned to the most recent marvels of entertainment—the radio, phonograph, and Hollywood spectacles, all of which created their own distinct brand of celebrities. But it was another world war that at last brought about a true boom and a return to the heroes of old—generals, politicians, and the engineers of ever more effective arms. The modern breed of scientists found the ultimate weapon—one of mass destruction.

As the hot war ended, a Cold War ensued, and the nuclear superpowers, America and the U.S.S.R., eyed each other warily and raced to get into space ahead of the other. America's hero of the moment became the astronauts. Its antiheroes were the countless writers, actors, government workers, and others who were accused of communist leanings by, among other organizations, Congress's now notorious House Un-American Activities Committee.

An unprecedented postwar prosperity had fanned the flames of American consumerism, but by the late 1950s and early 1960s the comfortable status quo—romanticized by the wildly popular, latest media, television—slowly gave way to an era of deep activism. African Americans launched a peaceful but defiant rebellion, forcing the nation to look at "separate but equal" for the false proposition that it was and to address the travesties of the Jim Crow South. Women activists, too, pushed for liberation from the traditions of a male-dominated social view. When the country began to slide into another war in Asia, many young men refused to honor the draft, and the country's brash young counterculture scorned middle-class values and celebrated "sex, drugs, and rock-and-roll," making legends of musi-

The iconic photo of U.S. Marines raising the American flag on February 23, 1945, after the critical World War II battle for Iwo Jima, Japan

cians. Meanwhile, assassinations of some of America's greatest figures and inner cities on fire in a rage against social injustice shook the nation at its core. Latino Americans, gay Americans, and Native Americans joined the movement for long-awaited justice as well. In 1973, members of the American Indian Movement occupied the town of Wounded Knee, South Dakota, for two months, demanding that the government honor long-ignored treaty obligations.

Although most of these mid-century movements were continuations of past battles for social justice, a different kind of movement emerged, with strong voices heralding its arrival. Environmentalism made America conscious of the fragility of the natural world and the effects of humankind on it. No longer could Americans blandly assume that nature could cope with excessive human exploitation. Suddenly, it became clear that natural features like the Everglades and a host of animal species could become extinct if they were not overtly protected.

The liberal revolutions of the 1960s and '70s resulted in a conservative backlash, and by 1980, the silent majority had begun to mobilize politically and to speak out in favor of a return to traditional values. Evangelical leaders took to the airwaves and attempted to roll back some of the liberal policies that had characterized the preceding decades. The conflict between conservative and liberal values became the next American battleground that only grew more strident when a farther, more ominous battleground opened on September 11, 2001. That morning al Qaeda terrorists hijacked four passenger planes, crashing one into the Pentagon and two others into the twin towers of the World Trade Center in Manhattan; a fourth crashed into a Pennsylvania field. Six years before, a homegrown terrorist had used a truck bomb to destroy a federal building in Oklahoma. The latest way of war—terrorism—had penetrated American shores and would lead to two more traditional wars of attrition—one in Iraq and another against Islamist factions in Afghanistan.

The threat of terrorism reordered politics and expectations, as did another 21st-century reality—the affordability of the home computer and the subsequent reliance on online communication. The appearance and popularity of the cell phone only solidified that kind of communication, fueling the rise of social media and changing America's human landscape more quickly and radically than anything in the past had ever done. Now politicians, marketers, and interest groups could reach a potential or existing audience with the touch of a button. The nation's new business barons were its tech gurus, and wealth gradually migrated away from a bricks-and-mortar-based economy toward cyberspace.

But a computerized planet also had its dark side. It allowed terrorism to grow and spread in the thickets of the World Wide Web, and it facilitated the convoluted and opaque business transactions that ultimately led to the Great Recession of 2008. Even as the implications of that recession grew—and almost a century and a half after the Emancipation Proclamation—the nation elected its first African-American president. During Barack Obama's two terms in office, the nation further fractured along socioeconomic, values-related, and racial lines. In yet another political backlash, a populist, nationalistic candidate—business magnate Donald J. Trump—emerged to head the Republican ticket in the 2016 presidential election. In contrast, the Democratic Party put forward the first woman ever to be nominated for president by a major political party—Hillary Rodham Clinton. Their unprecedented campaigns pointed to the deep divisions within the American body politic. Trump, seen as the candidate of change against longtime political player Clinton, appealed to disaffection with the status quo and took the race to be America's 45th president.

United Airlines Flight 175, hijacked by terrorists, crashes into the south tower of Manhattan's World Trade Center at 9:03 a.m., September 11, 2001.

Hillary Clinton, first woman to become the presidential nominee of a major American political party, at the Democratic National Convention in Philadelphia on July 28, 2016

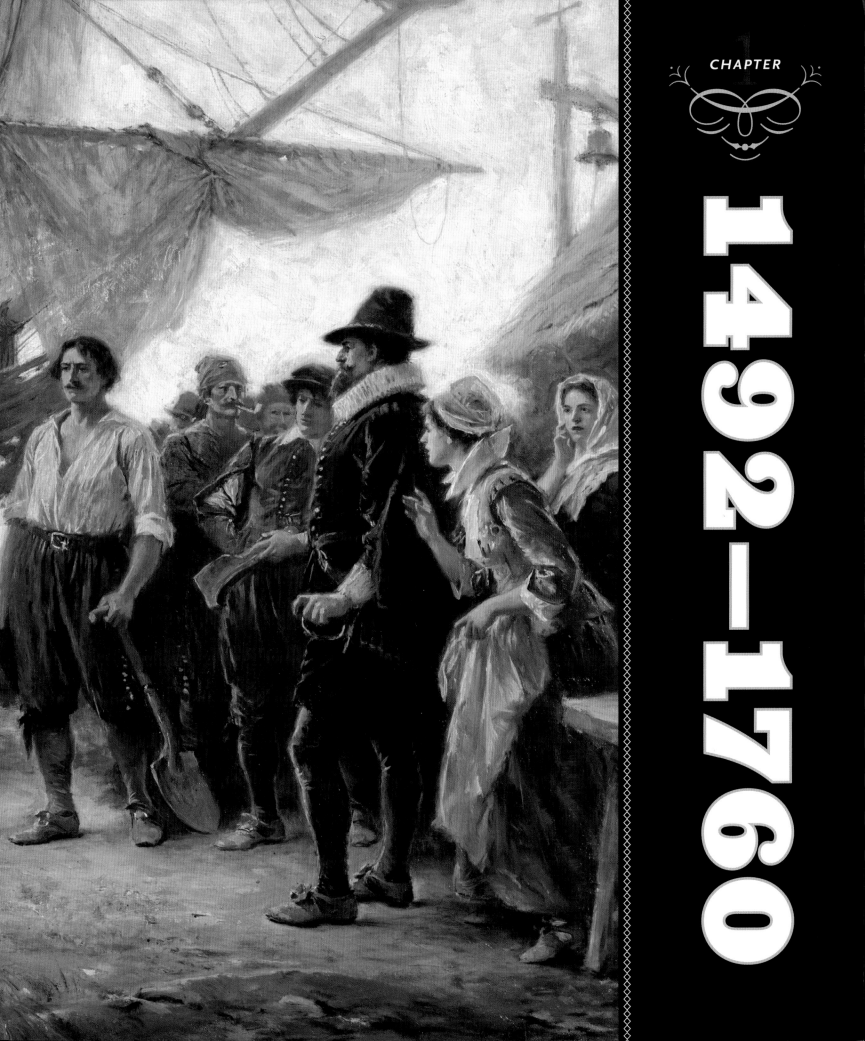

For we must consider that we shall be as a city upon a hill, the eyes of all people are upon us. So that if we shall deal falsely with our God in this work . . . we shall be made a story and a by-word through the world.

JOHN WINTHROP

THE OLD WORLD IN THE NEW

ALTHOUGH THE SECOND MONDAY IN OCTOBER HAS LONG BEEN CELEBRATED as Columbus Day—the day when America was "discovered" by Christopher Columbus's expedition—North America had been home to humans for thousands of years before that. Sometime between 40,000 and 15,000 years ago, the first humans had come to the Americas from Siberia. A long-held theory speculates successive waves of hunter-gatherers crossed a "land bridge" that appeared in the Bering Sea during the last ice age, linking Asia with northern North America. But more recently, scientists have begun to theorize that some intrepid prehistoric pioneers may have come by boat, because by at least 14,500 years ago, it is clear that human habitations were in Chile—a very long way by foot from Alaska. In any case, these paleohumans gradually spread across the continent and developed separate cultures, languages, and alliances. Most subsisted by seasonal farming as well as hunting and gathering, but the centuries-old traditions of the various groups were often shattered when they came in contact with Europeans and their territorial ambitions, hunger for riches, and unknown diseases.

Following in Columbus's wake, Spanish conquistadores explored much of southern North America in the 16th century and established forts and missions (one as far north as Virginia) as outposts from which to pursue their two overriding objectives—to find gold and gems and to convert the native populations to Christianity and exploit them for labor.

(previous pages) Pocahontas, daughter of Chief Powhatan, is abducted by Capt. Samuel Argall (left) for ransom.
(opposite) As the first Pilgrims reconnoiter in Plymouth Harbor, local Indians watch.

Intent on their own empire building, other European nations soon staked claims to various parts of North America—the French in the northeast and down the Mississippi River; the Russians in Alaska and the Pacific Northwest; the English, Dutch, and Swedes along the Atlantic seaboard. The colonists who crossed the Atlantic to establish the first footholds tended to be motivated to take on an unknown wilderness by two aims—either the promise of unprecedented opportunities for a better life in this New World or to escape persecution, political or, more often, religious. Puritans and other Separatists quickly inundated east-central New England in the mid-17th century, while Maryland became a haven for Catholics as well as smaller enclaves of persecuted Christians. Virginia, where England had attempted to establish a "plantation" of Englishness as early as the 1580s, operated as a commerce-driven concern and flourished as such. Each of these fledgling colonies could claim their own strong, visionary, and sometimes controversial leaders, who persevered against the odds to keep their colonies from collapse and, in so doing, forged a name for themselves in history.

As the new mercantilism of Europe and its growing wool trade pushed English tenant farmers off the land in favor of sheep, the displaced saw America as a bright beacon of hope, and English ships sailing for America grew more constant. Over the course of the 17th century, more and more British colonies took root along the eastern seaboard, and the British Empire became the dominant force there, eventually overwhelming the small outposts of other European powers. But Spain, through its network of missions and presidios, continued to hold sway in Florida, the Southwest, and California.

A calendar and astrolabe used by Virginia colonists. Astrolabes allowed mariners to calculate their latitude based on the position of celestial bodies.

Newly arrived colonists celebrate the establishment of Maryland, whose Catholic founders—the Calverts—promised religious freedom to all Christians.

CA 1000	1492	1539–1542	1585–1590	1607
Viking Leif Eriksson lands in northern North America	Columbus arrives in the West Indies and claims it for Spain	Hernando de Soto explores the American Southeast	English settlers establish Roanoke Colony	Jamestown established by Virginia Company colonists

Each new wave of European immigrants arriving in the East took as their due land long held by various native peoples. Powerful chiefs like Metacom in New England and Opechancanough in Virginia waged wars against the interlopers—to little ultimate effect. In Virginia, captured Indians were sometimes kept as slaves, but another group of enslaved humans was rapidly filling Virginia's need for labor in the tobacco fields—Africans who had been taken by force from their homelands or had been born into bondage in the West Indies. They were being imported to replace the indentured Europeans who had once been willing to take such work for sea passage and land in America.

As the first century of American colonization drew to a close, the hunger for slaves grew, fueling an insidious—and lucrative—trade in human beings. That trade soon became wrapped into a complicated network of commerce that moved American exports (flour, fish, furs, meat, lumber, tobacco, rum, and shipbuilding supplies) to Great Britain or the West Indies, whose major exports were slaves and the sugar and molasses needed to make rum. A new class of New England shipping merchants gradually developed around this trade, and the northern ports of Boston, New York, and Philadelphia became dynamic metropolitan centers.

By the beginning of the 1700s, 10 British American colonies were well established: Massachusetts Bay, Connecticut, Rhode Island, New York, Pennsylvania, East and West New Jersey, Maryland, Virginia, and Carolina. Their combined populations hovered at 260,000, but they would grow exponentially in the coming decades—by 1770, to more than two million in 13 colonies. And the port of Charleston, South Carolina, would develop into a colonial powerhouse second only to Philadelphia in wealth and size, thanks to its exports of indigo and rice. South Carolina's low-country rice fields relied on the countless slaves who worked them, and by the mid-1700s, blacks outnumbered whites two to one in the colony.

As the 18th century progressed, each of the colonies of British America increasingly developed its own distinctive culture, and life settled into less a daily struggle for survival and more a struggle to prosper for European Americans (though not for displaced native peoples or enslaved Americans). Throughout the colonies, agriculture provided the main livelihood. Small farms dominated most colonies, but in Virginia and South Carolina vast plantations gave rise to an aristocracy not unlike that of England. Still, land remained plentiful and hopes high. As Peter Kalm, a Swedish traveler to New Jersey, explained in 1748, "It does not seem difficult to find out the reasons why the people multiply faster here than in Europe. As soon as a person is old enough he may marry in these provinces without any fear of poverty. There is such an amount of good land yet uncultivated . . . the taxes are very low, and the liberties he enjoys are so great that he considers himself as a prince in his possessions."

Even in its first century, British America had engendered an expectation of liberty and individualism that broke all the precedents of the Old World. In succeeding generations, those expectations became bred in the bone—concepts worth fighting for.

A Pilgrim gives thanks after making landfall on Cape Cod in 1620. The "Saints"—as they called themselves—established the first English colony in New England.

1620	1630s	1634	1654	1732
Puritan separatists (Pilgrims) settle Plymouth Colony	Puritan Great Migration to New England	The Calvert family establishes colony of Maryland	Roger Williams establishes colony of Rhode Island	James Oglethorpe establishes colony of Georgia

BIOGRAPHIES

CONQUISTADORES, COLONISTS & SEEKERS 1492–1760

The Europeans who braved an ocean crossing for life in an unknown wilderness were a mixed lot. Some were motivated by ambitions for personal glory, and others wanted the opportunity to break free of Old World constraints. Although the courage and resolve of those early colonists cannot be doubted, neither can the valor of Native American leaders who fought to keep the European interlopers from destroying their centuries-old ways of life.

JEFFERY AMHERST
★ 1717–1797 ★
MILITARY COMMANDER OF BRITISH AMERICA

Born in England, Jeffery Amherst sailed to Canada in 1758 to serve as major general in America in the ongoing French and Indian War. His successful Siege of Louisbourg on Cape Breton Island elevated him to commander in chief of British forces in America. In September 1760, he defeated enemy forces at Montreal, and the French surrendered Atlantic Canada. Contemptuous of Native Americans and in charge of British policy toward them, Amherst ordered "measures to be taken as would Bring about the Total Extirpation of those Indian Nations." Those measures included the distribution of smallpox-infected blankets to Indians during the 1763 rebellion led by Chief Pontiac. During the American Revolution, George III several times urged Amherst to take command of British forces fighting in the former colonies, but he refused.

Jeffery Amherst He waged genocide against all Indians.

WILLIAM BRADFORD
★ 1590–1657 ★
LEADER, PLYMOUTH COLONY

As a young English orphan, William Bradford was drawn to one of the Separatist Puritan movements. Fleeing persecution by James I, the Puritans immigrated to the Netherlands until there, too, they were harassed by authorities. They determined to sail for the New World and settle "some place about Hudson's river." Thirty-year-old Bradford was instrumental in planning the undertaking and arrived aboard the *Mayflower* in late 1620. The settlers (now known as Pilgrims) took over a deserted Wampanoag camp on Plymouth Harbor as winter descended. Within five months, half the members of Plymouth Colony were dead of disease and starvation, including the governor. Bradford was elected to replace him and would serve in that capacity, with a few breaks, for 36 years. During that time, he encouraged a liberal, democratic approach to governance, including town meetings and the acceptance of non-Pilgrim groups and individuals into the colony.

CALVERT FAMILY
★ MID-17TH CENTURY ★
FOUNDERS OF MARYLAND

The state of Maryland owes its existence to George Calvert (ca 1582–1632), the First Lord Baltimore, and to his direct descendants. Having been granted the land between the Chesapeake Bay and the Potomac River by Charles I, Calvert, a Catholic, declared it a refuge for other English Catholics. At his death, the charter for the new colony passed to his son Cecilius. Like his father, "Cecil" was committed to the separation of church

George Calvert The English statesman received a royal charter to found Maryland.

and state and to religious tolerance for all Protestants coming to the colony. He appointed his brother Leonard governor of Maryland (named after Charles's Catholic queen, Henrietta Maria), and in 1633, Leonard led the first settlers there, establishing St. Mary's City as their settlement in 1634. In 1649, at the urging of Cecil, in England, the colony's House of Delegates passed the Act Concerning

Religion, which, among other things, declared that no Christian Marylander "be any ways troubled, molested, or discountenanced for or in respect of his or her religion." During the English Civil War, the Calverts twice lost, then regained control of Maryland. A third Calvert brother, Philip, served briefly as proprietary governor from 1660 to 1661. Cecil's son Charles assumed the governorship after Philip, but when Protestant rulers William and Mary ascended the throne, they placed Maryland under a royal governor.

In wilderness he [God] did me guide, And in strange lands for me provide. In fears and wants, through weal and woe, A pilgrim, past I to and fro.

WILLIAM BRADFORD

The Devil's Work
SALEM WITCH TRIALS
★ ★ ★

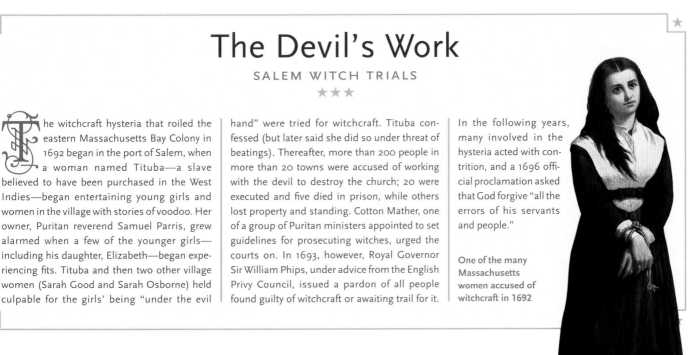

The witchcraft hysteria that roiled the eastern Massachusetts Bay Colony in 1692 began in the port of Salem, when a woman named Tituba—a slave believed to have been purchased in the West Indies—began entertaining young girls and women in the village with stories of voodoo. Her owner, Puritan reverend Samuel Parris, grew alarmed when a few of the younger girls—including his daughter, Elizabeth—began experiencing fits. Tituba and then two other village women (Sarah Good and Sarah Osborne) held culpable for the girls' being "under the evil hand" were tried for witchcraft. Tituba confessed (but later said she did so under threat of beatings). Thereafter, more than 200 people in more than 20 towns were accused of working with the devil to destroy the church; 20 were executed and five died in prison, while others lost property and standing. Cotton Mather, one of a group of Puritan ministers appointed to set guidelines for prosecuting witches, urged the courts on. In 1693, however, Royal Governor Sir William Phips, under advice from the English Privy Council, issued a pardon of all people found guilty of witchcraft or awaiting trail for it.

In the following years, many involved in the hysteria acted with contrition, and a 1696 official proclamation asked that God forgive "all the errors of his servants and people."

One of the many Massachusetts women accused of witchcraft in 1692

Christopher Columbus On October 12, 1492, his expedition made landfall in the West Indies.

CHRISTOPHER COLUMBUS

★ CA 1451–1506 ★

EXPLORER

Columbus's coat of arms referenced his fame.

Little else is known of the early life of the man who would change the face of the world except that he was Genoese by birth and later became a merchant sailor. Columbus eventually settled in Lisbon, Portugal, where his brother Bartholomew lived, and like him, became a maker of navigational charts. But Christopher continued as a seafaring merchant as well, sailing as far west as Iceland and south down the coast of West Africa.

As the age of discovery caught fire and Portugal and other western European countries engaged in a race to find a faster sea route to the Far East, the idea of sailing west rather than east to get there caught hold. Columbus approached Portugal's John II, seeking funding for an exploratory Atlantic crossing to find the legendary Cipangu (Japan) that Marco Polo had described as an island of "endless gold." Rebuffed by King John, Columbus approached Spain's King Ferdinand and Queen Isabella in the mid-1480s and was initially rejected. But with the help of allies who had the monarchs' ear, Columbus finally received funding for his voyage in January 1492.

On August 3, Columbus's small fleet—the *Niña, Pinta,* and *Santa María*—set sail, and two months later, on October 12, made landfall on what was probably San Salvador, in the Bahamas. Columbus spent little time there, anxious to move on to cities of gold. By month's end, the Spanish had landed on what is now Cuba, and Columbus believed he had reached Cathay (China), but he continued exploring. Pushed by winds toward a Taíno Indian island (Haiti), he at last found gold, christened the island Hispaniola, and established a makeshift base before sailing for Spain with his riches. On the return journey, weather forced him to put in at a Portuguese port, where he was briefly imprisoned and debriefed by John II. This cast a lasting pall on Columbus in Spain, but his cargo—gold, Indians, and spices—convinced Ferdinand and Isabella to continue their support.

As admiral of the Indies, Columbus made three more voyages to the Caribbean, in 1493, 1498, and 1502. Over the 10 years of his expeditions, his men, including his brothers Bartholomew and Diego, enslaved the Taíno and either exported them or forced them to work in gold mines. Spanish contact also spread diseases that decimated the native population.

In 1500, Columbus was arrested by his own men for his autocratic rule and returned to Spain in chains. But he had written to Ferdinand and Isabella, describing how his ships had climbed upward on his last voyage west, moving toward the heights of an "Earthy Paradise," from which rivers ran into the sea, and the Spanish monarchs sent him on a fourth and final voyage.

For centuries, Columbus was credited with having "discovered" the New World. It is clear, however, that Viking chieftain Leif Eriksson arrived in northern North America 500 years before Columbus, and today, Columbus's legacy is much tarnished by the destruction of native cultures, both advertent and inadvertent, that followed in his wake.

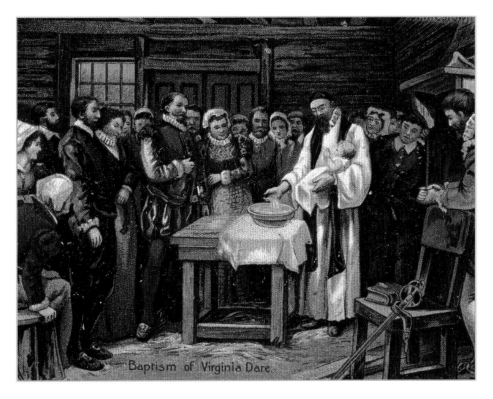

Baptism of Virginia Dare.

Virginia Dare Her 1587 christening at Roanoke Colony, in what is now North Carolina, marked a historic moment as she was the first English child born in North America.

> *Offend not the poore Natives, but as you partake in their land, so make them partakers of your precious faith: as you reape their temporalls, so feede them with your spirituals.*
>
> JOHN COTTON

JOHN COTTON

★ 1585–1652 ★

PURITAN LEADER

A respected Anglican theologian, the charismatic John Cotton began introducing Puritan ideas and rituals into his services at St. Botolph's church in Boston, Lincolnshire, where he was vicar for 21 years (1612–1632). He and Puritan leader John Winthrop had long been in contact, and Cotton delivered a soaring sermon to the first Puritans departing for the New World. When authorities in England began to maneuver against him for his Puritan views, Cotton sailed for Boston, where he became a leading minister in the First Church of Boston. His writings and piety inspired many in the Massachusetts Bay Colony, but Cotton was also embroiled in the religious controversies surrounding the banishment of Roger Williams and the official rejection of the antinomians, a dissident group led by Anne Hutchinson. Breaking with the teachings of the Puritan fathers, antinomians believed a person must have a direct experience of God to be saved.

John Cotton An early Puritan leader in Massachusetts

VIRGINIA DARE

★ 1587–?? ★

FIRST ENGLISH AMERICAN

Virginia Dare was the first English child born in the Americas, the daughter of Ananias and Eleanor Dare. The couple had joined the small band of colonists who arrived in what is now North Carolina to establish Roanoke Colony, a venture championed by Sir Walter Raleigh and endorsed by Elizabeth I. Virginia was born one month after Eleanor's arrival on Roanoke Island in 1587. Nine days later, John White, the colony's governor, and Eleanor's father departed for England to request more aid. His return was delayed, and when he finally arrived back at Roanoke Island, all of the colonists had disappeared. Their fate remains unknown.

JUAN DE OÑATE
★ CA 1550–1630 ★
CONQUISTADOR

The son of Spanish aristocrats living in New Spain (Mexico), Juan de Oñate spent his early adulthood protecting his family's silver mines and wresting territory in northern Mexico from native peoples to expand the Spanish hold on the area. In 1595, King Philip II placed de Oñate in charge of an expedition to explore north into what is now the American Southwest and to spread Catholicism to the American Indians there.

Hoping to find silver deposits as well, he and several hundred settlers set out in early 1598, and by summer had crossed the Rio Grande near present-day El Paso.

He claimed the area north of the river for Spain, calling it New Mexico, and the Spanish began establishing settlements there. In a letter to the pious Philip, de Oñate justified Spain's right and duty to the territory in part because of "the need for correcting and punishing the sins against nature and against humanity which exist among these bestial [Indian] nations." In the coming years, the Spanish subdued the native populations, extracting tributes and brutalizing Indians who would not comply. De Oñate also dealt harshly with disillusioned Spanish settlers who tried to return to Mexico. He was eventually tried and convicted for his cruelty and other crimes as governor of New Mexico and exiled for the rest of his life. He lived the remainder of his years in Spain.

HERNANDO DE SOTO
★ 1496/97–1542 ★
CONQUISTADOR

Hernando de Soto arrived in Spanish America in 1514 and explored parts of Central America before joining Francisco Pizarro's expedition to search for gold in the Andes. He returned to Spain a rich man, and after several years in Seville, he convinced Charles V to name him governor of Cuba and adelantado of Florida, an as-yet unconquered territory to the north of the Caribbean. De Soto financed his own expedition to the area in 1538 and arrived in Santiago de Cuba. In May of the following year, he set sail for Florida with almost 600 settlers and landed near present-day Tampa, Florida. For most of the next year, the Spanish explored northwest Florida, constantly battling the native peoples they encountered. Hoping to keep the Spanish moving away from their own territories, the natives told them tales of rich cities farther on.

By 1540, de Soto had made his way through the Southeast. Though his exact route is unknown, many scholars believe it took him into central Georgia and the Carolinas, then into south Alabama, where local tribes put up a fierce resistance to the conquistadores' presence. Despite his men's exhaustion, and knowing of their plots to abandon his expedition and return to ships waiting along the

Juan de Oñate The expedition led by the Spanish aristocrat arrives at El Paso del Norte in 1598, claiming this area north of the Rio Grande for Spain.

Hernando de Soto The first Europeans to reach the Mississippi River, de Soto's conquistadores explored its lower reaches during an expedition through southeastern North America from 1540 to 1542.

coast, de Soto pushed on into the northwestern corner of Arkansas, where his force spent the winter of 1541–42. He moved south again in the spring, into Louisiana and Texas. Later that spring, somewhere along the Mississippi River, de Soto died of fever.

JONATHAN EDWARDS
★ 1703–1758 ★
PHILOSOPHER, THEOLOGIAN

Educated at Yale, Jonathan Edwards at first resisted the Calvinism he had grown up with. But after an epiphany, he heartily joined the faith and eventually apprenticed as assistant minister to his grandfather Solomon Stoddard, at a church in Northampton, Massachusetts. Stoddard himself was a reformer, and Edwards followed in his footsteps. His

dispassionate yet moving sermons and writings extolled God's sovereignty and the beauty of his creation, and Edwards's justification of emotions, not solely intellect, in spiritual pursuits helped lead to the revivalist spirit of the first Great Awakening that swept through New England. He is considered one of America's greatest and most original philosophical theologians.

The Three Sisters
CORN, BEANS, AND SQUASH
★★★

The Iroquois, or Haudenosaunee, whose territories stretched from the Great Lakes south, relied on an innovative agricultural system that involved planting the "three sisters"—corn, beans, and squash—together, so that the cornstalks would act as supports for the climbing bean vines, and the squash would thrive as a ground crop in the semi-shade beneath them. The combination of the three species also helped ensure soil fertility and moisture. An acre planted in the three sisters yielded more than 10 times what European farmers were able to harvest from an acre planted in Old World techniques. Food stability allowed the Iroquois peoples to thrive, and in the mid-15th century, five tribes formed the Iroquois League, a confederation that promoted peace and cultural ties among the tribes and gave them dominion over a wide swath of land that extended south from Lake Ontario and from Lake Erie to the Hudson River in the west.

Autumn corn

Jonathan Edwards A towering intellect, the Calvinist theologian was a driving force behind the revivalism of America's first Great Awakening.

ANNE HUTCHINSON
★ CA 1591–1643 ★
PURITAN DISSIDENT

Anne Hutchinson, a devoted follower of Puritan leader John Cotton, arrived in Boston in 1634 with her husband, William, and their more than a dozen children, and quickly became a respected member of the Puritan community. Her father, Anglican clergyman Francis Marbury, had been an outspoken English clergyman, and though Hutchinson pursued the traditional woman's role of wife, nurse, and midwife, her inquiring mind led her to begin holding meetings in her home to discuss the teachings of John Cotton. Puritan leader John Winthrop, who was her neighbor, pronounced her "a woman of haughty and fierce carriage, of a nimble wit and active spirit, and a very voluble tongue, more bold than a man."

As Hutchinson's meetings attracted ever more people, Winthrop and other male leaders of the community began to take exception. Hutchinson only

Pedro Menéndez de Avilés Conquistadores led by Menéndez land on Florida's east coast in 1565 and establish a presidio on the site of present-day St. Augustine, claiming the area for Spain.

Now if you do condemn me for speaking what in my conscience I know to be truth I must commit myself unto the Lord.

ANNE HUTCHINSON

exacerbated them further by insisting to her gatherings that salvation came from divine grace, not the good works that she contended the Puritan fathers preached. In propounding her Covenant of Grace, she claimed that God had communicated with her through divine revelations. In 1637, she was banished from the colony for her heretical ideas, and she and her husband settled in nearby Providence Plantations, established by another banished Puritan, Roger Williams. After the death of her husband, she moved to New Netherland (New York) and was killed in an Indian raid.

PEDRO MENÉNDEZ DE AVILÉS
★ 1519–1574 ★
COLONIZER OF SPANISH FLORIDA

Spain's Philip II dispatched an expedition led by Pedro Menéndez de Avilés to Florida in 1565, with instructions to drive out the French and establish a colony there. The expedition landed on the shores of present-day Matanzas Bay in September, and Menéndez founded the Presidio of San Agustín near the site where Ponce de León had landed in 1513. St. Augustine, as it became known, served as the territorial capital and a stronghold that allowed Spain to control trade routes to and from Europe. Menéndez also explored the Atlantic coast and established a string of forts north to South Carolina's St. Helena Island.

Artifacts of the Timucua people of Florida and Georgia. Their 1,000-year-old way of life was upended after European contact.

Anne Hutchinson Her dissident Puritan movement threatened established church leaders.

METACOM

★ CA 1639–1676 ★

WAMPANOAG LEADER

Metacom—or King Philip, as he is also known—was a leader of the Wampanoag people in the Plymouth Bay area at a time when tensions with European settlers were mounting. Metacom's father, Chief Massasoit, had established friendly relations with the initial Pilgrim settlers and had shown the settlers how to farm productively in New England. But with the increasing influx of European migrants, the Wampanoag and other tribes in the region lost territory and independence. In June 1675, three Wampanoag men were hanged for a murder they did not commit. As a result, tensions increased, leading Metacom to head an uprising against the whites. Soon, other tribes in the region that had traditionally been rivals with one another joined in a confederation with the Wampanoag in what became known as King Philip's War. The

Peter Minuit In 1626, the Dutch governor general is believed to have bought Manhattan Island from Indians.

brutal, yearlong conflict "was attended by inexpressible calamities, each party making every possible effort for the total overthrow of its antagonist," wrote colonist James Thacher. In the end, the English prevailed. Metacom was killed and his head displayed on a pike in Plymouth. His wife and child, like other captives from the war, were sold into slavery in the West Indies, and Wampanoag hegemony was destroyed.

PETER MINUIT

★ CA 1580–1638 ★

GOVERNOR GENERAL OF NEW NETHERLAND

Either Walloon or French by birth, Peter Minuit became a successful merchant and joined the Dutch West India Company in the 1620s. The company sent him to New Netherland in 1625 to ascertain

its potential for exports other than animal pelts. A year later he was made the third governor general of the new colony, the only Dutch holding in North America. That same year, Minuit is believed to have purchased what is now the island of Manhattan from Native Americans for the equivalent of 60 guilders, roughly $24. (Exactly how the trade transpired remains unclear.) Minuit's roughly seven years as governor general were a peaceful time for the colony in its relations with New England settlements and local tribes. Why Minuit did not serve longer is unknown, but after he was relieved of his position, he began working with the Swedish to help establish a colony in North America. New Sweden, as it was called, was laid out near present-day Wilmington, Delaware, on territory claimed by the Dutch. As in the case of Manhattan, Minuit met with local native chiefs to "purchase" the land with European goods.

Metacom Also known as King Philip, he led a war against New England colonists in 1675.

CHRISTOPHER NEWPORT
★ 1561–1617 ★
A FOUNDER OF JAMESTOWN COLONY

Christopher Newport had a well-established reputation as an English adventurer and privateer when the Virginia Company chose him to lead a voyage to the New World in 1606. In 1607, his ships, the *Susan Constant, Godspeed,* and *Discovery,* reached the mouth of a bay they named the Chesapeake, sailed up a river they christened the James (after James I), and established the fort of Jamestown. In the coming years, Newport made the Atlantic voyage several times between England and the struggling colony, resupplying it. During his time in Virginia, he attempted to establish good relations with the Powhatan Indians and explored the area. He went on to serve with the East India Company, making several trips to Asia.

Susan Constant, one of three ships that carried the first settlers to Jamestown

James Oglethorpe Founder of Georgia

JAMES OGLETHORPE
★ 1696–1785 ★
FOUNDER OF GEORGIA

As a young man, James Oglethorpe fought the Turks in central Europe before returning to England to run successfully for the House of Commons. While he was serving in Parliament, a friend died in debtor's prison from smallpox, and the death led him to become a national champion of prison reform and a leading English humanitarian. Sympathetic to the hopeless conditions of England's "worthy poor," Oglethorpe and several colleagues contemplated the creation of a new American colony, where such people could become merchants, farmers, and artisans.

In 1732, at Oglethorpe's urging, George II granted a charter for the first new colony in North America in five decades. The next year, Oglethorpe led some 100 colonists to Georgia, where they laid out the town of Savannah on bluffs above a river by the same name. Still pursuing his humanitarian instincts, Oglethorpe treated tribes respectfully; welcomed Jews, Lutherans, and other persecuted religious minorities to the colony; and opposed slavery. He also defended the new colony from the Spanish, and when he returned to England in 1743, Georgia was flourishing.

OPECHANCANOUGH
★ ??–1646 ★
POWHATAN CHIEF

Opechancanough was the brother (or cousin) of the powerful Powhatan, chief of the Tsenacomoco Indians of coastal Virginia when the English established a struggling foothold in the New World at Jamestown. As Powhatan's power receded, Opechancanough became a greater force, working to consolidate the various tribes against the growing English presence, and at the same time, skillfully misleading the English as to his intent. On March 22, 1622, his planning came to brutal fruition, as Native Americans launched a well-coordinated assault at a number of locations, killing more than 300 colonists and burning homes to the ground. The Second Anglo-Powhatan War terrorized the English population of coastal Virginia for a year. When chieftains and English officials met, purportedly to discuss peace, the English served the Indians tainted wine and then fired on them. Opechancanough was wounded in the betrayal.

In the coming two decades, white settlers spread throughout Virginia's Tidewater region, claiming Native American territory as their own. Again, Opechancanough acted, planning a consolidated attack involving several tribes. They struck on April 18, 1644, killing some 400 colonists and setting off a third Anglo-Powhatan war. This one lasted two years and ended with Opechancanough's capture. Transported to Jamestown, he was fatally shot by a guard.

A Timeless Place

RE-CREATING THE PAST AT COLONIAL WILLIAMSBURG

★ ★ ★

In 1698, fire destroyed colonial Virginia's statehouse in Jamestown, and the capital was moved five miles inland to the hamlet of Middle Plantation, home to the newly established College of William and Mary. Royal Governor Francis Nicholson laid out a gridded baroque town there, anchored at one end by the college and at the other by the colonial capitol. Duke of Gloucester Street connected the two, and the governor's palace sat between them, fronting a broad green. Virginia's planters soon built elegant townhomes in Williamsburg (named for William III), and it became a seat of learning, commerce, and government, though lacking a port, never a major metropolis.

Williamsburg also became a hotbed of resistance and the scene of great history, thanks to the presence of the college and capitol. Among the luminaries who gathered, studied, or lived in Williamsburg were Thomas Jefferson, George Washington, Patrick Henry, James Madison, George Wythe, George Mason, and members of the Lee and Randolph families. These revolutionaries openly opposed British taxation and oppression of its American colonies and would become the Founding Fathers of a new nation.

In 1780, the capital shifted to Richmond, and over the ensuing 150 years, Williamsburg's 17th-century buildings fell to time or were embellished with modern features. But in the 1930s, the rector of historic Bruton Parish Church, W. A. R. Goodwin, convinced philanthropist John D. Rockefeller, Jr., to restore the town. Today, Colonial Williamsburg reigns as one of the world's preeminent historic sites, with more than 130 colonial buildings, spread over 300 acres, painstakingly reconstructed or restored, with ongoing archaeological excavations and reconstructions.

The Wren Building at the College of William and Mary ranks as the oldest academic structure now in use in America. Initial construction began in 1695, though fire damaged the Wren in ensuing centuries. Today, it looks as it did in 1732.

WILLIAM PENN
★ 1644–1718 ★
FOUNDER OF PENNSYLVANIA

Son of famous British admiral Sir William Penn, William Penn the younger suffered his family's and society's opprobrium when he joined the Society of Friends in the 1660s. Yet that did not deter him, and he published a number of pamphlets and broadsheets on the Quaker religion and traveled through Europe spreading its beliefs. In the late 1660s, he was briefly imprisoned in the Tower of London for his proselytizing, yet there he wrote perhaps his most famous work, *No Cross, No Crown.* In 1670, his father died, leaving Penn his estates and connections, and Penn became a regular at the court of Charles II. In 1681, in cancellation of a debt owed to Admiral Penn, Charles granted Penn's son a vast holding in America on the west side of the Delaware River, insisting that it be named Pennsylvania, after the admiral.

Penn planned a "holy experiment"—in Christian tolerance and equality, and he created a Frame of Government that ensured no leader would have the "power of doing mischief, that the will of one man may not hinder the good of a whole country." Penn also designed a layout for the colony's first city—Philadelphia, whose name means brotherly love—and when he arrived in 1682, he purchased a

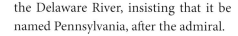

A doll that belonged to Penn's daughter, Letitia

> *Let the people think they Govern and they will be Govern'd. This cannot fail if Those they Trust, are Trusted.*
>
> **WILLIAM PENN**

tract for the city on the banks of the Schuylkill River from Lenape Indians. When he left two years later to return to his family and the needs of the Society of Friends in England, Philadelphia was flourishing spectacularly.

Once home, Penn was again caught up in British politics and accused of treason by the new king, William. He briefly lost proprietorship of the colony until his name was restored, but his clear title to the colony had become muddied. When Penn returned to Pennsylvania for two years in 1699, he found rifts within the colony's administration and its regions. Despite that, Philadelphia was thriving and had doubled in size to 5,000 people, making it second only to Boston in population.

Yet the colony's proprietary confusion and administrative malfeasances eventually led Penn into crippling debt and doubt, causing him to lament, "O Pennsylvania! what hast thou cost me?" He attempted to sell the colony to the crown, but he suffered a series of strokes from which he never recovered before negotiations were finalized. Proprietorship of Pennsylvania remained in the hands of the Penn family until the American Revolution.

PENNS TREATY with the INDIANS, made 1681 without an Oath, and never broken. The foundation of Religious and Civil LIBERTY, in the U.S. of AMERICA.

William Penn Legend records that he made a "memorable treaty" with various Delaware chiefs in 1683.

Pocahontas and John Rolfe The marriage of the young Native American woman and the English planter in 1614 engendered the "Peace of Pocahontas" between Indians and colonists.

POCAHONTAS

★ CA 1596–1617 ★

TSENACOMOCO WOMAN

Pocahontas, a Tsenacomoco woman intrigued by Virginia's first English settlers, is perhaps one of the most romantic figures in early American history, but the details of her life remain wrapped in legend. Her father, Powhatan, was the head of an alliance of Algonquian-speaking Indians in coastal Virginia when the English arrived and established Jamestown, and as a girl, Pocahontas was in attendance at various meetings among the English and Indians. Several accounts of the era mention her, most notably those of John Smith, who claimed Pocahontas had saved his life when he was taken captive by her people. (Historians now discount that story as well as others that describe her role as a diplomat to the English.)

Sometime after 1610, she is believed to have married an Indian warrior. In April 1613, the English took her prisoner and held her at Jamestown, demanding a ransom from her father. During the following year in semicaptivity, she was introduced to Christianity and fell in love with a widower named John Rolfe. The two were married in April 1614, with Powhatan's imprimatur. The marriage helped bring about what has been called the "Peace of Pocahontas," ending the fighting that had erupted between Powhatan's confederation and the settlers.

Rebecca (the Christian name given her at her baptism) Rolfe was invited to London by the Virginia Company and arrived with her husband and their son in the fall of 1616. The company hoped that her celebrity would allow them to raise further funds for the colony, and with this in mind, they created an engraving of her, dressed in the English clothes she then wore. She briefly became the darling of English society and met twice with King James I. However, she apparently became disillusioned with English society, and when her old friend John Smith finally met with her in January 1617, he said she ended their conversation with, "Your countrymen will lie much."

Having received a substantial grant from the Virginia Company to start a mission in America, the Rolfes sailed for home later that year. But as their ship moved down the Thames, Pocahontas fell fatally ill, possibly from hemorrhagic dysentery. She was buried at St. George's Church in Gravesend, England.

Pocahontas (Rebecca Rolfe) Shown here in Anglicized dress

POWHATAN (WAHUNSONACOCK)
★ ??-1618 ★
CHIEF OF POWHATAN CONFEDERATION

A member of the Tsenacomoco tribe, Wahunsonacock inherited the role of Powhatan—primary chief of a confederation of Algonquian-speaking tribes in southeastern Virginia. Through diplomacy and a sometimes brutal use of force, he had expanded it to roughly 30 tribes and some 15,000 people by 1607, the year the English arrived in the area. His principal residence at that time was at Werowocomoco, on the York River about 15 miles from Jamestown.

> *If your king have sent me presents, I also am a king, and this my land.*
>
> **POWHATAN TO JOHN SMITH, ACCORDING TO AN ENGLISH ACCOUNT**

Powhatan initially maintained cordial relations with the English, intent on learning their plans but wary of a prophesy he shared with John Smith—that strangers would arrive from the lower Chesapeake Bay and destroy his people. Smith described Powhatan as a "tall well proportioned man, with a sour look . . . his age near 60." At an audience with Powhatan, Smith said "this proud savage, having his finest women, and the principle of his chiefe men assembled, sat . . . as upon a Throne . . . with such a Majesty as I cannot express, nor yet have often seen, either in Pagan or Christian." When the English continued their inroads into

Powhatan The powerful chief of a confederation of tribes in the Chesapeake holds court among his other chiefs. When John Smith visited him in such a setting, the Englishman was impressed by Powhatan's regal bearing.

his territory without his consent, Powhatan grew ever more wary, particularly of Smith, whom he wanted killed. Smith returned safely to England in 1609, but by then the enmity between colonists and Indians had escalated into violence.

A seven-year peace ensued after one of Powhatan's favorite daughters, Pocahontas, married Englishman John Rolfe, sealing an alliance between the interlopers and Powhatan's confederation. When she died in England in 1617, reports indicate that Powhatan was deeply affected and died himself soon after. The mantle of power initially passed to an ineffective younger brother and then to Opechancanough, who would wage a losing war against the white population.

JOHN ROLFE

★ CA 1585–1622 ★

TOBACCO PIONEER,
HUSBAND OF POCAHONTAS

John Rolfe could be said to have saved the Virginia colony in a few ways. He arrived in Jamestown in 1610, when the fledgling colony was foundering, in part because it had found no lucrative export to ensure the Virginia Company's continued financial support. Rolfe began experimenting with cultivating "Spanish" tobacco *(Nicotiana tabacum)*, with seeds he had gotten from Trinidad. His first shipment to England in 1613 was well received but not considered as good as Spanish tobacco. In the same year, Rolfe met the adolescent daughter of Powhatan, who was being held captive in Jamestown. The following year, the two married, with Rolfe writing he did so "for the good of this plantation, for the honour of our countrie, for the glory of God, for my own salvations." Rolfe's hopes were realized: Pocahontas was baptized as Rebecca, and their marriage ended hostilities between the Powhatan confederation and the English for a number of years. Then in 1617, a shipment of 20,000 pounds of Rolfe's version of Spanish tobacco was enthusiastically received in England. Tobacco was soon growing on every available plot of land in the colony, sealing the fate of Virginia.

Yet 1617 also saw tragedy for Rolfe. The year before, he and Pocahontas and their young son, Thomas, had sailed to England as guests of the Virginia Company. As the family began their return voyage to America, Pocahontas died of a sudden illness while the ship was still in the Thames. Rolfe left Thomas in England and returned to Virginia and his duties as secretary and recorder general of the colony. He became a member of the governor's council and a planter. Thomas joined his father years later.

John Rolfe Rolfe and Pocahontas married in 1614 in Jamestown. Though she had converted to Christianity, the pious Rolfe worried about the biblical warning against "marrying strange wives."

"This Filthie Smoake"

TOBACCO'S MIXED LEGACY

★★★

Tobacco was initially introduced to Europe in the mid-1500s by the Spanish, who had brought back a Brazilian version of it *(Nicotiana tabacum)*. It was soon much sought after, initially for its purported medicinal properties, then for recreational use. But James I detested "this filthie smoake," believing it dangerous to the brain and lungs.

The early colonists to Virginia found that the Powhatan Indians used another tobacco *(N. rustica)*, which proved too harsh for European tastes. John Rolfe's 1612 discovery that he could grow the sought-after *N. tabacum* in Virginia changed the course of history. By 1630, the colony was exporting half a million pounds of tobacco to Europe.

Tobacco proved both blessing and curse to the Virginia colony. It made it a profitable concern at last, but it was a greedy crop, quickly depleting the soil of nutrients and requiring ever more land to be cleared. And it required backbreaking labor to sow, weed, and harvest. Initially, Virginia planters imported indentured white servants as laborers, but by 1700, African slaves dominated the tobacco fields. Tobacco set Virginia firmly on the road to the slave economy that would see generations of humans live in bondage.

Drying tobacco

discount). That same year, Smith was both briefly imprisoned in Jamestown and then made president of the governing council. Disgruntled by his fellow colonists' laxity in securing the stockaded village and in planting crops for survival, Smith declared, "He that will not work shall not eat." That only added to his unpopularity, as did his mixed

The men bestowe their times in fishing, hunting, wars, and such . . . The women and children do the rest of the worke. They make mats, baskets, pots, morters; pound their corne . . . prepare their victuals, plant their corne, gather their corne, beare al kind of burdens.

JOHN SMITH

John Smith A 19th-century painting depicts a romanticized scene of John Smith teaching Pocahontas to read.

JOHN SMITH
★ 1580–1631 ★
PRESIDENT OF JAMESTOWN COLONY

At a young age, this son of an English yeoman farmer became a soldier and adventurer, fighting in various parts of Europe, usually against the Ottoman Turks. In 1602, John Smith was wounded, captured, and sold into slavery in Turkey. After killing his master, he made his way back to England, where he was soon caught up in the plans of the Virginia Company to establish a new colony in America. In 1606, he sailed as a colonist aboard the *Susan Constant*. En route, he was arrested and put in irons, by his own account for plotting to "usurpe the governement, murder the Councell [of the colony], and make himselfe kinge." But he was released, because he had been named to the colony's seven-man governing council by the Virginia Company, who had instructed that the council members were to be announced only after the expedition reached America.

Smith remained a contentious figure during his brief time in Virginia. His braggadocio offended the other colonists, who may also have resented his survival skills and military experience, both of which proved vital. He was charged with trading with the Indians, and his initial relations with Powhatan, powerful chief of the region, were good—though he would later write that in 1607 he had been saved from death at Powhatan's hands by the chief's young daughter Pocahontas (a story historians now

relations with the Powhatan: Although he both admired and probably understood their culture better than the other colonists, he could be duplicitous and violent in his dealings with them.

In September 1609, Smith was severely injured when, traveling on the James, his gunpowder bag blew up, ignited by a match. Some historians believe the "accident" was a planned attempt to murder the much disliked Smith. He was removed as president of the colony and sent back to London. Perhaps the loss of Smith's brash but considerable leadership contributed to the tragedy the following winter—the "starving time," when 180 of the 240 colonists died.

Smith spent the next several years writing about Virginia (he had explored some 2,500 miles along the Chesapeake Bay and its tributaries and created a *Map of Virginia*). He returned to America in 1614 and 1615 to explore the coast well north of Virginia for a wealthy merchant. Smith named the area New England. In 1616, he was visited in England by Pocahontas—the Powhatan girl whom he had befriended and who had subsequently become a darling of the British aristocracy—but the visit was strained. Despite his problems, Smith's writings and maps of Virginia and New England remain critical historical documents, and his determination and leadership probably saved Jamestown from becoming no more than a historical footnote.

Fragment of a pear tree
from Peter Stuyvesant's farm

PETER STUYVESANT

★ CA 1592–1672 ★

DIRECTOR GENERAL
OF NEW NETHERLAND

A staunch adherent to the Dutch Reformed Church, Peter Stuyvesant became director general of the Dutch colony on the Hudson River—New Netherland—in 1647. The "peg-legged" Stuyvesant (he had lost a leg fighting in the Caribbean) proved to be an autocratic ruler, intolerant of those who did not follow the Dutch Reformed Church. He also exacerbated ongoing disputes with Connecticut over boundaries and lost territory for the Dutch colony as a result. Stuyvesant did, however, lead a successful invasion of New Sweden and claimed its territories along the Delaware River for the Dutch. He also brought in considerable profits from trade. Yet Stuyvesant's own disgruntled population became so disaffected with his leadership and the policies of the West India Company that they put up no resistance to a British demand to surrender New Netherland. After a brief return to Holland in 1665, Stuyvesant spent the rest of his life on his New Netherland's farm, the "Bouwerie"—the area of lower Manhattan now known as the Bowery.

Peter Stuyvesant The weak and contentious Dutch director general lost Manhattan to the British. A deed bears Stuyvesant's signature.

MYLES STANDISH

★ CA 1584–1656 ★

MILITARY LEADER
OF PLYMOUTH COLONY

While serving with Elizabeth I's army in Holland, Myles Standish was approached by Separatists (Pilgrims) in exile there to serve as military captain or adviser to their new colony. He sailed aboard the *Mayflower* in 1620 and remained the military leader of the Plymouth Colony for the rest of his life, launching strikes against local American Indians when he suspected brewing hostility. In 1858, Henry Wadsworth Longfellow's poem, *The Courtship of Miles Standish,* earned Standish a place in American history—though the details of the poem are believed to be strictly fiction.

ROGER WILLIAMS

★ CA 1603–1683 ★

FOUNDER OF RHODE ISLAND

A pioneer of religious freedom, Roger Williams was initially attracted to Puritan tenets as a young man in London. There, he served as chaplain in the household of William Masham and was exposed to such Puritan activists as Oliver Cromwell, John Winthrop, and John Cotton. In 1631, he emigrated to the Massachusetts Bay Colony but once there, he found himself at odds with Puritan fathers, who had not separated officially from the Church of England.

Williams refused a position as a pastor in Boston. He moved to nearby Salem, where he again clashed with local Puritan leaders over beliefs; then he briefly settled with the avowed Separatists of the Plymouth Colony. But there, his beliefs that Indian lands must be purchased directly from the tribe (rather than taken under the imprimatur of the king's charter to the colony) again set him at odds with his fellow colonists. He returned to Salem for three years, but his outspoken religious ideas ultimately led to his banishment from the Massachusetts Bay Colony, whose authorities planned to exile him back to England.

Warned of their plans by Puritan leader John Winthrop, Williams fled the colony in January 1636 and managed to survive a winter on his own along Narragansett Bay, helped by local Indians in the area. In the spring, he purchased land from the Narragansett Indians and founded the town of Providence and subsequently the colony of Rhode Island, where, he proclaimed, "none be accounted a Delinquent for Doctrine." He petitioned Parliament for a colonial charter, which

An uncompromising visionary, Roger Williams ran afoul of Salem's Puritan fathers for his beliefs. He arrived in America in 1631 and survived a bitter winter with help from the Narragansett.

> *An enforced uniformity of religion throughout a nation or civil state, confounds the civil and religious, denies the principles of Christianity and civility.*
>
> **ROGER WILLIAMS**

was finally confirmed in 1663. But word of Williams's tolerance had spread long before the official charter, and others suffering persecution for their religious beliefs had flocked to Providence soon after its founding and continued to do so through the 17th century. Williams himself briefly espoused Baptist ideas and founded the first Baptist church in America in 1638. But he later rejected all organized doctrine and declared himself a "Seeker." He consistently sought peaceful relations with the Narragansett Indians, except during King Philip's War, when he was ready to defend Providence against violence. He died several years later in his Providence home. Williams's ardent belief in religious tolerance and the separation of church and state continues to resonant in American thought and justice.

Roger Williams His Rhode Island colony pioneered American ideals of religious freedom.

JOHN WINTHROP
★ 1588–1649 ★
PURITAN LEADER

A member of the English gentry, John Winthrop had became a respected London lawyer and ardent Puritan by the 1620s, when economic depression and Charles I's repression of religious nonconformists began to upend his world and led him to thoughts of emigration. In 1629, he met with the Massachusetts Bay Company, who held a charter to function as a commercial venture and establish a colony between the Charles and Merrimack Rivers in New England. A year later, as elected governor of the new colony, Winthrop led an expedition of some 700 to 1,000 people aboard four ships to what is now the Boston area. Under Winthrop's guidance, the colony flourished and never suffered the near-fatal privations that other early colonists had suffered. By the mid-1640s, new arrivals in the Great Migration and new births had expanded the population in the Massachusetts Bay Colony to 20,000.

Winthrop was reelected governor 12 times in the 1630s and '40s, though not for consecutive terms. His governance was wedded to Calvinist beliefs on predestination and to a community of "living saints" elected by God to be saved; Winthrop believed the power to govern should reside in this religious oligarchy. In 1631, the colony limited the vote to male members of the Puritan church.

Winthrop's style of governance and what was viewed as his somewhat despotic leadership were periodically challenged by others, but he remained an exceedingly popular leader, even during early religious conflicts that roiled the colony. In the controversy with the outspoken and nonconformist Roger Williams, Winthrop warned Williams that the colony's magistrates planned to force him to return to England, allowing Williams to escape to what is now Rhode Island. Yet after the dispute with the antinomians, led by Anne Hutchinson, Winthrop grew inclined to prosecute religious dissenters more harshly. He also declared that the colony's charter, which had been brought to America with the first group of Puritans, gave the Holy Commonwealth of Massachusetts absolute sovereignty over its internal affairs. Historians generally view Winthrop as the pivotal figure in the early history of Massachusetts.

> *This liberty is the proper end and object of authority and cannot subsist without it; and it is a liberty to that only which is good, just, and honest.*
>
> **JOHN WINTHROP**

This bowl and spoon were crafted around 1702 by a Native American in the Massachusetts area named Papenau. He carved them from the breastbone of a large bird.

John Winthrop Powerful Puritan governor of the Massachusetts Bay Colony, Winthrop is shown here tending his flock of "living saints" by performing apothecary services in his home.

Spanish Missions

A MIXED LEGACY

The Spanish presence in America predated that of the English, and unlike England, Spain was committed to spreading Christianity to native peoples. With that in mind, in the late 16th and 17th centuries, it established missions in the East from Florida to Virginia and in the Southwest and West. Father Eusebio Francisco Kino (1644–1711) was the force behind the missions of the Sonoran Desert, while in California, Father Junípero Serra (1713–1784) established a series of Franciscan missions. New Mexico and Texas also saw the development of missions. Those early outposts functioned both for religious instruction and to subsume native populations under the colonial structure. Though local American Indians who had converted were introduced to European crops and livestock, they were frequently treated almost as slave labor and succumbed to poor treatment and European diseases that decimated their populations.

French-Canadian mercenary Louis St. Denis helped with the founding of Spanish missions in east Texas.

Founded in January 1691, San José de Tumacácori Mission ranks as the one of the oldest in Arizona.

The San Agustín de la Isleta Mission was established in New Mexico in 1622, on the site of an old pueblo.

Over the course of 54 years, Spanish Franciscans established 21 California missions that stretched from San Diego in the south to San Francisco in the north.

Spanish Missions Founded in Alta California

🔵 Order of mission establishment

San Francisco Solano
21 1823

San Rafael Arcángel
1817 20

San Francisco de Asis
(Mission Dolores) 1776 6

San José
1797

14

Santa Clara de Asis
8 1777

Santa Cruz
1791 12

San Juan Bautista
15 1797

San Carlos Borromeo de Carmelo 2
1770

Nuestra Señora de la Soledad
13 1791

San Antonio de Padua 3
1771

San Miguel Arcángel
16 1797

San Luis Obispo de Tolosa
5 1772

La Purísima Concepción
1787

Santa Inés
1804

11 19

Santa Bárbara 10
1786 9
San
Buenaventura
1782

San Fernando Rey de España
1797

17

San Gabriel Arcángel
4 1771

San Juan Capistrano
1776

7

San Luis Rey de Francia
18 1798

San Diego de Alcalá
1 1769

0   100   200 Miles

Bartolomé de las Casas denounced Spanish exploitation of native peoples in the Americas, perpetuated by the mission system, and called for a more humane approach to evangelizing.

Santa Barbara Mission was founded in 1786 as the 10th mission on El Camino Real. The mission became a major archival repository in 1833.

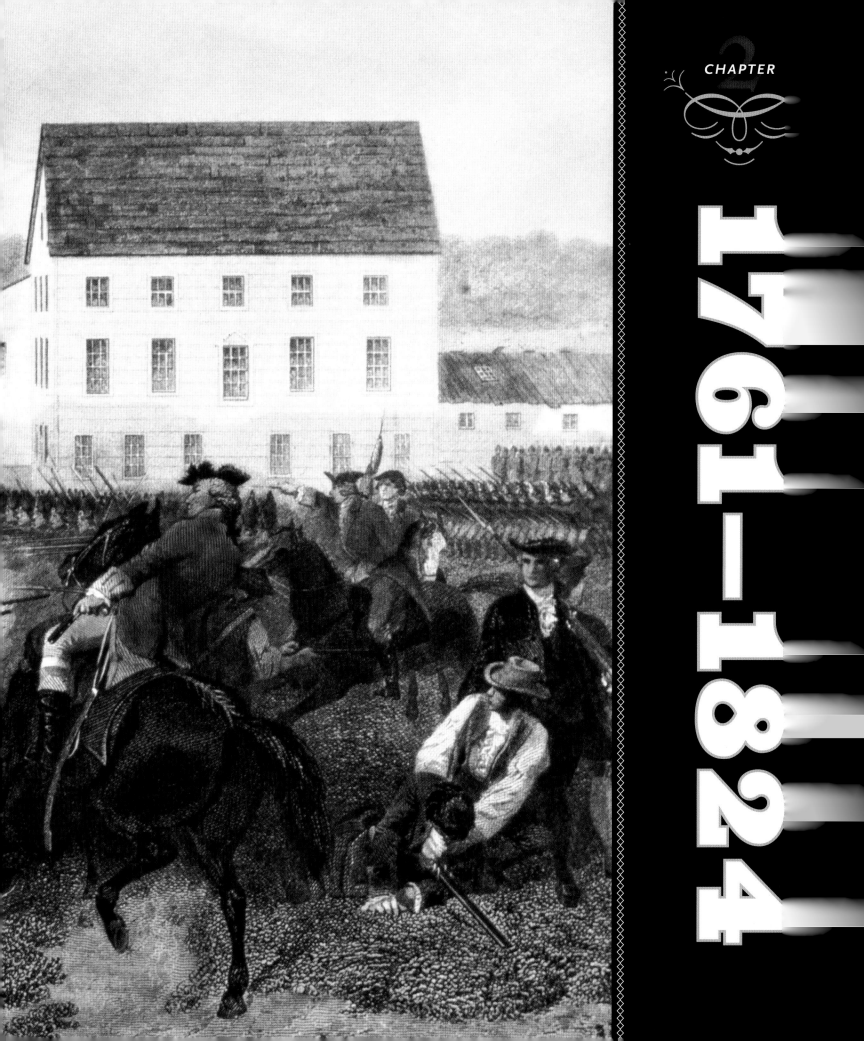

> *When in the Course of human events it becomes necessary for one people to dissolve the political bands which have connected them with another and to assume among the powers of the earth, the separate and equal station to which the Laws of Nature and of Nature's God entitle them...*
>
> THOMAS JEFFERSON, DECLARATION OF INDEPENDENCE

FORGING A NEW NATION

BY THE MID-18TH CENTURY, THE 13 COLONIES OF BRITISH AMERICA HAD BECOME a disjointed conglomeration of peoples, religions, aspirations, and cultures. In general, Britain had left the colonists to their own devices, making little demand on them beyond loyalty and obedience to British law. But the French and Indian War had been costly, and victory in that war had proved a blessing and a curse: The 1763 Treaty of Paris more than doubled the size of British America, making its administration more expensive and unwieldy. Hoping to generate funds to help with that expense, Parliament passed the Sugar Act in 1764. The Stamp Act quickly followed, and suddenly, the affection between colonists and crown began to fray. From America, the cry of "taxation without representation" carried across the Atlantic to Parliament. In Boston, mobs attacked British agents and launched a "tea party," throwing tons of British tea into Boston Harbor. In Virginia, firebrand Patrick Henry spoke out against George III. Still, most colonies were far from contemplating the unthinkable—a break with the mother country. But in the coming decade, mounting taxes and British rigidity engendered a growing unrest. Redcoats occupied Boston, and Sons of Liberty and other American patriots railed against the oppression. In September 1774, delegates from 12 of the 13 colonies convened in Philadelphia at the First Continental Congress, hoping to find a way to resolve differences with the crown and at the same time looking to forge a deeper sense of union among the colonies.

(previous pages) On April 19, 1775, British redcoats and colonial militiamen clash in Lexington, Massachusetts, igniting a revolution.
(opposite) America had no navy when it went to war against Britain, Earth's greatest naval power.

A silver-plated button from a British soldier's uniform. Unlike the well-equipped redcoats, the Continentals often lacked uniforms, and even shoes.

Then, on a cold New England morning in April 1775, redcoats exchanged fire with Massachusetts minutemen and militiamen in Lexington and Concord. Returning to Boston, the British found themselves under siege. Striking out at the patriot's protoarmy, the British attacked on June 17, but the Americans, dug in on Breed's Hill, held their ground. After a bloody fight, the redcoats prevailed, but barely. The Battle of Bunker Hill, as it came to be known, was an ignominious moment for the British that amazed the European and American world. Two weeks later, George Washington arrived in Boston to take command of the freshly minted Continental Army and the some 20,000 New Englanders who had joined the Boston siege. Somehow, this combined force was to take on the most powerful military in the world—Britain's.

By March, the Americans had dislodged the British from Boston, but it was far from the end of the fight—just a repositioning that began the long, brutal years of revolution. The war moved to New York, and as Washington waited on Manhattan Island for the British to make a move, the Second Continental Congress acted, adopting a Declaration of Independence that signaled America's determination to break with the mother country. Throughout the colonies, the patriotic cause caught fire in the "spirit of '76," but the enthusiasm was short-lived. By fall, New York had been lost, George Washington was under attack by his own peers, and his army was desperately moving across New Jersey, attempting to avoid obliteration.

The only thing holding it together was Washington himself—his men, "naked and starving," fought on out of a deep loyalty and respect for the man they called the "old boss." On

The Second Continental Congress appointed five delegates to draft a declaration of independence: Robert Livingston, Roger Sherman, John Adams, Thomas Jefferson, and Benjamin Franklin.

1763–65
Colonists object to new taxes

1773
Boston Tea Party ignites revolutionary spirit

1775
Battles of Lexington and Concord

1776
Declaration of Independence is adopted

1777
Battle of Saratoga is a pivotal victory

Christmas Day, they braved a blizzard to cross the ice-choked Delaware River on a mission Washington characterized as "Victory or Death." Taking a Hessian mercenary force fighting for the British by surprise in Trenton, New Jersey, the Americans scored a victory—not of great military significance but enormous for the morale of the army and the public. The Revolution would go on after all.

And it did—for almost five more years, with fierce fighting in and around Philadelphia and a pivotal American victory at Saratoga, New York, in large part because of the daring of American officer Benedict Arnold. The war of attrition wore down both sides, but the Americans slowly gained ground in the South. And France had at last joined the American cause, thanks to Benjamin Franklin's diplomacy in Paris. Then suddenly, in the fall of 1781, all elements coalesced in the patriots' favor. With his French allies, Washington advanced on Cornwallis's force, pinned down at Yorktown, Virginia, and on October 19, the British surrendered, effectively if not officially ending the war.

Peace proved almost as fraught as war, as the newly independent states lacked unity and a common purpose. "Our federal government is a name, a shadow, without power, or effect," Henry Knox, the Revolution's great artillery commander, worried. Many state leaders shared his concern, so in May 1787, Philadelphia once again became the setting for a historic convention. After rancorous months, the convention delegates agreed to a Constitution for the new country. There followed an even more rancorous ratification process in the states before the Constitution was finally adopted.

In 1789, Washington became the nation's first president and John Adams his vice president. In the coming decade and a half, the rancor continued as the Federalists, led by Alexander Hamilton and John Adams, and the anti-Federalist Democratic-Republicans, led by Thomas Jefferson and James Madison, attempted to define the limits of national government. Meanwhile, the territorial limits of the nation swelled to cross the continent, from ocean to ocean, with President Jefferson's Louisiana Purchase.

War with Britain came again in 1812, but the young country survived—if barely. By the time James Monroe assumed the presidency in 1817, the Federalist Party was essentially a thing of the past, and the nation had settled into a so-called Era of Good Feeling. Although it was short-lived, it nonetheless marked something of a coming of age for the newly forged experiment in democracy that was the United States.

Yet that democracy, determined by the right to vote, extended only to white men, and in a number of states, only to those who paid taxes (six states even required property ownership). Women had no official voice in government, and enslaved African Americans had no voice even in the course of their own lives. Native Americans, meanwhile, had seen their lives, lands, and traditions decimated. For them, there would be no eras of good feeling again.

Still, the republic blundered on, into the new century.

George Washington's leadership inspired his men and kept them fighting against all odds until they finally prevailed over the British.

1778	1781	1783	1789	1791
France joins the war as an American ally	Cornwallis surrenders at Yorktown, Virginia	Treaty of Paris officially ends the war	Constitutional government begins	Bill of Rights amended to the Constitution

BIOGRAPHIES

FOUNDING FATHERS & MOTHERS 1761-1824

The American Republic was an unprecedented idea, fueled by thinkers, writers, merchants, farmers, and militarists who, in the legendary words of one patriot, were willing to choose liberty or death. The following men and women led that fight, and founded a new nation. They were not perfect, nor was their nation, but they were brave, resolute, and visionary.

ABIGAIL SMITH ADAMS

★ 1744-1818 ★

FIRST LADY, FOUNDING MOTHER

The daughter of a Congregational minister in Weymouth, Massachusetts, Abigail Smith had no formal education yet became one of the most influential women in early America. She married John Adams in 1764, and the two had a deep relationship based on shared intellectual, moral, and political concerns. John's long absences during the Revolutionary War years required Abigail to maintain their family farm and raise their children mostly on her own as she dealt with deprivation and outbreaks of disease and passing troops who camped on her land.

Throughout those years, she and John corresponded often, and politics, governance, and diplomacy were much discussed topics in the letters. Most historians agree that Abigail was John's closest confidante and adviser on the pressing issues of the day. In 1776, as Adams pushed for independence at the Second Continental Congress, Abigail famously advised him to tell his fellow delegates to "remember the ladies, and

Abigail Adams's embroidered leather slippers (late 1790s) are typical of the period.

be more generous and favorable to them than your ancestors . . . Remember all Men would be tyrants if they could."

Abigail joined her husband in Europe during his final diplomatic years (1784–88). During Adams's presidency of the United States, Abigail continued to advise him, though she was often unwell and spent a good deal of her time at the family farm in Braintree. Noted for her blunt style, sharp intellect, and principled beliefs, she championed such cases as public education for women and an end to slavery. Her eldest son, John Quincy Adams, served as sixth president.

Abigail Adams Husband John's trusted adviser and the nation's second first lady

JOHN ADAMS
★ 1735–1826 ★
FOUNDING FATHER

Throughout his life, John Adams reflected his proud ancestry—a "line of virtuous, independent New England farmers" whose roots lay in the Puritan Great Migration of the 1630s. Harvard-educated, Adams combined the family tradition of farming with law and settled into his hometown of Braintree, Massachusetts, with his wife, Abigail.

History soon overtook them, however, and in 1770, the disputatious Adams took on the unpopular role of defending British soldiers who had fired on rabble-rousers in what became known as the Boston Massacre. His efforts won most of the men acquittal and Adams grudging admiration as a man of principle. Later, he would remember the case as "one of the best pieces of service I ever rendered my country."

For the rest of his life, Adams continued to render such service. He was a delegate to both the First and Second Continental Congresses and established himself as an ardent, if pugnacious, patriot. He headed the Board of War, which supplied the Continental Army's needs, and was appointed to the Committee of Five charged with drafting a declaration of independence; Adams, along with Franklin, advised Jefferson on his final draft.

In 1778, Adams spent a brief period in France as an American commissioner, then returned to Massachusetts in 1779 and devoted himself to writing a constitution for the commonwealth. Returning to Europe, he served as one of three commissioners who negotiated critical treaties of peace and commerce with the British after

John Adams An outspoken member of the Continental Congress, Adams (center), along with Benjamin Franklin, made minor changes to Jefferson's draft of the Declaration of Independence. *Inset:* His spectacles

the war. Adams also took on loan negotiations with the Dutch before becoming the first American minister (ambassador) to Britain. During his years in Europe, Adams became close friends with Thomas Jefferson, also an American minister.

Returning to America, Adams, then 52, longed for a simple life devoted to "my farm, my family and goose quill" pen. Instead, he would serve for eight years as the nation's first vice president, then for four (1797–1801) as its second president. His tenure was marred by passage of the Alien and Sedition Acts—which tempered free speech and immigrants' rights—and his own battles with other

members of the Federalist Party. Yet Adams managed to keep America out of a European war and, at the same time, to build up the country's naval defenses. He lost his second run for the presidency to his former friend turned political enemy, the populist Democratic-Republican candidate Thomas Jefferson.

The final years of John Adams's life were spent on his beloved family farm, where he reconciled at last with Jefferson. The two began a historic and affectionate correspondence and died within hours of each other on July 4, 1826—exactly 50 years after the signing of the Declaration of Independence.

SAMUEL ADAMS
★ 1722–1803 ★
PATRIOT LEADER

Harvard-educated and puritanical, Bostonian Samuel Adams had little early success, foundering as a businessman, tax collector, and maltster. He found his true calling as a political leader, first elected to public office in 1747. In the years leading up to the Revolution, he came into his own as an outspoken patriot and agitator against the British. A delegate to the Massachusetts House, Adams loudly protested new taxes and duties and later the British occupation of Boston. He was a driving force behind the Circular Letter sent by the Massachusetts legislature to other colonial legislatures in 1768, proclaiming recent parliamentary acts unconstitutional.

An ardent member of Boston's Sons of Liberty, Adams is often credited with playing a leading part in organizing the Boston Tea Party, although historians disagree about his actual role. In 1775, he, along with John Hancock, fled British-occupied Boston and only evaded capture thanks to the "midnight ride" of Paul Revere and William Dawes. As a delegate to the First and Second Continental Congresses, Samuel—like his distant cousin John Adams—argued for war with Britain and signed the Declaration of Independence. In 1781, he helped draft the Articles of Confederation and later that year left Congress to return to Boston, where he continued to agitate for public virtue in politics.

Samuel Adams A firebrand in the early days of unrest against the British, the former Boston maltster helped shape the Sons of Liberty into an effective covert force against the crown.

ETHAN ALLEN
★ 1738–1789 ★
COMMANDER, AMERICAN REVOLUTION

One of the earliest settlers in the Burlington, (now) Vermont area, Ethan Allen is forever associated with the Green Mountain Boys, a paramilitary force of frontiersmen he founded in the years before the Revolution. The "boys" fought to protect settlers in the Green Mountains from being evicted or subject to onerous fees, due to a land dispute with neighboring New York. Allen made his mark in May 1775, when, at age 37, he was commissioned by the Connecticut Committee of Safety to secure the Lake Champlain region and its British-held forts for the patriot cause. The prize among these—Fort Ticonderoga—anchored the southern end of Lake Champlain and held

A silver bowl crafted by Paul Revere to honor Massachusetts's legislators who voted not to rescind the Circular Letter

Ever since I arrived to a state of manhood and acquainted myself with the general history of mankind, I have felt a sincere passion for liberty.

ETHAN ALLEN

Ethan Allen Taking the British commander of Ticonderoga by surprise on May 10, 1775, Allen and his Green Mountain Boys, with help from Benedict Arnold, claimed the fort for the American cause.

much needed armament. On May 5, Allen, partnering with Benedict Arnold—who had suddenly appeared near Ticonderoga—took the lightly garrisoned fort for the Americans and followed up that victory by securing strategic Crown Point as well. However, Allen's ill-conceived and unsuccessful attack on Montreal ended in his captivity and time spent in a British prison in Cornwall.

He was repatriated in 1778 and became commander of Vermont's forces. By the early 1780s, Allen, along with other Vermonters, had become disillusioned by New York's attempts to block Vermont statehood, and Allen began secret negotiations with the British that achieved little except to tarnish his reputation for a period of time. A self-styled philosopher and frontiersman, Allen generally championed individualism and continues to be the vaunted folk hero of the Green Mountain State.

Homegrown Agitators
SONS AND DAUGHTERS OF LIBERTY
★ ★ ★

Associated with such Boston patriots as Samuel Adams, John Hancock, and Paul Revere, the Sons of Liberty probably took form sometime in 1765, in reaction to the unpopular Stamp Act. Before Parliament that year, Isaac Barré, a parliamentarian and strong advocate of the colonists, had called them "Sons of Liberty," and the patriot paramilitarists may have taken their name from his speech. The Sons' exact origins and membership are unknown as they composed a secret, and disparate, paramilitary brotherhood committed to harassing the British. Although the Boston chapter played a key role in the very early history of the revolt against Britain, chapters operated in other colonies as well, notably Connecticut, New York, and South Carolina.

The Sons overtly agitated against the British, often using intimidation tactics on customs agents and tax collectors and forming networks of communication among the various chapters. Each chapter attracted men from all walks of life who had come to believe British rule was unjust and oppressive. The Boston Sons sometimes met at night under the "Liberty Tree," an old elm in Hanover Square, but more frequently at local taverns, particularly the Green Dragon (sometimes called the "headquarters of the Revolution") in the city's North End. Most historians believe the Sons were the agitators dressed as Mohawk Indians who precipitated the 1773 Boston Tea Party.

The Sons' counterpart, the Daughters of Liberty, held spinning bees to engender zeal for the patriotic movement and to create homespun fabrics, in lieu of British imports. They also experimented with local substitutes for heavily taxed goods, such as tea and sugar.

RICHARD ALLEN
★ 1760–1831 ★
AFRICAN-AMERICAN LEADER, FOUNDER OF A.M.E. CHURCH

Born into slavery in 1760, Richard Allen rose to become a leader of the African-American community. As a boy, he was sold by his Philadelphia owner to Delaware planter Stokeley Sturgis, and it was in Delaware that Richard was exposed to Methodism and became an itinerant preacher for the faith, converting Sturgis to the religion as well. With his conversion, Sturgis "could not be satisfied to hold slaves, believing it wrong," and he encouraged Allen to do odd jobs as a way to purchase his freedom. Allen did so, working for the patriot forces during the Revolution.

Once free, he took the last name "Allen" and continued preaching, riding a wide circuit through eastern states as an itinerant minister. He returned to Philadelphia in 1786, where he supported himself as a shoemaker while preaching at St. George's United Methodist Episcopal Church, holding a 5 a.m. service for black congregants only. Although the church was attended by both blacks and whites, as its African-American congregation grew, so too did racial tensions. By 1794, Allen and other members of the new Free African Society had formed the first African-American Methodist church in America, Bethel African Methodist Episcopal Church, where Allen was pastor. More such churches were founded in the mid-Atlantic states, and in 1816, they united to form the first independent black denomination—the African Methodist Episcopal Church—with Allen as bishop. Aside from his official duties with the church, Allen was an abolitionist and worked on the Underground Railroad.

Richard Allen An early abolitionist and founder of the African Methodist Episcopal Church

> *I was confident that there was no religious sect or denomination would suit the capacity of the colored people as well as the Methodist; for the plain and simple gospel suits best for any people.*
>
> **RICHARD ALLEN**

BENEDICT ARNOLD
★ 1741–1801 ★
SOLDIER/TRAITOR, AMERICAN REVOLUTION

Benedict Arnold was an ambitious young Connecticut merchant who sometimes captained his own trading ships when tensions between Britain and its American colonies first flared. Though he had no previous military training, Arnold threw himself into the conflict, organizing a local foot guard that marched to aid other militia surrounding Boston after the Battles of Lexington and Concord. In 1775, he was commissioned a colonel by the Massachusetts Committee of Safety and charged with capturing British-controlled Fort Ticonderoga. With the help of Ethan Allen and the Green Mountain Boys, Arnold took the fort, which anchored the south end of Lake Champlain, and its critical armaments in May 1775. Later that year, he led a legendary expedition through the Maine wilderness to wrest Quebec City from the British. The patriots' attack, launched during a driving blizzard, failed and Arnold was wounded, though he refused to quit the field. His heroics gained him further standing as a military commander, and he was put in charge of an American fleet being assembled in Lake Champlain to block British advances south from Canada into New England. Again, Arnold showed bravery and a strong strategic talent. But his greatest moment came at the 1777 Battle of Saratoga, when he led pivotal assaults against the British that spurred their defeat and in many ways turned the tide of the war.

In 1778, Arnold became military governor of Philadelphia and soon married Margaret Shippen, a Loyalist. Possibly her influence, as well as Arnold's own vainglorious nature and sense that he had not been given enough recognition by

ARNOLD'S ROUTE THROUGH THE WILDERNESS.

Benedict Arnold's arduous 1775 winter march with his men through the Maine wilderness into Canada secured his reputation as a valiant leader.

In a 1780 proclamation, Arnold exhorts Continental soldiers to "reflect on what you have lost . . . repel the ruin that still threatens you" and defect to the British, as he had done.

Benedict Arnold Initially a hero of the Revolution, Arnold later switched sides and became America's most famous traitor.

the Continental Congress or George Washington, led to his growing disillusionment with the American cause. Yet Washington considered Arnold a trusted member of his inner circle, and thus privy to military plans and secrets. It was those plans that Arnold contrived to sell to the British, passing them off to spymaster John André.

Though Washington offered Arnold a command position in the field again, Arnold refused, instead lobbying to become commander of West Point, a strategic American stronghold on the Hudson. Once there, Arnold conspired to turn it over to the British, but his plans were foiled when André was captured with documents that could have only come from Arnold. Arnold escaped capture himself and was given a generalship in the British Army. His defection and treachery shocked the American military, leading Gen. Nathanael Greene to say, "Never since the fall of Lucifer has a fall equaled his."

In late 1780, Arnold sailed up the James under the British flag, and the force he commanded took the Virginia capital, Richmond. He continued to fight on the British side until Cornwallis's surrender at Yorktown in October 1781, after which Arnold and his family sailed for England. Arnold had expected British admiration for his defection to their side but instead was scorned as a turncoat. Always a controversial and contentious figure, he remained so the rest of his life, and after a brief few years in Saint John, New Brunswick, Arnold returned to London and died there at age 60.

MARGARET ARNOLD
★ 1760–1804 ★
WIFE OF BENEDICT ARNOLD

Margaret Arnold played her own part in the drama surrounding her husband, Benedict. Before her marriage, as the daughter of a prominent Philadelphia Loyalist, "Peggy" Shippen had been a sought-after local belle, sometimes escorted by the British major John André. After her marriage to Arnold in 1779, Peggy at times acted as a conduit, passing her husband's traitorous letters on to André. When Arnold's treason was discovered by George Washington at West Point, Peggy Arnold briefly distracted him and waylaid his party with a histrionic performance that involved pointing to the ceiling and keening, "The spirits have carried him [Arnold] up there." Her acting saved her, and after the war, she was given an annual pension by the British "for her services."

CRISPUS ATTUCKS
★ CA 1723–1770 ★
PATRIOT

Believed to have been the son of an African father and Native American mother, Crispus Attucks spent his early years as a slave in Framingham, Massachusetts. He managed to escape slavery and supported himself either as a sailor on a whaler or as a ropemaker in Boston. On March 5, 1770, Attucks was in a group of men who began taunting a British guard at the Boston customhouse. The British opened fire, killing five of the men, including Attucks. The incident became known as the "Boston Massacre" and fueled patriotic outrage. Attucks is believed to have been the first American to die in the conflict with Britain.

BENJAMIN BANNEKER
★ 1731–1806 ★
SCIENTIST, SURVEYOR

Born a free black man in Maryland, Benjamin Banneker was taught to read by his grandmother, an English woman who had come to America as an indentured servant. Banneker's precociousness in mechanics and mathematics was apparent early on, and by the age of 22, he had designed and built a striking clock. He also had a keen interest in astronomy and advanced mathematics and pursued both, predicting the April 1789 solar eclipse. In 1791, President Washington appointed Banneker to the three-man

Benjamin Banneker An admired scientist, abolitionist, and surveyor

team tasked with surveying the site of the new federal capital city on the banks of the Potomac. The *Georgetown Weekly Ledger* reported that the team leader, Andrew Ellicott, was accompanied by Benjamin Banneker, "an Ethiopian, whose abilities, as a surveyor, and an astronomer, clearly prove that Mr. Jefferson's concluding that race of men were void of mental endowments, was without foundation." That same year, Banneker published his *Almanack and Ephemeris* and sent a copy to Jefferson, along with

> *Would to God that I did stand on the same ground with every other man! This is the first time that I have been permitted to enjoy the rights of a citizen.*
>
> **AARON BURR**

a 12-page letter that challenged Jefferson on slavery: "Sir, how pitiable is it to reflect, that although you were so fully convinced of the benevolence of the Father of Mankind, and of his equal and impartial distribution of these rights and privileges, which he hath conferred upon them, that you should at the same time counteract his mercies, in detaining by fraud and violence so numerous a part of my brethren, under groaning captivity and cruel oppression."

In surveying the federal city, Banneker and Andrew Ellicott had worked with Pierre L'Enfant, who designed the city plan. When the hot-tempered L'Enfant was fired and took his plans with

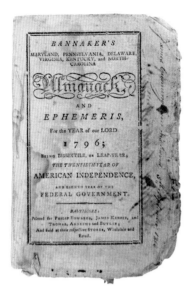

Banneker's *Ephemeris* served as an almanac.

him, Banneker was able to reconstruct them from memory and the project continued. In his later years, Banneker wrote an antislavery treatise and continued his scientific investigations, conferring with other scientists of his day.

AARON BURR

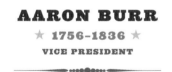

★ 1756–1836 ★

VICE PRESIDENT

Like his historic rival, Alexander Hamilton, Aaron Burr fought valiantly in the American Revolution and then became a prominent New York lawyer and national political figure. Charismatic and flamboyant, he came within a vote or two of winning the nation's third presidential election in 1800, losing to Thomas Jefferson and serving instead as his vice president. After his tenure, Burr began colluding with New England secessionists, who wanted to establish a Northern Confederacy. When Alexander Hamilton publicly maligned Burr's character, Burr challenged his longtime foe to a duel. On July 11, 1804, he inflicted a wound that led to Hamilton's death. Now a political outcast, Burr fled New York to avoid an indictment for murder.

For some time before the duel, Burr had been corresponding with James Wilkinson, governor of the newly acquired Louisiana Territory, and others who were anxious to create a separate western kingdom encompassing Mexico and the Southwest, with Burr at its head. In 1806, Burr and a group of armed men were captured on the Ohio River, presumably on their way to attack New Orleans. Burr was arrested and held in Richmond, Virginia, pending trial. Chief Justice John Marshall, on circuit duty, oversaw the trial, and thanks in large part to his legal machinations, Burr was acquitted. After spending some years in Europe, Burr returned to New York and reestablished himself as a successful lawyer.

Aaron Burr At Burr's trial on charges of conspiracy in Richmond, Chief Justice John Marshall found insufficient evidence of treason.

JOHN SINGLETON COPLEY

★ 1738-1815 ★
ARTIST

Widely considered the first American master, painter John Singleton Copley was exposed to artists' prints during his Boston boyhood, as his stepfather was a London-trained engraver. Copley borrowed techniques from those printers and other painters, evolving into a sought-after Boston portraitist in the English style. Among his works are paintings of patriot leaders Paul Revere and Samuel Adams and British commander Gen. Thomas Gage. In 1774, Copley settled in London and became a respected member of the artistic establishment, expanding his range to historical scenes as well as portraiture.

John Singleton Copley The respected Boston portraitist went on to become a leading figure in British art circles.

JOHN DICKINSON

★ 1732-1808 ★
FOUNDING FATHER

John Dickinson was a respected Philadelphia lawyer and colonial legislator when he published the first of his now famous *Letters From a Farmer in Pennsylvania* in the late 1760s. The letters argued against British taxation of the colonists without representation and enjoyed a wide audience in America and in Europe. Yet in the mid-1770s, Dickinson argued against a total break with the mother country and was chosen by the Continental Congress in 1775 to draft the unsuccessful "Olive Branch Petition" to George III. He also refused to sign the Declaration of Independence and did not attend the Second Continental Congress session, so that the signing could be unanimous. But as revolution overtook the colonies, he joined the patriot cause, participating in military campaigns and eventually chairing the committee to write the Articles of Confederation. After the war, he was president, or governor, of both Delaware and Pennsylvania, an ardent supporter of a strong central government, and a signer of the Constitution.

> *He certainly is not a wise man who folds his arms and reposes himself at home, seeing with unconcern the flames that have invaded his neighbor's house.*
>
> **JOHN DICKINSON**

Olaudah Equiano Noted for his *Interesting Narrative . . .* of his life as a captured African, a slave, and a freedman

E. I. DU PONT

★ 1771-1834 ★
INDUSTRIALIST

Founder of one of America's oldest and most prominent corporations, Éleuthère Irénée du Pont de Nemours emigrated to the United States in 1800. As a young man, he had apprenticed to a chemist involved with gunpowder production, and once in America, du Pont saw the need for good quality gunpowder. Within two years of his arrival, he had established a gunpowder mill on Brandywine Creek, just north of Wilmington, Delaware. By the mid-19th century, E. I. du Pont de Nemours and Company had become the U.S. military's largest supplier of gunpowder. Today, DuPont ranks as one of the world's largest chemical companies.

OLAUDAH EQUIANO
★ 1745–1797 ★
ABOLITIONIST

The story of Olaudah Equiano's early life comes from his autobiography, *The Interesting Narrative of the Life of Olaudah Equiano, or Gustavus Vassa, the African* (1789). In it, he says he was the son of a respected elder among the Ibo tribe in West Africa and was sold into African slavery as a boy, then sold to a European slave ship making passage to America. Bought by a British naval officer, he spent seven years sailing to ports worldwide. In 1766, he purchased his freedom, settling in London and participating in a 1773 expedition searching for the Northwest Passage. Returning to London, he became an abolitionist. In his autobiography's foreword, addressed to Parliament, Equiano explains he wrote this "genuine Narrative...to excite in your august assemblies a sense of compassion for the miseries which the Slave-Trade has entailed on my unfortunate countrymen."

Of Human Bondage
SLAVERY IN 18TH-CENTURY AMERICA
★ ★ ★

At the outbreak of the Revolution, African Americans accounted for roughly 20 percent of the population in the colonies. The South had a far higher proportion—some 60 percent in South Carolina and 40 percent in Virginia. In northern cities as well, including Boston, Philadelphia, and New York, and in New York's Hudson River Valley, slaves were an integral and not insignificant part of the population. Some, notably men, were able to earn funds to buy their freedom, but most remained in bondage throughout their lives, as did their children. They have also remained largely unknown to history as individuals, given that most were illiterate and their "masters" generally left little record of them beyond a passing reference or their first name on a list of taxable property.

During the Revolution, the British, understanding that the slave population presented a vulnerability to the Continentals, sometimes promised freedom in exchange for a slave's joining forces with them against the patriots. The patriots' own Declaration of Independence, with its proclamation of inalienable rights, rang hollow, given the presence of slavery in America. Some Founding Fathers argued for manumission, many favoring the idea of colonization—shipping freed slaves to West Africa. George Washington stipulated in his will that his slaves should be emancipated after his wife's death. James Madison, according to a friend, declared himself almost in despair over slavery and "talked more on the subject...than on any other, acknowledging, without limitation or hesitation, all the evils with which it has ever been charged."

The British occasionally promised freedom to slaves in the Revolution, enticing them to escape their shackles and join the redcoats' ranks.

BENJAMIN FRANKLIN

★ 1706–1790 ★

FOUNDING FATHER

Though firmly associated with Philadelphia, Benjamin Franklin grew up in Boston, the youngest son in a Puritan family of 13 children. Even as a boy, Franklin's precocious and questing nature was apparent, yet he had little formal schooling. By 10, he was working in his father's tallowmaking business, though he dreamed of going to sea. His father prevented that by apprenticing the boy to his older brother James, a printer. Franklin made the most of his apprenticeship by reading and writing a series of popular spoofs for his brother's paper, the *New-England Courant*. But by his midteens, Franklin was chafing at the apprenticeship and ran away before serving its full term. Dirty, hungry, and almost penniless, he eventually landed in America's largest city, Philadelphia, where he again took up the trade of

Benjamin Franklin
Revered Founding Father

printing. In the next quarter century, he established himself as a successful businessman and writer of the popular *Poor Richard's Almanack*. A civic leader, Franklin pushed for city improvements, served as postmaster of Philadelphia, and championed a sanitation system and firefighting force for the city and a militia system for the colony.

Franklin's business success allowed him to retire at 42 and devote himself to

Benjamin Franklin's
air pump

Americans in Paris

EARLY MINISTERS TO FRANCE

★★★

Knowing that European allies were key to the Revolution's success, the Continental Congress dispatched a series of ministers to Paris. One of the first, Silas Deane, was a diplomat engaged in complicated financial dealings that ultimately discredited him. But the situation was saved by the appointment of Benjamin Franklin, who reveled in his Parisian life as Paris reveled in him. John Adams found both wanting when he joined Franklin as fellow minister. He disapproved of what he considered Franklin's dissolute lifestyle, and Adams' own ham-fisted diplomacy offended the French.

Thomas Jefferson became minister to France after the war and wrote to a friend, "Were I . . . to tell you how much I enjoy their architecture, sculpture, painting, music, I should want for words." His experience with French viticulture and neoclassical architecture lives on in American wine traditions and in such landmarks as Monticello and the University of Virginia.

This battery is just one of Franklin's many inventions.

This electrostatic machine, which dates from about 1750, appears to be Franklin's design.

Porcelain saucer and cup with portrait of Franklin

Robert Fulton built the North River Steamboat (sometimes called the *Clermont*), which traveled successfully up and down the Hudson, making it the first commercially viable steamboat.

intellectual pursuits, particularly science. He gained international renown with his experiments on electricity. That acclaim, along with his knowledge of London—he had lived there in his late teens—served him well as he began a second career representing the interests of various colonies in London. In London, as tensions grew between Parliament and the colonies, he argued for moderation, but by 1774, he no longer trusted the British and returned to America ready for revolution.

Though almost 70, Franklin reigned as elder statesman among the patriots at the Second Continental Congress and counseled Thomas Jefferson on his draft of the Declaration of Independence. Yet Franklin's greatest contribution was as American minister to the French court during the Revolution. Enormously popular in Paris, owing to his style and his reputation as a scientist, he succeeded in persuading France to join the former colonists in making common cause against their mutual enemy, Britain. Without France and its skilled officers, gunpowder, troops, and ships, the American victory would not have been possible. Franklin also negotiated, along with John Adams and John Jay, the treaties of peace and commerce that came at war's end.

Despite his age, his public service continued after the war, when he became president (similar to governor) of Pennsylvania and the oldest delegate at the Constitutional Convention, convincing doubters there of the need to adopt the Constitution. Franklin's role as statesman, inventor, entrepreneur, civic-betterment engineer, and diplomat has earned him the sobriquet the First American.

ROBERT FULTON
★ 1765–1815 ★
INVENTOR, DIPLOMAT

Pennsylvania-born Robert Fulton hoped to be a portrait painter and went to Europe to pursue his dream. There, he became enthralled with shipbuilding and the newly invented steam engine. In France, Fulton designed the first successful submarine and became acquainted with American ambassador Robert Livingston. In 1811–12, the two men, along with Nicholas Roosevelt, worked to design and build a reliable steamboat. Initially lampooned as "Fulton's Folly," the *North River Steamboat of Clermont* made its first run from New York to Albany in 1807. By 1812, Fulton's steamboats were operating on rivers throughout the mid-Atlantic.

HORATIO GATES
★ 1727–1806 ★
GENERAL, AMERICAN REVOLUTION

English-born Horatio Gates settled in Virginia in 1772, and when revolution with Britain became a reality, he joined the patriot cause, becoming a major general. Gates's pivotal moment came at the 1777 Battle of Saratoga. Though he failed to act decisively as commander of the American forces, the Continental Army nonetheless defeated John Burgoyne's army. Gates's limited command abilities became evident at the 1780 Battle of Camden, South Carolina, one of America's worst defeats in the war.

NATHANAEL GREENE

★ **1742–1786** ★

GENERAL, AMERICAN REVOLUTION

A Rhode Island blacksmith and politician with an interest in military matters (though he was raised a Quaker), Nathanael Greene became the youngest brigadier general in the Continental Army in 1775, then its youngest major general. His bravery during the 1775–76 Siege of Boston impressed George Washington, who would, in the years to come, rely on Greene as perhaps his most trusted commander. Greene's leadership and military acumen proved invaluable at decisive moments early in the war—Trenton, Princeton, Monmouth. In 1780, he assumed command of American forces in the South, and his strategy for battling the British in the Carolinas in the first half of 1781 weakened Cornwallis's army, convincing him to move north into Virginia. There, his force was ultimately trapped at Yorktown. Even after that decisive British defeat, Greene kept up the fight in the South, freeing Georgia of the enemy and settling there until he suffered an untimely natural death in 1786. Had he lived, many historians believe Washington would have appointed him the nation's first secretary of war.

NATHAN HALE

★ **1755–1776** ★

PATRIOT SPY

Nathan Hale is probably best remembered for his alleged final words, "I only regret that I have but one life to lose for my country." After the American defeat at the Battle of Long Island in 1776,

Nathan Hale He was hanged as a spy for the Revolution.

George Washington asked for volunteers to infiltrate enemy lines in New York and spy on the British. Hale may have been the only officer in the Continental Army to respond, and on September 12, began his mission. On September 21, the Great Fire of New York led the British to round up all possible patriots, and Hale was quickly found out. A day later, he was publicly hanged, having first uttered, according to legend, his famous quote. His statue is on the grounds of the CIA.

Nathanael Greene North Carolina innkeeper Elizabeth Steele offers Greene funds for the Continental cause. As commander of American forces in the South, Greene outmaneuvered the British.

ALEXANDER HAMILTON

★ **1755/57–1804** ★

FOUNDING FATHER

The man who would engineer many of America's abiding federal institutions came from a difficult boyhood in the British West Indies. By his early teens, he and his brother were penniless orphans. A prosperous merchant family eventually took Hamilton in, and he had access to a private library that stimulated his native intellect. In 1773, Hamilton arrived in New York to attend King's College (now Columbia University). He became a full-throated patriot and, in 1776, captain of an artillery company.

Though Hamilton was a slight, short man, he was a fierce fighter and strong commander, and in 1777, Washington invited Hamilton to be one of his aides-de-camp. For much of the rest of the war, he would be at the choke point of problems, decisions, defeats, politics, and power. Despite Washington's regard and trust in him, Hamilton "felt no friendship for him and have professed none." Hamilton also chaffed to get back into the field, and he was allowed to do so near war's end, distinguishing himself during the Siege of Yorktown.

Hamilton's marriage to Elizabeth Schuyler—daughter of Gen. Philip Schuyler, a prominent New Yorker—elevated his social standing, and after the war, he became a successful New York lawyer and member of the Confederation Congress. As such, he was deeply concerned about how little true authority the federal government enjoyed. "I fear that we shall let slip the golden opportunity of rescuing the American empire from disunion,

> *You are called upon to deliberate on a new Constitution for the United States of America. The subject speaks its own importance . . . nothing less than the existence of the UNION, the safety and welfare of the parts of which it is composed, the fate of an empire in many respects the most interesting in the world.*
>
> **ALEXANDER HAMILTON**

Alexander Hamilton An officer in the Revolution (his powder horn, right), he later became the great architect and champion of strong federal government.

anarchy, and misery," he wrote to George Washington. A strong voice at both the Annapolis Convention and the resulting Constitutional Convention, Hamilton argued forcibly for a strong federal government. When the Constitution went to the various states for ratification, Hamilton was determined to see it succeed. His determination resulted in one of America's most enduring documents, the *Federalist* papers—a series of 85 essays that appeared in New York newspapers under the pseudonym Publius. Hamilton wrote 51 of them, and James Madison and John Jay the remainder.

With a viable Constitution at last in place, Hamilton served in Washington's Cabinet as the first and probably most forceful secretary of the treasury. He worked mightily to create a strong federal government with a budget and tax system, a central bank, a funded debt, a customs service, and a coast guard. But his pugnacious and outspoken federalism and his sometimes devious tactics alienated Thomas Jefferson, James Madison, James Monroe, Aaron Burr, and others. Burr ultimately challenged Hamilton to a duel, and on the morning of July 11, 1804, the two faced off along the Hudson River Palisades. Though duels were rarely fatal, Burr's shot found its mark, and Hamilton died a day later of his wound.

JOHN HANCOCK
★ 1737–1793 ★
FOUNDING FATHER

John Hancock is best remembered for his defiantly bold signature on the Declaration of Independence. He was, at the time, president of the Second Continental Congress, a leading member of Boston's patriot force—the Sons of Liberty—and one of the wealthiest men in the colonies. He had inherited a shipping business engaged in overseas trade from the uncle who raised him and had spent 1760 to 1761 in London on business.

Hancock took exception to the new, aggressive breed of customs agents imposed on the colonies by the British in the late 1760s and early 1770s, and two of his ships were involved in incendiary incidents over customs inspections. Hancock's defiance of the British made him a popular hero and a foe sought by the British. As tensions with Britain moved toward open rebellion, Hancock was elected to both Continental Congresses and served as president of the second. He hoped to be made commander in chief of the Continental forces, but when that position went to George Washington, Hancock continued as president of the Congress for another year. In 1778, he briefly assumed command of a military force charged with retaking Newport, Rhode Island. That attempt failed, and with it, Hancock's military aspirations. In 1780, the ever popular Hancock was elected the first governor of Massachusetts (1781–85) and returned to that office in 1787 and helped quell distrust of government that had led to the populist uprising known as Shays's Rebellion. In 1789, he was one of the candidates in the first U.S. presidential election.

John Hancock Founding Father and one of New England's wealthiest men

Hancock's signature, first on the Declaration of Independence

SALLY HEMINGS
★ 1773–1835 ★
PROBABLE MOTHER OF CHILDREN
BY THOMAS JEFFERSON

Perhaps one of America's least known yet much discussed historical figures, Sally Hemings was an enslaved house servant owned by Thomas Jefferson and believed by many historians to be the mother of six children by him. Hemings had come to Monticello as a young child, as part of the estate of Jefferson's wife, Martha (1748–1782). In fact, Hemings is believed to have been Martha's half sister, the child of Martha's father and an enslaved black woman belonging to him. The first of the Jefferson-Hemings children was born at Monticello in 1795. Rumors of the relationship between Jefferson and Hemings became public in an article published by James Callender in a Richmond newspaper in 1802. In the decades after, several Hemings children claimed Jefferson as their father. In addition, Hemings's children were the only Monticello slaves Jefferson ever freed. In 1998, DNA tests done on Hemings and Jefferson descendants established a conclusive link between the families.

PATRICK HENRY
★ 1736–1799 ★
ORATOR OF THE EARLY REVOLUTION

Patrick Henry's fiery speeches against British oppression became a clarion call for the American Revolution. A self-taught Virginia lawyer, Henry delivered the first of those speeches to a small

Whether this [independence] will prove a blessing or a curse, will depend upon the use our people make of the blessings which a gracious God had bestowed on us. If they are wise, they will be great and happy. If they are of a contrary character, they will be miserable.

PATRICK HENRY

Patrick Henry He delivered his 1775 "Liberty or Death" speech to the Second Virginia Convention.

group of Virginia burgesses (legislators) in May 1765—"Caesar had his Brutus, Charles the First his Cromwell, and George the Third . . ." Legend has supplied the final line: "If this be treason, make the most of it." In 1775, speaking before the Second Virginia Convention in Richmond, Henry is said to have delivered his immortal lines: "Is life so dear, or peace so sweet as to be purchased at the price of chains and slavery? Forbid it, Almighty God! I know not what course others may take; but as for me, give me liberty, or give me death!"

Henry continued as a revolutionary firebrand and Virginia's first governor (1776–79). A strong anti-Federalist, he argued against state ratification of the U.S. Constitution unless a bill of individual rights was included. His final speech, given in 1799, argued eloquently for national unity. A much quoted though unsubstantiated line from it argues, "United we stand, divided we fall."

"We the People . . ."
DRAFTING THE DECLARATION OF INDEPENDENCE
★ ★ ★

On June 7, 1776, Virginian Richard Henry Lee introduced a resolution to the Second Continental Congress: "That these United Colonies are, and of right ought to be, free and independent States." The Congress delayed a vote on the resolution and instead appointed John Adams, Roger Sherman, Robert Livingston, Benjamin Franklin, and Thomas Jefferson to a declaration committee. Three of the members had assignments they felt were more important, and Franklin was ill, so the 33-year-old Jefferson, known to be a poor public speaker but "had the reputation of a masterly pen," was chosen to write the document.

Jefferson drew on both the ideas of the Enlightenment and George Mason's Virginia Declaration of Rights. Adams and Franklin both made small changes to Jefferson's draft, and when Congress reviewed the declaration, it condensed the final five paragraphs. On July 4, Congress adopted the 1,817-word Declaration of Independence and a Philadelphia print shop quickly created broadsides that riders carried through the colonies. On July 8, church bells rang out in celebration and Jefferson's words were read in public gatherings.

JOHN JAY
★ 1745–1829 ★
FOUNDING FATHER

One of the lesser known Founding Fathers, John Jay made significant contributions to the American fight for freedom from Britain and the early shaping of the country. During the Revolution, his oversight of a network of informers led the modern CIA to label him America's first counterintelligence chief. He also served as a delegate to the First Continental Congress and president of the Second Continental Congress from 1778 to 1779. At the Revolution's end, Jay was sent to Paris as one of three American ministers charged with negotiating peace terms with the British, which resulted in the Treaty of Paris.

John Jay Spymaster, statesman, jurist, and Founding Father

A gold snuffbox presented in gratitude to John Jay by New York City officials

Under the Articles of Confederation, Jay served as secretary of foreign affairs (now secretary of state) from 1784 to 1789, and during those years Jay contributed several essays to Hamilton's *Federalist* papers, arguing for a strong federal government and ratification of the Constitution. In the years following ratification, Jay became a prominent member of the Federalist Party, first Chief Justice of the United States (1789–1795), and immediately following that, governor of New York (1795–1801). In that position he pushed to realize a long-held dream—the emancipation of African-American slaves. Jay had owned slaves but explained, "I purchase slaves and manumit them at proper ages and when their faithful services shall have afforded a reasonable retribution." In 1799, he signed into law the New York Act for the Gradual Abolition of Slavery.

THOMAS JEFFERSON
★ 1743–1826 ★
FOUNDING FATHER

At his death, John Adams declared, "Thomas Jefferson still survives." And certainly the Jeffersonian legacy continues to this day in American architecture, in the words of the Declaration of Independence, and in the ideals of a populist republic. Yet Jefferson was not born a "common man." A member of Virginia's aristocracy, he showed himself early on to be an intellectual, reveling in his six years at the College of William and Mary in Williamsburg before settling into a planter's life in the Virginia Piedmont. As a member of the House of Burgesses, Jefferson stood firmly with the colonists demanding more rights from the crown. In 1774, he wrote his *A Summary View of the Rights of British America*, which led to his being chosen to draft the Declaration of Independence in the summer of 1776.

During the next three years of war, Jefferson devoted himself to his family, his estates, and to ideas on the postcolonial governance of Virginia. After serving as its second governor (1779–1781), Jefferson planned to retire from public life. But when his wife, Martha, died in 1782, it left him in despair and devoid

A late 1700s surveying compass that may have been used by Thomas Jefferson of a direction. In 1784, he sailed for France as American foreign minister. He was in Europe when the U.S. Constitution was drafted, but he was kept informed of the arguments surrounding its ideas by close friend James Madison.

Returning to America, Jefferson became the country's first official secretary of state and was increasingly troubled by the antirepublican stance of the Federalists. Along with Madison, Jefferson took on Alexander Hamilton and others who

I hold it that a little rebellion now and then is a good thing, and as necessary in the political world as storms in the physical.

THOMAS JEFFERSON

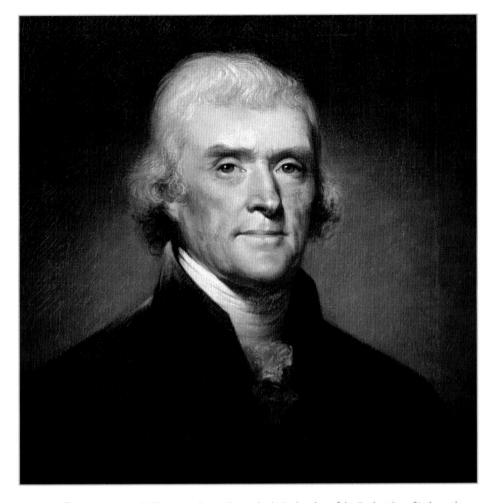

Thomas Jefferson America's brilliant Founding Father and principal author of the Declaration of Independence

were arguing for a strong central government over states' rights. In 1796, the new Democratic-Republican Party pushed Jefferson, "the man of the people," to be their candidate. He lost to Federalist John Adams but had the votes to become vice president. Four years later, he was elected third president of the nation. During two terms in office, he engineered the Louisiana Purchase, which almost doubled the size of the United States, and he worked persistently to keep America out of war, using commerce rather than guns as a weapon against Britain.

In 1809, Jefferson returned to his beloved mountaintop estate, Monticello, and spent his final 17 years there or at a more remote estate—Poplar Forest. He continued to work on their gardens and grounds. He also healed his relationship with former friend turned political foe, John Adams. Jefferson devoted himself to an educational system for the state and planned and oversaw the building and implementation of what is now the University of Virginia. Always plagued by debt, Jefferson sold his vast collection of books to the U.S. government to restock the Library of Congress after the British torched the original collection in the War of 1812.

Despite his great achievements, Jefferson did little to improve the conditions of the enslaved people he controlled, and his writings on the topic of slavery and enslaved people are mixed. Historians generally agree that he fathered several children by one of his slaves, Sally Hemings.

According to Jefferson's own instructions, his gravestone at Monticello describes him as author of the Declaration of American Independence and the Virginia Statute for Religious Freedom, and father of the University of Virginia.

Jefferson's "perspective"—or magnifying—glass

JOHN PAUL JONES
★ **1747–1792** ★
NAVAL HERO

Scottish by birth, John Paul Jones went to sea as a young teenager, serving on merchant ships and slavers, though he hated the latter. He immigrated to America in 1773 and became a first lieutenant in the fledgling Continental navy. Soon captain of his own ship, Jones sailed to France, America's ally, in 1778. There, he made a strong impression on the court and public and became part of a joint Franco-Spanish invasion of Britain. He was put in command of a squadron of five ships and rechristened his flagship, an old Indiaman, the *Bonhomme Richard,* in homage to his champion at court, Benjamin Franklin, and Franklin's alter ego, Poor Richard.

In September, off the Yorkshire coast, Jones's small fleet came upon the British Baltic Fleet—44 merchant ships carrying critical supplies and guarded by two warships. Jones determined to take on one of them, the formidable *Serapis,* and the two ships engaged in a brutal and legendary battle in the heat of which Jones apparently did *not* say the famous line for which he is remembered, "I have just begun to fight." He did, however, emerge victorious, taking the *Serapis* as a rich prize of war. Today, Jones is often called the founder of the U.S. Navy.

Unlikely Allies
VIRGINIA'S ARISTOCRATS AND MASSACHUSETTS'S POST-PURITANS
★ ★ ★

Virginia and Massachusetts supplied many leaders in the Revolution, yet these men came from deeply different worlds. The Virginia planters lived an almost feudal life, the lords of vast estates run on the labor of enslaved African Virginians. This New World aristocracy was close-knit, bound by shared land and commerce concerns, social customs, marriage, and time spent together in the colony's House of Burgesses. Although Anglicanism was Virginia's religion, great piety was not its hallmark. The colony had been founded as a commercial venture, and its eye was still on accruing personal wealth and enjoying its rewards—foxhunts, horse races, balls, and manors.

In contrast, religion had been the driving force that had brought the great migration of Puritans to the Massachusetts Colony in the 1630s. Puritan ardor and abstemiousness initially flavored all aspects of life, but by the mid-1700s, that had relaxed somewhat. Most people lived simple lives as small farmers, teachers, lawyers, and tradesmen, though a rich merchant class flourished in eastern towns. Still, ostentation was frowned on and hard work and education highly prized.

Despite their differences, Virginia's aristocrats and Massachusetts's Puritan-imbued patriots shared a deep respect for each other and a distinctly American sense of individual freedom.

John Paul Jones Aboard the *Bonhomme Richard,* he battles the *Serapis.*

Jones's sword at the U.S. Naval Academy, where he is considered a founder of the Navy

FRANCIS SCOTT KEY
★ 1779–1843 ★
AUTHOR OF "THE STAR-SPANGLED BANNER"

In September 1814, Francis Scott Key, a young American lawyer in Washington, D.C., found himself aboard a British ship off Baltimore, negotiating the release of a friend of his who had been taken captive. He was still on the British ship when the bombardment of Fort McHenry, off Baltimore, began a week later. After 25 hours of cannonading, the fighting lulled, and in the predawn light Key went on deck, waiting apprehensively to see if the American flag was still flying above McHenry. The sight of it waving there inspired Key, an amateur poet, to write what is now known as "The Star-Spangled Banner." Immediately popular, Key's song was not adopted as the national anthem until 1931.

The tattered but beloved star-spangled banner

And the star-spangled banner in triumph shall wave/ O'er the land of the free and the home of the brave!

FRANCIS SCOTT KEY

HENRY KNOX
★ 1750–1806 ★
FOUNDING FATHER

From the earliest days of the Revolution, Boston bookseller Henry Knox proved himself an indispensable part of America's military effort. A large, impressive man who weighed in at close to 300 pounds, he fought in the Battle of Bunker Hill and quickly came to the attention of George Washington when the general took command of the patriot forces encamped around Boston in the summer of 1775. In early December of that year, Washington sent Knox on an almost impossible mission, but one that Knox himself may have initiated: to travel the 300 miles to Fort Ticonderoga, at the southern end of Lake Champlain, and transport the armament there through the winter wilderness and back to the Continental Army in Boston. Knox's epic feat put some 40 cannon, 8 mortars, 6 coehorns, and 2 howitzers into the Continentals' hands and allowed Washington's army to drive the British out of Boston in March 1776.

Henry Knox An often overlooked redeemer of the Revolution, his feats with artillery kept the patriot cause alive.

Knox went on to take part in most of the major battles of the War of Independence, often handling logistics, as he did at the legendary crossing of the Delaware River in December 1776 and the decisive Siege of Yorktown in 1781. When Washington resigned as commander of the Army at the Revolution's end, Knox stepped into that role. A close friend and adviser to Washington, Knox was appointed the nation's first secretary of war and remained in that position throughout Washington's presidency.

MARQUIS DE LAFAYETTE

★ 1757–1834 ★

AMERICAN REVOLUTIONARY ALLY

A young French marquis who volunteered his services in the Revolution, Lafayette became an indispensable element to its success. From an old, vastly wealthy, and much venerated family of aristocrats, Lafayette could claim ancestors who had fought in the Crusades and with Joan of Arc. His own father had died in the Seven Years' War, when the marquis was only two, and the boy longed to continue the tradition of military service. In the early 1770s, the American fight for independence captured his imagination, and he made secret plans (against Louis XVI's orders) to join the American Revolution and bought a ship to transport him and a handful of others across the Atlantic. By mid-June 1777, he was anchored off Charleston, and then he set off on an 800-mile overland march to Philadelphia. "We traveled a great part of the way on foot, often sleeping in the woods, starving, prostrated by the heat," a member of his group wrote.

In Philadelphia, Lafayette was initially rebuffed in his efforts to join the fight, as he was one of a number of young Frenchmen attempting to do so (many of them unskilled poseurs insinuating themselves into the officer corps). But Lafayette refused to be deterred and proved himself a worthy officer. In his first fight in the Battle of the Brandywine in September 1777, he was shot in the leg. Washington was immediately impressed with the young marquis and developed a father's affection for him. "I do not know a nobler, finer soul, and I love him as my own," Washington told a visiting French diplomat. In the battles to come, Lafayette would continue to distinguish himself.

In 1779, he returned to France and helped convince Louis XVI to send a large fleet and a thousand men in support of the Revolution. "I had left as a rebel and fugitive," Lafayette wrote of that trip home, "and returned in triumph as an idol." In the final months of America's fight, he again played a critical role by harassing Cornwallis and pinning him down at Yorktown, Virginia, in September 1781.

Returning to France at war's end, Lafayette helped precipitate the French Revolution. But as an aristocrat, he was suspect. Fleeing, the nobleman was captured by the Austrians and imprisoned for five years. He was released in 1797, to

Commemorative gloves bear Lafayette's likeness.

He has left a young wife and a fine fortune . . . to come and engage in the cause of liberty.

GEORGE WASHINGTON ON LAFAYETTE

Marquis de Lafayette
The French nobleman proved an invaluable ally.

find the great family fortune confiscated by the French government.

In 1824, Lafayette made a final triumphal tour of America as a great hero of independence. "We shall look upon you always as belonging to us, during the whole of our life, as belonging to our children after us," President John Quincy Adams proclaimed. Lafayette left America with sacks of Bunker Hill soil with which he was buried. "The welfare of America is intimately linked with the happiness of all mankind," Lafayette once stated. "She will become the respectable and safe asylum of virtue, integrity, tolerance, equality, and a peaceful liberty."

CHARLES LEE
★ 1732–1782 ★
REVOLUTIONARY GENERAL

Gen. Charles Lee remains an enigmatic figure from the American Revolution. As a British officer, he fought in the French and Indian War, and then he settled in Virginia. He joined the patriot cause with the expectation of being appointed commander in chief; instead, he served as a commander under Washington. In the fall of 1776, Lee procrastinated in joining his forces with Washington's desperate army in New Jersey, despite Washington's entreaties that he quickly do so. When Lee finally moved into New Jersey, he was taken prisoner at a crossroads tavern. Freed in the spring of 1778, Lee rejoined the fight, but his lackluster performance at the Battle of Monmouth Court House led Washington to an unusual show of fury and Lee's dismissal from the Army. Historians speculate that he may have actually been a British insurgent rather than a patriot.

Richard Henry Lee A respected member of Virginia's planter aristocracy and the Continental Congress, he argued for independence from Britain—and an end to slavery in America.

RICHARD HENRY LEE
★ 1732–1794 ★
PATRIOT

A leading voice among the Virginia patriots protesting British taxation, Richard Henry Lee also challenged his fellow Virginia planters on the issue of slavery. As early as 1759, when he was a new member of the House of Burgesses, he introduced a failed bill that proposed a heavy duty on the importation of slaves so as "to put an end to that iniquitous and disgraceful traffic within the colony of Virginia." In 1774, Lee was elected to the First Continental Congress, and at the 1776 Second Continental Congress, he introduced a bill urging a final break, which resulted in the Declaration of Independence.

Lee's cousin Henry "Light-Horse Harry" Lee (1756–1818), was one of Washington's most trusted officers in the Revolution, governor of Virginia, and father of Robert E. Lee.

Meriwether Lewis and William Clark on the lower Columbia River during their expedition that explored the newly acquired territories between the Mississippi and the Pacific

The country on both sides of the missouri from the tops of the river hills, is one continued level fertile plain as far as the eye can reach.

MERIWETHER LEWIS

A telescope from the Lewis and Clark expedition

MERIWETHER LEWIS & WILLIAM CLARK

★ LEWIS, 1774–1809 ★
★ CLARK, 1770–1838 ★
EXPLORERS OF THE AMERICAN WEST

The names of Lewis and Clark have become synonymous with their exploration of the American West, thanks to the expedition they jointly led from 1803 to 1806, and yet the two were very different men.

Meriwether Lewis grew up less than a dozen miles from Thomas Jefferson's Monticello; the two knew each other and were connected by marriage. In 1801, newly elected President Jefferson sought out Lewis, then a captain in the Frontier Army, to be his personal secretary because the young man had "a knowledge of the Western country, the army & it's [sic] situation" and because he was, like Jefferson, a strong advocate of republicanism. Jefferson directed Lewis to begin planning an "exploring party" to return to the western country. But two years later, when the Louisiana Purchase more than doubled the size of the country, Lewis's assignment morphed into an urgent expedition into the vast, new American West, which now stretched through little-known territory to the Pacific. In preparation for the expedition, Lewis learned navigational, cartographic, and astronomical skills.

While in the Army, Lewis had served under William Clark, and he contacted his former officer, proposing that they jointly command the upcoming expedition. Clark responded, "My friend I assure you no man lives with whome I would perfur to undertake Such a Trip &c as your self." Though Lewis could be melancholic and difficult, he was a natural leader and keen observer, and sharing command of the Corps of Discovery with Clark worked reasonably well. Clark undertook the cartographic aspects of the expedition, creating detailed maps of natural features, while Lewis served as naturalist and diplomat to the various native tribes the expedition encountered. At its end, both men were lauded for their part in a victorious endeavor.

Lewis made a halfhearted effort to see the notes from the expedition on the regions and their flora and fauna and peoples published, but the effort never bore fruit. He also served as governor of the Louisiana Territory, but his emotional health and future prospects dimmed in the years after the expedition, and his drinking increased. After two failed attempts, he took his life in a roadhouse on the Natchez Trace in 1809.

A Journey of Discovery

THE LEWIS AND CLARK EXPEDITION

★ ★ ★

President Jefferson sent the Corps of Discovery into the uncharted new American lands west of the Mississippi with instructions to make allies of the native tribes, to record the flora and fauna and natural features, and to find waterways linking the Missouri River to the Pacific. On May 15, 1804, the 29 men of the expedition started up the Missouri River outside St. Louis. In the next 28 months, they traveled some 8,000 miles through what Lewis described hyperbolically as "country . . . on which the foot of civilized man had never trodden." Often guided by Indians, most famously a young Shoshone mother named Sacagawea, the corps met with some 50 tribes and charted and described the American plains, the vast seas of buffalo, great rivers and mountain ranges, the grandeur of the Pacific coast, and more than 300 species previously unknown to science. Today, *The Journals of Lewis and Clark* are considered an American classic.

Clark's life was not as fraught as Lewis's. His family were successful planters on the western frontier of Virginia, then in Kentucky, and his brother, George Rogers Clark, was the Revolutionary hero of the western fight for freedom from Britain. Much younger, William served in militias in the late 1700s, fighting Native Americans in the Ohio Valley. It was during this time that he had met Lewis.

With Lewis's death, the task of organizing and publishing the journals and records of scientific discoveries made during the Corps of Discovery's expedition fell to Clark. Not the wordsmith that Lewis had been, Clark enlisted the help of Nicholas Biddle, a lawyer, writer, and magazine editor in Philadelphia (and later president of the Bank of the United States).

Clark spent the two decades after the expedition working mostly in Indian affairs. He first served as principal Indian agent for the Louisiana Territory and commander of its militia, then as governor of the newly designated Missouri Territory. His last years were spent in St. Louis on Indian affairs in that region.

ROBERT LIVINGSTON

★ 1746–1813 ★

STATESMAN, INVENTOR

A member of the Continental Congress, Robert Livingston, a New York lawyer, was on the committee charged with drafting the Declaration of Independence, though he played little role. In the Revolution, he became what was essentially the first secretary of state, and in April 1789, he administered the first presidential oath of office to George Washington. As minister to France under Jefferson, he negotiated the 1803 Louisiana Purchase and later worked with inventor Robert Fulton on developing the first successful steam-powered vessel, the *Clermont*, which made its maiden voyage in 1807 on the Hudson River.

The compass used by Lewis and Clark during their journey

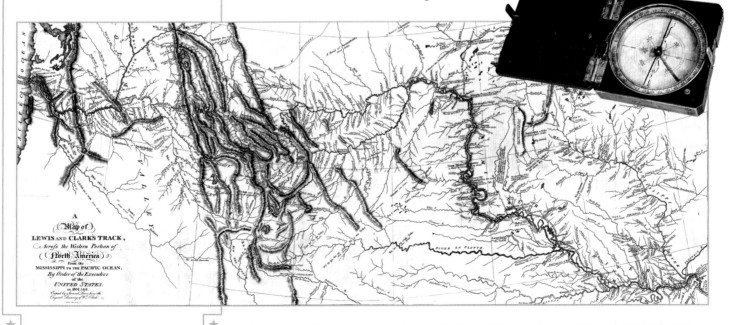

A map showing the circuitous routes taken by the Corps of Discovery during its 28-month, 8,000-mile saga

THOMAS MACDONOUGH
★ 1783–1825 ★
REVOLUTIONARY NAVAL HERO

A U.S. Navy lieutenant who served with Stephen Decatur in the First Barbary War of 1801–05, Thomas Macdonough was only 28 when he was asked to take command of the American naval defense of Lake Champlain in the War of 1812. Macdonough oversaw the building of a small American fleet on a tributary of the lake, and in early September 1814, his masterful victory over a British naval force marked a turning point in the war. Winston Churchill later called it "the most decisive engagement of the War of 1812."

DOLLEY MADISON
★ 1768–1849 ★
FIRST LADY, FOUNDING MOTHER

Dolley Madison arguably reigns as America's most revered and influential first lady (1809–1817). She was the young widow of a Philadelphia Quaker lawyer when she married James Madison in 1794. During Madison's years as secretary of state, Dolley often serviced as stand-in first lady for President Thomas Jefferson, a widower. When Madison succeeded him in office, his wife became a Washington force, essentially defining the role of first lady (she was the first to spend her tenure in Washington). In 1814, when the British attacked Washington, she saved several portraits in the White House and in so doing, became a legendary hero. Returning to the city after its burning, she lobbied

Dolley Madison The influential first lady may have made this gown (below) from White House drapes she took as the British invaded.

> Liberty is to faction what air is to fire, an aliment without which it instantly expires. But it could not be less folly to abolish liberty, which is essential to political life, because it nourishes faction, than it would be to wish the annihilation of air.
>
> JAMES MADISON

successfully to rebuild the federal city rather than move it to another location. Even after Madison's death, she wielded great respect and authority, though she was plagued by debts, owing in part to the economic failings of the Madison plantation, Montpelier. Yet she continued to work on finishing and seeing published her husband's critical papers, including his copious notes on the Constitutional Convention.

JAMES MADISON
★ 1751–1836 ★
FOUNDING FATHER

Another Virginia aristocrat, James Madison could have spent his life in the "Solitude and Contemplation" he loved had not the Revolution intervened. Slight (five feet four) and hypochondriacal, Madison never served on the battlefield, but he did become deeply involved in crafting the laws under which the new state of Virginia should operate. After serving on the Virginia Council of State, he was elected to the Continental Congress in 1779, and once there, he began taking careful notes on congressional debates, and he served on numerous committees. As the war drew to an end, Madison continued on as a respected figure in the Confederation Congress. When he returned to Virginia in 1784, he served in the state legislature, but his thoughts were focused on how to cement the union of states. He attended the Annapolis Convention called to discuss that in September 1786, where he formed a bond with Alexander Hamilton over the issues facing the new nation.

The following spring Madison wrote his groundbreaking "Vices of the Political System of the United States," based on his experiences in state and federal government and on his own thinking. His original outline soon became the backbone of the Virginia Plan for national government, presented at the opening of the Constitutional Convention in Philadelphia in May 1787. Madison's ideas—that the independence of states would prove "utterly irreconcilable with the idea of an aggregate sovereignty" but that the states needed to maintain some autonomy— became the much debated themes of the convention. Madison made it his duty to take copious notes on the convention's proceedings, and they remain the document of record for that historic moment.

Once the fight for states' ratification began, Madison contributed to Alexander Hamilton's *Federalist* papers project, writing 29 of the 85 essays arguing for a strong federal government. Madison's masterpiece, *Federalist* no. 10, written in November 1787, begins, "Among the numerous advantages promised by a well constructed Union, none deserves to be more

James Madison Often called the Father of the Constitution, Madison's ideas infuse American government.

accurately developed than its tendency to break and control the violence of faction." Once ratification was achieved, Madison was committed to adding language to the Constitution that would protect individual rights. His original proposal for 19 changes was whittled down in congressional committee to 12, and presented as amendments to the Constitution. Ten of those were ratified, to become the U.S. Bill of Rights. As the new nation took form, Madison became, with Jefferson, an ardent republican opposed to what he saw as the overweening desires of the Federalists for a dominant central government. He served as Jefferson's secretary of state

and then succeeded him as fourth president (1809–1817).

More scholarly than an overt leader, Madison was not well suited to the position, and his Cabinet was weak and fractious, refusing to fund the military adequately, even in the face of tensions with Britain and France. By 1812, Britain and America were again at war, and in 1814, the British had taken over the new capital city and burned the few federal buildings then standing. Despite that, the Madisons returned to Washington and worked to resurrect the federal city. His final years were spent at his Montpelier estate.

FRANCIS MARION

★ CA 1732–1795 ★

SOLDIER, AMERICAN REVOLUTION

Francis Marion is remembered by history as the Swamp Fox, owing to his tactical brilliance in irregular warfare against the British during the American Revolution. A native of South Carolina, he first fought in the French and Indian War, and then in 1780–81, he organized a small, mobile militia—Marion's Men—that effectively harassed British forces during their southern campaign for the Carolinas. Today, he is considered one of the fathers of modern guerrilla warfare.

Marion's decanter box, essentially a traveling liquor cabinet to be used while in the field

Francis Marion In a scene from legend, the wily "Swamp Fox" invites a British officer to share a meal of sweet potatoes and cold water. Inspired by the spirit of Marion's Men, the officer joined their cause.

JOHN MARSHALL

★ 1755–1835 ★

CHIEF JUSTICE OF THE UNITED STATES

Known as the "Great Chief Justice," John Marshall served as a soldier under Washington during the Revolution, enduring the brutal winter at Valley Forge. Following his battlefield years, he had a brief formal introduction to legal studies as a student of George Wythe at the College of William and Mary. Marshall became a lawyer in Richmond, Virginia, a member of the House of Delegates, and a strong Federalist. President Adams sent him as an envoy to Paris as part of a successful diplomatic mission that managed to diffuse tensions with the French. On his return, Adams offered him a seat on the Supreme Court, but Marshall refused, preferring to run for the House of Representatives. After a brief tenure there, he became secretary of state. In 1801, Marshall was nominated Chief Justice of the United States and won unanimous Senate confirmation, though he continued to serve as secretary of state as well.

> *The power to tax involves the power to destroy.*
>
> JOHN MARSHALL

During his 34 years (1801–1835) as Chief Justice, Marshall strengthened the judicial branch of government, creating a truly tripartite form of federal government, and expounded and extended the theories of constitutional law. In an early and pivotal case before him—*Marbury* v. *Madison* (1803)—Marshall ruled that the Supreme Court could invalidate an act of Congress if it violated the Constitution. He also later ruled that the federal judiciary had the power to overrule a state court's decision. While on the Virginia circuit, Marshall also presided over the Aaron Burr treason trial of 1807, and his contention that the prosecution had not established an "overt act" of treason, as the Constitution required, led to the former vice president's acquittal. It also increased tensions between Marshall, a Federalist, and his Democratic-Republican cousin, President Thomas Jefferson. Marshall was a supporter of the American Colonization Society, which advocated resettling freed American slaves in Liberia.

One of the longest serving Chief Justices to date, Marshall was involved in more than a thousand decisions while on the court, and he authored 500 opinions.

GEORGE MASON

★ 1725–1792 ★
FOUNDING FATHER

Though George Mason does not enjoy the same prominence as other pivotal figures in the American fight for independence, his thoughts and writings on law and governance had a great influence on his fellow Founding Fathers and ultimately the founding documents of the nation. In his formative years, he had exposure to legal thinking from the extensive library of his uncle, colonial lawyer John Mercer. From his father, Mason had inherited extensive landholdings on the Potomac River, and at the age of 30, he began constructing an estate, Gunston Hall, not far from George Washington's Mount Vernon. The two young men developed a friendship based on mutual respect and interests.

Mason became a member of the Virginia House of Burgesses in 1759, and in the next decade, he wrote critical papers regarding the overreach of the British government in its dealings with the American colonies, including the Fairfax Resolves (1774) and the seminal Virginia Declaration of Rights (1776). His language in that declaration—"All

> No free government, or the blessing of liberty, can be preserved to any people but by a firm adherence to justice, moderation, temperance, frugality, and virtue, and by frequent recurrence to fundamental principles.
>
> GEORGE MASON

men are by nature equally free and independent, and have certain inherent rights . . . namely, the enjoyment of life and liberty, with the means of acquiring and possessing property, and pursuing and obtaining happiness and safety"—would be echoed by Thomas Jefferson, when Jefferson drafted the Declaration of Independence.

During the Revolution, Mason was influential in Virginia affairs and in creating a system of governance. In the years that followed, Mason helped reach a compromise on Virginia's claims to western lands that in turn led to the Constitution. In 1787, Mason was a vocal member of the five-man delegation to the Constitutional Convention. He refused to sign the final version, as he believed it gave the senate too much power, the federal judiciary too much power over state judiciaries, and most important, that it lacked a declaration of individual rights. Mason's Master Draft of a bill of rights, prepared during the Constitutional Convention, later found voice in the U.S. Bill of Rights, ratified as the first amendments to the Constitution in 1791.

George Mason His Virginia Declaration of Rights was echoed by Jefferson in the Declaration of Independence. Mason later exercised similar influence over the language in the Bill of Rights.

James Monroe Affable and popular, Monroe (waving)—the fourth Virginian to be president—won an easy election in 1816, launching a short-lived "Era of Good Feelings."

JAMES MONROE
★ 1758–1831 ★
FOUNDING FATHER

Slightly younger than the early founders of the American nation, James Monroe has been called the last president among the Founding Fathers. He was a student at the College of William and Mary in 1774 when tensions with the colonists led the royal governor to flee Williamsburg. Two years later, Monroe joined the Continental Army and served with distinction as an officer under George Washington, fighting in a number of critical battles. At Trenton in early 1776, he suffered a near-fatal injury while leading a charge against a British cannon position.

After the war, Monroe studied law under Thomas Jefferson, became a prominent Virginia politician, and was elected to the Confederation Congress in 1783. A delegate to the Virginia ratifying convention, he voted against ratification of the Constitution, objecting to the lack of a bill of rights and direct election of senators. He ran and narrowly lost to James Madison in the first election for the House of Representatives, but the state legislature appointed him to the U.S. Senate. As the Federalists argued for an ever stronger central government, Monroe joined his fellow Virginians Jefferson and Madison in opposing them and instead espousing republican, populist ideals.

In 1794, President Washington appointed Monroe American minister to France. Returning to Virginia in 1796 for a few brief years, Monroe served as governor (1799–1802) before being again dispatched to France to negotiate the Louisiana Purchase. He later served as secretary of state, then secretary of war under Madison, then succeeded him as fifth president. Though Monroe's two terms in office (1817–1825) have been labeled the "Era of Good Feelings," they

America Claims Dominion
MONROE'S LASTING DOCTRINE
★ ★ ★

In President Monroe's 1823 message to Congress, he concluded with language that has since become known as the Monroe Doctrine: "We owe it, therefore, to candor and to the amicable relations existing between the United States and [European] powers to declare that we should consider any attempt on their part to extend their system to any portion of this hemisphere as dangerous to our peace and safety." Monroe had laid down a historic gauntlet, warning Europe that the United States claimed the Western Hemisphere as its sphere of influence and that European expansionism or interventionism would not be tolerated. Monroe's decree had its roots in Spanish Florida, where a fluid border allowed Spanish raids into U.S. territory in Florida and Georgia and encouraged runaway slaves to escape into swamps, where the Seminole offered them support. In 1818, Monroe dispatched Gen. Andrew Jackson to the area and Jackson invaded Spanish Florida, creating an international incident. Meanwhile, Spain's Latin American colonies were struggling for independence, and the United States was sympathetic to their plight. These, and other geopolitical considerations, were much on the mind of Monroe and his forceful secretary of state, John Quincy Adams, when they jointly conceived of the Monroe Doctrine.

A bicorne hat worn in Monroe's era

got off to a rocky start, with an economic crisis and dissension over the admission of Missouri to the union as a slave state. The resulting Missouri Compromise was supported by Monroe as a means to quell tensions between North and South.

Monroe's presidency is perhaps best known for its decisive foreign policy and for the lasting effects of the Monroe Doctrine, still a cornerstone of American foreign policy. He was the last of the "Virginia dynasty"—the Virginians who served as four of the first five presidents.

Gouverneur Morris Drafter of the Constitution

> *In adopting a republican form of government, I not only took it as man does his wife, for better, for worse, but what few men do with their wives, I took it knowing all its bad qualities.*
>
> **GOUVERNEUR MORRIS**

GOUVERNEUR MORRIS
★ 1752–1816 ★
FOUNDING FATHER

Gouverneur Morris, part of the wealthy New York elite and a lawyer by training, was instrumental in New York State governance and as a member of the Continental Congress. But his greatest role was as a leading voice at the Constitutional Convention, where he argued for religious liberty and the rights of property and against slavery. He drafted much of the final version of the Constitution, including its ringing preamble: "We the People of the United States, in Order to form a more perfect Union . . ." He later served as minister to France (1792–94), U.S. senator (1800–1803), and chairman of the Erie Canal Commission.

ROBERT MORRIS
★ 1734–1806 ★
FINANCIER OF THE REVOLUTION

Born in England, Robert Morris moved to the colonies at 13 years of age and eventually became one of Philadelphia's most prominent businessmen.

Robert Morris The "financier of the American Revolution" helped fuel it with his own funds.

A delegate to the Second Continental Congress, he initially argued against independence but later signed the Declaration of Independence. When the Revolution faltered, he loaned money from his personal funds to the struggling cause, bankrolling and supplying American fighting forces to become known as the "financier of the Revolution."

Yet after the Revolution, even though he had given America critical support, Morris was the subject of the first congressional investigation, involving his financial dealing during the war. Though exonerated, he declared bankruptcy in 1798, owing to bad investments, and served three years in debtor's prison. After his release, he led a modest life in Philadelphia until his death in 1806.

Thomas Paine The political activist whose 1776 opus, *Common Sense* (above), fired the American public to revolt against Britain and helped pave the way to independence.

THOMAS PAINE
★ 1737–1809 ★
"PEN" OF THE AMERICAN REVOLUTION

Thomas Paine arrived in Philadelphia, Pennsylvania, in December 1774, having failed at almost every occupation he had tried in his native England—except for an attempt at pamphlet writing. He was 37 and desperately ill with typhus, but he did have one saving grace: a letter of introduction from his London friend Benjamin Franklin, extolling him as "an ingenious worthy young man." Impressed by that, a local doctor nursed Paine back to health, and Paine took a job as editor of a new magazine devoted to "utility and entertainment." He soon broke out of that mold, writing invectives against the slave trade that were very convincing; then he turned his pen on Britain and began work on what would become his first masterpiece, *Common Sense*. In prose easily accessible to the common man, he preached that "the cause of America is, in a great measure, the cause of all mankind," then went on to assert that "government, even in its best state, is but a necessary evil; in its worst state an intolerable one."

Common Sense changed both Paine's life and the course of history. Americans were captivated and inspired by it, as was much of the Western world. After its release, Paine briefly served as an aide-de-camp to his great hero, George Washington, but was unsuited to soldiering and returned to writing. Late in 1776, he released the first of his *American Crisis* essays, which began, "These are the times that try men's souls. The summer soldier and the sunshine patriot will, in this crisis, shrink from the service of their country; but he that stands by it now, deserves the love and thanks of man and woman." When Washington's troops attacked Trenton that December, their battle cry was, "These are the times that try men's souls."

> *Government, like dress, is the badge of lost innocence; the palaces of kings are built on the ruins of the bowers of paradise.*
>
> **THOMAS PAINE**

Paine's pen earned him widespread celebrity, and he spent some years in France, where the French Revolution inspired him to write *Rights of Man,* which defended the revolution. Yet he also spoke out against the planned execution of Louis XVI, and that landed him in a Paris prison for most of 1794. While he was there, the first sections of his masterwork, *The Age of Reason,* were published, arguing against organized religion. He also composed an open letter to George Washington, his former hero, castigating him as a poor leader.

Throughout his life, Paine was often undisciplined and dissolute. John Adams once described him as "a mongrel between pig and puppy, begotten by a wild boar on a bitch wolf." In 1802, the poverty-stricken Paine returned to America and settled on a farm given him by the state of New York, in appreciation for his revolutionary work. A few years later he moved to the city itself, where he died in 1809. In the early days of the American Revolution, he had written, "I am neither a farmer, mechanic, merchant nor shopkeeper. I believe, however, I am of the first class. I am a *farmer of thoughts,* and all the crops I raise I give away."

CHARLES WILLSON PEALE & JAMES PEALE

★ CHARLES, 1741–1827 ★
★ JAMES, 1749–1831 ★
AMERICAN PAINTERS

The Peale family became synonymous with art in the early decades of the new nation, but brothers Charles and James began as saddlemakers after they lost their father at an early age. Charles, the older of the two, yearned to paint, and in the late 1760s, he went to London and studied under fellow American Benjamin West. James became a cabinetmaker,

Charles Willson Peale In the early days of the American Republic, Peale became a prolific portraitist of presidents and other founders.

James Peale Although not as well known as his brother, James was also a respected artist.

and when Charles returned to Maryland and opened a studio, James worked there, making frames for Charles's art.

Charles also began to teach James to paint and draw, until war intervened. In 1776, James joined a Maryland regiment and fought with Washington at all the major early battles of the Revolution. In the dire winter of 1776, Charles's militia unit joined Washington's force, and Charles later recalled spotting Washington's desperate men crossing the Delaware River in early December. One "was in an old dirty blanket jacket, his beard long, and his face so full of sores that he could not clean it." The man, Peale suddenly realized, was James.

In 1779, James resigned his commission and joined Charles in Philadelphia. Both brothers painted historical scenes, still lifes, and miniature portraits. Charles became a leading American portraitist, painting seven portraits of Washington, as well as six other presidents and several other Founding Fathers. In 1786, Charles enlarged his gallery to accommodate a museum of art and natural history. His son, Rembrandt Peale, also enjoyed a wide artistic reputation.

OLIVER HAZARD PERRY

★ 1785–1819 ★

NAVAL HERO, WAR OF 1812

Oliver Hazard Perry was from a family of seafaring men. His father served in the American Revolution as a captain in the U.S. Navy. He secured his eldest son, Oliver, a midshipman's warrant during tensions with France at the turn of the 19th century. Oliver also saw action during the First Barbary War (1801–05), and after that war, he was eventually given command of his own ship. Perry left the Navy briefly, but as war with Britain loomed, he returned. In the winter of 1813, he was posted to Erie, Pennsylvania, as a master commander and oversaw the construction of a small fleet of ships. His defeat of the British squadron at the September 1813 Battle of Lake Erie earned him a place in history and led him to write his commander the legendary line, "We have met the enemy and they are ours."

Oliver Hazard Perry His defeat of the British navy in the 1813 Battle of Lake Erie was a critical victory.

Pontiac The Odawa (Ottawa) chief launched his own war against the British during the larger Seven Years'—or French and Indian—War.

PONTIAC

★ CA 1714/1720–1769 ★

ODAWA (OTTAWA) CHIEF

Born somewhere along the Detroit River, where the French had influence in the colonial era, Pontiac became a young leader among the Odawa and aligned his people with New France against the British, particularly during the Seven Years' War (1756–1763). As British domination of the Great Lakes increased near the war's end, Pontiac helped instigate a rebellion that has come to bear his name. His warriors captured a series of British forts in what is now the Midwest, and the uprising spread to the Virginia and Pennsylvania frontiers. Pontiac himself participated in a short-lived siege of British-held Detroit that ended with the end of the Seven Years' War.

EDMUND RANDOLPH

★ 1753–1813 ★

PATRIOT AND STATESMAN

When Edmund Randolph's Loyalist father, John, returned to England in 1775, Edmund moved into the Virginia household of his prominent patriot uncle, Peyton Randolph. In the early days of the Revolution, when Edmund became an aide-de-camp to George Washington, then in Boston, his father wrote him, "For God's Sake, return to your Family & indeed to yourself." But Randolph remained a patriot and served as a delegate to the Virginia Constitutional Convention and the Continental Congress. With independence, he became governor of Virginia and was deeply involved in establishing a viable federal union. He opened the Constitutional Convention in 1787 by introducing the Virginia Plan, which outlined a new system of national governance. Though he refused to ratify the convention's final version of the Constitution, Randolph ultimately worked for its ratification and became the first U.S. attorney general (1789–1794), then secretary of state (1794–1795).

They came with a Bible and their religion, stole our land, crushed our spirit, and now tell us we should be thankful to the Lord for being saved.

PONTIAC

HEARTH & HOME

Virginia's Dynastic Heritage

THE PRIVATE HOMES OF FIRST PRESIDENTS

★ ★ ★

Virginia was once dotted by the great plantations of the Virginia aristocracy, and some still stand, including the homes of four of the first five presidents—Washington, Jefferson, Madison, and Monroe. They offer intimate glimpses into the private lives of these celebrated men and of life in their time, an era marked by slavery, hospitality, ravaging illnesses, and grand dreams.

George Washington's Mount Vernon, on the Potomac 15 miles south of Washington, D.C., is a much revered national icon, reflecting its owner's patrician tastes and practicality. Like Jefferson's and Madison's estates, it was run on slave labor, and like them, its grounds reflect plantation life—outbuildings where slaves lived and worked as blacksmiths, millers, and other craftsmen. The rooms of the mansion echo Washington's love of stately decorum.

By contrast, Monticello is symbolic of Jefferson's restless intellect. Filled with items that speak to his interests in natural history, science, architecture, and invention, the domed classical revival home occupies a hilltop above the city of Charlottesville and the University of Virginia. Gardens and plantings of all kinds reflect Jefferson's love of horticulture. Plagued by visitors, Jefferson often escaped to his more remote estate, Poplar Forest, near present-day Lynchburg. Very near Jefferson's palatial Monticello is Highland, the simple clapboard farmhouse of fifth president James Monroe. The family lived here in Monroe's "cabin-castle" from 1799 to 1823.

Roughly 30 miles northeast, Madison's Georgian mansion, Montpelier, overlooks the rolling Virginia Piedmont. Madison's father, James Sr., built the original house, but James and Dolley added the grand portico as well as additions. More additions were built by owner William du Pont after he purchased the home in 1901, but the house is now slowly being restored to its appearance during the Madisons' final years there.

Thomas Jefferson was perpetually changing and refining his beloved Monticello—"little mountain"—above Charlottesville, Virginia. It now ranks among UNESCO's World Heritage sites.

PEYTON RANDOLPH
★ CA 1721–1775 ★
PRESIDENT, CONTINENTAL CONGRESSES

Peyton Randolph, a respected member of colonial Virginia's planters' society and an early and insistent voice for the rights of the colonists, had objected to taxes imposed by the royal governor as far back as 1751. As tensions with Britain grew in the 1760s, he was elected speaker of the House of Burgesses and continued to oppose increasing British taxation. At the First Continental Congress in 1774, Randolph was unanimously elected president and presided over the Second Continental Congress as well, until his sudden death of a stroke in 1775. For his service, he earned the sobriquet "father of the country" (later passed to his colleague, George Washington).

Paul Revere In this romanticized version of his ride, redcoats try to head him off as he races to warn that the British are coming.

PAUL REVERE
★ 1735–1818 ★
PATRIOT LEADER

At the outset of hostilities with the British, Paul Revere was a prosperous Boston silver- and goldsmith, having learned the crafts from his French Huguenot father, an emigrant to America. In the years prior to the Revolution, Revere also learned copperplate engraving and put that skill to use in his endeavors as an early patriot, creating incendiary engravings of the British occupation of Boston. His "Bloody Massacre in King Street," produced three weeks after the "massacre" of March 1770, fueled anti-British sentiments among the colonists. Many of his works, as a smith and engraver, are now considered early American masterpieces.

However, his reputation rests with his work as messenger and spy for the early patriots. After the 1773 Boston Tea Party, he rode to New York to spread news of its success, and the following year, he rode to New York and Philadelphia, "Calling a Congress" of all the colonies. But the ride with which he is most associated is his "midnight ride," made famous in an 1860 poem by Henry Wadsworth Longfellow.

The ride resulted from Revere's clandestine activities undertaken with other Boston Sons of Liberty. In 1775, the group determined to keep an eye on the movement of British soldiers in the occupied town. They agreed on a signal, should the British march from the town: "If the British went out by Water, we would shew two Lanthorns in the North Church Steeple;

& if by Land, one." On the night of April 18, suspicious movements were observed and two lanterns appeared. Revere rode ahead of the British to Lexington to warn John Hancock and Samuel Adams, then in hiding, that a British contingent was on its way, presumably to capture them. According to Revere's own account, he "alarmed almost every House, till [he] got to Lexington" and successfully delivered the warning. As he attempted to ride on to Concord to alert patriots there, he was briefly apprehended by the British before returning to Boston. During the war years, Revere served with the Massachusetts artillery, and after the Revolution, he opened the first copper rolling mill in North America, which produced copper for the hull of the U.S.S. *Constitution*.

BETSY ROSS
★ 1752–1836 ★
FOLK HERO

Betsy (Elizabeth) Ross is a figure shrouded in legend. What is definitively known about her is that she was a Philadelphia widow and seamstress who made ship's colors for Pennsylvania ships in the first years of the Revolution. In 1870, however, a grandson, William Canby, reported to the Historical Society of Pennsylvania that his grandmother did sewing and embroidery for George Washington on his stays in Philadelphia during the Revolution, and that in June 1777, he, with Robert Morris and another member of Congress, visited her and requested that she create the first American flag. The story took on a life of its own, but most scholars reject its validity, as no historical documentation has come to light to substantiate it.

BENJAMIN RUSH
★ 1746–1813 ★
MEDICAL PIONEER, FOUNDING FATHER

The son of a widowed mother who ran a grocery store, Benjamin Rush was taken under the care of his uncle, a medical doctor, and went on to apprentice respected physicians in Philadelphia. He earned a medical degree from the University of Edinburgh and trained at a hospital in London. While there, he met Benjamin Franklin, who would become his friend and fellow patriot.

Returning to Philadelphia, Rush treated mainly the poor but also taught chemistry at what is now the University of Pennsylvania, and he became a respected

Mirth, and even cheerfulness, when employed as remedies in low spirits, are like hot water to a frozen limb.

BENJAMIN RUSH

local leader. In the fall and early winter of 1776, Rush worked with Thomas Paine in refining and finding a printer for Paine's opus *Common Sense*. The following summer, as a delegate to the Second Continental Congress, Rush became a signer of the Declaration of Independence. He then served for several years as a surgeon general in the Continental Army and attempted, generally unsuccessfully, to raise its medical standards and hygiene practices. In 1787, he was elected to the Pennsylvania ratifying convention for the U.S. Constitution and was a leader of the movement for ratification.

Benjamin Rush Physician and Founding Father

In his later life, Rush served as treasurer of the U.S. Mint and continued to pursue his interests in medicine (focusing particularly on a mind-body connection and on purging and bloodletting treatments), in the abolition of slavery, and in education. He was a founder of Dickinson College and what is now Franklin and Marshall University, as well as chair of various departments at the University of Pennsylvania.

Betsy Ross Despite the lack of historical evidence, she gained fame for making the first U.S. flag.

and her infant also helped disarm other Indians encountered.

In August, the party reached the Montana plains, thanks to Sacagawea's guidance. She and her family remained there with the Mandan, and Charbonneau was paid $500 for his services, horse, and tepee. Sacagawea received nothing—except the enduring respect of the Corps of Discovery and an enduring place in the history of America.

> [Sacagawea], we find, reconciles all the Indians, as to our friendly intentions—a woman with a party of men is a token of peace.
>
> **WILLIAM CLARK**

Sacagawea The Shoshone teenager proved invaluable as a guide to Lewis and Clark on their expedition.

SACAGAWEA
★ CA 1786–1812 ★
GUIDE, LEWIS AND CLARK EXPEDITION

Sacagawea, a Shoshone, is thought to have been born in what is now Idaho. As a girl she was kidnapped by Hidatsa, who sold her a few years later to French-Canadian trapper Toussaint Charbonneau. During November 1804, Charbonneau offered himself and his two "squaws" as guides to Meriwether Lewis and William Clark and their Corps of Discovery. The explorers, anxious to have the Hidatsa-speaking Sacagawea as a guide, waited until she gave birth before continuing west into the Rockies. The teenage Sacagawea, her infant son "Pomp" strapped to her back, proved critical to the expedition. With her knowledge of the natural world and terrain and Native American ways and languages, she acted as interpreter, translator, trader, and guide for the expedition. At one point, she even saved the expedition's journals from floating away on the upper Missouri River. The presence of a mother

ELIZABETH ANN SETON
★ 1774–1821 ★
FIRST AMERICAN SAINT

The daughter of a prominent New York physician, Elizabeth Bayley married businessman William Seton in 1794. In 1803, William faced serious financial and health problems, and the couple sailed for Italy, where William soon died. Remaining in Italy, Elizabeth became attracted to Catholicism. She returned to America and joined the Catholic Church in 1805. In 1808, she established the first free Catholic school in America in Baltimore and then a year later founded with others the Sisters of St. Joseph. She was canonized by Pope Paul VI in 1975.

DANIEL SHAYS
★ CA 1747–1825 ★
LEADER OF SHAYS'S REBELLION

Having served as an officer in the Revolution, Daniel Shays returned to his farm in western Massachusetts and found himself saddled with what he believed were unreasonable tax obligations imposed by the state government. In September 1786, he joined fellow farmers in an armed

Daniel Shays Shown at left in a 1787 woodcut

protest against land foreclosures. Word of "Shays's Rebellion" spread through the new nation, alarming George Washington and other leaders. The rebellion was put down the following February, and Shays (who was only one of its leaders) escaped. However, the rebellion's consequences were far-ranging, as it pointed out the weaknesses in the federal government and was an impetus behind the 1787 Constitutional Convention.

FRIEDRICH VON STEUBEN
★ 1730–1794 ★
AMERICAN REVOLUTION ALLY

A German by birth, Friedrich von Steuben became an officer on the General Staff of the Prussian Army, serving in the Seven Years' War. He was discharged for unknown reasons in 1763, and in 1777, contemplating joining the American Revolutionary effort, he traveled to Paris, hoping to be endorsed by American foreign minister Benjamin Franklin.

Steuben presented himself to George Washington in February 1778, during the dire winter at Valley Forge,

Friedrich von Steuben He shaped Washington's army into a disciplined fighting force.

offering a somewhat overblown letter of introduction from Benjamin Franklin. By March, Steuben had embarked on a training program for Washington's troops that would teach and impose critically needed military discipline. He first trained a "model company," who then trained other troops. With no more English at his command than "God damn," Steuben introduced close-order drill, bayonet training, and new sanitation measures, creating the kind of professional army Washington had always longed for. Steuben went on to fight alongside Nathanael Greene in the South, and he was at Washington's side during the victorious Siege of Yorktown in 1781. In an early letter to Washington, Steuben had said he desired only to "render your Country all the Services in my Power, and to deserve the title of the Citizen of America by fighting for the Cause of your Liberty." He in fact died a U.S. citizen on his farm in New York.

The Second Great Awakening
AMERICA'S EVANGELICAL ROOTS
★ ★ ★

s the United States struggled to find its national soul, Americans struggled with their own souls. Historians call the half century beginning in 1790 the Second Great Awakening. During this period, the more established Anglican and Congregationalist churches found themselves in competition with Methodists and Baptists, as throughout the states itinerant preachers held emotional revivals and camp meetings that drew large crowds and a growing flock to their religions.

This populist message of personal salvation and the exercise of free will for all people led to an evangelical groundswell, which attracted the lower classes—African Americans as well as whites. The "awakening" began in the rural South; then it spread to the Midwest and New England. There, visionary Congregationalist theologians, like Lyman Beecher and Nathaniel Taylor, embraced it to temper the doctrine of predestination and create New Light Calvinism.

GILBERT STUART
★ 1755–1828 ★
PORTRAITIST

Even as a young teenager, Gilbert Stuart showed strong artistic talent, and by the age of 20 he had moved to London to pursue a career as a painter. There, he studied with American expatriate Benjamin West, and at the end of his five-year apprenticeship to West, he painted what is now considered one of his masterpieces: "The Skater," a full-length portrait that broke with the established grand manner of portraiture and received wide acclaim at the 1782 exhibition of the Royal Academy. In 1793, Stuart returned to the United States and continued his reputation as a leading portraitist. His paintings of American presidents and first ladies—Washington, Jefferson, both Adamses, and both Madisons—as well as other founders, have become icons of American art.

What a . . . business is that of a portrait painter! You bring him a potato and expect he will paint you a peach.

GILBERT STUART

JOHN SULLIVAN
★ 1740–1795 ★
POLITICIAN, SOLDIER

After serving as a delegate at the First Continental Congress, John Sullivan was appointed a brigadier general in the Continental Army. He was with Washington's army at the Siege of Boston and the Battles of Long Island and Trenton. In 1779, after botching a combined Franco-American attack on Newport, Rhode Island, he led a campaign against the Iroquois Confederation in Pennsylvania and New York, with orders from Washington to "lay waste all the settlements . . . that the country may not be merely *overrun* but *destroyed*." Sullivan's ignominious campaign displaced some 4,000 people. He returned to politics in 1780, serving in the Continental Congress and as New Hampshire's attorney general and governor.

John Sullivan More liability than asset, the Revolutionary commander mismanaged most of his campaigns.

TECUMSEH
★ 1768–1813 ★
SHAWNEE CHIEF

As a boy and young man, Tecumseh watched as European encroachment changed the traditional Shawnee way of life. His father died warring with Virginia settlers in what is now Ohio, and Tecumseh vowed to become a warrior himself in the last decades of the 1700s.

He based himself in Prophetstown (also known as Tippecanoe, in the Indiana Territory), whose name derived from Tecumseh's brother, Tenskwatawa, a powerful spiritual leader and "prophet." Tecumseh, himself a compelling orator, began traveling the region, north to Canada and south to Alabama, recruiting warriors in a campaign of massive resistance. While he was away on such a mission, William Henry Harrison attacked and destroyed Tippecanoe.

In 1811, as Tecumseh, whose name means "shooting star," was attempting to convince the Creek to join his pan-Indian alliance, a comet streaked across the night sky and became a lasting part of his legend. In the War of 1812, Tecumseh's pan-Indian force in the southern Great Lakes region sided with the British, and it was a major factor in the successful capture of Detroit. On October 5, 1813, on the Thames River in southern Ontario, Tecumseh died in battle against William Henry Harrison. His death marked the end of Indian resistance in a broad swath of territory, from the Ohio River Valley south.

Tecumseh The charismatic Shawnee leader united other tribes in a war against white settlers in the Ohio Valley region. The war ended at his death in 1813.

John Trumbull His paintings of the Revolution have become national treasures.

JOHN TRUMBULL
★ 1756–1843 ★
PAINTER, ARCHITECT

As an aide-de-camp for George Washington in the early years of the Revolution, aspiring artist John Trumbull sketched scenes of the conflict. Later, after studying with Benjamin West in London, he turned those scenes into paintings that have become part of the American artistic legacy. Four now hang in the Capitol Rotunda—"Declaration of Independence", "Surrender of General Burgoyne," "Surrender of Lord Cornwallis," and "Washington Resigning His Commission to Congress." In 1832, Yale University established an art museum to house some 100 more of Trumbull's historical paintings, donated by the artist himself.

NANCY WARD
★ ca 1738–1822 ★
CHEROKEE LEADER

Nan'yehi (her given name) was a member of the Cherokee of East Tennessee in a chaotic period, as newly arrived white settlers, Creek, and Cherokee battled for land and smallpox decimated tribes. Nan'yehi became a *Ghighau,* "beloved woman," of the matriarchal Cherokee, with a position of power on tribal councils and in tribal and ritual affairs. At one point, she intervened in the execution of a white woman, a Mrs. Bean, who taught her how to weave and how to raise milk cows and use diary products. These lessons were passed on to others in her tribe, both helping the Cherokee and contributing to their Europeanization. In the 1750s, Nan'yehi married trader Bryant Ward and also become known by the Anglicized name Nancy Ward. For the remainder of her life, she served as a Cherokee leader and an influential moderator between Cherokee and whites, taking part in critical negotiations between the two and advocating strongly for peace.

George Washington During the brutal winter of 1777–78 at Valley Forge, George and Martha comforted the men.

GEORGE WASHINGTON

★ 1732–1799 ★

FOUNDING FATHER

George Washington is perhaps America's most revered figure, hailed as "father of the country" both for his unrelenting fight against the British in the Revolution and for his leadership in the early days of the nation. Washington's drive to succeed was clear even in his boyhood: His father died when he was 11, and his mother, disinterested in education or social hierarchy, focused her efforts on piety and the family farm. But her eldest son slowly established himself among the Virginia gentry and fought as an officer with the British during the French and Indian War. Of his first battle, he famously wrote in a letter: "I have heard the bullets whistle; and believe me, there is something charming in the sound."

After his half brother Lawrence died of tuberculosis in 1752, Washington took over his large estate on the Potomac; Mount Vernon would become one of the great loves of Washington's life. Soon after, he met and married a wealthy young widow, Martha Dandridge Custis, and settled into the life of a respected planter and member of the Virginia House of Burgesses. Like his fellow burgesses, Washington became increasingly concerned by the political situation under the new king, George III. In 1774, he went to Philadelphia as a delegate to the First Continental Congress. Though

Civilian clothing worn by Washington, who believed in formality and decorum

Washington preferred a holster-style flintlock pistol in the early years of the war.

he was not an inspired speaker, his stateliness and height (six feet two) impressed others, and when the Second Continental Congress convened in 1775, it appointed him commander in chief of the Continental Army.

For the next almost six years, Washington held the British at bay against all odds, gradually developing a defensive strategy that led to a war of attrition the British couldn't sustain. Washington had taken command of untrained troops, and with little political support and few funds for uniforms, armament, or salaries for his men, he slowly turned them into a formidable fighting force. His men revered him for his courage, calm, determination, and, above all, his presence at

At a time when our lordly Masters in Great Britain will be satisfied with nothing less than the deprivation of American freedom . . . no man shou'd scruple, or hesitate a moment to use a[r]ms in defence of so valuable a blessing, on which all the good and evil of life depends.

GEORGE WASHINGTON

their side battle after battle, year after grueling year. Despite that, he was often attacked by military or political enemies who, at various times (especially early in the war), called for his demotion. With victory, however, Washington became more icon than man to most of the Western world. One Dutch visitor to Philadelphia, on seeing Washington pass in the city, wrote that he had seen "the greatest man who has ever appeared on the surface of this earth."

Though he had hoped to retire to a quiet life at Mount Vernon, Washington was soon serving the country again, first as president of the 1787 Constitutional Convention and then as first president of the nation (1789–1797). Faced with the task of defining that role, he chose a decorous and balanced approach that helped mitigate the growing political factionalism between republican and federalist approaches to government (Washington himself held with the federalist belief in a strong central government).

He refused a third term and spent the last three years of his life at Mount Vernon with Martha, who had been a lifelong companion and partner. As she had helped tend the wounded and despairing in winter camps during the war, she now helped him host the endless stream of visitors who came to Mount Vernon to pay respects to the great man. In mid-December 1799, she was at his side when a sudden illness took his life. In his will, Washington had stipulated that all the slaves he owned be freed at Martha's death, but she freed them in 1800.

In his farewell address to the nation, Washington had said, "I shall carry . . . with me to my grave . . . unceasing vows that . . . the happiness of the people of these States, under the auspices of liberty, may be made complete."

NOAH WEBSTER
★ 1758–1834 ★
AMERICAN LEXICOGRAPHER

Raised on a Connecticut farm, Noah Webster attended newly established Yale University, after which he became a schoolteacher in postrevolutionary America. He soon realized that American education needed to lay down its own roots, rather than rely on British texts and teachings. To answer that need, he wrote *A Grammatical Institute of the English Language,* which remained a critical textbook for a century.

In 1801, Webster began work on another dictionary that reflected distinctly American spellings. His first edition was published in 1806, and for the next two decades, he worked on refining and adding to it. In 1828, he published a second version, *American Dictionary of the English Language,* which included some 65,000 words and their definitions.

Webster was committed to education throughout his life and helped found Amherst College and advocated for universal education as well as for the abolition of slavery.

Noah Webster The New England teacher compiled the first American grammar book and dictionary.

PHILLIS WHEATLEY

★ CA 1753–1784 ★

POET

Taken by slavers on the West African coast as a child, Phillis Wheatley was brought to Boston and purchased by the relatively progressive Wheatley family, who recognized her intellect. They taught her to read and write and introduced her to literature. In 1770, she wrote *An Elegiac Poem, on the Death of . . . George Whitefield,* which gained her international fame. Yet a year later, she was unable to find an American publisher for her poetry collection and sailed for London. There, her classic, *Poems on Various Subjects, Religious and Moral,* was published in 1773, the first published poetry volume written by an African American. Returning to America, she was manumitted by the Wheatleys and continued to write poetry, though most remained unpublished.

Benjamin West Pennsylvania-born West became a leading figure in British art and a founder of the Royal Academy and National Gallery.

BENJAMIN WEST

★ 1738–1820 ★

ARTIST

Born in America to an innkeeping family, Benjamin West left the colonies as a young man to study painting in Italy and was soon part of artistic circles there. His works impressed English society as well, and he settled in London in 1763. West's romantic scenes from classical history and myth earned him an enthusiastic following, but in 1770, he broke new ground with a contemporary historical moment—the "Death of General Wolfe" outside Quebec in 1759. The first American painter with an international reputation, West co-founded the British Royal Academy and the National Gallery in London.

ELI WHITNEY

★ 1765–1825 ★

INVENTOR

Massachusetts native Eli Whitney graduated from Yale before moving to a Georgia plantation as a tutor in the early 1790s. There, he invented a simple gin to separate the sticky green seeds of short-staple cotton from the cotton boll. His invention saved the southern economy but encouraged the growth of slavery. Whitney himself saw little profit from his invention. Returning to New England, he pioneered an early version of mass production, inventing metal milling machines to produce patterned parts for a musket that could be assembled in a factory setting.

> *Where e'er Columbia spreads her swelling Sails: / To every Realm shall Peace her Charms display, / And Heavenly Freedom spread her gold Ray.*
>
> PHILLIS WHEATLEY

GEORGE WYTHE

★ 1726–1806 ★

JURIST

Born on a Virginia plantation, George Wythe became a prominent lawyer and burgess. Eventually settling in Williamsburg, he taught law at the College of William and Mary. As revolution threatened, Wythe became a fervent patriot, delegate to the Second Continental Congress, and signer of the Declaration of Independence. During the war years, he continued to teach law, helped George Mason draft the Virginia Constitution, and designed the state seal. In 1789, he was appointed judge of Virginia's Court of Chancery in Richmond, and in that capacity, he argued that the Virginia Declaration of Rights applied to African Americans as well as whites and that they should thus "be considered free." His ruling did not withstand the appeals process, but Wythe freed several of his slaves in his lifetime, and all in his will. Historians believe that he was administered fatal poison by his grandnephew, George Wythe Sweeney, in his Richmond home. Wythe's most enduring achievement was the influence he exerted on the legal thinking of such leaders as Thomas Jefferson, John Marshall, and Henry Clay.

The Continental Congress

AN EXPERIMENT IN AMERICAN DELIBERATION

★ ★ ★

Surely the 55 delegates who convened in Philadelphia in September 1774 had no idea that their First Continental Congress would herald a new world order. They represented 12 of the 13 British colonies, and they had met to discuss how to deal with unfair tax laws recently imposed on them. But they also wanted to cement ties among the American colonies and so agreed to meet again in early May 1775. By then, the "shots heard 'round the world" had been fired at Lexington and Concord, and New England militiamen had the British Army in Boston under siege.

The Second Continental Congress approved a Continental Army with George Washington at its head and sent the king the "Olive Branch Petition," which George III refused even to receive. When Congress convened a year later, its members boldly signed a declaration of independence from Britain. For the next five years, the Congress continued to serve, though ineffectually, as a de facto government. Washington complained bitterly of its lack of support for his army and of the general caliber of its later delegates. "Where are our Men of abilities?" he wrote in 1779, "Why do they not come forward to save their Country?" By then, most of the towering figures who had attended the early congresses—many now known as America's founders—had moved on to other public service. Despite its weaknesses, the Second Continental Congress did manage to adopt Articles of Confederation uniting the former colonies. When they became effective in March 1781, the Continental Congress ceased to be, replaced by the Confederation Congress.

Virginians George Washington (left), Patrick Henry, and Richard Henry Lee were among the 55 delegates to attend the First Continental Congress in Philadelphia's Carpenters' Hall, September 1774.

A Defining Role
THE FIRST FIRST LADIES

The first three of America's first ladies stepped into a role that had yet to be defined. Moving to New York (the temporary seat of government) with her two grandchildren, Martha Washington was the first to take on the mantle of the nation's "Lady Presidentess," and she determined to hold a weekly reception in the president's house for anyone who would like to attend. Abigail Adams, who followed her in the role, said that Martha's behavior made her "the object of Veneration and Respect." Abigail herself was not well for much of her husband's single term in office and spent much of the time on the family farm in Massachusetts. Dolley Madison, however, relished the role. Moving into the President's House in the new federal city, she used her charm, political savvy, and social gatherings to exert an influence on national affairs.

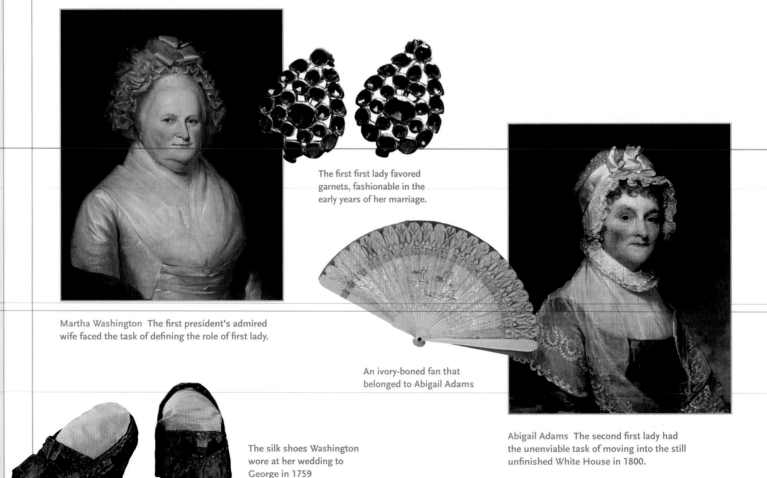

The first first lady favored garnets, fashionable in the early years of her marriage.

Martha Washington The first president's admired wife faced the task of defining the role of first lady.

An ivory-boned fan that belonged to Abigail Adams

The silk shoes Washington wore at her wedding to George in 1759

Abigail Adams The second first lady had the unenviable task of moving into the still unfinished White House in 1800.

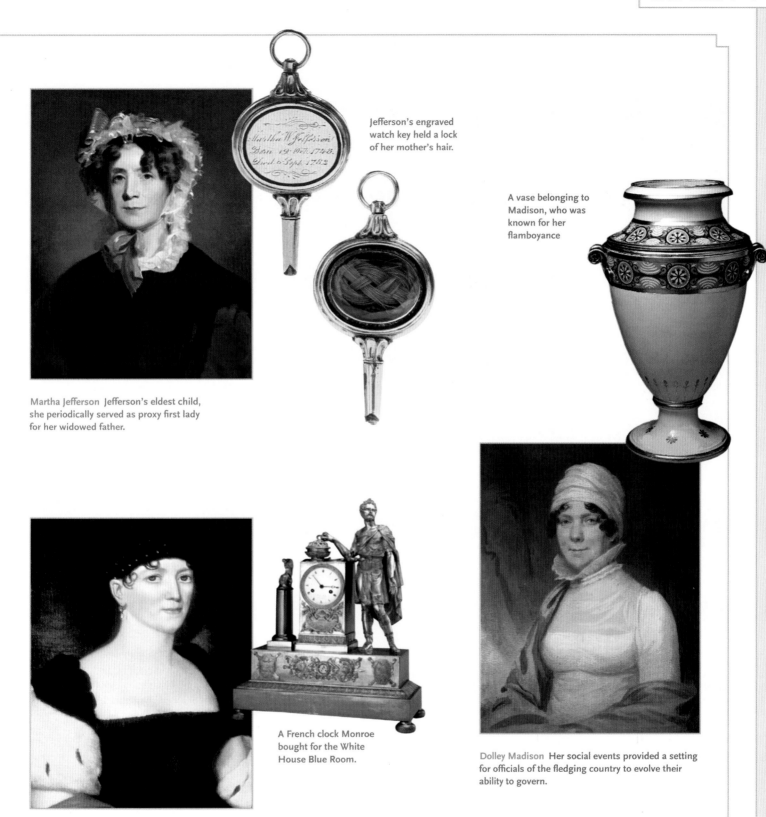

Jefferson's engraved watch key held a lock of her mother's hair.

A vase belonging to Madison, who was known for her flamboyance

Martha Jefferson Jefferson's eldest child, she periodically served as proxy first lady for her widowed father.

A French clock Monroe bought for the White House Blue Room.

Dolley Madison Her social events provided a setting for officials of the fledging country to evolve their ability to govern.

Elizabeth Monroe From a wealthy New York family, she charmed the French when James Monroe served as minister there.

1825–1860

YOUNG AMERICA: AMBITIOUS & AMBIVALENT

AMERICA OPENED ITS SECOND 50 YEARS IN RELATIVE PROSPERITY—ITS INTER-national reputation, its territories, and its future looking ever expansive. Yet, the political and regional battles that had marked the early Republic were still simmering, and one issue began to fester like a cancer that could not be healed—slavery. Four of the first five presidents of the United States had been Virginians, with ties to an old aristocracy that relied on slavery for its existence. The single exception had been John Adams, a Massachusetts lawyer and diplomat. In 1825, his son John Quincy, also a lawyer and diplomat, became the sixth president. His narrowly close election had been decided by the House of Representatives, and Henry Clay, speaker of the House, had cast the determining vote in what another presidential contender, Democrat and slaveholder Andrew Jackson, called a "corrupt bargain" as Clay became Adams's secretary of state. In the next election, Jackson—hero of the 1815 Battle of New Orleans, a renowned "Indian fighter," and a frontier "man of the people" from west of the Appalachians—easily swept Adams from office. The age of "Jacksonian democracy" had begun, and the common man, believing Jackson's populist message, rejoiced, happy to see the cabal of "Eastern elite" broken at last.

(previous pages) Settlers follow the Oregon Trail through a land of beauty in this painting by American master Albert Bierstadt.
(opposite) One of the countless forty-niners—men who hoped to strike it rich in the California gold rush

Sac leader Black Hawk surrendered at Fort Crawford, Wisconsin, on August 27, 1832, having lost a short but valiant war against white expansion.

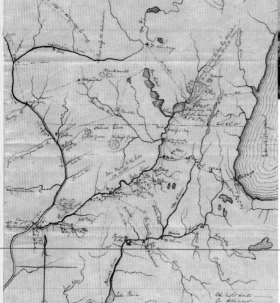

A map showing the 1832 military campaign fought against Indians in northern Illinois and southern Wisconsin during the Black Hawk War. Lt. Col. Edwin Rose drew the map based on his firsthand knowledge of the conflict.

For eight years, Jackson, by dint of charm, native intelligence, and imperiousness, held much of the country in thrall. He preached the rights of the underclass, yet his policies decimated Native American cultures and kept slavery alive and well. He preached states' rights and decentralization, eviscerating the Bank of the United States (which helped bring on a financial panic), yet when South Carolina put forward the idea of nullification and began murmuring about secession, Jackson threatened a swift federal response.

The nullification crisis had been brought on by new tariffs believed to favor northern industrialists over southern planters. In 1832, South Carolina, urged on by her favorite son—Vice President John Calhoun—passed an Ordinance of Nullification that allowed a state, through complicated procedural steps, to nullify any federal law it considered unconstitutional. As in most every area of his presidency, Jackson prevailed in the nullification crisis, and his forces prevailed in the short-lived Black Hawk War against the final remnants of the Sac and Fox peoples. Jackson left office enormously popular, but his "reign," as his opponents saw it, had only stoked sectional tensions. It had also led to the formation of a new political party—the Whigs, who believed in a strong federal system and expanding infrastructure.

No president in the coming two decades ever enjoyed Jackson's popularity or dominance. But all of them faced the most critical problem he had faced: a nation, barely formed and on the point of fracturing, despite—or perhaps because of—its enormous successes.

The United States grew phenomenally and in diverse ways in the first half of the 19th century. Texas became part of the Union, and President Polk (1845–49), having won his war against Mexico, vastly increased America's holdings in the West, adding the Southwest and the Pacific coast, and parts of the Mountain West. Innovations in transportation (from canals to a national highway to railroads) and in farming (from the steel plow to the reaper to the

1829–1836
Jacksonian era, under populist Andrew Jackson

1830–1838
Native tribes forced out of Southeast

1837
Financial panic leads to years of recession

1846–1848
Mexican-American War

1848
Gold discovered in California

thresher) encouraged families to push ever west and settle new lands. And in 1849, the gold rush sent hundreds of thousands of dream seekers from throughout the world racing to California. But that westward surge only exacerbated the issue that hung over America like a threatening storm—slavery, and more particularly its expansion into the new territories.

The 1820 Missouri Compromise had affected a fragile balance between North and South on the issue: Territory west of Missouri and above latitude 36° 30 N was to be free; below that latitude, slavery was allowed. But the newly acquired territories threatened to upset the balance in the number of new free states versus the number of new slave states. In the wake of the Mexican-American War, another compromise was needed to restore equilibrium, and after much heated debate, a series of bills collectively known as the Compromise of 1850 passed Congress. Among them was the deeply controversial Fugitive Slave Act. It effectively drowned the hopes of millions of enslaved Americans, who dreamed of escaping to the North to a final freedom.

Then, in 1854, the Kansas-Nebraska Act broke all precedents, allowing each territorial legislature to decide for itself whether or not to allow slavery. It was a final nail in the sectional divide. "Bleeding Kansas" erupted in a guerrilla war of pro- versus antislavery violence. Free-soil advocates and abolitionists called for an end to all slavery, and a strange-looking Illinois lawyer named Abraham Lincoln took on Senator Stephen Douglas, champion of the Kansas-Nebraska Act, in a series of debates across Illinois during their race for the U.S. Senate. Through the summer of 1858 the polished orator Douglas argued for states' rights on the issue of slavery and assured his crowds that the "negro . . . belongs to an inferior race, and must always occupy an inferior position." The less polished Lincoln nonetheless forcefully declared that the "covert real zeal for the spread of slavery, I cannot but hate. I hate it because of the monstrous injustice of slavery itself. I hate it . . . especially because it forces so many really good men amongst ourselves into an open war with the very fundamental principles of civil liberty." Thousands came to hear Douglas and Lincoln debate the spread of slavery, and thousands more avidly read their arguments in newspapers across the country.

A year later, Americans had other news to occupy them. Abolitionist John Brown had taken the fight from Bleeding Kansas, where he and his sons had murdered settlers in a pro-slavery town, to Virginia and attempted a failed attack on the federal arsenal in Harpers Ferry, hoping to foment a slave insurrection. As John Brown hung, the nation hung in the balance, North and South gripped in a visceral, long-festering resentment of one another. In November 1860, the strange-looking lawyer from Illinois, running on the ticket of the fledgling Republican Party, won the presidency. A month later, South Carolina seceded from the Union.

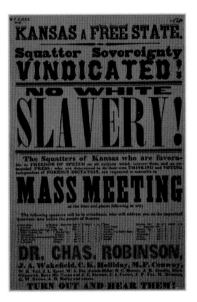

A handbill rallies Kansas free staters to a meeting. Fighting between pro- and antislavery factions resulted in "Bleeding Kansas."

Dr. John Doy (seated) with the "Immortal Ten," antislavery men who rescued him from jail after his conviction for abducting slaves. He was trying to free them.

1850	1854	1857	1858	1860
Compromise of 1850 includes Fugitive Slave Act	Kansas-Nebraska Act expands slavery in territories	Dred Scott case ruling denies African Americans rights	Abraham Lincoln, Stephen Douglass debate slavery	Lincoln elected president; South Carolina secedes

BIOGRAPHIES

POLITICAL GIANTS & A BREWING STORM 1825–1860

The leaders who followed in the footsteps of the Founding Fathers found themselves locked in a new conflict—not with Britain but with each other, as regional interests and arguments threatened disunion. Larger-than-life figures again stepped forward to champion a great America, or in the case of Native American leaders, to protect their own people, excluded from the American dream. As new technologies and new territory fueled that dream for many, it left others mired in bondage. Slavery stained the very concept of America and a reckoning was at hand.

JOHN QUINCY ADAMS
★ 1767–1848 ★
SIXTH U.S. PRESIDENT

As the son of Founding Father John Adams and Founding Mother Abigail Adams, John Quincy Adams was immersed in politics from a young age. He spent his formative years in Europe with his father, then an American diplomat. From age 10 to 17, John Quincy lived in Paris, Amsterdam, and St. Petersburg. Despite his youth, he was a secretary to America's emissary to St. Petersburg and to his father during the Paris negotiations ending the American Revolution.

Returning to America for nine years in 1785, he completed a Harvard degree and practiced law. He then served in the U.S. Senate for five years but by 1809 was again in St. Petersburg as American minister and close confidant of Tsar Alexander. Five years later, President Madison dispatched Adams, as America's leading diplomat, to head a delegation charged with negotiating an end to the War of 1812. A hard-nosed negotiator, Adams argued for a return to conditions as they were in the United States before the war. His arguments ultimately won out, and the Treaty of Ghent was seen as a victory for America's standing in the world. In 1817, President Monroe appointed Adams secretary of state, and his impact in that role would endure far

John Quincy Adams The quintessential diplomat, Adams served one term as president.

beyond his eight-year tenure. He built a solid diplomatic corps; helped craft the Monroe Doctrine; and negotiated the Adams-Onís Treaty of 1819, in which Spain ceded Florida and the United States assumed Spain's claim to the "Oregon Country."

In 1824, Adams ran for president along with three other candidates—Andrew Jackson, Henry Clay, and William Crawford. When the election results proved indecisive, the House of Representatives decided the outcome, and Speaker Henry Clay cast the decisive vote for Adams. Jackson accused the two of a "corrupt bargain" when Adams made Clay his secretary of state. Though a consummate diplomat, Adams was not an effective politician and never had the congressional support he needed for his initiatives. After one term in office, he lost to Andrew Jackson in a resounding defeat. Yet Adams went on to serve nine consecutive terms as a Massachusetts representative in the House, where his speeches against slavery became legendary. It was on the House floor that he suffered a fatal stroke, ending literally a lifetime in public service.

Louis Agassiz The Swiss-born paleontologist pioneered the science of glaciology and, as a professor at Harvard, greatly influenced younger American scientists.

LOUIS AGASSIZ
★ 1807–1873 ★
PALEONTOLOGIST, GLACIOLOGIST

JOHN JACOB ASTOR
★ 1763–1848 ★
FINANCIER

Jean Louis Agassiz was born in Switzerland and studied paleontology in Paris under the field's founder, Baron Georges Cuvier. Agassiz quickly gained standing as a paleontologist and, after returning to Switzerland, as a founder in the science of glaciology and a pioneer in the concept of ice ages. In 1848, Agassiz accepted a professorship at Harvard, where he influenced generations of American scientists. Though he was a contemporary of Charles Darwin, Agassiz rejected the theory of evolution throughout his career, maintaining that the "evidence of the existence of a Creator, constantly and thoughtfully working among the complicated structures that He has made" could be found throughout nature.

Son of a German butcher, John Astor left his village to join his brother as a maker of musical instruments in London. After several years, he emigrated to New York, hoping to sell his instruments to finance a fur-trading business. He was quickly successful and expanded his business concerns to Montreal. By the 1790s, Astor became the leading trader there and in London. By the century's end, he was involved in trade with China, exporting furs and American ginseng and importing teas and cloth. He also acquired an impressive amount of New York City real estate and cultivated leading politicians of the day. Astor expanded his reach in 1815—with ships serving markets in Hawaii, Latin America, and Europe.

Audubon's paint box. He took simple equipment into the wilderness in search of his wild subjects. English admirers labeled him the American woodsman.

John James Audubon, a self-trained artist, documented the wonders of avian America in his classic, *The Birds of America*, whose color engravings included this tricolored heron.

JOHN JAMES AUDUBON
★ 1785–1851 ★
WILDLIFE ARTIST

The man who would become perhaps America's most famous wildlife artist was born Jean Rabin in Haiti, the illegitimate son of a French planter and slave trader and a Creole mother. John James Audubon (Audubon was his father's name) was raised in France on his father's estate, where at an early age, he showed an interest in drawing and in the natural world, particularly birds. At 18, his family sent him to Philadelphia to avoid conscription in Napoleon's army.

Audubon lived outside the city on a family property called Mill Grove. While there, he continued to pursue his interest in birds, even banding eastern phoebes to study their habits. As he entered manhood, Audubon attempted to establish himself in business in various locations but never enjoyed much success. By 1820, he was living in Henderson, Kentucky, with his wife and two children and supporting his family by teaching drawing, portrait painting, and taxidermy, as well as continuing to amass an impressive portfolio of bird images. Hoping to

add to it, he set off down the Mississippi with a young assistant and lived off the land while he sketched the avifauna of the South.

Settling his family in New Orleans, he again turned to portrait painting as a livelihood but remained determined to continue his artistic "collection of the Birds of our Country, from Nature, all of Natural Size." By 1824, he felt he had amassed enough engravings to publish his bird collection. Failing to find U.S. backers, he sailed for England, where he launched a successful traveling exhibition of his large bird portraits and was soon hailed as the "American woodsman." He also found a printer for his *Birds of America;* it would ultimately

> *A true conservationist is a man who knows that the world is not given by his fathers, but borrowed from his children.*
>
> JOHN JAMES AUDUBON

comprise 435 hand-colored plates, the last issued in 1838.

During the years of its publication, Audubon continued to travel to America, drawing birds. On his final expedition to the West, he switched his focus to mammals, and those works are included in *Viviparous Quadrupeds of North America,* completed by his sons. Twentieth-century historian Lewis Mumford proclaimed Audubon "an archetypal American who astonishingly combined in equal measure the virtues of George Washington, Daniel Boone and Benjamin Franklin."

HENRY WARD BEECHER
★ 1813–1887 ★
ABOLITIONIST

In an age of great American orators, Henry Ward Beecher ranked among the greatest. His father, Lyman Beecher, was a renowned Calvinist evangelist, but Henry showed no inclination in that direction during his rather lackluster years as a student. However, once he took the pulpit as a pastor himself, he developed his remarkable talent for moving and dramatic speech. In 1847, the young man was called to preach at a new Congregational church in Brooklyn, New York. There, at Plymouth Church, Beecher gained such a reputation that his services were sometimes attended by up to 2,500 people, and the fledging congregation soon became one of the largest in America. Mark Twain, a sometime attendee at Plymouth, described Beecher as "sawing his arms in the air, howling sarcasms this way and that, discharging rockets of poetry and exploding mines of eloquence, halting now and then to stamp his foot." His sermons, rather than threatening doom, promised redemption and God's love.

Beecher also used his sermons to attack the institution of slavery from the pulpit, and with characteristic dramatic flair, he started selling slaves into freedom from his pulpit. At about the same time, his sister Harriet Beecher Stowe, published her groundbreaking work, *Uncle Tom's Cabin,* which fired the antislavery cause throughout America and Europe.

Henry's own words reached far beyond New York, and as the slavery question began to tear at the national fabric, abolitionists moved into "Bleeding Kansas" armed with "Beecher's bibles"—rifles to take on the pro-slavery faction. Throughout the Civil War, Beecher continued his role as a public figure and advocate. His 1863 trip to England became an impromptu campaign for selling the northern cause to the British, and Lincoln later credited its success with helping win the war. After the war, Beecher continued to advocate—for women's suffrage, temperance, and even the compatibility of the theory of evolution with biblical teaching. In 1874, rumors of his adultery came to a head when he was tried for it. Though a New York jury exonerated him of the charges, Beecher's potential womanizing remains an issue of historical speculation.

Henry Ward Beecher Though he remains one of America's greatest orators, his reputation for womanizing sullied his legacy.

BLACK HAWK

★ 1767–1838 ★

CHIEF, SAC AND FOX INDIANS

Black Hawk's leadership abilities had earned him the status of war chief among the Sac and Fox Indians by the time the War of 1812 erupted. He and his warriors fought on the side of the British, and their efforts thwarted American expansion up the Mississippi. After the war, he and his tribe were forced off their ancestral lands in Illinois and into territory west of the Mississippi.

> *The earth is our mother—we are now on it . . . I hope we are all friends here.*
>
> **BLACK HAWK**

Black Hawk The Sac warrior's innate dignity impressed the crowds he appeared before when he was forced to tour on public display after his 1832 defeat.

Andrew Jackson's policy of Indian removal was aimed at dislodging the last enclaves of woodland Indians from their eastern lands, but Black Hawk refused to recognize a treaty ceding Illinois to the federal government. In April 1832, bolstered by the promise of help from the British and other tribes, he led some Sac and Fox—many of them women, children, and elders—from Iowa Territory east across the Mississippi to their traditional homeland in northern Illinois, where they planned to plant corn. Local militia soon appeared, determined to kill the "bandit collection of Indians." Black Hawk raised a flag of truce, but the militia fired anyway and the Indians returned fire, setting off the Black Hawk War.

Despite being pursued by some 7,000 troops (including a young Abraham Lincoln), Black Hawk and his people held their own until August 1, when they were pinned down by approaching troops at the Bad Axe River. Some women and children tried to swim to safety on the other side, but there the Dakota, allies of the government, were waiting and bludgeoned them to death.

Black Hawk surrendered three weeks later when the last of his warriors abandoned him. President Jackson ordered that he and his son Whirling Thunder be sent on tour through eastern cities and displayed as trophies of war. Rather than facing public opprobrium, the two warriors won public respect for their innate dignity. Black Hawk won an extended legal battle regarding his right to petition the government and traveled to Washington to press his concerns. His case raised questions about the rights of Indians under U.S. law. After being released from custody, Black Hawk was placed under the supervision of a rival chief, as a form of humiliation, but he spent his final years without animosity. His life story, *Autobiography of Ma-Ka-Tai-Me-She-Kia-Kiak,* became one of the first published Native American autobiographies.

JOHN BROWN
★ 1800–1859 ★
ABOLITIONIST

John Brown was born into a committed antislavery family in Connecticut, and he would take that tradition to radical extremes. As a young man, he tried and failed at various occupations and continually moved his growing family (eventually numbering 20 children) to Ohio, Massachusetts, Pennsylvania, and New York. His focus remained on the plight of enslaved humans, and he gave land to fugitive slaves, worked on the Underground Railroad, and helped found the League of Gileadites, which protected escaped slaves from capture.

> *Now, if it be deemed necessary that I should forfeit my life for the furtherance of the ends of justice, and mingle my blood . . . with the blood of millions in this slave country . . . let it be done.*
>
> **JOHN BROWN**

In 1855, Brown moved to Kansas Territory at the urging of his grown sons, who wanted his help in fighting proslavery settlers. On the night of May 24, 1856, Brown and his sons attacked a settlement at Pottawatomie Creek and brutally killed five men. Brown evaded capture and even toured the Northeast, raising money for a war on slavery. By 1859, he was in Harpers Ferry, Virginia (now West Virginia), where a federal arsenal was located. Brown planned to raid the arsenal and then arm local slaves to form his army.

On October 16, 1859, Brown and 21 of his followers—5 blacks and 16 whites—launched their attack, but local militia and federal troops under Col. Robert E. Lee quickly overwhelmed them. Wounded and captured, Brown was tried for murder, slave insurrection, and treason against Virginia. He was hanged in December 1859, but in a final statement given to his jailer, he predicted that "the crimes of this *guilty land will* never be purged *away* but with Blood."

John Brown A militant abolitionist known for his raid on Harpers Ferry in 1859

We Hold These Truths . . .
THE SENECA FALLS CONVENTION
★ ★ ★

The progressive manufacturing town of Seneca Falls, New York, is considered the birthplace of the women's rights movement, owing to a conference convened there on July 19, 1848. The two-day meeting had been quickly organized by women's rights advocates, including Elizabeth Cady Stanton and Lucretia Mott. Though it was barely publicized, the conference drew together some 300 men and women to discuss the "social, civil, and religious conditions of woman." Stanton and Mott presented their "Declaration of Sentiments," modeled on the Declaration of Independence. It averred that the "history of mankind is a history of repeated injuries and usurpations on the part of man toward woman, having in direct object the establishment of an absolute tyranny over her," and insisted that "[women] have immediate admission to all rights and privileges which belong to them as citizens of these United States." The declaration was signed by 68 women and 32 men, including abolitionist Frederick Douglass.

THE FIRST CONVENTION

EVER CALLED TO DISCUSS THE

Civil and Political Rights of Women,

SENECA FALLS, N. Y., JULY 19, 20, 1848.

WOMAN'S RIGHTS CONVENTION.

A Convention to discuss the social, civil, and religious condition and rights of woman will be held in the Wesleyan Chapel, at Seneca Falls, N. Y., on Wednesday and Thursday, the 19th and 20th of July current; commencing at 10 o'clock A. M. During the first day the meeting will be exclusively for women, who are earnestly invited to attend. The public generally are invited to be present on the second day, when Lucretia Mott, of Philadelphia, and other ladies and gentlemen, will address the Convention.*

*This call was published in the *Seneca County Courier,* July 14, 1848, without any signatures. The movers of this Convention, who drafted the call, the declaration and resolutions were Elizabeth Cady Stanton, Lucretia Mott, Martha C. Wright, Mary Ann McClintock, and Jane C. Hunt.

A pamphlet celebrating the high points of the first women's rights convention

James Buchanan Preceded Lincoln in office

JAMES BUCHANAN
★ 1791–1868 ★
15TH U.S. PRESIDENT

James Buchanan was the son of an Irish immigrant who became a wealthy Pennsylvania merchant. Buchanan chose law as a profession and was also very successful. After his engagement to a wealthy social elite ended in scandal and her unexpected death, he vowed he would not marry. Instead, he plowed his energies into a career in politics and served five terms in the U.S. House of Representatives, a tenure as American envoy to Russia, and a decade in the Senate. In 1852, he attempted to secure the Democratic nomination for president, but the nomination went to Franklin Pierce, a compromise candidate. When Pierce won the presidency, he appointed Buchanan minister to Britain. In the following election of 1856, the 65-year-old Buchanan finally achieved the presidency.

Despite his long experience in government, Buchanan was unable to deal with the mounting rift between North and South over the question of slavery in the western territories. He unrealistically believed it could be settled by the Supreme Court, but two days after his inaugural, the Supreme Court under Chief Justice Roger Taney handed down the controversial Dred Scott decision, which fanned the flames of factionalism. As Buchanan's one-term presidency ground on, government ground to a virtual standstill.

In his final months in office—after Lincoln's election but before his inaugural—Buchanan had to deal with the threat of Southern secession, and while he denied that a state had the legal right to leave the Union, he also asserted that the federal government could not step in to prevent a state from doing so. When South Carolina seceded, however, Buchanan attempted to send provisions to federally held Fort Sumter. As civil war engulfed the country, Buchanan was publicly maligned for weakness in not having prevented it and accused of pro-southern leanings. His last years were spent in relative isolation at Wheatland, his Pennsylvania home.

JOHN C. CALHOUN
★ 1782–1850 ★
VICE PRESIDENT, AMERICAN STATESMAN

Born in South Carolina, John Calhoun was elected a representative to Congress in 1810 and soon became a member of the War Hawks, pushing for war with Britain because of, in part, British impressment of American sailors. In 1817, he was appointed Monroe's secretary of war and supported the Monroe Doctrine and the Missouri Compromise, which limited the unbridled expansion of slavery into the western territories.

The young Calhoun considered a run for president in 1824 but instead ran as vice president and served as such during John Quincy Adams's presidency and in Andrew Jackson's first term in office. During that time, Calhoun led the opposition to tariffs seen to cripple southern planters and further the interests of

Our Federal Union—next to our liberties the most dear! May we all remember that it can only be preserved by respecting the rights of the States and distributing equally the benefits and burdens of the Union!

JOHN C. CALHOUN

John C. Calhoun The South's most forceful orator for states' rights, he was a lion of the Senate.

Kit Carson Symbol of the West, Carson had been a trapper, guide, rancher, and U.S. soldier and Indian fighter.
Inset: Carson's leather pouch

Noted Western artist Charles M. Russell captured the Kit Carson mystique in "Carson's Men," depicting Carson and two other frontiersmen patrolling the Santa Fe Trail in the 1840s.

northern industrialists. His nullification stance argued that if a state felt a federal law was unconstitutional, it could hold a special convention and declare the law null and void—for all states. Publicly breaking with Jackson over nullification, Calhoun returned to the Senate in 1832, where he continued to defend what he called the "peculiar institution of slavery."

In 1843, he made a final attempt to launch a presidential campaign but withdrew before the nomination cycle. Again returning to the Senate in 1845, he became part of the Great Triumvirate, along with Daniel Webster and Henry Clay, which dominated the Senate. Dying of tuberculosis in 1850, Calhoun nonetheless had a final message. As another senator delivered it, Calhoun sat in attendance to hear his warning to the North: "If you who represent the stronger portion, cannot

agree to settle . . . on the broad principle of justice and duty, say so; and let the States we both represent agree to separate and part in peace. If you are unwilling we should part in peace, tell us so; and we shall know what to do, when you reduce the question to submission or resistance." In 1957, the Senate recognized Calhoun as one of the five greatest senators of all time.

CHRISTOPHER "KIT" CARSON
★ 1809–1868 ★
SOLDIER, WESTERN LEGEND

Raised in rural Missouri, Kit Carson became a fur trapper in the West as a young man, and in 1842, he served as a

guide for western explorer John C. Frémont. Through his writings, Frémont made Carson famous as a mountain man. Carson married three times—to an Arapaho woman, a Cheyenne, and finally a Hispanic woman. During the Mexican-American War, Carson fought with federal forces in California before becoming a New Mexico rancher. During the Civil War, he fought with the Union and was also ordered to head up a campaign to force the Navajo off their traditional lands in Arizona. Though sympathetic to the Navajo, Carson followed orders, launching a brutal campaign to destroy crops and livestock. In 1864, 8,000 Navajo surrendered and began the "Long Walk"—some 300 miles from Arizona to Fort Sumner, New Mexico.

HENRY CLAY
★ 1777–1852 ★
U.S. SENATOR

Henry Clay was a major force during one of the most critical eras of United States history. Born on a Virginia farm during the American Revolution, he became a Kentucky lawyer and successful politician, despite a strong antislavery stance and his defense of Aaron Burr in Burr's 1807 trial for treason. In 1811, Clay was elected to the U.S. House of Representatives and immediately voted its speaker. A great orator and a dynamic and charming figure, he became a persistent voice among the War Hawks pressing for war with Britain. He was also a close friend of First Lady Dolley Madison and President Madison, who appointed him a member of the Ghent delegation negotiating an end to the War of 1812.

In the 1824 presidential election, Clay entered the race but made a weak showing. Instead, President-elect John Quincy Adams, with whom he had negotiated the Treaty of Ghent, made Clay his secretary of state. In the following election of 1831, Clay ran for and won a seat in the U.S. Senate, where he ardently promulgated his three-pronged "American system": a tariff to promote American industry, a national bank to enable commerce, and federal funds for such internal improvements as roads and canals.

In the 1832 presidential race, he ran against his political nemesis, Andrew Jackson, and lost. Returning to the Senate in its so-called golden era in the 1830s and 1840s, he became one of the Great Triumvirate of intellect and oratory that included John Calhoun and Daniel Webster. A leading founder of the Whig Party, he ran again for president in 1844 and lost to James Polk.

Clay remained in the Senate the rest of his life, where he was known as the Great Compromiser for his efforts to soothe the growing rift between North and South. In 1850, ill with tuberculosis, Clay introduced another compromise that began: "It being desirable, for the peace, concord, and harmony of the Union of these States, to settle and adjust amicably all existing questions of controversy between them arising out of the institution of slavery upon a fair, equitable and just basis . . ."

Henry Clay The Kentuckian was the Senate's Great Compromiser. Inset: A Clay campaign button

> *Alas! who can realize that Henry Clay is dead! Who can realize that never again that majestic form shall rise in the council-chambers of his country to beat back the storms of anarchy?*
>
> **ABRAHAM LINCOLN'S EULOGY TO HENRY CLAY**

Though Clay pleaded for an end to sectional hostility, no compromise had been reached when, six months later, his illness forced him to take respite outside Washington. But his compromise did prevail, and he returned to the city over which he had exercised such influence. He died there in 1852.

SAMUEL COLT
★ 1814–1862 ★
INVENTOR, INDUSTRIALIST

As a young boy, Samuel Colt was inspired by the work of inventors such as Robert Fulton, and at the age of 21, he opened a plant in Paterson, New Jersey, to produce his innovative revolving-cylinder pistol. Heralded by Texas Rangers and federal forces, it could be fired multiple times without reloading. Impressed, the Army enlisted Colt to design a more powerful revolver. By the 1850s, Colt was mass-producing revolvers with interchangeable parts and aggressively marketing them to aspiring settlers, lawmen, and cowboys. By the time the Civil War

become a land agent, but by then, Texas was fighting for its soul. Though Texas was technically part of Mexico, the large contingent of American settlers there had declared it an independent republic. Only a few weeks after Crockett arrived in San Antonio, the Mexican dictator, Antonio López de Santa Anna, arrived as well, leading a large force. Crockett joined the small band of Americans who had taken up positions in San Antonio's Alamo Mission, and when the Mexicans attacked, Crockett fought fiercely. To no avail. The Alamo fell, and some accounts say Crockett died defending it, while others report he was taken captive, brought before Santa Anna, and ordered bayoneted, then shot. Crockett's brutal demise only added to his legend as the great American frontiersman.

Samuel Colt His mass-produced repeating revolver revolutionized the firearms industry.

erupted, he was one of the wealthiest men in America. Though he died early in the conflict between the North and South, his company continued to produce firearms for the Union until Colt's Hartford, Connecticut, factory burned down in 1864.

DAVY CROCKETT
★ 1786–1836 ★
FRONTIERSMAN, SOLDIER, POLITICIAN

Frontiersman David "Davy" Crockett became a member of Congress in 1827, but in the years that followed, he grew to be a national legend as a backwoodsman and tale-teller, thanks in part to a book titled *Sketches and Eccentricities of Col. David Crockett of West Tennessee*. When Crockett lost his 1834 bid for reelection to a lawyer with a peg leg, he announced, "Since you have chosen to elect a man with a timber toe to succeed me, you may all go to hell and I will go to Texas."

Crockett reached San Antonio de Béxar in early February 1836, hoping to

Davy Crockett The legendary frontiersman and soldier died a hero, having fought to save San Antonio's Alamo.

Stephen Douglas He famously debated Lincoln.

STEPHEN DOUGLAS

★ 1813–1861 ★

U.S. SENATOR

The "Little Giant," as the five-foot-four Stephen Douglas became known, was born in rural Vermont and quickly exhibited his talents for success, studying law and eventually settling as a lawyer in Illinois. While in his 20s, he was elected to the state legislature, then in his early 30s, to the U.S. House of Representatives. By 1847, he was a U.S. senator and would remain a powerful voice in the Senate for the rest of his life.

In 1854, as tensions between North and South grew, Douglas championed the Kansas-Nebraska Act, which essentially repealed the Missouri Compromise of 1820 and allowed the spread of slavery into the western territories. Passage of the act ultimately led a relatively unknown Illinois lawyer, Abraham Lincoln, to challenge Douglas for his U.S. Senate seat, a contest that became a verbal duel over the morality and spread of slavery. The seven Lincoln-Douglas debates, held during the summer and fall of 1858, remain a high-water mark in American oratory.

In the 1860 presidential election, the two men faced off again. When Lincoln won, Senator Douglas became an ardent ally, backing Lincoln fully in his attempts to bring the South back into the Union. When Douglas died unexpectedly of typhoid fever in June 1861, an influential Republican editor wrote, "The loss at this crisis must be regarded as a national tragedy."

RALPH WALDO EMERSON

★ 1803–1882 ★

TRANSCENDENTALIST PHILOSOPHER, POET

A towering figure in America's intellectual firmament, Ralph Waldo Emerson was no doubt spurred to scholarly pursuits by his father, a Congregationalist minister in Boston who had a keen—and for that time, unusual—interest in Asian literature and thought. At Harvard, Ralph Waldo pursued those interests himself before following his father into the ministry at the Second Church of Boston. When his wife died in 1831, Emerson left the pulpit, explaining that he could no longer administer Communion because he did not believe in the unique divinity of Jesus. He took a trip through Europe and then in 1836 published a small book, *Nature,* which coalesced his ideas.

He had settled in Concord, Massachusetts, outside Boston, in 1834, and remarried in 1835. Concord would remain his home for the rest of his life. Once there, Emerson began to gather around him a group that called themselves the New England Transcendentalists and included Henry David Thoreau, Margaret Fuller, Bronson Alcott, and others. Confident that a new future was at hand, the Transcendentalists extolled nature and rejected unexamined conformity in all areas of life, preaching that each individual should develop what Emerson called "an original relation to the universe."

Emerson became the grand man of American literary thought in the mid-19th century—and beyond. His extensive lectures, essays, and poetry celebrated nature as an impetus for spiritual inspiration and posited an impersonal God, as well as introducing audiences to Asian and Middle Eastern worldviews.

Ralph Waldo Emerson
The great Transcendentalist
and poet

> *Standing on the bare ground, — my head bathed by the blithe air, and uplifted into infinite space, . . . I become a transparent eye-ball; I am nothing; I see all . . . ; I am part or particle of God.*
>
> RALPH WALDO EMERSON

Unsolitary Confinement

THE PRESIDENT'S HOUSE

★ ★ ★

George Washington selected the site for the president's house, and Irish-born architect James Hoban won the competition to design it, submitting a far more modest structure than the capital's overall designer, Pierre L'Enfant, had envisaged. First and briefly occupied by the Adamses, it became a pet architectural project of the third president, Thomas Jefferson, who added colonnaded wings on the east and west. After the British set fire to the White House, as it had become known, in 1814, Hoban was hired to salvage it. He restored its Georgian symmetry, and it was reoccupied by the fifth president, James Monroe, in 1817. Monroe put his own touches on the White House, adding the south portico and the elaborate French Empire pieces that still form the heart of the home's furnishings. During Theodore Roosevelt's tenure, the Executive Offices were moved to the newly constructed West Wing.

The early years of the building presaged its future. Succeeding administrations variously added to it, renovated it, allowed it to fall into disrepair, opened it to the public, or kept the public at bay. Funding for its structural integrity and refurbishing generally depended on the inclinations of Congress and the political-fiscal whims of the time. During the Truman Administration, a major renovation left only the outer walls in place. In the early 1960s, First Lady Jacqueline Kennedy launched a campaign to refurnish the White House. With the help of a curatorial staff, she looked for pieces of historic and artistic interest, making sure those objects reflected the evolution of the White House over time. President Johnson created the Committee for the Preservation of the White House in 1964. Today, the white stone building has 132 rooms and 35 bathrooms. Most of its first family occupants would probably agree with former First Lady Michelle Obama that the White House is "a really nice prison."

In 1821, the president's house was still a work in progress, newly rebuilt after a British fire destroyed it in 1814. In the two centuries since, 40 presidents have left their mark on the ever evolving White House.

MILLARD FILLMORE
★ 1800–1874 ★
13TH U.S. PRESIDENT

Poor and poorly educated as a child in central New York, Millard Fillmore was apprenticed by his father to a clothmaker who essentially treated him as a bondsman. Fillmore managed to pay off the apprentice obligation and, obsessed with education, went on to study law. He rose to become a highly successful Buffalo lawyer, national politician, and prominent leader of the Whig Party in the U.S. Congress.

In 1848, he ran as vice president on the Whig ticket with Zachary Taylor. When Taylor died in 1850, Fillmore assumed the presidency and threw his support behind the Compromise of 1850, which included the controversial Fugitive Slave Act and was intended to quell factional tensions over slavery. It did not, and North-South hostilities only increased during Fillmore's two years in office. He lost the Whig nomination to Gen. Winfield Scott in the next election season, but he did run for president again in 1856, as the candidate for the Whig-American

Party, a coalescing of the dying Whigs and the newly conceived, anti-immigrant Know-Nothings. His defeat signaled the end of the Whig Party, but his run had taken votes away from Republican candidate John C. Frémont, whom Fillmore deeply opposed, and the election went to Democrat James Buchanan.

Though Fillmore was a strong supporter of the Union cause during the Civil War, his support as president of the Fugitive Slave Act seriously diminished his legacy.

Millard Fillmore Zachary Taylor's running mate, he became president when Taylor died in 1850.

JESSIE BENTON FRÉMONT
★ 1824–1902 ★
POLITICAL ACTIVIST

Raised to privilege, Jessie Benton was the daughter of Missouri senator Thomas Hart Benton. Despite his strong advocacy for westward expansion, Benton initially objected to his daughter's marriage to western explorer John C. Frémont in 1841 but then supported Frémont's

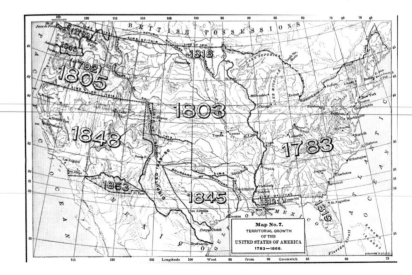

Pushing West
AMERICA'S "MANIFEST DESTINY"
★★★

Even the first colonists to America carried with them some sense of their God-given destiny to settle this land, and subsequent generations pushed ever west into the heartland. In the years before the Revolution, Carolina frontiersman Daniel Boone blazed a trail into eastern Tennessee, then on to Kentucky, opening the area to settlement. The itch for new lands grew in the decades after independence, and in 1845, New York journalist John O'Sullivan gave it clear voice, writing that America's "manifest destiny" was "to overspread the continent allotted by Providence for . . . our yearly multiplying millions." A mid-century depression and the California gold rush encouraged the quest for new opportunities in the West, and in 1850, some 65,000 people pushed more than 2,000 miles across the plains and Rockies on the Oregon-California Trail. Their numbers would only grow in the coming decades.

An archival map shows the territorial growth of the United States from the late 1700s into the period known as Manifest Destiny.

career. The well-educated and talented Jessie helped her husband craft some of his expedition reports, and they enjoyed commercial success.

Always her husband's champion and a steely personality in her own right, Jessie Frémont became part of his unsuccessful 1856 bid for president, whose slogan was "Frémont and Our Jessie." After the couple suffered financial reversals in the early 1870s, Jessie's writings supported the family. With her husband's death in 1890, Jessie moved permanently to Los Angeles.

John C. Frémont The western pathfinder, and later politician, plants the flag atop a Rocky Mountain peak.

Jessie Benton Frémont Frémont's influential wife

JOHN C. FRÉMONT
★ 1813–1890 ★
EXPLORER, SOLDIER, POLITICIAN

Savannah-born John C. Frémont spent his early years working for the military as an instructor and topographical engineer, and in that capacity, he explored the American West, searching for an expedient overland route from the Mississippi River to the Pacific and thus exploring little-known tracts of Wyoming, Idaho, Nevada, and Oregon. In 1845, he led an armed expedition to California, then Mexican territory. Frémont rallied local American settlers against the Mexicans, and with help from a naval expedition, he led a successful insurrection. By 1847, California was in American hands, with Frémont as its disputed military governor.

Court-martialed in a highly public trial in Washington, D.C., for his insubordination for attempting to govern without proper authority, Frémont was found guilty; then he returned to California after a pardon by President Polk. He became one of its first senators and an extremely wealthy man, thanks to a rich vein of gold on his lands in the Sierra Nevada foothills. By then a legend, Frémont ran as the first Republican candidate for president in the 1856 election, with his strong-willed wife, Jessie, a critical player in the campaign. When he lost, he did not step out of the public spotlight. During the Civil War, Frémont served as a major general in the Union Army and the commander of the Western Department, where his controversial 1861 move to emancipate all slaves in the region caused Lincoln to rescind his command.

After the war, Frémont accrued more wealth from the railroad boom but suffered financial disaster during the depression of 1873. His last public role was as territorial governor of Arizona (1878–1881), where charges of malfeasance led to his resignation. He died in New York City nine years later.

Margaret Fuller The pioneering social activist became America's first female foreign correspondent.

MARGARET FULLER
★ 1810–1850 ★
TRANSCENDENTALIST, ACTIVIST

The only daughter of a Cambridge, Massachusetts, lawyer, Sarah Margaret Fuller was rigorously schooled in the classics as a girl, making her a formidably educated woman for her time. Seeking out Ralph Waldo Emerson and the New England Transcendentalists, she became one of their circle, and though her intellect was not in question, she had, according to Emerson, "an overweening sense of power, and slight esteem for others." Nonetheless, she served as editor of the Transcendentalists' *Dial* magazine, and in 1844, her work there earned her a position as the first full-time female employee at the *New York Tribune,* where she crusaded for social reforms for the urban poor and prostitutes, and published one of

America's earliest works on women's rights, *Woman in the Nineteenth Century.*

Posted to Europe in 1846 by the *Tribune,* Fuller became America's first female foreign correspondent. In Italy, she married an Italian marchese secretly, as his family would have opposed a foreign, non-Catholic wife. Fuller covered the Italian revolution of 1848–49; then while sailing to America in 1850, she and her husband and their young son died in a shipwreck off New York.

> *As men become aware that few men have had a fair chance, they are inclined to say that no women have had a fair chance.*
>
> **MARGARET FULLER**

WILLIAM LLOYD GARRISON
★ 1805–1879 ★
ABOLITIONIST

The man who would become one of America's leading abolitionists struggled through his childhood. His family had been abandoned by their father, a sea captain, before Garrison was three, and the boy had little educational opportunities. He was an apprentice to a newspaper editor in his hometown of Newburyport, Massachusetts, and the newspaper business would remain his occupation. As a young man, Garrison moved to Boston and joined the growing abolitionist movement. After being accused of libel by a Newburyport slave trader, he spent seven weeks in prison.

Garrison initially embraced the American Colonization Society, which advocated for shipping American slaves and free blacks to Africa for resettlement.

In the initial issue of the *Liberator,* editor William Lloyd Garrison declared he "would not retreat a single inch." His stance made him a leading voice among American abolitionists.

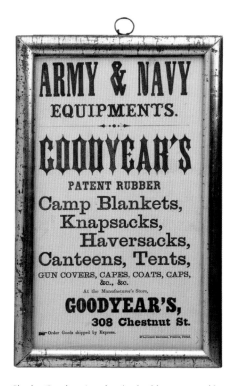

Charles Goodyear's vulcanized rubber was used in the Union's military camp equipment.

He soon rejected that idea, however, and by 1831, he had begun publishing his own abolitionist newspaper, the weekly *Liberator*. Through it and his public speeches, he quickly became a leading force in the movement to free American slaves. Garrison's belief that freed bondsmen would assimilate into the broader American culture was considered radical at the time, even in northern antislavery circles, but he was resolute and often self-righteous and rigid in his beliefs.

The American Anti-Slavery Society that he helped found in 1833 called for the immediate emancipation of all people held in bondage in America. That society suffered a schism, as Garrison also fell out with other abolitionist comrade in arms, including Frederick Douglass. Yet Garrison never yielded in his beliefs (one of which was that the Constitution was a pro-slavery document). In December 1865, after ratification of the 13th Amendment ending slavery, Garrison published his final issue of the *Liberator*, which had appeared continuously for 35 years. He died 14 years later in New York City.

CHARLES GOODYEAR
★ 1800–1860 ★
INVENTOR

Charles Goodyear, a failed Philadelphia hardware merchant, was an ardent inventor by nature. When imported waterproof gum from Brazil created a "rubber fever" in the 1830s, Goodyear was infected, even though the fever soon ended when the gum failed to hold its shape under changing temperatures. But Goodyear remained captivated by the gummy "inert substance which so excites the mind." For the next 20 years, even as his health and finances deteriorated, he continued experimenting on ways to make the gum less sticky and more rigid, discovering by happenstance that heat and sulfur vulcanized rubber. Though he ushered in a new age of rubber, Goodyear died in debt, owing to his poor business acumen and numerous patent infringements on his inventions. Neither he nor his family was associated with the company that bears his name.

WILLIAM HENRY HARRISON
★ 1773–1841 ★
NINTH U.S. PRESIDENT

William Henry Harrison was born into one of Virginia's most respected families (his father Benjamin Harrison had been a signer of the Declaration of Independence). Harrison chose the military and set off to fight Indians in the Northwest Territory (later Ohio and Indiana). He eventually settled in Indiana and served as territorial governor, engineering highly questionable treaties with regional Sac chiefs that essentially deprived them of Illinois and parts of Wisconsin and Missouri. In 1811, Harrison, in the absence of Shawnee leader Tecumseh, led a force against his brother, Tenskwatawa, at Tippecanoe and routed the Indians. Reveling in his sudden fame, Harrison gave up the military and for the next 25 years tried to build a political career. At 67, as a Whig, he was elected president under the slogan "Tippecanoe and Tyler too" (John Tyler was his running mate). Harrison fell ill immediately after his inaugural and died in 32 days, making him the first president to die in office.

William Henry Harrison His presidency lasted only 32 days before he died of pneumonia.

Forty-Niner Fever

STAKING A CLAIM IN CALIFORNIA'S GOLD RUSH

★ ★ ★

In the winter of 1848, John Sutter, who held vast lands in what was then Mexican California, hired John Marshall to build and operate a sawmill on the South Fork of the American River, in the Sierra Nevada foothills. While doing so, Marshall discovered pieces of yellow metal in the tailrace of the mill and told others working with him that he thought they could be gold. Although some of them laughed at him and called him crazy, Sutter himself tested the metal and found that it was indeed gold. By late summer, news of the discovery had reached the East Coast and beyond. Within a year, "forty-niners" from across the continent were leaving families, farms, and jobs behind to make the long journey to California, some overland on the California-Oregon Trail, some by sea.

In part to shorten the six-month ocean voyage from the eastern United States around South America to California, the Panama Canal Railway was built. But gold fever also impacted people across the globe, bringing emigrants from China, Europe, and Latin America. Most never found a fortune in gold, but their quest created boom times for many. The population of San Francisco increased 20-fold in two years, going from 1,000 in 1848 to 20,000 in 1850, and such iconic businesses as Levi Strauss & Co., Ghirardelli Chocolate, and Wells Fargo grew out of the gold rush. Yet the need for laborers (caused by so many men having left jobs to search for gold) led to the passage of a California law that forced orphaned Native Americans or those accused of "loitering" into forced labor—one more dubious legacy of gold fever.

Prospectors from across America and beyond converged on the Calaveras River in California's Sierra Nevada, hoping its abundant gold would make them rich.

NATHANIEL HAWTHORNE

★ 1804–1864 ★

NOVELIST

Nathaniel Hawthorne was descended from the 17th-century Puritan fathers who founded Massachusetts. After graduating from Bowdoin College in Maine, Hawthorne returned to his hometown of Salem, intent on writing fiction. In 1837, his *Twice-Told Tales* won acclaim. After marrying into the respected Peabody family, he moved to a Peabody family home—the "Old Manse" in Concord, Massachusetts. There he became well acquainted with Ralph Waldo Emerson and Henry David Thoreau, though he never embraced their Transcendentalism. Unable to support his family as a writer, Hawthorne took a job in the Salem customhouse in 1846 but lost it in 1849 to patronage. Although the loss embittered Hawthorne, it led him to write two of his greatest works, *The Scarlet Letter* (begun soon after his dismissal from the customhouse) and *The House of the Seven Gables* (which details the hypocrisy of a judge). Hawthorne wrote the latter in the Berkshires, where he befriended the younger novelist Herman Melville.

In 1852, Hawthorne's longtime friend Franklin Pierce became president and appointed the writer as American consul to Liverpool. The family spent seven years abroad, and Hawthorne's experiences inspired a final novel, *The Marble Faun*. In failing health from an unidentified malady on his return to New England in 1860, he died in his sleep four years later. His novels, which probe the nature of good and evil, rank among America's classics.

Nathaniel Hawthorne
His novels detailed life
in New England.

Samuel Houston He served as Texas' president, then governor. *Inset:* An 1860 election proclamation by the then governor

SAMUEL HOUSTON

★ 1793–1863 ★

SOLDIER, POLITICIAN

As a teenage boy in East Tennessee, Sam Houston left home to live with the Cherokee for three years and never lost his affinity for their culture. He subsequently represented Tennessee in Congress (1823–27) before serving as governor of the state for two years. When his marriage failed, he resigned from office and returned to the Cherokee, who adopted him into the tribe. In the early 1830s, Houston went to Washington twice, to inform officials that government agents were defrauding the Indians.

In 1832, President Jackson sent Houston to Texas, then a part of Mexico, to negotiate treaties with tribes there. Houston remained in Texas and during the war for independence from Mexico, he became commander of the Texan Army. After the American debacle at San Antonio's Alamo, Houston took on the forces of Mexican commander Santa Anna at the Battle of San Jacinto in April 1836. Though outnumbered two to one, Houston routed the Mexicans and with his victory, won independence for Texas. He served as president of the republic until 1844. The following year, Texas joined the United States as the 28th state, and in 1846, Houston was elected senator. His support of Native American rights and opposition to the Kansas-Nebraska Act and its expansion of slavery made him unpopular with his constituency, and he was not reelected in 1859. He was, however, elected governor that same year and argued strongly but vainly against the secession of Texas from the Union. He was deposed in 1861 when he refused to swear allegiance to the Confederacy and died two years later in Huntsville, Texas.

Julia Ward Howe The prolific writer and activist is best known for her poem "The Battle Hymn of the Republic."

JULIA WARD HOWE
★ 1819–1910 ★
WRITER, SOCIAL ACTIVIST

The daughter of a wealthy Wall Street Banker, Julia Ward Howe was surrounded by some of the most influential people of her era as a young woman, including Emily Astor (John Jacob's grandchild), Henry Wadsworth Longfellow, and Margaret Fuller. In 1843, she married Samuel Gridley Howe, a philanthropist who had fought in the Greek Revolution and the Polish Revolt. Although Julia Howe had enjoyed independence as a single woman, her husband had traditional expectations of his wife, and the marriage would be deeply—and publicly—fraught. Her anonymously published volume of poetry *Passion-Flowers* (1854) openly defied a husband's authority, and she also became involved in social causes such as the abolition of slavery, women's rights, and education. Also an ardent abolitionist, her husband backed John Brown's rebellion, and when that failed, he moved to Canada briefly to avoid prosecution.

In 1862, Howe's poem, "The Battle Hymn of the Republic," was published in the *Atlantic Monthly*. Set to the tune of "John Brown's Body," it soon became the battle song of the North in the Civil War. Later, the women's suffrage movement, of which Howe was a part, adopted the song. She continued writing poetry and books throughout her life, and in 1908, she became the first woman elected into the American Academy of Arts and Letters.

WASHINGTON IRVING
★ 1783–1859 ★
WRITER

Washington Irving grew up in a well-heeled New York family and became a lawyer. But his passion lay in writing, and his work generally parodied pretentions, as was the case with his popular *Diedrich Knickerbocker's History of New York* (1809). He traveled to England on business in 1815 and joined literary circles there. In 1819, he published his masterpiece, *The Sketch Book of Geoffrey Crayon, Gent,* a collection of essays, satirical pieces, and a new literary form—the short story; "The Legend of Sleepy Hollow" first appeared in *The Sketch Book*. His sequel, *Bracebridge Hall,* was equally successful. After travels in western Europe, Irving returned to New York in 1832 and spent most of the rest of his life writing biographies in his home on the Hudson.

Washington Irving The writer forged a new literary genre—the short story.

Irving's Gothic masterpiece, "Rip Van Winkle," inspired artists such as Arthur Rackham to match the story's building suspense in their illustrations.

ANDREW JACKSON

★ 1767–1845 ★

SEVENTH U.S. PRESIDENT

Raised in the borderlands between North and South Carolina, Andrew Jackson was captured as a teenager by the British during the Revolutionary War; his mother and two brothers died in the conflict. After the war, he studied law, started a practice in Nashville, and married Rachel Robards, who had been married before. Jackson and Robards believed her divorce had been granted when they married, but that was not so, and this would plague them in the years to come.

You must pay the price if you wish to secure the blessing.

ANDREW JACKSON

Andrew Jackson He won the day for America at the 1815 Battle of New Orleans and became a national hero.

In 1796–97, Jackson made his initial foray into national politics, serving for a year as the first congressman from the new state of Tennessee, then for a year in the Senate before personal financial pressures and a distaste for Washington politics led him to resign. When the War of 1812 erupted, Jackson became commander of a militia and sent his forces against the Creek, allies of the British. After crushing their resistance, he imposed a treaty that wrested an enormous tract of land (some 23 million acres) in western Georgia and Alabama from them. On January 8, 1815, he also defeated the British in the Battle of New Orleans. The victory catapulted Jackson to the status of national hero. He was made commander of the southern district, and as such, was instructed to invade Spanish Florida to fight the Seminole, precipitating an international outcry but also hastening the U.S. accession of Florida.

Elected senator again in 1823, Jackson ran for president the following year. Though he received the most electoral votes, he did not have the necessary majority, and ultimately John Quincy Adams prevailed. Jackson ousted Adams in the next election, and his inaugural ushered in the age of Jacksonian democracy (1829–1837). Though in fact politically conservative, Jackson positioned himself as a self-made populist from outside eastern power circles, who championed the rights of the common man. His presidency was propelled by his forceful, often autocratic personality and characterized by inconsistent policies. "King Andrew I," as his opponents called him, supported a strong union and threatened military intervention when South Carolina passed its nullification resolution. Yet in his second term as president, Jackson vigorously opposed paper money and the recharter of the Bank of the United States. In the ensuing "bank war," inflation spiraled, leading to financial panic as the enormously popular Jackson left office in 1837. For the next two years, the policy of Indian removal pursued by Jackson and Congress saw some 15,000 Cherokee pushed from their Appalachian homeland to what is now Oklahoma. More than 4,000 died on the Trail of Tears.

HENRY WADSWORTH LONGFELLOW
★ 1807–1882 ★
POET

The man who reigns as one of America's iconic poets grew up in Portland, Maine, the son of a prominent attorney. After graduating from nearby Bowdoin College, Longfellow spent three years on a European tour, enthralled by learning other languages and pursuing his own passion to write. He returned to Bowdoin, where he taught Italian, Spanish, and French, and wrote six textbooks on foreign languages. That work resulted in the offer of a professorship at Harvard.

While on another European trip in 1835 with his new wife, Mary, and two friends, Mary died, leaving Longfellow deeply depressed. On his return to Harvard, he began writing the kind of poetry that would gain him increasing

> *The true glory of a nation consists not in the extent of its territory, the pomp of its forests, the majesty of its rivers, the height of its mountains, and the beauty of its sky; but in the extent of its mental power—the majesty of its intellect—the height and depth and purity of its moral nature.*
>
> **HENRY WADSWORTH LONGFELLOW**

Henry Wadsworth Longfellow His epic poems were recited by generations of schoolchildren.

fame. "I read your poems over and over . . . Nothing equal to some of them was ever written in this world, this western world," former classmate Nathaniel Hawthorne wrote in praise. Yet Longfellow was in the throes of emotional pain, owing to his failed courtship of heiress Frances "Fanny" Appleton. Finally, in 1843, the two were married and settled into Craigie House, a gift from Fanny's father. It would become the intellectual hub of Cambridge, host to Ralph Waldo Emerson, Hawthorne, Oliver Wendell Holmes, and others.

By 1847, Longfellow's success as a poet allowed him to leave Harvard and devote himself to writing, producing long-form poems that mythologized American figures and moments (among them, *Evangeline: A Tale of Acadie, The Courtship of Miles Standish, The Song of Hiawatha,* and "Paul Revere's Ride"). In 1861, he suffered another overwhelming loss when Fanny's dress caught fire. Longfellow attempted to save her, but she died of her injuries, and he suffered permanent scars that he covered with what became his signature, flowing beard. Though devastated by the loss of his wife, he continued to live in Craigie House and

to write, but his greatest works were behind him. His fame, however, continued, and his 70th birthday became a national celebration.

CYRUS MCCORMICK
★ 1809–1884 ★
INVENTOR

Cyrus McCormick grew up in Virginia's Shenandoah Valley on the farm of his father, Robert, who had spent several decades attempting to make a mechanical reaper. McCormick continued his father's work both as a farmer and as an inventor, and in 1834, he patented a design for a mechanical reaper but initially found no buyers in his area. In the next decade, he made modifications to the original design as his time allowed, and by 1845, he was selling a few reapers a year, initially made by hand on his farm and later by shops he contracted with in the Northeast. As orders increased—many of them from the Midwest—Cyrus

Cyrus McCormick The Virginia farmer changed American agriculture.

McCormick's reaper made harvesting wheat vastly easier than it had ever been and opened the prairie to greater production.

> *Trying to do business without advertising is like winking at a pretty girl through a pair of green goggles. You may know what you are doing, but no one else does.*
>
> **CYRUS MCCORMICK**

moved operations to a factory he established in 1847 in Chicago, where water and rail transportation made for easy shipment into the grain-producing heartland. Though his patent expired a year later and McCormick had to deal with competitors, he had a strong talent for marketing and his company flourished, producing more than 2,500 reapers annually by the end of its first decade.

The McCormick reaper quickly revolutionized agriculture, allowing six or seven men to harvest in a day as much wheat as would have been harvested in the past by 15 men working with sickles and a cradle. More than 100,000 mechanical harvesters were in use on farms throughout the West by 1864.

OSCEOLA
★ 1804–1838 ★
SEMINOLE WARRIOR CHIEF

Born Billy Powell in Tallassee, Alabama, Osceola was the son of a part Muscogee and part white mother and a father whose identity remains unknown. Mother and son moved to Florida when Osceola, the name the boy chose for himself, was about 10, and thereafter he claimed an Indian identity. As a young man, Osceola refused to acknowledge the Indian Removal Act of 1830, written to force Native Americans out of the Southeast. The Seminole came to consider him "the master spirit and leader of the tribe," according to artist George Catlin. Osceola's eloquence also gained a following among the American press.

In 1835, he and his followers ambushed and killed several men, including a government agent. The event set off the Second Seminole War, during which some 1,000 to 1,500 Seminole warriors and their allied runaway slaves (to whom the Seminole offered safe haven) waged a guerrilla-style war and successfully held an army of thousands at bay for about two years. But by autumn 1837, the army was prevailing, and Osceola's followers were deserting or losing hope. The chief sent word that he wanted a parley with the army, but in October, when he appeared in St. Augustine under a flag of truce, he was captured. He died in prison only months later, and his family was ultimately forced west on the Trail of Tears.

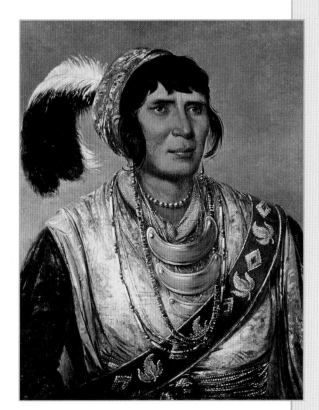

Osceola The warrior's guerrilla tactics thwarted U.S. forces fighting the Seminole.

MATTHEW PERRY
★ 1794–1858 ★
COMMODORE

A native of coastal Rhode Island, Matthew Perry was the son of a Revolutionary War naval captain and the brother of Oliver Hazard Perry, who would become famous for his naval victory on Lake Erie in the War of 1812. Matthew himself went on to a stellar naval career, hunting slave traders, pushing for the adoption of steam warships, and commanding the Gulf Squadron in the Mexican-American War.

In 1852, President Fillmore dispatched Commodore Perry and his small squadron of four warships to isolationist Japan on a quasi-diplomatic mission. At the time, all trade with Japan was filtered through the Dutch, but Perry was to present the emperor with a letter from Fillmore proposing that "the United States and Japan should live in friendship and have commercial intercourse with each other"—without Dutch intermediaries. Initially greeted with armed Japanese waiting for him when he anchored

in Edo (now Tokyo) Bay, Perry persisted in his assignment and succeeded in presenting the letter to princely representatives of the emperor. He gave them a period of time to respond but said he would return with a squadron of "black ships," as the Japanese called his vessels, and that their refusal to comply would result in war. The following spring, he returned with nine ships, and the Japanese signed the Treaty of Kanagawa, opening Japan to trade with America and eventually leading to a liberalizing of Japanese society and the demise of centuries of shogun hegemony.

FRANKLIN PIERCE
★ 1804–1869 ★
14TH U.S. PRESIDENT

Like many presidents of his era, Franklin Pierce was a Northerner and a lawyer who began his career in state politics. In 1829, he was elected to the New Hampshire legislature and soon became its speaker. He went on to serve in the U.S. House and Senate and then in the Army during the Mexican-American War. The Democrats put the inoffensive but well-spoken Pierce forward as their candidate in 1852, and despite being relatively unknown, he won. Pierce was ill suited to deal with the growing tensions between North and South over the expansion of slavery, though he attempted to direct attention away from that rift by promoting American expansionism (including a suggestion to buy Cuba). His attempts failed, and after the passage of the Kansas-Nebraska

Franklin Pierce His presidency exacerbated the North-South rift.

Act, Pierce threw federal support behind the pro-slavery faction and violence spread through "Bleeding Kansas." He was not renominated by his party for a second term, and his death in 1869 received little attention.

EDGAR ALLAN POE
★ 1809–1849 ★
WRITER

One of America's most imaginative writers, Edgar Allan Poe himself lived a somewhat tragic life. His parents, both actors, had died by the time he was three, and he was raised in the family of wealthy Richmond, Virginia, merchant John Allan. Poe's childhood with the Allans allowed him a fine education, and he attended the University of Virginia. He did well but incurred debts, some from gambling, and Allan refused him support, forcing him to leave school. In 1827, Poe both enlisted in the Army and published his first collection of poems, *Tamerlane and Other Poems,* soon following it with a second volume; neither enjoyed strong sales.

By the 1830s, Poe had given up the military to devote himself to literature,

Charged with opening relations with Japan, Matthew Perry and his fleet set sail in November 1852, arriving in Japan in July 1853.

The Way West

A TALE OF INGENUITY, GRIT, AND OPPORTUNITY

★ ★ ★

The early 19th century saw a great migration of Americans. A 1785 ordinance had divided lands west of the Ohio River into rural "townships" with sections that could be sold to large or small landowners. Thus, a gridded farmland, where title would not be disputed, encouraged land-poor Eastern-ers to move west. By mid-century, the steel plow, the automatic reaper, and the thresher had also revolutionized grain farming. Meanwhile, riverboats and canals allowed for the easy transport of goods in the early part of the century, while in the 1840s railroads began to crisscross the landscape, opening the Plains and West even farther. Telegraph lines soon followed the train tracks, linking the continent in ways unimaginable just decades before.

Pioneering families pushed ever west, carving farms out of the bountiful wilderness.

writing short stories in Baltimore and Philadelphia newspapers. In 1835, he became editor of the Richmond-based *Southern Literary Messenger,* where he gained national prominence. Poe had been living with his aunt Maria Clemm and her young daughter, Virginia, for several years, and in 1836 he married 13-year-old Virginia.

In the early 1840s, Poe edited and wrote for other magazines and formu-lated the horror and detective genres that would become his hallmark, publishing such classics as "The Tell-Tale Heart," "The Black Cat," and "The Raven." Poe's pioneering style was intended to portray the essence of the human condition and evoke in readers an understanding of "terror, or passion, or horror." His own brief life ended in tragedy. His wife died

In the contemplation of Beauty we alone find it possible to attain that pleasurable elevation, or excitement of the soul, which we recognise as the Poetic Sentiment.

EDGAR ALLAN POE

at age 24, and two years later, Poe was found semiconscious in Baltimore, which he had visited for unknown rea-sons. Four days later he was dead. The facts of his death remain unresolved.

Edgar Allan Poe The writer's life and death were as strange as those of one of the characters in his tales of mystery and horror.

A campaign banner with an extra star shows Polk's support for adding Texas.

James Polk Under Polk's presidency, American territorial holdings were greatly expanded in the Pacific Northwest and Southwest, but the new territories only fueled tensions over the spread of slavery.

JAMES POLK

★ 1795-1849 ★

11TH U.S. PRESIDENT

James Polk moved with his family from North Carolina to the Tennessee frontier when he was 10, and the family managed to acquire thousands of acres and a plantation reliant on slave labor. Despite his isolation, Polk received a good education and graduated from the University of North Carolina. After studying law in the office of a Nashville attorney, he established his own practice in Columbia, Tennessee, and entered state politics as a representative. An ardent Jacksonian, Polk was elected to the U.S. Congress in 1825 and remained for 14 years, with two terms as speaker of the House and the sobriquet of "Young Hickory," because of his close ties to President Jackson ("Old Hickory"). Polk then served as a one-term governor of Tennessee but failed in two other gubernatorial bids. In 1844, he emerged as the unexpected Democratic candidate for president. He ran against powerful Whig senator Henry Clay in a brutal election, in which he scored an upset victory by a very thin margin. Polk's well-educated wife, Sarah, proved an asset to him in all of his political endeavors.

In his presidential campaign, the energetic Polk had preached American expansionism and Manifest Destiny, and he pursued that once in office. He reached a compromise agreement with Britain over the Oregon Territory early in his tenure. But the Southwest was a different matter. The vast territory of Texas had been annexed by Polk's predecessor, John Tyler, just before he left office, and territorial tensions and border disputes with

There is more selfishness and less principle among members of Congress . . . than I had any conception of, before I became President of the U.S.

JAMES POLK

Mexico escalated in the mid-1840s, leading Polk to ask Congress for a declaration of war in 1846.

As commander in chief, Polk took a strong hand in directing the military strategy of the Mexican-American War ("Mr. Polk's War"), and it ended in victory. The 1848 Treaty of Guadalupe Hidalgo allowed the United States to purchase California and New Mexico and established the Rio Grande as Texas' southern border. It did not, however, give expansionists "All of Mexico!" as their slogan had demanded.

Although Polk could revel in his territorial victories, they also posed problems. Were the new territories to be free or slave states? The Wilmot Proviso, an amendment to an appropriations bill that had been introduced to Congress in 1846, had stipulated that "neither slavery not involuntary servitude shall ever exist" in the territories acquired under the Treaty of Guadalupe Hidalgo. Though it did not pass both houses of Congress, it raised sectional tensions to new heights. Polk himself supported extending the Missouri Compromise line to the Pacific, thus allowing slavery in the newly added southern territories but not in the northern ones.

Polk had promised to remain in office only one term, and he did not pursue reelection, though his popularity would have almost certainly meant easy victory. He left office having enlarged the nation by more than a million square acres, bringing in most of the Southwest and Pacific coastal states, as well as Nevada and parts of the Mountain West. But his four-year term had also seen the sectional divide over slavery grow and a man he disliked, his former commander, Whig Zachary Taylor, elected president. Polk lived only three months beyond his own presidency, dying of an illness that may have been cholera. Polk left his estate to his wife, with the request that she free all slaves at her death.

The abolitionists surely have a work to do now in influencing and directing the bloody struggle, that it may end in Emancipation, as the only basis of a true and permanent peace.

AMY KIRBY POST

AMY KIRBY POST
★ 1802–1889 ★
SOCIAL ACTIVIST

Raised as a Quaker, Amy Post eventually settled in Rochester, New York, with her husband, Isaac Post, a Hicksite Quaker, who believed in following an "inner Light" rather than a formalist approach to spirituality. Amy embraced both Hicksite beliefs and the antislavery movement but gradually fell out with the Hicksite community over her ardent and public abolitionist activities and fund-raising for the cause. The Post home was used as a frequent station on the Underground Railroad, and at times as many as 20 fugitive slaves heading for Canada took refuge there in a given night. Such celebrated abolitionists as William Lloyd

Amy Kirby Post An abolitionist and women's rights leader

Garrison and Frederick Douglass were also guests during their lecture appearances in Rochester. Harriet Jacobs, a slave who lived with the Posts for nearly a year, was encouraged by Amy Post to write her autobiographical *Incidents in the Life of a Slave Girl,* and Post helped her publish it.

A proponent of women's rights as well, Post attended the seminal 1848 Seneca Falls Convention and signed the Declaration of Sentiments. At the subsequent Rochester Convention, Post took a leading role. She continued to be a leader in the abolitionist movement and in women's rights and helped found the Working Women's Protective Union. She was also an ardent spiritualist and temperance advocate.

JOHN ROSS
★ 1790–1866 ★
CHEROKEE CHIEF

John Ross was raised in Alabama in a mixed Scottish-and-Cherokee milieu that reflected his own lineage. Although his mother was part Cherokee, his father, a white trader, wanted his children raised as whites and sent his son to a white academy for his education. As an adult, Ross became a prosperous slave-holding planter and one of the wealthiest men in the Cherokee Nation. He gradually began to play a part in Cherokee politics, and in 1828, he became the Cherokee's first elected principal chief. During the 1830s, Ross fought President Jackson's attempts to take the Cherokee's Georgia lands for white settlement and secured a Supreme

Dred Scott v. Sandford went to the U.S. Supreme Court, which was divided over major issues. The majority opinion denied Scott his freedom.

Court ruling in the Cherokee's favor, though Jackson and Georgia ignored the ruling. Undaunted, Ross also opposed the 1835 Treaty of New Echota, which had been signed by other Cherokee leaders and called for Indian removal from the tribal homeland. When forced to comply in 1838, Ross was put in charge of organizing the tribe during the tragic Trail of Tears from the Appalachian South to Indian Territory (Oklahoma).

Once settled in Indian Territory, Ross attempted to establish a new Cherokee government, but a faction of Cherokee "Old Settlers" opposed him and bloodshed ensued for years. Ultimately, Ross prevailed, establishing a stable political system and a free public school system. His efforts to secure a treaty guaranteeing a permanent Cherokee homeland in Indian Territory were realized days before his death.

Dred Scott After spending years living in a free state, Scott, a slave born in Virginia, sued for his freedom.

John Ross Part Cherokee, the chief led the legal battle to protect native lands.

In truth, our cause is your own; it is the cause of liberty and of justice; it is based upon your own principles, which we have learned from yourselves; for we have gloried to count your Washington and your Jefferson our great teachers.

JOHN ROSS

DRED SCOTT

★ CA 1800–1858 ★

SLAVE, PLAINTIFF IN LANDMARK SUPREME COURT DECISION

Born a slave, Dred Scott moved several times with his original master, Peter Blow, before Army surgeon John Emerson bought him. During his time with Emerson, Scott spent two and a half years in the free state of Illinois and two in the free territory of Wisconsin. After Emerson's death in 1843, Scott tried to buy his freedom from Emerson's wife, Irene, but she refused. In 1846, Scott attempted to win his freedom through the courts in a tangled process that would shape America's history.

In 1847, Scott lost his initial trial in St. Louis on a technicality, but the Missouri Supreme Court ruled in 1848 that the case should be retried. In that instance Scott and his wife were granted their freedom, though again the state supreme court reversed the lower court's decision. Scott's lawyer turned to the federal court system, but the federal circuit court in Missouri did not overturn the state Supreme Court decision.

In 1856, *Dred Scott* v. *Sandford* went to the U.S. Supreme Court (John Sandford was Irene Emerson's brother). Five justices on the court owned slaves, and the court divided over major issues in the case. Chief Justice Roger Taney read the majority opinion, which held that as a black, Scott had no rights as a citizen, and therefore could not bring suit, and that African Americans had historically been viewed as "beings of an inferior order . . . so far inferior, that they had no rights which the white man was bound to respect."

The decision also held that as slaves were property, and as the Constitution prohibited Congress from taking property, the Missouri Compromise of 1820, limiting slavery in certain western territories, was unconstitutional. The ruling ignited northern antislavery sentiment and elated the South.

After the case, Irene Emerson's abolitionist husband gave Scott back to the Blow family, who gave Scott and his wife their freedom at last, but he lived only nine months as a free man.

SEQUOYAH

★ CA 1770–1843 ★

INVENTOR OF THE CHEROKEE SYLLABARY

Many childhood details of the man who changed the Cherokee Nation remain unclear, but it is known that his birth name was George Gist or Guess. Childhood lameness, possibly from an accident or a health condition, led to his Cherokee name—Sequoyah—"pig's foot." When his family moved to Georgia, he became intrigued by the "talking leaves" the English used to communicate. He had further exposure to written English when he fought with Andrew Jackson's forces in the War of 1812.

Though Sequoyah could not read or write English, after the war he devoted himself to creating an alphabetic writing system for Cherokee. After a dozen years of work, he produced a "syllabary" of 85 symbols that captured the syllables of Cherokee. For his labors, he was initially tried for witchcraft, but his judges (Cherokee warriors) were easily convinced of the advantages of such a written system, and it spread quickly in the 1820s. Sequoyah's syllabary allowed the Cherokee to print their own newspaper and prosper more easily in a white-dominated world, though it did not save them from forced removal to Indian Territory (Oklahoma). Honored by both whites and his own tribe, Sequoyah died in Mexico, when he and a small band went on an expedition to visit displaced Indian communities.

Sequoyah The symbols he created for Cherokee syllables gave that nation a written language and with it, more advantages in the dominant white culture.

JOSEPH SMITH

★ 1805–1844 ★

FOUNDER OF MORMONISM

As a farm boy in the Northeast, Joseph Smith was exposed to the evangelical spirit of the Second Great Awakening then sweeping rural America. According to his own account, while praying in the woods in Palmyra, New York, in 1820, he was visited by God and Jesus, who instructed him not to join any existing church. Three years later, Smith announced that a figure he identified as the Angel Moroni came to him and explained that an ancient record existed, detailing how one of the lost tribes of Israel had fled to the American continent and given rise to the Native American peoples. Another four years passed before Smith claimed to discover the record written on thin golden plates in a buried stone box near the family farm.

Though the language was unknown, four years later Smith said he was given divine guidance in translating the plates. In early 1830, the Book of Mormon (named after an ancient prophet) was published and Smith founded the Church of Jesus Christ of Latter-day Saints.

In the coming years, Smith led his burgeoning flock to Ohio, then Missouri, then Illinois, but suspicion and prejudice dogged the polygamous Mormons because they were unknown. Smith traveled to Washington "to lay before the Congress of the United States, the grievances of the Saints while in Missouri." He also lobbied President Van Buren but received little reassurance.

Back in their prospering town of Nauvoo, Illinois, Smith and his followers organized a militia, and Smith announced himself as a candidate in the 1844 presidential race. But that June, local citizens accused him and his brother of inciting riot and arrested them. While in jail in Carthage, Illinois, both were shot by a mob. Yet Smith remains to this day the Prophet of the Saints.

> *Until colored men manage by dint of hard acquisition to enter the ranks of skilled industry, very little substantial respect will be shown them, even with the ballot-box and musket in their hands.*
>
> **WILLIAM STILL**

WILLIAM STILL

★ 1821–1902 ★

ABOLITIONIST

A freeborn black man, William Still taught himself to read and write and in 1847 was hired as a clerk for the Pennsylvania Society for the Abolition of Slavery. Still's parents had been slaves prior to his birth, and Still well understood the

Joseph Smith Founder of a distinctly American religion—the Church of Jesus Christ of Latter-day Saints—Smith preached that Native Americans were descended from one of the lost tribes of Israel.

Smith said an angel directed him to the ancient text that became the Book of Mormon.

William Still Leader on the Underground Railroad

horrors of slavery, so he took a leading role in the abolitionist movement and the Underground Railroad, working with Harriet Tubman and others in the dangerous business of assisting fugitive slaves. In the midst of his other endeavors, Still managed as well to become one of the most successful black businessmen Philadelphia has ever known, dealing in real estate and coal. But he is best remembered as author of a definitive, self-published history, *The Underground Rail Road* (1872). After the Civil War, he continued to work on freedmen's aid and pressed for universal suffrage.

LUCY STONE
★ 1818–1893 ★
ABOLITIONIST, WOMEN'S RIGHTS

Lucy Stone's upbringing in rural Massachusetts clearly influenced her later life, as she was discouraged from education, owing to traditional gender expectations. Nonetheless, she attended Oberlin

College in Ohio, and after her graduation in 1847 at 29, she became the first woman from Massachusetts to earn a college degree. Her abilities, particularly as a public speaker, led to a job as an agent/speaker for the American Anti-Slavery Society.

In the early 1850s, she participated in National Women's Rights Conventions, where her powerful speech apparently converted Susan B. Anthony to the cause and inspired English social philosopher John Stuart Mill. Choosing not to take her husband's name after marriage, she inspired other "Lucy Stoners" to keep theirs. After emancipation, Stone lobbied for the 15th Amendment, which gave African-American men the right to vote, though not women. Stone's support of the amendment as it stood and her push thereafter for suffrage at the state rather than federal level led to a schism in the movement between her faction and such well-known members of the American suffrage movement as Anthony and Elizabeth Cady Stanton.

Lucy Stone She argued forcibly for the rights of African Americans and women.

Through Artists' Eyes
PAINTERS PORTRAY AMERICA
★★★

As Americans embraced the rich possibilities of their vast new country, artists began to celebrate its beauty. In 1825, English-born Thomas Cole hiked into the Catskills above the Hudson River in autumn and understood immediately its artistic potential. His canvases of nature in all its romantic grandeur inspired artists such as Frederic Edwin Church, John Frederick Kensett, and Albert Bierstadt in what became known as the Hudson River school. After traveling into the American West in 1857, Bierstadt continued the grand romantic tradition, creating enormous Western landscapes that became the impetus for another artistic movement, the Rocky Mountain school, whose other famous proponent was Thomas Moran. Meanwhile, George Catlin was committed to capturing the lives of Plains Indians, hoping with his simple style "to rescue from oblivion their primitive looks and customs." In the 1830s and 1840s, he displayed his Indian Gallery throughout eastern and European cities.

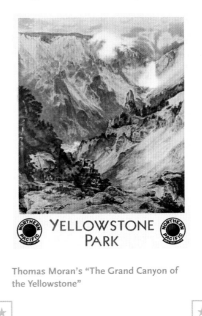

Thomas Moran's "The Grand Canyon of the Yellowstone"

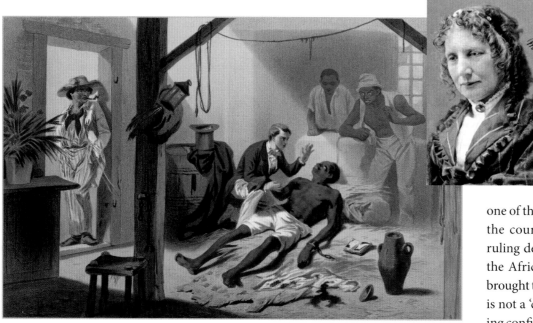

Harriet Beecher Stowe Her classic, *Uncle Tom's Cabin*, brought the cruelties of slavery to life for thousands of readers worldwide and served as a critical tool in the fight for abolition.

The "Death of Uncle Tom" is an illustration from Stowe's masterwork published in 1852.

HARRIET BEECHER STOWE
★ 1811–1896 ★
WRITER

The daughter of prominent abolitionist minister Lyman Beecher, Harriet Beecher Stowe grew up in an intellectual household in Litchfield, Connecticut. She became a teacher herself, but her passion was writing. After marrying Calvin Stowe, a theology professor, she continued her writing, despite the demands of a large family. In 1851, following the passage of the Fugitive Slave Act, Gamaliel Bailey, editor of the abolitionist periodical the *National Era,* contracted with Stowe to write a story that would "paint a word picture of slavery." The 40 installments of Stowe's *Uncle Tom's Cabin,* published in a single volume later that year, brought Stowe international fame and financial security. It also brought the torments of slavery to life for thousands, as did the preaching of her brother Henry Ward Beecher. The often told story that Lincoln met Stowe in 1862 and greeted her by saying, "So you're the little woman who wrote the book that started this great war" is apocryphal.

ROGER TANEY
★ 1777–1864 ★
CHIEF JUSTICE OF THE UNITED STATES

Born to tobacco planters in Maryland, Roger Taney was initially a Federalist when he served five years in the Maryland senate. Yet under Andrew Jackson's administration, Taney threw his support behind Jackson's Democrats and was appointed attorney general, then secretary of the treasury. In both capacities, he worked with Jackson to dismantle the Bank of the United States. In 1836, he became Chief Justice of the United States, having failed in 1835 to be confirmed by the Senate for a seat on the court. In 1857, he delivered the opinion of the Court in one of the most volatile cases ever before the court: *Dred Scot* v. *Sandford.* The ruling declared, "A free negro [Scott] of the African race, whose ancestors were brought to this country and sold as slaves, is not a 'citizen.'" Taney professed "abiding confidence that this act of my judicial life will stand the test of time." Yet under him, with the Dred Scott ruling, the Supreme Court's reputation fell to a low point, and his obituary in the *New York Times* concluded that Taney "was by many suspected of leaning strongly in his sympathies toward the Southern side of the great issues which divide the nation."

Roger Taney Fifth Chief Justice of the United States

ZACHARY TAYLOR
★ 1784–1850 ★
12TH U.S. PRESIDENT

Zachary Taylor was raised to the life of a wealthy Kentucky planter, but as a young man, he chose a career in the Army. He was put in command of a series of frontier posts in the Midwest and the South and gained a reputation as an "Indian fighter." Yet Taylor's goal was to keep white settlers and Native Americans separated, to lessen tensions, and to prevent white settlers from encroaching on Indian lands. In 1845, President Polk ordered Taylor to Texas, where territorial disputes with Mexico were increasing. When Taylor's troops were attacked near the Rio Grande, Polk asked for and got a declaration of war.

During the conflict, "Old Rough and Ready," as his men called Taylor, won critical victories at Palo Alto and Monterrey, against Mexican forces that far outnumbered his. At Buena Vista, Mexican general Santa Anna suffered his final defeat and Taylor emerged as a national hero.

Though he had no political experience, Taylor responded to the clamor that he run for president in 1848, and somewhat surprisingly, was tapped by the Whig

> *It would be judicious to act with magnanimity towards a prostrate foe.*
>
> **ZACHARY TAYLOR**

Party as its candidate. Because his stance on national issues straddled both parties' beliefs, Taylor offered no platform during his campaign, even in regard to the expansion of slavery into the western territories, and was positioned as the ideal candidate, "without regard to creeds." However, after he emerged victorious, he maneuvered to have California and New Mexico apply for statehood (both newly acquired territories from the Mexican-American War), assuming they would bar slavery in their constitutions. In reaction, some Southern Democrats began threatening secession, and Taylor in turn threatened to hang anyone who unbalanced the Union. He also threatened to lead an army himself into Texas if the new state did not respect the border with Mexico.

As 1850 opened, congressional leaders strove to craft legislation that would quell sectional tensions. Taylor watched and waited. He did not support solutions that would make their way into the final Compromise of 1850, which included the Fugitive Slave Act, but he would never have the chance to react officially. After attending Independence Day ceremonies that year, he fell ill with what was probably cholera. He died on July 9, after only 16 months in office.

Zachary Taylor "Old Rough and Ready" (at right in a daguerreotype, above on the white horse at the Battle of Buena Vista) became a national hero in the Mexican-American War.

Henry David Thoreau Iconoclastic and visionary, Thoreau lived his Transcendentalist views, extolling nature and rejecting the usual paths to success.

HENRY DAVID THOREAU

★ 1817–1862 ★

TRANSCENDENTALIST PHILOSOPHER

One of America's most revered writers, Henry David Thoreau lived almost his entire life in his hometown of Concord, Massachusetts. After graduating from Harvard, he founded a school in Concord with his brother John and taught for a few years before moving on to sporadic work in the family's pencilmaking business. He gave that up to become the live-in handyman for his neighbor and mentor, Transcendentalist Ralph Waldo Emerson, and to write. During this period, Thoreau published a few poems and essays in the Transcendentalists' journal, *The Dial.* He returned briefly to his parents' home and pencilmaking, but as Emerson later said of him, Thoreau "declined to give up his large ambition of knowledge and action for any narrow craft or profession, aiming at a much more comprehensive calling, the art of living well."

In 1845, he began building a cabin on Walden Pond, on the outskirts of Concord. During his two years there, he wrote his contemplation on life and the natural world, *Walden.* He also wrote *A Week on the Concord and Merrimack Rivers.* The latter was published first and did not sell well, so Thoreau could not find a publisher for *Walden.* He revised it seven times before it was finally published, to positive critical reviews. Thoreau's other writings included travel/nature pieces and essays. He was also a committed abolitionist and conductor on the Underground Railway. When Thoreau died at 45 of tuberculosis, Emerson called him "the captain of a huckleberry party," and declared, "The country knows not yet . . . how great a son it has lost."

SOJOURNER TRUTH

★ CA 1797–1883 ★

ORATOR

Isabella Baumfree was born into slavery in the Dutch-American enclave of the Hudson River Valley. Her native language was Low Dutch, and she had little exposure to other African Americans beyond her family. In 1826, having borne five children, she walked away from her then master, carrying her infant daughter. After some months of uncertainty, she was about to return to her former owner when "God revealed himself to her, with all the suddenness of a flash of lightning." The vision gave her the strength to continue as a free woman, and she settled in New York City, working as a domestic. In 1843, she determined to change her name to Sojourner Truth and become an itinerant lecturer "testifying of the hope that was in her–exhorting the people to embrace Jesus, and refrain from sin." She was well received in Connecticut and Massachusetts, and in 1850, her dictated memoir, *The Narrative of Sojourner Truth,* gained her widespread recognition. A year later, she delivered her iconic speech at the Women's Rights Convention in Akron, Ohio. "That man over there says that women need to be helped into carriages, and lifted over ditches . . . Nobody ever helps me . . . And ain't I a woman? Look at me! Look at my arm! I have ploughed and planted, and gathered into barns, and no man could head me! And ain't I a woman?"

Truth settled in Battle Creek, Michigan, in the 1850s and was active in the Underground Railroad. She continued to lecture, becoming an iconic figure. After the Civil War, she pushed for desegregation and helped newly freed blacks find jobs and establish new lives. She died at her Battle Creek home in 1883.

Sojourner Truth She was an eloquent speaker on the humanity of women and blacks.

HARRIET TUBMAN

★ CA 1820–1913 ★

ABOLITIONIST, CONDUCTOR ON THE
UNDERGROUND RAILROAD

The woman who would go down in American history as "Moses," for leading her people to freedom, was born Araminta Ross, a slave on Maryland's Eastern Shore. Her early life was characterized by all the hardships of bondage—separation from her family, endless labor, poverty, brutality. In the early fall of 1849, she

> *I grew up like a neglected weed. Ignorant of liberty, having no experience of it . . . Every time I saw a white man I was afraid of being carried away.*
>
> **HARRIET TUBMAN**

followed the North Star and the Underground Railroad, escaping to freedom. Under the name Harriet Tubman (Harriet was her mother's name and Tubman her husband's, though he was not with her), she settled in Philadelphia but two years later returned to Maryland to lead her first group of bondsmen to freedom. She risked that trip at least a dozen times in the coming decade, and all of her attempts were successful, making her the most famous conductor on the Underground Railroad.

Tubman also became a prominent abolitionist, with ties to major figures in the movement. During the Civil War, she

Harriet Tubman A fearless conductor on the Underground Railroad, an abolitionist, and a Union spy, she will be featured on the new $20 bill.

served as a spy for the Union in South Carolina and was the first woman in that conflict to lead an armed raid, on plantations along the Combahee River. After the war, she settled in Auburn, New York, and struggled to support her extended family. Still she remained a crusader, working for the suffragist movement and education and aid for former slaves.

Tubman never received a government pension for her war work, but in 2016, the U.S. Treasury Department announced that Tubman's likeness would replace Andrew Jackson's on the front of the $20 bill.

Nat Turner An engraving depicts the capture of Turner, who led a slave rebellion in Virginia in 1831. The successful rebellion ended in his eventual hanging.

As I was praying one day at my plough, the Spirit spoke to me, saying, "Seek ye the kingdom of heaven, and all things shall be added unto you."

NAT TURNER

NAT TURNER

★ CA 1800–1831 ★

LEADER OF SLAVE INSURRECTION

African-Virginian Nat Turner led the only successful slave rebellion in his state. A self-styled preacher and prophet, Turner had learned to read and write and spent much time in study and prayer. In the 1820s, he said he "saw white spirits and black spirits engaged in battle." Inspired, in August 1831 Turner began planning an insurrection for southeastern Virginia with four other slaves. Almost 60 whites were killed in the short-lived uprising, quickly put down by militia and federal troops. Local vigilantes took revenge on black people in the area, killing dozens. Before Turner was hanged, lawyer Thomas Ruffin Gray recorded what he said were Turner's verbatim confessions. The resulting pamphlet, "The Confessions of Nat Turner," served as a weapon against northern abolitionists.

JOHN TYLER

★ 1790–1862 ★

10TH U.S. PRESIDENT

A member of Virginia's aristocracy, John Tyler grew up on a tobacco plantation on the James River. He briefly practiced law before entering state then national politics. Tyler served in the U.S. Congress between 1816 to 1821, then the Senate from 1827 to 1836, where he was a states' rights, limited-government, pro-slavery member. In the 1836 presidential race, Tyler ran unsuccessfully as a Whig vice presidential candidate. But in 1841, he became William Henry Harrison's vice president.

When Harrison died after a month in office, Tyler ascended to the presidency and spent four fraught, ineffectual years in that office; three days before leaving office, he signed the Texas statehood bill. In 1860, Tyler chaired a peace convention, hoping to head off war, but when the convention achieved no results, Tyler fully supported southern

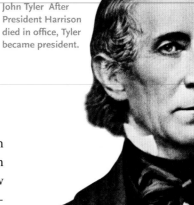

John Tyler After President Harrison died in office, Tyler became president.

secession. Soon after he was elected to the Confederate Congress, he died at his Virginia home.

MARTIN VAN BUREN
★ 1782–1862 ★
EIGHTH U.S. PRESIDENT

Martin Van Buren grew up on politics, in his Dutch immigrant parents' tavern/inn in largely Dutch Kinderhook, New York, near Albany—a stopover for politicians and government workers. He became an attorney and a political force in New York's Jeffersonian-style Democratic-Republican Party before being elected to the U.S. Senate in 1821. He quickly established himself as a strong anti-Federalist voice, and after Andrew Jackson's 1828 election, Van Buren was appointed secretary of state. A close presidential confidant, Van Buren helped Jackson craft policy on such vital issues as nullification. In 1832, he was elected Jackson's vice president and continued to advise him during his contentious second term, in which the "Bank War"—over rechartering the Bank of the United States—created deep political divisions and led to the emergence of the Whig Party.

In 1836, Van Buren followed Jackson into the presidency as his handpicked successor. Yet two months after he took office, the nation was faced by a financial panic brought on in part by Jackson's fiscal policies. Van Buren's contentious solution, the establishment of an independent treasury, did not improve conditions, and for his entire term, the nation remained in a depression. Implementing Jackson's Indian removal policies, Van Buren went to war with the

Martin Van Buren He followed Jackson as president and continued many of his policies.

Seminole of Florida and forced all Cherokee east of the Appalachians onto the infamous Trail of Tears.

By the time Van Buren stood for reelection in 1840, the Whig Party had become a formidable force. Its aggressive campaign against "Martin Van Ruin"—along with tensions over slavery and the moribund economy—led to his resounding defeat in the electoral college.

A political animal, Van Buren kept his hand in Democratic Party politics and came close to receiving the presidential nomination in 1844. His lack of support for the annexation of Texas probably cost him the nomination, but Van Buren was not done, even then, with politics. In the 1848 election, he ran as the new Free Soil Party's candidate, opposing the spread of slavery into the western territories. Losing again, Van Buren spent the following years writing a definitive history of political parties, and prior to his death in 1862, he supported Lincoln's stand against southern secession.

Broken Promises
BETRAYAL OF THE FIVE "CIVILIZED" TRIBES
★ ★ ★

The British and Americans named the Cherokee, Chickasaw, Choctaw, Creek, and Seminole of the American Southeast the "civilized" tribes, conferring that stature on them because they were willing to adapt to European ways. Over the 18th and early 19th centuries, these tribes (though less so the Seminole) adopted European-style clothing, Christian teachings, representative government, farming techniques, and even, in some cases, slavery of blacks. Their accommodations were strategic, a way to mollify and coexist peacefully with whites and at the same time learn from them. In many areas in the Southeast, intermarriage between whites and Native Americans led to a population that was largely mixed blood. In the end, none of this helped secure their future. President Andrew Jackson's Indian removal policies, implemented through the 1830s, saw their homelands lost and their displacement to Indian Territory (Oklahoma). The Seminole of Florida held out the longest against removal, resulting in the Second (1835–1842) and Third (1855–58) Seminole Wars.

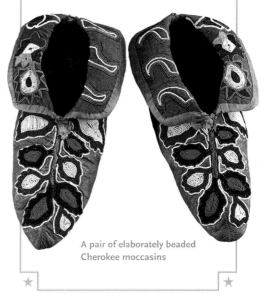

A pair of elaborately beaded Cherokee moccasins

Daniel Webster The great American statesman was a highly regarded attorney.

DANIEL WEBSTER

★ 1782–1852 ★

STATESMAN

From a farm family on the New Hampshire frontier, Daniel Webster graduated from Dartmouth and moved on to the law, where his gift for oratory fueled a successful career. He represented New Hampshire in the House of Representatives for two terms. After settling in Boston, he was elected a Massachusetts member of the U.S. House of Representatives (1823–27), then the Senate (1827–1841). He argued for federal jurisdiction over states during the nullification crisis, and in 1836, he was one of four Whig candidates for president. With his loss, he remained in the Senate another five years. After the 1841 election, Webster became secretary of state for two years

and negotiated the Webster-Ashburton Treaty, which resolved issues with Great Britain along the contentious Maine-Canada border. He resigned his position in 1843, disagreeing with President Tyler over the annexation of Texas.

In 1845, Webster returned to the Senate for five more years. Part of the Great Triumvirate, with Henry Clay and John Calhoun, Webster argued against war with Mexico and for the 1850

Instead of speaking . . . of secession, instead of dwelling in those caverns of darkness, instead of groping with those ideas so full of all that is horrid and horrible, let us . . . enjoy the fresh air of Liberty and Union.

DANIEL WEBSTER

Compromise as a way to diffuse tensions between the North and South. His famous, and in some circles infamous, "seventh of March" speech to the Senate in support of compromise as a means to preserve the Union evoked strong criticism from antislavery factions, as it tacitly endorsed the Fugitive Slave Act. From 1850 to 1852, Webster served a second term as secretary of state under Millard Fillmore and died while in office.

HARRIET WILSON

★ 1825–1900 ★

NOVELIST

Born in New Hampshire, "Hattie" Wilson was forced into indenture as a girl after her African-American father died and her Irish mother disappeared. Her early life and her years as a young mother were filled with hardship, and she had to leave her young son in a poorhouse while she made a thin living as a dressmaker in Boston. While there, she wrote an

One of America's greatest orators, Webster delivers a sweeping defense of the Union and against secession to his fellow senators. He also served twice as secretary of state.

autobiographical novel—*Our Nig or, Sketches from the Life of a Free Black, in a Two-story White House, North. Showing that Slavery's Shadows Fall Even There.* Published in 1859, it ranks as the first novel published in America by an African-American woman. The work disappeared from historical memory but was rediscovered and resurrected in the 1980s by scholar Henry Louis Gates. Wilson spent the remainder of her life in Boston, but there is indication that she wrote other works.

The Mormons were forced ever west. Under Brigham Young's leadership, they settled in the Utah Territory.

BRIGHAM YOUNG

★ 1801–1877 ★

LEADER OF THE CHURCH OF JESUS CHRIST OF LATTER-DAY SAINTS

Brigham Young met Joseph Smith in the early 1830s, soon after Smith founded his new religion. Young soon converted to Mormonism, and after missionizing briefly in Canada, he led a group of family and friends to Smith's new community in Ohio. By 1835, Young had become one of the 12 apostles of the burgeoning new religion, spreading the message of Mormonism throughout the eastern states. When Smith's Missouri community again met with local hostility, Young was instrumental in orchestrating the move to Nauvoo, Illinois.

Young spent part of 1840–41 in Liverpool, England, proselytizing and creating new branches of the church. When he returned to Nauvoo, he endorsed, though initially with some reluctance, Smith's new stance on polygamy. Soon after, Smith appointed him president of the Quorum of the Twelve Apostles, which governed the church. Young was on another proselytizing mission to the East Coast in 1844,

when Smith was assassinated by an Illinois mob. Returning to Illinois, Young, now head of the church, organized an exodus west, and in 1846, some 5,000 Mormons set out for a new and unidentified promised land. Young led the advance band, and a thousand miles into the pilgrimage, on July 24, 1847, his group reached a remote valley dominated by a great salt lake. Young reportedly said, "It is enough, this is the right place."

The newly arrived settlers set to work planting crops, creating an irrigation system, and founding the city of Salt Lake. In 1850, Young became governor of the new Utah Territory. A talented organizer, Young oversaw all aspects of the LDS church in those formative years, establishing local industries and educational institutions that would allow the Mormon community to be self-sufficient and insulated. He also used church funds to assist more Mormon immigration into Utah and surrounding territories.

When President Buchanan attempted to ignite a "Mormon War" in the mid-1850s, Young assiduously sidestepped

open conflict by cutting off federal supply lines instead of engaging in battle. The "war" did, however, result in the Mountain Meadows Massacre, in which 120 new emigrants were attacked by Mormons under John Lee, who claimed to be acting under Young's orders. In his lifetime, Young took at least 20 wives, 16 of whom bore him a total of 57 children.

Brigham Young
Second leader of
the Mormons

Gateway to Freedom
ABOLITIONISTS AND THE UNDERGROUND RAILROAD

s with much of the history of American slavery, details and hard facts about the Underground Railroad are hard to come by, but by the early 1800s, a network of "stations"—homes and churches of courageous free blacks, white abolitionists, and other slaves—gave escaping slaves safe haven as they followed the North Star toward the Mason-Dixon Line separating the slave-holding South from the North. "Conductors," the most famous of whom was Harriet Tubman, led small groups of escapees north. Railroad operatives often used a clever, covert system of signals to communicate with one another and with slaves hoping to flee. After the passage of the Fugitive Slave Act in 1850, even America's free states were no longer free to African Americans, as slave catchers and bounty hunters prowled every corner of the country, looking for fugitives. Canada West, as Ontario was called, offered the only hope of real liberation for escaped slaves. The route there generally took slaves across New York State, where abolitionists operated the Underground Railroad at great personal risk, as anyone discovered harboring escapees faced punishment.

"Depots" on the Underground Railroad were often rooms like this, secreted behind walls or in cellars to hide them from slave catchers.

This Wisconsin inn was a depot; a tunnel connected it to a cellar where slaves hid.

Fugitive slaves on the Maryland coast head for Delaware and an Underground Railroad depot—a safe haven where they could rest before continuing north.

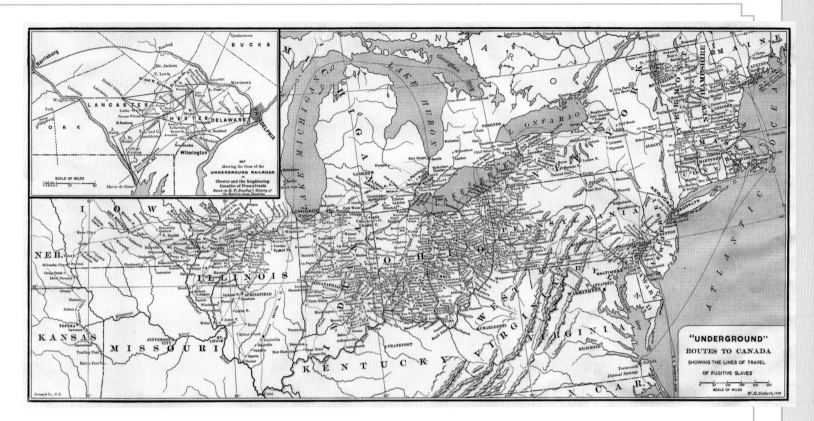

The Underground Railroad (red) wove across the United States. With the 1850 Fugitive Slave Act, the free states no longer provided freedom, and an escaped slave's only hope was to make it to Canada.

Operatives on the Underground Railroad help a fugitive slave on his perilous way.

Code for the Underground Railroad, the "Liberty Line" advertised "Seats Free, irrespective of color" and a route "between the Patriarchal Dominion and Libertyville, Upper Canada."

U.S. congressman and ardent abolitionist Thaddeus Stevens offered his Pennsylvania home as a depot on the railroad and hired spies to keep an eye out for slave catchers on the prowl.

CHAPTER 4

1861–1876

We here highly resolve that these dead shall not have died in vain,
that this nation under God shall have a new birth of freedom,
and that government of the people, by the people,
for the people shall not perish from the earth.

ABRAHAM LINCOLN, GETTYSBURG ADDRESS

THE TERRIBLE SWIFT SWORD

N MARCH 4, 1861, ABRAHAM LINCOLN STOOD IN THE BLUSTERY WINDS sweeping Washington and took the oath of office. Already, seven southern states had seceded from the Union to form the Confederate States of America, but the new president nonetheless appealed to the "better angels" of America's collective nature. The angels apparently were not listening. Within a few months, six more states had joined the Confederacy, and the young nation was at war with itself.

Few people—including the members of his own Cabinet—thought Lincoln up to the task of uniting the North's fractious elements, let alone saving the Union. Although his oratory could be soaring, he cultivated his backwoods image and homespun style. Yet on April 12, when the Confederates threatened federally held Fort Sumter off Charleston, South Carolina, Lincoln acted decisively, then called for 75,000 northern militiamen to come to the aid of their country—if only for 90 days. Those three months extended into four years of brutal battles and bruising politics that neither North nor South could have foreseen.

By July, the armies of each were facing off virtually on Washington's doorstep. Under pressure to attack the Confederate forces at Manassas Junction, about 30 miles west of the capital, Union general Irvin McDowell marched his army out to meet the enemy. He knew his men were untrained and raw, but the northern public disagreed. A crowd that included congressmen and senators followed in his wake to enjoy the sight of a sure Confederate defeat.

(previous pages) **Ulysses S. Grant and Robert E. Lee meet at the village of Appomattox on April 9, 1865, to discuss terms of Lee's surrender.**
(opposite) **Enslaved African Americans await the hour of emancipation—January 1, 1863.**

First Manassas did prove a rout—of the North. The South—Virginia—had been invaded, and southern manhood would protect it, or die trying.

In November, Lincoln replaced an aging but venerated Winfield Scott, hero of the Mexican-American War, with George McClellan as head of all Union armies. McClellan, vainglorious and a darling of the North, organized and trained the army around Washington—then did it some more. Despite Lincoln's exhortations to act and bring the war to an end, McClellan stalled, even as little-known Union commander Ulysses S. Grant scored decisive victories in Tennessee. Finally, in March 1862, McClellan transported his army to Fort Monroe and then marched it up the Virginia Peninsula toward the Confederate capital, Richmond.

Meanwhile, a Confederate commander known as Stonewall Jackson was waging a cat-and-mouse game with Union forces in the Shenandoah Valley, keeping them from reinforcing McClellan, who was again stalling. McClellan should have been more aggressive, because in June the South unleashed an unexpected weapon—Robert E. Lee, who took command of the forces defending Richmond. By the beginning of July, Lee had McClellan in retreat, and Lincoln briefly replaced him with John Pope, who promptly lost the Second Battle of Manassas. By late summer, when the Army of Northern Virginia again met Lee in Maryland, McClellan was back in charge. The battle on September 17, on the banks of Antietam Creek, would prove the single bloodiest day in American military history, with 22,720 casualties—some 12,400 Union to 10,320 Confederate. The North, nonetheless, claimed the field and victory, and Lincoln used the rare Union success to issue the Emancipation Proclamation: "That on the 1st day of January, in the year of our Lord one thousand eight hundred and sixty-three, all persons held as slaves within any State . . . in rebellion against the United States shall be then, thenceforward, and forever free." Already, thousands of enslaved peoples in the South had flocked behind Union lines, where they were considered "contraband of war." Now, they would be free; others, still enslaved, would need a final Union victory before they could claim freedom.

By late 1862 and into the spring of 1863, northern victory seemed more and more doubtful, as the South made brutalizing conquests at Fredericksburg and Chancellorsville, Virginia. Then on July 4, the tide turned. Lee was in retreat, having suffered a critical and overwhelming defeat after days of fighting outside the Pennsylvania village of Gettysburg. And in the western theater, Grant's siege of Vicksburg had ended in victory, giving the North control of the Mississippi. The threat of intervention from England and France on the side of the cotton-rich Confederacy now seemed unlikely.

As the war ground on, the North gained ground—more and more in the western theater. In early 1864, Lincoln, frustrated by years of

Pins from Abraham Lincoln's second presidential campaign, 1864

The Confederate bombardment of Union-held Fort Sumter, Charleston Harbor, April 1861

1860	1861	1861	1862	1863
Abraham Lincoln elected president of United States	Jefferson Davis becomes president of Confederacy	Bombardment of Fort Sumter, South Carolina	Battle of Antietam, bloodiest day in U.S. military history	Emancipation Proclamation issued

Under the 15th Amendment, black men could not be denied the right to vote on account of race.

Union commander Ulysses S. Grant brought long-sought victory to the North in the Civil War.

weak commanders in the East, gave Grant command of all northern forces, and Grant moved to the eastern theater. Lee's army was his objective and through the spring he chased Lee relentlessly through southeastern Virginia, in battle after torturous battle. By late summer, Lee's army was bottled up in Petersburg, a communications and rail center close to Richmond. Grant's victories and the capture of Atlanta virtually ensured Lincoln's reelection in 1864, and the two men who had pushed and prodded the war toward a Union victory faced a spring of hope.

On April 9, Lee surrendered to Grant at the village of Appomattox, Virginia. Eleven days later, Lincoln was assassinated by actor John Wilkes Booth, and a shocked nation watched as a weak Democratic vice president, Andrew Johnson, ascended to the presidency. In Lincoln's final speech on April 11, he had said, "Let us all join in doing the acts necessary to restoring the proper practical relations between these [southern] States and the Union." His plans for Reconstruction called for that, but Johnson had little facility for working with the Republican Congress (the House ultimately voted to impeach him, but not the Senate) or generally mending the country. He was also openly hostile to extending rights to freed slaves, while in the South, states enacted "Black Codes" that would deeply restrict those rights.

Johnson lost his bid for the Democratic nomination in 1868, and Ulysses S. Grant took the reigns with good intentions but little talent for political maneuvering. Corruption plagued his two-term administration in North and South, but in the South, Reconstruction added turmoil, yearning, and often, deprivation. In 1873, a financial panic plunged the country into four years of depression. Yet a reunited America, despite itself, slowly edged forward. The railroad and communication networks Lincoln had so long envisioned began to grow, Congress passed the 15th Amendment, extending suffrage to all men (but not women); and a new birth of prosperity and freedom, if still distant, began to seem possible.

The Emancipation Proclamation freed only Confederate slaves.

1863	1864	1865	1870	1873–79
Union victories at Gettysburg & Vicksburg	Sherman's March across Georgia	Lee & Johnston surrender; Lincoln assassinated	Grant begins two-term presidency	Financial panic & economic depression

BIOGRAPHIES

WARRIORS, SHOWMEN, MAGNATES & REFORMERS 1861–1876

The mid-19th century produced a riotous mix of Americans. Possibility and technological innovation permeated the air, as did, in the early 1860s, war. Battlefield heroes from both North and South vied with railroad barons and showmen for public attention, while social reformers gave voice to the rights of women, African Americans, and the poor, and visionaries gave birth to new, distinctly American forms of poetry, fiction, and design.

P. T. BARNUM
★ 1810–1891 ★
SHOWMAN, CIRCUS PIONEER

When Phineas Taylor Barnum's father, a Connecticut farmer, died in 1825, Barnum, age 15, began working in a general store, where his reputation for dealmaking was quickly established. Having bought Joice Heth, an African-American woman who was being displayed for profit as some 160 years old and the former nurse of George Washington, Barnum marketed her as "the greatest curiosity in the world." Finding profit in "humbugging" the public, Barnum opened his American Museum in 1842 on the Lower East Side of Manhattan. The public came in droves to see his giants, performing animals, Native Americans, and even a mermaid. Barnum later made international sensations of

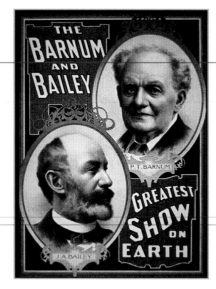

P. T. Barnum His showmanship humbugged the public with sensationalist entertainment.

Mr. and Mrs. Tom Thumb, and Swedish "nightingale" Jenny Lind.

Barnum also pursued a stint in politics, championing social causes that benefited the common man before returning to showmanship. In 1874, his New York Hippodrome opened on what is now the site of Madison Square Garden. There, Barnum launched the "Greatest Show on Earth." Worried about the rival Great London Show, under manager James Bailey, Barnum negotiated to combine the shows into a traveling extravaganza called the Barnum & London Circus, later the Barnum & Bailey Circus. Ringling Bros. and Barnum and Bailey Circus continued to tour as "The Greatest Show on Earth" until 2017.

CLARA BARTON
★ 1821–1912 ★
FOUNDER OF THE AMERICAN RED CROSS

Clara Barton worked as a teacher (unusual for a woman then) in her home state of Massachusetts before moving to

Washington, D.C., in 1854 to become a recording clerk at the U.S. Patent office. She was in that position when the Civil War began, and she immediately began aiding wounded soldiers quartered into the city. In 1862, Barton received permission to transport supplies directly to the front and from that time forward, the "Angel of the Battlefield," as she became known, provided medical supplies and nursing in major battles. The war and its aftermath took a toll on her health, and in 1869, she went to Europe to recuperate.

Five years before, the Red Cross had been established in Geneva, Switzerland, and Barton became captivated by the organization. After volunteering with the International Red Cross in the Franco-Prussian War, she returned to the Washington area. In 1881, Barton and her colleagues founded the American Red Cross, and she was elected president, leading it for nearly a quarter century. Her work made her an international figure and a force in the women's movement. In 1975, Barton's Glen Echo, Maryland, home became the first national historic site dedicated to the accomplishments of a woman.

Albert Bierstadt's grand canvases (here depicting Yosemite) enthralled viewers with the pristine majesty of the American West.

ALBERT BIERSTADT

★ 1830–1902 ★

ARTIST

German-born Albert Bierstadt moved as a young child to New Bedford, Massachusetts, but returned to Germany as a young man. Having already established a reputation in New Bedford as a painter, Bierstadt befriended other painters in Germany, including Emanuel Leutze (who painted the iconic "Washington Crossing the Delaware"). Back in America, Bierstadt joined the Lander expedition heading west on the Overland Trail in 1859. Returning to New York, he used the sketches he had made to create dramatic, sweeping panoramic scenes of the American West. Bierstadt made several more trips west, including to Alaska. His monumental western landscapes remain his signature works.

Clara Barton No stranger to the battlefield, she served as an angel of mercy ministering to the wounded and went on to found the American Red Cross.

Contraband of War

FINDING FREEDOM BEHIND UNION LINES

★★★

In the spring of 1861, in the first weeks of the Civil War, three slaves escaped to Union-held Fort Monroe, at the tip of the Virginia Peninsula. When their owner, a Confederate colonel from nearby Hampton, came to demand his property back under the Fugitive Slave Act, the fort's commander, Benjamin Butler, refused. A lawyer by training, Butler argued that because Virginia had seceded from the United States, federal law no longer applied. Instead, Butler labeled the slaves "contraband of war," thus creating a precedent that would inspire many thousands of enslaved people to flee behind Union lines.

The influx of thousands of civilians was not necessarily welcomed by officers of an army at war, and escaped slaves were sometimes turned away. But many worked behind the lines as cooks, nurses, boatmen, and fortification builders. An 1862 act of Congress deemed contraband "forever free of their servitude, and not again [to be] held as slaves." In 1863, the Union finally allowed African Americans to join the Army as soldiers.

JOHN WILKES BOOTH
★ 1838–1865 ★
ACTOR, LINCOLN'S ASSASSIN

John Wilkes Booth grew up in rural northern Maryland, the son of the respected but mentally unstable Shakespearean actor Junius Brutus Booth. John followed his father into the theater and often performed in the South, finding appreciative audiences there. When the Civil War tore the nation in two, Booth remained in the North, continuing to act but also spying for the Confederacy.

Histrionic and ever in need of adulation, Wilkes hit upon a plan in 1864 to kidnap President Lincoln and ransom him for southern soldiers held as prisoners. The abduction, set for March 17, 1865, failed when Lincoln changed his schedule, but Booth would not be deterred in his determination to avenge the South against the "false president." On April 14, he saw his chance, when the Lincolns attended a performance at Ford's Theatre. Booth was not acting that night but waited just outside Lincoln's box; then stealthily entering, he shot Lincoln in the head. Jumping to the stage, and breaking a leg as he did so, Booth exclaimed *"Sic semper tyrannis—Thus ever to tyrants"* before hopping to a waiting horse. Lincoln died the following morning.

Booth escaped capture until April 26, when soldiers and secret service surrounded the Virginia barn he was hiding in. Fatally shot, Booth delivered his final line: "Tell Mother I died for my country."

John Wilkes Booth An actor, Booth also spied for the South, and with its defeat, he assassinated its enemy—Abraham Lincoln—in April 1865.

BELLE BOYD
★ 1844–1900 ★
CONFEDERATE SPY

At 17, Maria Isabella "Belle" Boyd killed a Union soldier who insulted her and her mother in their occupied hometown—Martinsburg, Virginia. Thereafter, Boyd determined to become a spy. The Union knew the flirtatious "Siren of the Shenandoah" was passing information to Confederate generals, notably Stonewall Jackson, and though she was arrested several times, she was not actually jailed until July 1862 and for only a month. Jailed again briefly in 1863, she continued working for the Confederacy, before moving to England in 1864. Returning to America after the war, she became an actress.

Belle Boyd The "Siren of the Shenandoah" spied on Union occupiers for the Confederacy.

MATHEW BRADY
★ CA 1823–1896 ★
PIONEERING PHOTOGRAPHER

Mathew Brady was the son of Irish immigrants who settled in east-central New York. As a young man in New York City, he is thought to have learned from artist (and later inventor of the telegraph) Samuel Morse about the new technology of daguerreotype photography. Brady earned an early reputation designing small, intricate cases, sold in his Daguerrean Miniature Gallery on Broadway. He also began making photographic portraits, and by the late 1840s, he had opened a Washington, D.C., studio. Brady quickly established himself as the leader in creating daguerreotypes of well-known politicians, including Abraham Lincoln. His 1860 "Cooper Union" image of Lincoln remains a hallmark.

At the inception of the Civil War, Brady organized and financed a cadre of photographers to follow Union forces and document the war, the first field reporting of its kind. Among this group was Brady himself, Alexander Gardner, and James F. Gibson. Their photography, exhibited in various venues, brought the life on the front to the northern public, but the endeavor sent Brady into serious debt. The $25,000 he received for the sale of his war collection to the federal government after the war just barely covered the debts he had incurred in creating the photographs. He continued to live in Washington for the rest of his life, but his years of fame and financial comfort were behind him.

AMBROSE BURNSIDE
★ 1824–1881 ★
UNION COMMANDER

A graduate of West Point, Indiana-born Ambrose Burnside served in the Mexican-American War before resigning his commission in 1853 and settling in Rhode

Ambrose Burnside His checkered service as a commander of Union forces included victories and defeats, including two badly failed attempts to invade Virginia from the north and take Richmond.

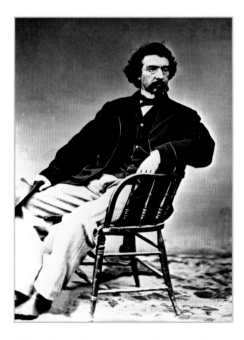

Mathew Brady He sent a corps of photographers to the battlefront to capture the essence of war.

Island. At the onset of the Civil War, he organized the First Rhode Island Infantry, one of the first units to arrive in Washington, D.C. From the war's inception, Burnside saw action at First Manassas, along the North Carolina coast, and at Antietam. Impressed by Burnside and somewhat desperate for a commander, Lincoln put him in charge of the Army of the Potomac in November 1862. Burnside's ill-fated march on Richmond ended in a Union debacle at the Battle of Fredericksburg the next month. Nonetheless, he tried again later that winter, and his "Mud

March" south again only got as far as Fredericksburg. Burnside lost his command of the Army of the Potomac, moving instead to commander of the Department of the Ohio. After he successfully defended Knoxville in autumn 1863, he was moved back to a position with the Army of the Potomac and fought under Ulysses S. Grant in the final march on Virginia in the spring of 1864. After the war, he served as a U.S. senator from Rhode Island and became a successful businessman. His signature hairstyle gave rise to the term "sideburns."

BENJAMIN BUTLER
★ 1818–1893 ★
UNION COMMANDER

Benjamin "Beast" Butler had been a Massachusetts lawyer, politician, and brigadier general in the state militia before the Civil War. Though he was no supporter of President Lincoln, Lincoln nonetheless appointed him a major general almost immediately and put him in command of Fort Monroe, a Union inholding on the coast of otherwise Confederate Virginia. While there, Butler determined that three slaves who had escaped from nearby Hampton to the fort were "contraband of war" and did not need to be returned to their owner. His precedent-setting decision encouraged slaves from throughout the South to attempt to escape behind Union lines.

Benjamin Butler He declared escaped slaves "contraband of war."

Butler was appointed military governor of New Orleans after it fell to the Union in 1862, and his harsh treatment of the vanquished residents—including pilfering their property and declaring that any woman who disdained his occupying forces should be treated like a prostitute—led Confederate president Jefferson Davis to call him "Beast Butler." Removed from his New Orleans post in January 1865, Butler eventually resigned under pressure in November of that year. He did, however, resurrect his political career in the late 1860s through the early 1880s, serving as a member of Congress and governor of Massachusetts. He also stood as a candidate in the 1884 presidential election, losing the nomination to Democrat Grover Cleveland.

SALMON P. CHASE
★ 1803–1873 ★
STATESMAN

A political leader and outspoken abolitionist in mid-19th century Washington, D.C., Salmon P. Chase became treasury secretary in Lincoln's Cabinet. Throughout the war years, Chase worked to see that the war was financed and a national banking system established. Yet he had an obvious disdain for the folksy, rawboned Lincoln, and Chase's daughter and acclaimed hostess, Kate Chase, and Mary Lincoln were rivals for social prominence in the capital. In early 1864, Chase maneuvered behind the scenes, hoping to replace Lincoln as the Republican presidential candidate. Later that year, he resigned from the Cabinet. In December 1864, Lincoln nominated Chase for Chief Justice, and he held that role until his death, ruling on issues pertaining to the

war, Reconstruction, and finance. Even as Chief Justice, Chase continued to hope for a presidential nomination.

COCHISE
★ ??–1874 ★
APACHE CHIEF

Leader of the Chiricahua band of Apache Indians, Cochise resisted white settlement in the Southwest in the 1860s. Though details of his early years are unknown, he was described as tall and muscular. His name meant "having the quality or strength of oak." In the 1850s, the Chiricahua lived relatively peacefully with settlers who moved into their territory in southern Arizona and New Mexico. Some supplied firewood for the Apache Pass stagecoach station. Then, in 1861, a group of Apache stole cattle that belonged to a white settler and kidnapped his son. They were part of another band of Apache, but the Chiricahua were accused.

A contingent of U.S. Army troops arrested Cochise, killing one Indian in the process. Cochise managed to escape and, possibly wounded by a bullet, was able to flee to the safety of the hills. The federals captured some of Cochise's relatives; Cochise in turn took hostages to use in negotiations. Both sides ended up killing all their hostages, and 11 years of bloody warfare ensued. Hundreds of people died.

During the Civil War, the region was mostly abandoned to the Apache, but when a high-ranking Chiricahua was killed in 1863, Cochise renewed his violent campaign, taking refuge in the Dragoon Mountains of Arizona. He finally surrendered in 1871 and settled on a reservation the following year.

CHARLES CROCKER

★ 1822–1888 ★

RAILROAD & BUSINESS MAGNATE

Originally from New York and Iowa, Charles Crocker joined the flood of forty-niners heading to the California gold-fields. He soon gave up the search for gold and instead supplied miners with dry goods. In Sacramento, he befriended fellow Republicans and businessmen Collis Huntington, Leland Stanford, and Mark Hopkins. The Big Four, as they are known to history, established the Central Pacific Railroad in 1860. Crocker, a physically enormous man, oversaw construction, resigning from the railroad board to run Charles Crocker & Company. It built the Central Pacific line over the Sierra Nevada at Donner Pass and linked with the Union Pacific on May 10, 1869, in Promontory Summit, Utah Territory, to form America's first transcontinental railroad. In 1871, Crocker became president of the Southern Pacific line, which eventually absorbed the Central Pacific. He also made a fortune in California real estate, established the Crocker Bank, and endorsed grand irrigation projects for the state.

GEORGE CUSTER

★ 1839–1876 ★

CAVALRY OFFICER

George Armstrong Custer was born in Ohio and became a Civil War hero, but he ended up becoming infamous for leading his men into disaster at the Battle of the Little Bighorn in Montana. Graduating at the bottom of his class from West Point in 1861, Custer joined the

Custer's Last Stand at the Battle of the Little Bighorn on June 25, 1876, was one of the riveting dramas of the period, when news reports trickled in several days later.

staff of Gen. George B. McClellan. Within two years, he was in command of a brigade of Michigan cavalry; he distinguished himself in battle and helped bring about the eventual surrender of Robert E. Lee.

After the war, Custer was sent to the Great Plains as part of the Army's effort to subdue hostile Indians and protect white settlement in the territories. In 1868, his troops routed Cheyenne Chief Black Kettle's village along the Washita River in Kansas. He then had five years during which he largely worked on his book, *My Life on the Plains*. In 1876, in command of the Seventh Cavalry Regiment, he joined with Gen. Alfred Terry to try to force the free-roaming Sioux and Cheyenne in the Montana Territory onto reservations.

On the morning of June 25, Terry ordered Custer to take up a position to the south of the Indians camped along the Little Bighorn River. Custer was in charge of 650 soldiers, a force he thought large enough to handle the 800 warriors he believed were massed in a riverside village. But the Army scouts were wrong. What awaited was perhaps the biggest army of Indians ever assembled in North America—some 2,000 warriors. Making matters worse, Custer decided to split his force into three units.

Critics would later blame Colonel Custer for attacking instead of waiting for Terry, as instructed. Although some blamed Terry for underestimating the Indian contingent, Custer's other two units were crippled and unable, or unwilling, to join the fight, and Custer and all 210 of his men were killed in the most stunning defeat of the Army at the hands of the Indians. The entire battle lasted perhaps an hour.

A striking figure with long curling locks, Custer was considered both gallant and vainglorious, fearless and reckless. He is remembered in history after "Custer's Last Stand" as a flawed hero.

George Custer The officer, posing in 1863, led 210 men to their deaths at the battle in Montana.

The inauguration of Confederate president Jefferson Davis, Montgomery, February 1861

JEFFERSON DAVIS

★ 1808–1889 ★

PRESIDENT OF THE CONFEDERATE STATES OF AMERICA

Jefferson Davis claims one of the most mixed legacies in American history. His father, a Mississippi planter, had fought with distinction in the American Revolution, and Jefferson Davis himself was a West Point graduate who served in the U.S. military, initially in the Black Hawk War. Fighting under Zachary Taylor, Davis met and married Taylor's daughter Sarah, but she soon died of malaria, and Davis, overcome with grief, spent the next seven years in isolation, creating a plantation outside Vicksburg, Mississippi. In 1845, he broke his isolation and was elected to the U.S. House of Representatives but served only one year before volunteering in the Mexican-American War. Lauded as a national hero for his exploits at the Battle of Buena Vista, he was elected to the Senate in 1848 and then became President Pierce's secretary of war in 1853. Well suited to the position, Davis strengthened coastal defenses and ironically, given the events to come, enlarged the U.S. Army.

Returning to the Senate in 1857, Davis was an ardent proponent of slavery yet also attempted to smooth growing regional tensions and spoke out against secession. But when his home state of Mississippi seceded in January 1861, Davis resigned his Senate seat. In his impassioned farewell speech, he asserted the rights, under the Constitution, for a state to withdraw from the Union and wished the North well. Within the month, Jefferson Davis had been inaugurated president of the newly formed Confederacy. Among his initial acts, he sent a peace delegation to Washington, but the gesture was rebuffed. The war that had been brewing for a decade became a reality that spring.

A military man at heart, Davis had wanted command of southern forces rather than the presidency, and he set to work dealing with the South's unpreparedness for war. Throughout his presidency, he dealt with that issue and a lack of manpower, as well as internecine fighting among his advisers and serious and recurring, although never diagnosed, health problems. The odds were against Davis and the South, and on April 2, 1865, he was given a message from commander Robert E. Lee that Richmond, the Confederate capital, could no longer be defended. Davis ordered its evacuation and fled with his Cabinet, hoping to reach the trans-Mississippi area and continue to prosecute the war. His plans—and Confederate hopes—ended with his capture in Georgia on May 10. He was held for two years as a prisoner at Fort Monroe on the Virginia Peninsula, where his dank prison cell further damaged his health. He was standing trial for treason in late 1868 when he was released under President Johnson's grant of amnesty to all those involved in the conflict.

Davis spent his final days living on Mississippi's Gulf Coast and writing a justification of the Confederacy under constitutional law, *The Rise and Fall of the Confederate Government*.

> *I am sure I feel no hostility to you, Senators from the North . . . I hope, and they [the people of Mississippi] hope, for peaceful relations with you, though we must part.*
>
> **JEFFERSON DAVIS'S FAREWELL SPEECH TO THE U.S. SENATE**

Jefferson Davis A former U.S. secretary of war, Davis became president of the Confederacy.

HEARTH & HOME

The Home Front

NORTHERNERS AND SOUTHERNERS SURVIVING WAR

★ ★ ★

The Civil War tore at the very fabric of life as men of every age went off to fight and women and children—and in the South, enslaved African Americans—were left to fend for themselves in the face of shortages and rampant inflation. The South became an invaded land, and as the war progressed, clothes, shoes, salt to cure meat, wheat, and other foods became the dreamed-of luxuries of a lost world. Virginia devolved into a killing ground, where armies decimated the landscape like plagues of locusts, leaving nothing for locals. Fighting in Tennessee along the Ohio and Mississippi corridors also left behind devastation, as did the 1863 siege of Vicksburg, and the fighting at Gettysburg, Pennsylvania. Then in 1864, Sherman scorched the earth across Georgia in his March to the Sea, while Sheridan made Virginia's Shenandoah Valley "a barren wasteland."

The industrial North experienced the war in a very different way. A wartime boom in manufacturing created a nouveau riche class but did little to better the lives of the average workers, whose wages remained stagnant even as the price of beef, rice, and sugar doubled. Often those average workers were women, filling workplace slots vacated by men. Women also organized aid societies for the troops, sewing, rolling bandages, collecting clothing, and generally worrying over their sons and husbands at war. Some returned, but vast numbers did not, taken in battle or by disease. In all, the Civil War is now believed to have claimed somewhere between 752,000 and 850,000 souls. The men who survived on both sides were often plagued by wounds—physical and emotional—that hobbled them. The home front became a new front in the battle to live beyond the bitterness of war.

On April 2–3, 1865, Southerners fled the Confederate capital of Richmond as Grant's forces advanced on it. To keep supplies out of enemy hands, warehouses were burned, and the spreading fire left most of the business district in ruins.

EMILY DICKINSON
★ 1830–1886 ★
POET

Though she spent nearly her entire life in her hometown of Amherst, Massachusetts, Emily Dickinson and her poetry have had an impact on readers around the globe. Her family was prominent in the region, and her grandfather the driving force in founding Amherst College. Emily spent less than a year at nearby Mount Holyoke College before returning to her parents' home and living there the rest of her life, eventually becoming reclusive. She filled her days caring for her invalid mother, cooking, gardening, reading, and writing letters and poetry, generally themed around nature and mortality. Only a few of her some 1,800 poems were ever published in her lifetime and those anonymously.

After her death, her sister, Lavinia, discovered the trove of hidden poetry, and Mabel Todd—an accomplished local woman and the lover of Dickinson's married brother—was enlisted to help with the poems' publication. Todd changed some of Dickinson's wording, and the first volume, *Poems of Emily Dickinson,* met with success; it was soon followed by a second. Owing to a bitter feud over ownership of the poet's works, Dickinson's final known poems were not published until 1945.

Dorothea Dix A pioneer of social activism, Dix repeatedly pushed to improve conditions in institutions for those with mental illness. Her activism led to her appointment as superintendent of Army nurses during the Civil War.

Emily Dickinson Unknown during her lifetime, her poetry is now revered worldwide.

DOROTHEA DIX
★ 1802–1887 ★
SOCIAL REFORMER

Raised on the Maine coast, Dorothea Dix became a Boston teacher and opened a school there for young women. Tuberculosis led her to give up teaching, and for more than a decade she was debilitated by poor health. In 1841, her health restored, she became aware of the poor conditions in jails, prisons, poorhouses, and mental hospitals. After visiting scores of such facilities in the Midwest and South, she lobbied Congress for federal funds to improve conditions for treating mental illness. In 1860, legislation for that purpose finally became law, but the Civil War thwarted further reform, and Dix was appointed superintendent of Army nurses. After the war, she continued to champion the cause for those with mental illness.

FREDERICK DOUGLASS
★ CA 1818–1895 ★
ABOLITIONIST

Frederick Douglass was born into slavery on Maryland's Eastern Shore, very close to the place and time Harriet Tubman was born. At eight, Douglass was sent to serve

> *Those who profess to favor freedom, and yet deprecate agitation, are men who want crops without plowing up the ground.*
>
> **FREDERICK DOUGLASS**

in the household of a Baltimore ship captain and learned to read and write there. Seven years later, he was hired out as a farmhand under a violent slave master who regularly beat him and fed him little. Douglass attempted an escape but was caught and jailed for two years and then sent to a shipyard in Baltimore.

In 1838, at age 20, he made it to freedom in the North, eventually settling in New Bedford, Massachusetts, headquarters of outspoken abolitionist William Lloyd Garrison. Within a few years, Douglass had become a figure in the abolitionist movement. His *Narrative of the Life of Frederick Douglass, an American Slave, Written by Himself* established his reputation in national and international circles.

Using funds from a speaking tour in Great Britain and Ireland, Douglass began publishing *North Star,* an antislavery paper in 1847 in Rochester, New York. He also became involved with the women's movement. During the Civil War, Douglass met with and advised President Abraham Lincoln, and at war's end continued his fight for African-American and women's rights, though some suffragettes objected to his support of the 15th Amendment, which extended the vote to black men but not to women.

Frederick Douglass Though born into slavery, Douglass became an internationally recognized abolitionist and unofficial adviser to a sometimes reluctant President Lincoln.

White Whale to Tell-Tale Heart
AMERICA'S LITERARY GOLDEN AGE
★★★

America produced 19th-century giants in literature whose works are still read and cherished as classics. New York and particularly Massachusetts nourished this exceptional crop of talent. Nathaniel Hawthorne (*The House of the Seven Gables, The Scarlet Letter*) and Herman Melville (*Moby-Dick*) both wove their New England roots into their groundbreaking novels, while Washington Irving lampooned his New York Dutch ancestry and James Fenimore Cooper spun mesmerizing tales of the New York wilderness in his *Leatherstocking Tales*. The Concord, Massachusetts-based Transcendentalists—most notably, Ralph Waldo Emerson (*Nature*) and Henry David Thoreau (*Walden*)—elevated life to a finer shade of meaning in their essays, and America's poets parsed life's small details and large dramas to create a largess of soaring verse: In eastern Massachusetts, Henry Wadsworth Longfellow's epic poems (*The Courtship of Miles Standish, The Song of Hiawatha,* and "Paul Revere's Ride") made heroes of little-known Americans, while in western Massachusetts, Emily Dickinson pondered life, mortality, and nature in a poetic form never before attempted ("Hope Is the Thing With Feathers," "Because I Could Not Stop for Death"). New York–born Walt Whitman, too, celebrated life in his poems with an abandonment and abundance that broke all traditions (*Leaves of Grass*). Edgar Allan Poe defied regional and literary labels. He moved back and forth from Virginia to New York and from poetry ("The Raven," "Annabel Lee") to essays to short stories ("The Black Cat," "The Tell-Tale Heart") that gave rise to today's horror genre.

Melville's *Moby-Dick* became the great American novel.

JUBAL EARLY
★ 1816–1894 ★
CONFEDERATE COMMANDER

One of the Confederacy's most skilled commanders, Jubal Early, a Virginian, was a graduate of West Point and initially was posted to fight against the Seminole in Florida. After a brief period as a civilian lawyer and state politician, he led Virginia volunteers in the Mexican-American War. At the 1861 Virginia Convention, he voted against secession, yet became an officer of distinction in the southern army. From the First Battle of Manassas in July 1861 on, he fought in major engagements in Virginia and Maryland. In July 1864, Early led the only Confederate force to come close to Washington, D.C. After the war, Early moved to Mexico, then Canada, but eventually returned to Virginia and continued to prosecute the war with words, defending Lee and blaming others for the Confederacy's loss.

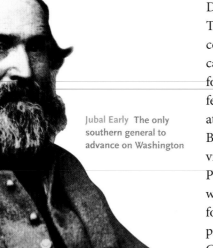

Jubal Early The only southern general to advance on Washington

Nathan Bedford Forrest The Confederate general and his men were renowned for their cruelty, particularly to African Americans. After the war, Forrest, shown leading his troops, was associated with the Ku Klux Klan.

NATHAN BEDFORD FORREST
★ 1821–1877 ★
CONFEDERATE COMMANDER

During the Civil War, Nathan Forrest, a Tennessean who had made a fortune in cotton and slaves, raised and equipped a cavalry unit with his own funds. Noted for audacity, speed, and flaunting of Confederate orders, Forrest's cavalry fought at Shiloh, Vicksburg, Chickamauga, and Brice's Cross Roads, and it perpetrated a vicious slaughter of Union soldiers at Fort Pillow, Tennessee, of whom 64 percent were black. After the war, Forrest helped found the Ku Klux Klan, purportedly to protect southern women and orphans. As Grand Wizard, he was unable to prevent the Klan's growing acts of violence, and he ordered it disbanded in 1869. The Klan was resurrected in 1915.

ALEXANDER GARDNER
★ 1821–1882 ★
PHOTOGRAPHER

Scottish-born Alexander Gardner became assistant to photographer Mathew Brady in 1856 and was managing Brady's Washington, D.C., studio when the Civil War struck. He went into the field to cover the North's Army of the Potomac. After photographing the 1862 Battle of Antietam, Gardner decided to work for himself and capture the horrors of battle. He took the last formal portrait made of Lincoln in his Washington studio in February 1865. After the war, *Gardner's Photographic Sketch Book of the Civil War* became the first published collection of Civil War photographs. He spent his final years photographing the West for the Union Pacific Railroad.

Alexander Gardner His darkroom on wheels

ULYSSES S. GRANT
★ 1822-1885 ★
COMMANDER OF THE UNION ARMY,
18TH U.S. PRESIDENT

The son of an Ohio tanner, Hiram Ulysses Grant grew up around the noxious smell of animal carcasses and chemicals and wanted nothing to do with the tanning occupation. A quiet child, Grant was reticent in school, leading other children to call him "Useless." Yet he lost his retiring nature around horses and early on distinguished himself as an exceptional horseman. His father encouraged him to apply to West Point, and Grant reluctantly did. The application filed by his congressman mistakenly listed him as Ulysses Simpson (his mother's family name) Grant, and the name stuck.

After graduation, Grant fought in the Mexican-American War and then returned to marry Julia Dent. Posted to forts throughout the country, Grant spent his final postings in the West, without his wife. During that time, he began to drink heavily and eventually resigned from the Army in 1854. He struggled for the rest of the decade to support his family and ultimately failed. With the advent of the Civil War, he returned to the military and led a volunteer regiment in Illinois, where the family was then living. In fighting in the western theater, Grant showed himself to be a strong commander not afraid to fight. His critical, and rare for the Union, victories at Fort Henry and Fort Donelson gained him a national reputation. Though he lost the 1862 Battle of Shiloh, in 1863 he finally brought down Vicksburg, the South's Gibraltar on the Mississippi. After more victories in East Tennessee, President Lincoln named him commander of all Union forces in 1864, and Grant came east, relentlessly chasing and engaging Robert E. Lee's army until it was trapped at Petersburg, Virginia. On April 9, 1865, Lee surrendered to Grant in the village of Appomattox, Virginia, and Grant's place in history was secure.

In 1866, Grant was named general of the armies, and in 1868, he was elected president on the Republican ticket. Grant's abilities as a commander did not translate well in the political arena. His administration was plagued by corrupt players, though not Grant himself, and the financial panic of 1873 thrust the country into a depression. But Grant was a strong champion of the rights of African Americans and the 15th Amendment, which had been ratified in 1870. He also advocated more tolerant and just treatment of Native Americans.

Grant spent his final years battling throat cancer and struggling again to provide for his family after his death. To that end, he dictated his *Personal Memoirs,* finishing them days before he died. The book became an enormous financial success.

Ulysses S. Grant The 18th president, at left, sits for a family portrait. He was a devoted father to his four children and loving husband to his wife, Julia.

HORACE GREELEY

★ 1811–1872 ★

NEWSPAPER EDITOR

A New England boy with some background in newspapers, Horace Greeley arrived in New York City in 1831, at 20, and soon made a mark as a writer and editor. Ten years later, he had established his own newspaper, the *New York Tribune*. An enormous success, it thrust the eccentric Greeley into the national spotlight, but his calls for an immediate end to slavery probably exacerbated sectional tensions. Before and during the Civil War, Greeley criticized Lincoln and did not endorse him for a second term. In 1872, as a nominee of the Democratic Party, Greeley ran against Grant for president and lost overwhelmingly. Immediately after, he lost control of the *Tribune* and, suffering a mental and physical breakdown, died later that year.

Horace Greeley Editor of the *New York Tribune*, he exercised enormous influence on politics.

Benjamin Harrison The one-term 23rd president scored an upset victory and left a mixed legacy.

BENJAMIN HARRISON

★ 1833–1901 ★

23RD U.S. PRESIDENT

The grandson of President William Henry Harrison, Benjamin Harrison was raised in Ohio, beside his grandfather's estate. As a young man, he moved with his wife to Indianapolis, began practicing law, and became part of the new Republican Party. During the Civil War, he achieved the rank of brigadier general, and after it, he returned to politics, eventually serving in the U.S. Senate from 1881 to 1887.

The year after losing his Senate seat, Harrison ran for president. Though support for him was tepid, he scored an upset victory against incumbent President Grover Cleveland by winning the electoral, but not the popular, vote. Harrison's one-term presidency left a mixed legacy: He supported the Sherman Antitrust Act and the building of a canal across Nicaragua, and he convened the 1889 Pan-American Conference. He negotiated strong trade deals and treaties that made the Samoan Islands an American protectorate; he also attempted but failed to bring the Hawaiian Islands under American control. Yet his domestic fiscal policies, including his support for high tariffs, may have been a factor in the later depression of 1893. In the election of 1892, his former opponent, Grover Cleveland, prevailed. Harrison continued to be a voice in American public affairs until his death.

Agnes Darling, if such should be we never meet again, while firing my last shot, I will gently breathe the name of my wife—Agnes—and with wishes even for my enemies I will make the plunge and try to swim to the other shore.

WILD BILL HICKOK

WILD BILL HICKOK

★ 1837–1876 ★

WESTERN LEGEND

James Butler Hickok, the western dandy and gunslinger who would become known as "Wild Bill," spent his boyhood in rural Illinois, where his family's farm served as a stop on the Underground Railroad. During the Civil War, Hickok worked for the Union Army as a spy, scout, and sharpshooter, and at war's end he guided Union heroes Sherman and Custer on western tours. An 1867

The Big Four

A RAILROADING WEB

★★★

Though they became iconic figures in the West, the Big Four—Leland Stanford, Mark Hopkins, Collis Huntington, and Charles Crocker—were all Easterners drawn to California by the gold rush. The men became affluent Sacramento merchants, selling to prospectors. In 1860, Huntington proposed that the four invest in an idea proposed by engineer Theodore Judah—to build a Pacific railroad that would cross the Sierra Nevada at Donner Pass and connect to lines on the eastern side. In 1862, President Lincoln signed a bill giving them approval for the Central Pacific Railroad, and on May 10, 1869, in Promontory Summit, Utah Territory, it linked with the Union Pacific to form America's first transcontinental railroad. The Big Four went on to create the Southern Pacific Railroad, which ran south to Arizona, and eventually established a web of rail lines in the West. Each of the four amassed vast wealth, making them both admired and maligned as "robber barons."

Workers on the Big Four's Central Pacific lay track through the Nevada desert in 1868.

Harper's article grandly exaggerated Hickok's exploits and sealed his reputation as a gunslinger and the quintessential Western man. Hickok worked off and on as a U.S. marshall, showman, and gambler and was in countless gunfights. His enemies were legion, and when he arrived in Deadwood, Dakota Territory, in 1876, the town's underworld plotted to take him down. He was fatally shot in the back of the head while playing poker in a local saloon.

A. P. HILL

★ 1825-1865 ★

CONFEDERATE COMMANDER

Robert E. Lee considered fellow Virginian and West Point graduate Ambrose Powell Hill one of his best commanders, but military historians do not generally agree. At the outbreak of the Civil War, Hill resigned from the U.S. Army to join Confederate forces and fought in the defense of Richmond during the North's 1862 Peninsula Campaign. He went on to play a role at Cedar Mountain, Second Manassas, Antietam, and Fredericksburg. In 1863, at Chancellorsville, Hill moved into Stonewall Jackson's place after Jackson was mortally wounded. After Chancellorsville, he was given command of the III Corps, but his performance at Gettysburg, particularly his premature engagement of Union forces, contributed to the South's loss. In the final stages of the war, Hill fought in the Wilderness Campaign and was killed at Petersburg while checking defensive lines.

Wild Bill Hickok He was as legendary for his good looks as his gunslinging exploits.

MARK HOPKINS
★ 1814–1878 ★
RAILROAD BARON

Raised in the eastern Appalachians, Mark Hopkins joined the gold rush to California but soon gave up prospecting and opened a grocery store, and then he expanded his mercantile interests by partnering with Collis Huntington. The two were wealthy by the time they joined with Leland Stanford and Charles Crocker to found the Central Pacific Railroad. Hopkins was involved in overseeing the company's accounting and discouraged the more speculative investments his bolder partners favored. When he died, he was building a grand house at the top of San Francisco's Nob Hill, now the site of the InterContinental Mark Hopkins hotel.

COLLIS HUNTINGTON
★ 1821–1900 ★
TRANSPORTATION MAGNATE

Born into a Connecticut farm family, Collis Huntington early on evinced his talent for capitalism, becoming an itinerant peddler by age 16. In 1849, he followed the flood of forty-niners to the California goldfields, sailing by way of Panama. Delayed there for months, he

Collis Huntington The quintessential robber baron, he forged a vast and questionable industrial empire.

again turned to itinerant peddling, selling merchandise to others on the isthmus. Once in California, Huntington forwent gold fever and established himself as a hardware merchant in Sacramento, eventually partnering with Mark Hopkins. The two, along with another local merchant, Charles Crocker, helped establish the California Republican Party, soon led by Leland Stanford.

Huntington was the initial impetus behind the four establishing the Central Pacific Railroad, and he went to Washington to lobby on its behalf. Subsequent legislation awarded his company and the Union Pacific favorable loans and enormous land grants to create a transcontinental railroad.

As construction began, Huntington settled in New York to handle policy and financing and buy equipment. His aggressive business practices resulted in some government scrutiny, but it also made him a major force in American enterprise. In the early 1870s, he expanded his railroading empire, building the Chesapeake and Ohio Railway and expanding his western railroad interests. But by the early 1880s,

Mark Hopkins Like Collis Huntington, Hopkins was one of the Big Four, but, disinclined to engage in the bold and often nefarious business tactics Huntington preferred, Hopkins played a lesser role in empire building.

his often questionable practices had resulted in a congressional hearing. Huntington evaded questioning and generally found ways to delay repaying government loans; his final days were spent under a shadow of public opprobrium. Novelist Frank Norris modeled the protagonist in his 1901 classic, *The Octopus,* after Huntington, saying of the character, "No one individual . . . was more hated, more dreaded, no one more compelling of unwilling tribute to his commanding genius."

STONEWALL JACKSON

★ 1824–1863 ★

CONFEDERATE COMMANDER

Stonewall Jackson Eccentric but brilliant at military strategy, Jackson (left) was perhaps Robert E. Lee's (right) most valuable weapon. *Inset:* A Confederate jacket

The man who would become the South's "Stonewall" spent his early years in western Virginia (now West Virginia) and was poorly prepared for the world that awaited him when he entered West Point in 1842. Most of his fellow cadets found "Old Jack" "cold and undemonstrative" yet "absolutely honest and kindly, intensely attending to his own business." The description would fit Thomas "Stonewall" Jackson throughout his life.

In the Mexican-American War, Jackson proved to be courageous and calm under fire. In 1851, he resigned from the Army and received an offer to teach at the Virginia Military Institute. From that position, he watched the nation begin to unravel, writing a friend in early 1861, "I am in favor of making a thorough trial for peace, and if we fail in this, and the state is invaded to defend it with terrific resistance—even to taking no prisoners."

Soon Jackson was an officer in the Confederate Army, and within months

All Old Jack gave us was a musket, a hundred rounds . . . and he druv us like hell.

CONFEDERATE SOLDIER

he was given a chance to mount his terrific resistance. At the First Battle of Manassas in July 1861, as his brigade held a critical hill in the face of enemy fire, Gen. Barnard Bee told his own disorganized troops, "Look, men, there stands Jackson like a stone wall! Rally behind the Virginians." The following spring, Jackson, now commanding roughly 17,000 men, launched his legendary Valley Campaign. For 10 weeks in the spring of 1862, he outmaneuvered more than 50,000 Union soldiers and kept them

occupied in the Shenandoah Valley. He and his men covered hundreds of miles and were exhausted from the campaign's long marches when they arrived in the Richmond area to defend the Confederate capital that June, and their performance in the Seven Days' Battle marked the low point in Jackson's otherwise remarkable record. Yet, he had established himself as Robert E. Lee's most indispensable general.

Jackson's II Corps would see more Virginia victories at Cedar Mountain, Second Manassas, and Fredericksburg and an inconclusive yet horrific draw at Antietam. In the spring of 1863, Jackson engineered an almost impossible flanking maneuver and surprise attack on the Union Army at Chancellorsville, Virginia. The following evening, while reconnoitering in the dark, Jackson was mistakenly shot by Confederate forces and died a week later. His last words were: "Let us cross over the river and rest in the shade of the trees."

ANDREW JOHNSON
★ 1801–1875 ★
17TH U.S. PRESIDENT

Raised in rural poverty in North Carolina, Andrew Johnson did not truly learn to read or write until age 17, when he was taught by his wife, Eliza. By then, he was living in Greeneville, Tennessee, and working as a tailor. He gradually became involved in politics as a Jacksonian Democrat, serving in the state legislature, the U.S. Congress, and as Tennessee governor. When the Civil War erupted, he was in his first term in the U.S. Senate. Though a pro-slavery, states' rights advocate, he did not believe in secession and remained in Congress even after the secession of Tennessee. Lincoln appointed him military governor of that deeply contested Border State, and in the presidential election of 1864, he tapped Johnson as his running mate, in a calculated gesture to appeal to War Democrats. A month after their inaugural, Lincoln was assassinated and Johnson, a man of little leadership ability, assumed the presidency.

Andrew Johnson
He was elected 17th president and was one of the weakest.

Joseph Johnston One of the South's great generals, he beat back Sherman's offensive at Kennesaw Mountain, north of Atlanta, on June 27, 1864.

Pro-South and racist, Johnson's plans for Reconstruction differed radically from those of Lincoln and of Congress, with whom he clashed repeatedly. In February 1868, the House voted 126 to 47 to impeach him, but his conviction in the Senate was defeated by one vote. Johnson lost his bid to run for a second term. Tennessee returned him to the Senate in 1875, but he suffered a stroke soon thereafter. Most historians view him as one of the nation's weakest presidents.

JOSEPH JOHNSTON
★ 1807–1891 ★
CONFEDERATE COMMANDER

As the Civil War began, Joseph Johnston, a West Point–educated Virginian, was quartermaster general of the U.S. Army. Resigning, he joined the Confederacy, organized the Army of the Shenandoah, and then was put in charge of the Army of Northern Virginia. He was wounded in the Union advance on Richmond in 1862 and replaced by Robert E. Lee. After recovering, Johnston moved to the western theater and fought Grant and Sherman in battles in Tennessee and Georgia. Considered overly cautious, he was removed from command in July 1864, but only briefly. Back in the field for the final months of war, he fought a losing battle against Sherman's army. On April 26, 1865, after Lee's surrender, Johnston surrendered the largest Confederate force, almost 90,000 men, in North Carolina. After the war, he served one term representing Virginia in the Congress and as railway commissioner under Grover Cleveland.

ROBERT E. LEE
★ 1807–1870 ★
COMMANDER OF THE CONFEDERATE ARMY

Robert E. Lee's prominent Virginia family included Richard Henry and Francis Lightfoot Lee, the only brothers to sign the Declaration of Independence, and his father, "Light-Horse Harry," a governor and one of George Washington's most trusted commanders. However, when Robert was still a child, his father, burdened by debt, left his wife and children, who had to rely on other family members. Robert went to West Point and then remained in the Army, marrying Mary Custis, great-granddaughter of Martha Washington. In the Mexican-American War, Lee proved to be an outstanding soldier, and with the advent of the Civil War, he was offered command of Union forces. Instead, he resigned from the Army, explaining, "though opposed to secession and a deprecating war, I could take no part in an invasion of the Southern States."

Joining the Confederate Army, Lee was appointed commander of the Army of Northern Virginia in June 1862 and effectively ended the Union advance on Richmond. In the coming three years, he would hold out against a Union Army three times larger and far better equipped than his, scoring historic victories in Virginia at Second Manassas, Fredericksburg, and

Robert E. Lee The Confederacy's most revered figure, Lee resigned himself to its defeat and counseled his fellow Southerners to see themselves as Americans again.

Chancellorsville, and an inconclusive and brutal stalemate at Antietam. In July 1863, owing to his own tactical missteps, he suffered a defeat at Gettysburg from which his army never fully recovered. The following spring, Ulysses Grant pursued Lee's army through eastern Virginia in a series of brutal battles known as the Wilderness Campaign, ending with Lee's army besieged in Petersburg.

Lee was appointed commander in chief of all Confederate forces in early 1865, but by then it was a moot point. Knowing that he had neither the men nor matériel to prosecute the war further, Lee told his inner circle, "There is nothing left for me to do but to go and see General

Grant, and I would rather die a thousand deaths." He surrendered at the village of Appomattox, Virginia, on April 9, 1865.

Lee's strategic genius and audacity as a commander have been much studied and much admired, though they cost an enormous amount in human lives. To the South, however, he remained the consummate hero, and after the war, he urged his fellow Southerners to set aside bitterness and see themselves again as Americans. Lee spent his final years as president of Washington College (now Washington and Lee University) in Lexington, Virginia. His application to have his citizenship reinstated was lost and not acted upon until 1975.

Abraham Lincoln Abraham and Mary were devoted parents, particularly to their younger sons, Tad and Willie. *Inset:* Lincoln favored top hats, which only increased his height.

ABRAHAM LINCOLN

★ 1809-1865 ★

16TH U.S. PRESIDENT

Abraham Lincoln's hardscrabble childhood in the wilderness of Kentucky and Indiana became the stuff of American legend. Barely schooled, young Abe nonetheless had a thirst for knowledge and talent for leadership. In his young adulthood, he managed to escape the farm labor imposed on him by his father and begin a new life in New Salem, Illinois. He earned his living as a shopkeeper and owner, postmaster, and surveyor, reading prodigiously as he did so and eventually settling on a life in law and politics.

An ardent Whig with a deep belief in internal improvements such as canals and railroads, Lincoln was elected to the Illinois General Assembly in 1834. Three years later, he moved to the new state capital, Springfield, as a lawyer, often riding circuit, which he loved. Despite his unsophisticated awkwardness, he made his way in Springfield social circles, where the reigning belle was an opinionated young Kentuckian named Mary Todd. After a troubled and unlikely courtship, the gangly, struggling Lincoln married Mary, and the two settled in Springfield. Mary shared Lincoln's love of Whig politics and was an asset as he made his mark in political circles. In 1846, he was elected to the U.S. House of Representatives for one term; then he returned to law. In 1854, his political instincts were reawakened with the introduction of the Kansas-Nebraska Act, which proposed expanding slavery in the western states. Lincoln was incensed by the idea and

spoke out forcibly against it. He hoped for a U.S. Senate seat that year, but he was not elected. Four years later, he tried again, this time challenging incumbent Senator Stephen Douglas—champion of the Kansas-Nebraska Bill and an old suitor of Mary—to a series of debates. Though the bombastic Douglas was a more skilled debater, "Honest Old Abe," awkward and odd in his gestures, "always touched sympathetic chords."

Newsmen closely covered the debates and thousands came to hear them. Lincoln lost the election, but his national reputation was made. In November 1860, he was elected president on the Republican ticket. With his characteristic, folksy humor, he told the press, "Well,

> *We are not enemies, but friends . . . The mystic chords of memory . . . will yet swell the chorus of the Union, when again touched, as surely they will be, by the better angels of our nature.*
>
> **ABRAHAM LINCOLN'S FIRST INAUGURAL ADDRESS**

boys, your troubles are over now, but mine have just begun." Before Lincoln could take the oath of office in March 1861, seven states had seceded from the Union and six more would follow. By April, Confederate forces had bombarded Union-held Fort Sumter, and Lincoln had ordered a blockade of the South and a suspension of habeas

He Belongs to the Ages

THE DEATH OF FATHER ABRAHAM

★ ★ ★

The Lincolns were enjoying a rare night out on April 14, 1865, when actor John Wilkes Booth snuck into their box at Ford's Theatre and shot the president. He was taken across the street to the Petersen House as most of his Cabinet rushed to his side. He died just after seven the following morning, and Secretary of War Edwin Stanton, tears streaming, delivered a benediction: "Now he belongs to the ages."

Throughout the North—and the world—mourners gathered and wept openly for "Father Abraham." After a funeral in the White House East Room, his body first lay in state in the Capitol Rotunda, and from there, traveled some 1,700 miles in a nine-car funeral train that, over two weeks, stopped at 10 cities in the East and Midwest. In each, the open casket was placed on view and well over a million came to pay their respects. Lincoln was finally laid to rest in a temporary grave beside his son, Willie. An elaborate tomb for the Lincolns was ultimately built in Springfield.

The President's Box at Ford's Theatre in Washington, D.C., where Lincoln was fatally shot

---

corpus. If it took war, so be it. The Union must be maintained.

For the next four years, Lincoln battled the South, his commanders and Cabinet, and northern detractors who opposed his policies. In January 1863, he issued the Emancipation Proclamation, freeing slaves in the Confederacy still under rebel control, and in November he delivered the speech for which he would be most remembered—the Gettysburg Address. In 1864, Lincoln won a second term; a month after his March 1865 inaugural, Lee surrendered to Grant. The war was effectively over, the Union preserved. Six days later, Lincoln was dead.

JAMES LONGSTREET

★ 1821–1904 ★

CONFEDERATE COMMANDER

Robert E. Lee's "Old War Horse," James Longstreet, like Lee, graduated from West Point and distinguished himself in the Mexican-American War. He fought at Lee's side from the summer of 1862 on—in the defense of Richmond, at Second Manassas, Antietam, Fredericksburg, and Gettysburg, where Longstreet objected to Lee's bold, and ultimately failed, plan to attack well-fortified Union positions. With peace, Longstreet became a Republican and Grant supporter, leading to his vilification in the South.

James Longstreet Lee's right-hand man, respected by military historians for his tactical acumen

Billy the Kid Much of the "Kid's" life remains shrouded in mystery.

WILLIAM HENRY MCCARTY (BILLY THE KID)

★ CA 1859–1881 ★

WESTERN OUTLAW

The outlaw who would become known as Billy the Kid was the son of an Irish immigrant mother and is believed to have been born in New York City, though details of his early life are uncertain. William Henry McCarty, who changed his name at some point to William Bonney, first got into trouble with the law in New Mexico as a teenager. He escaped jail a number of times, and his exploits as a horse thief, rustler, and gunslinger became legendary in the Southwest. A New Mexico posse headed by Sheriff Pat Garrett apprehended the "Kid" and his gang in late 1880. However, Billy escaped once more while awaiting execution. Almost three months later, he was fatally shot by Garrett in Fort Sumner, New Mexico.

GEORGE MCCLELLAN

★ 1826–1885 ★

UNION COMMANDER

The Union Army's "Young Napoleon" was, like so many other Civil War commanders, a graduate of West Point and veteran of the Mexican-American War. At the onset of the Civil War, George McClellan was appointed major general of Ohio Volunteers, but President Lincoln soon gave McClellan that rank in the regular army, reporting directly to Union commander Winfield Scott. McClellan scored early victories in western Virginia, clearing the area of Confederate sympathizers and thus allowing the formation of West Virginia as the newest Union state. After the North's ignominious defeat at First Manassas, Lincoln made McClellan commander of the Army of the Potomac. Arriving in the capital, the 34-year-old, fatally vainglorious commander wrote to his wife, "I seem to have become the power in the land."

But he was a strong organizer and planner, and he spent many months training and drilling the Army before launching his spring 1862 campaign to take the Confederate capital, Richmond. A cautious commander reluctant to act aggressively, McClellan failed in that attempt, which could have brought the war to a swift conclusion. A frustrated Lincoln replaced him—but only briefly. After the Army of the Potomac under John Pope lost at Second Manassas, McClellan was again put in charge and faced off against Lee's forces at Antietam, Maryland, in September 1862. The Confederates were forced out of Maryland and dangerously weakened by a battle that remains the bloodiest single day in American history. Yet McClellan refused to follow up and permanently damage Lee's army, despite Lincoln's entreaties to do so. He was relieved of his command in November and never again served in the Army.

Now openly opposed to Lincoln and his policies, McClellan, ever pompous but popular with the northern public, entered politics, and in 1864, he ran as a Democrat against Lincoln. His platform promised a negotiated peace with the

George McClellan The North's vainglorious "Young Napoleon" did little for the Union cause.

South and an end to the war. But as the campaign began, the tide of war shifted distinctly, with northern victories in Atlanta and Virginia. Lincoln's electoral vote tally was 212 to McClellan's 21. After the war, McClellan worked for various engineering firms and served as governor of New Jersey.

> *Wherever Lee goes,*
> *there you will go also.*
>
> UNION COMMANDER GRANT
> TO GENERAL MEADE

GEORGE MEADE
★ 1815–1872 ★
UNION COMMANDER

A West Point–trained Army topographical engineer, George Meade initially worked on the defenses around Washington before joining the Army of the Potomac and fighting in the Peninsula Campaign. He went on to battle at Second Manassas, South Mountain, Antietam, Fredericksburg, and Chancellorsville, steadily rising through the ranks. After the North suffered yet another humiliating defeat at Chancellorsville, Lincoln replaced Joseph Hooker with Meade as commander of the Army of the Potomac. As Meade told a confidant, "Well, I've been tried and convicted without a hearing. I suppose I shall have to go to the execution." Execution of sorts awaited him that summer in the small Pennsylvania town of Gettysburg, when his army and Lee's collided. After three grueling days of battle, Lee's force, defeated and badly damaged, retreated toward Virginia. Meade, recognizing that his own

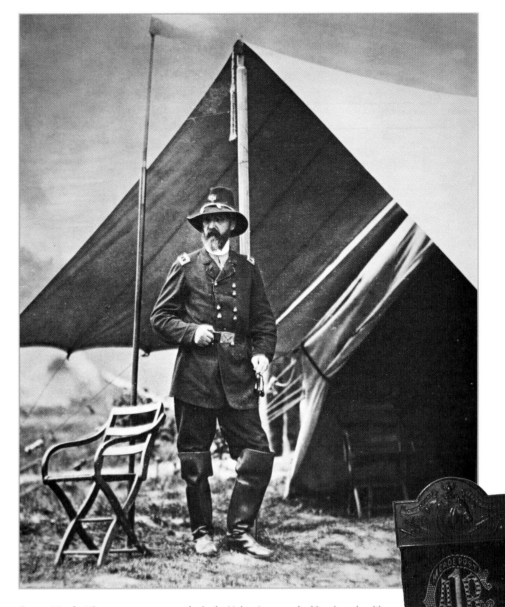

George Meade His career as a commander in the Union Army reached its pinnacle with his 1863 victory at Gettysburg, but he refused to press his advantage in its aftermath. *Inset:* A medal commemorating Meade

men were spent, gave desultory chase, and once again, Lee's army survived to fight another day. Hearing the news, Lincoln lamented, "We had only to stretch forth our hands and they were ours."

Yet Lincoln would not accept Meade's proffered resignation, and he continued in command of the Army of the Potomac until the end of the war, if only nominally. After Grant was put in charge of all Union forces in the winter of 1864, he effectively made the command decisions, but Meade followed them well enough for Grant to request that he be promoted to major general. Meade continued to serve as a commander in the U.S. Army after the war.

HERMAN MELVILLE

★ 1819–1891 ★

NOVELIST

Herman Melville's early childhood in New York was privileged until about age 11, when the family import business failed and young Herman had to work to help support the family. By his early 20s, he had taken to the sea, sailing on whalers through the South Seas for some three years. Already interested in writing, Melville used his adventures as fodder for two reasonably well received novels—*Typee* and *Omoo.* As his family's ever vacillating fortunes again took a downturn, he began to write as a means of supporting them, himself, and his new wife, Elizabeth, the daughter of Massachusetts's chief justice. After completing three more novels that met with mixed success, Melville began another he called *The Whale.* While writing it, he grew to be friends with the esteemed older novelist Nathaniel Hawthorne and bought a farm near him in the Berkshires. According to Hawthorne's wife, Sophia, the "generally silent and uncommunicative" Melville poured out to his friend "the rich floods of his mind and experience . . . so sure of apprehension, so sure of a large and generous interpretation, and of the most delicate and fine judgment."

Melville's novel, renamed *Moby-Dick,* was published in 1851 and its failure to receive critical acclaim threw Melville into a depression. Though he continued to write novels through the 1850s, he enjoyed no success and many disappointments in the years to come, including the early deaths of both of his sons. From 1866 to 1885, he worked as a customs inspector in New York Harbor, occasionally writing verse. In retirement he wrote another work, *Billy Budd,* which is now ranked as a literary achievement, but Melville's masterpiece, *Moby-Dick,* sits at the pinnacle of American literature.

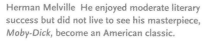

Herman Melville He enjoyed moderate literary success but did not live to see his masterpiece, *Moby-Dick,* become an American classic.

Samuel Morse's telegraphic receiver recorded the Morse code dots and dashes he invented to send via wire.

SAMUEL F. B. MORSE

★ 1791–1872 ★

INVENTOR OF TELEGRAPH, ARTIST

The son of a well-regarded Massachusetts geographer, Yale-educated Samuel Morse initially saw himself as an artist and in 1811 sailed for England and studied art there for four years. Most of his canvases in those early years reflected the epic historical scenes then popular in Britain. His work, however, did not sell well in America, and Morse became an itinerant portraitist and the friend of various writers, artists, and intellectuals. In 1825, he and other artists founded the National Academy in New York City to make fine art more accessible to the average person "through instruction and exhibition." Morse served as its first president from 1826 to 1845, and during that time, he returned to Europe, again to study art.

While sailing back to America, he discussed the new discovery of electromagnetism with other passengers. Through those conversations Morse is believed to have conceived the idea of sending coded messages over a wire using electromagnetic currents. Knowing he had little true understanding of electricity, he sought help from New York scientist Leonard Gale. Gale's help and that of his own technical assistant,

Alfred Vail, along with the pioneering work of scientist Joseph Henry, led to Morse's ultimate invention of his own telegraph system. Although other, older systems already existed, Morse came up with the idea of coded dots and dashes as a means of messaging. Through the 1830s, however, a poor economy thwarted his efforts to build an actual line. Finally, in 1843, Congress appropriated funds to build a line between Washington, D.C., and Baltimore. On May 24, 1844, Morse sat in the Supreme Court chamber, then in the Capitol, and sent the now legendary message "What have God wrought" to Baltimore. The moment would revolutionize communications, as overhead lines interlaced the country and allowed people at great distances to communicate via telegraph operators using Morse code. In the decade to come, Morse was involved in numerous patent suits regarding the telegraph; they were generally settled before the Supreme Court in 1854, in his favor.

JOHN MOSBY
★ 1833–1916 ★
CONFEDERATE OFFICER

The man who would become the Confederate's Gray Ghost had been a sickly and frequently bullied child and young man in rural Virginia. At the onset of the Civil War, John Mosby was an attorney and, though he had not been a supporter of secession, he joined the Confederate Army as a private. He quickly proved his worth in intelligence gathering, and in January 1863, J. E. B. Stuart made him

commander of the 43rd Virginia Cavalry. "Mosby's Rangers" soon became legendary for their seemingly invisible movements and guerrilla-like harassment of Union supply and communication lines in northern Virginia.

After the war, Mosby became a full-throated Republican and the campaign manager and close friend of Ulysses S. Grant. He eventually served as American consul to Hong Kong and assistant attorney general.

It is a classical maxim that it is sweet and becoming to die for one's country; but whoever has seen the horrors of a battlefield feels that it is far sweeter to live for it.

JOHN MOSBY

John Mosby The South's Gray Ghost served in the Grant Administration after the Civil War.

LUCRETIA MOTT

★ 1793–1880 ★

ABOLITIONIST, WOMEN'S
RIGHTS ACTIVIST

Strongly influenced by her Quaker upbringing in the Northeast, Lucretia Mott was recognized as a minister in the faith. She was a member of the more liberal Hicksite Quakers and became a sought-after abolitionist and founder of women's groups opposed to slavery. Increasingly, her speaking and public stances intertwined the rights of enslaved peoples and the rights of women. In 1848, Mott and Elizabeth Cady Stanton helped to organize the first women's rights convention in Seneca Falls, New York.

Lucretia Mott Quaker beliefs inspired her work as an abolitionist and warrior for women's rights.

After the Civil War, Mott became embroiled in the controversy over the 15th Amendment, which guaranteed all men, regardless of race—but not women—the right to vote. In 1869, Mott was involved, along with Stanton and Susan B. Anthony, with founding the National Woman Suffrage Association. She and her husband, James, were also instrumental in establishing Swarthmore as a coeducational Quaker college.

THOMAS NAST

★ 1840–1902 ★

ILLUSTRATOR

German-born Thomas Nast came with his family to New York City at the age of 6 and by 15 was working as a reportorial newspaper artist. In 1862, he began covering the Civil War from the frontlines for the newly established *Harper's Weekly.* A fierce supporter of the Union and the Republican Party, Nast allegorized the war in ways that captured the northern public's imagination. His "Compromise with the South" cartoon, which ran in *Harper's Weekly* in early September 1864 and showed a Union soldier surrendering to the South, was believed to have helped Lincoln win his second term.

At war's end, Nast continued as a book and magazine illustrator and again played an instrumental role in American politics with his *Harper's* cartoons lampooning the corruption of New York's Tammany Hall and its ringleader, William Magear "Boss" Tweed. Nast also helped establish the donkey and elephant as symbols of the two national political parties, as well as popularizing the chubby-cheeked, bearded version of the American Santa Claus. However, by

Thomas Nast His political and wartime cartoons in *Harper's Weekly* combined humor, outrage, and pathos.

1886, he had lost some of his following and left *Harper's,* having clashed with the new editor. In 1902, President Theodore Roosevelt appointed Nast, by then in dire need of work, as consul general to Ecuador. He served only six months before dying of yellow fever.

FREDERICK LAW OLMSTED

★ 1822–1903 ★

LANDSCAPE ARCHITECT

Frederick Law Olmsted grew up in Hartford, Connecticut, and spent his early adult years traveling to Europe and Asia, touring the American South and writing about his travels (including his acclaimed *Cotton Kingdom*), and running an experimental farm. In the late 1850s, he began working with established landscape architect Calvert Vaux, and the two won a design competition to create a "rural park" on a vast swath of rocky wasteland in upper Manhattan.

Central Park was still a work in progress when the Civil War began, and a

Frederick Law Olmsted New York's Central Park—and countless other urban and rural green spaces across the country—owes its existence to Olmsted's groundbreaking ideas on landscape design.

It is a scientific fact that the occasional contemplation of natural scenes of an impressive character . . . is favorable to the health and vigor of men.

FREDERICK LAW OLMSTED

group of influential New Yorkers, including Olmsted, established the Sanitary Commission to organize the efforts of relief societies. Olmsted agreed to serve as secretary general and moved to Washington to lobby for official sanction of the commission. In June 1861, Lincoln reluctantly agreed, and for the next two years, Olmsted and his supplies and aides were at the battlefront.

In 1863, Olmsted moved to Northern California and for two years managed Mariposa Estate, now Mariposa Grove, an enormous gold-mining concern. When he returned to New York, he and

Vaux completed Central Park and designed Brooklyn's Prospect Park. For the next 30 years, Olmsted forged a new vision of the interface between people and nature, designing landscape plans for parkways, park systems, public and private complexes, the 1893 World's Columbian Exposition, and the iconic scenic preserves at Yosemite Valley, Mariposa Grove, and Niagara Falls.

A Promise Broken

FORTY ACRES AND A MULE

★ ★ ★

In January 1865, Union general William Tecumseh Sherman, having taken Atlanta and made his infamous March to the Sea, issued Special Field Orders, No. 15. It set aside a 30-mile-wide stretch of the southern Atlantic coast from the St. Johns River in Florida north to Charleston, for the "settlement of negroes now made free." The heads of African-American families could claim 40 acres to establish a farm there. In the next several months, some 20,000 people settled in the area and another 20,000 followed later in 1865. Although mules were not part of the bargain, Army surplus animals were given out to some of the settlers.

An unapologetic racist who generally used derisive terms for African Americans, Sherman had issued the orders under the explicit directive of Secretary of War Edwin Stanton, who had heard of Sherman's prejudice in Washington. Yet, as Washington politics changed, so did support for the plight of freed blacks. By 1867, most of the enclave's settlers had been forced off their 40 acres by previous white owners who returned to claim their lands.

Gen. William Tecumseh Sherman on horseback in 1864

GEORGE PICKETT

★ 1825–1875 ★

CONFEDERATE COMMANDER

————— ·••◦◦◦•·• —————

Last in the West Point class of 1846, the Virginian fought, like many of his fellow alumni, in the Mexican-American War and remained in the Army at war's end. With the advent of the Civil War, Pickett resigned his U.S. commission and joined the Confederate Army. As a brigadier general, he fought in defense of Richmond during most of the major battles of the 1862 Peninsula Campaign. In July 1863, Pickett led a division into south-central Pennsylvania, where the Battle of Gettysburg had been ongoing for two days. Robert E. Lee's Army of Northern Virginia had initially prevailed in the fighting, but the federal army held the heights on the north side of the battlefront. Lee determined to attack Cemetery Ridge, the Union center, and ordered Pickett's division, not yet battle-fatigued, to undertake the assault. Pickett led some 5,500 soldiers in the assault across open ground and toward the Union's well-fortified ridge. Pickett's Charge, as it became known, ended in utter failure for the Confederacy and remains a signature moment of defeat in the war. Pickett's last years in the war were plagued by more defeat and ignominy, and his postwar years were spent farming and nursing a bitterness regarding the events of the war. His reputation was resurrected posthumously by his widow, LaSalle Corbell Pickett, who became a popular author by depicting her husband as the hero of Gettysburg.

George Pickett The Virginian is best known for his failed attack on Cemetery Ridge.

A colored etching depicts Pickett's Charge, the Battle of Gettysburg, 1863. The Confederate commander led some 5,500 soldiers in the assault, which ended in failure for the Confederacy.

> *I have several female operatives. If you agree to come aboard you will go in training with the head of my female detectives, Kate Warne. She has never let me down.*
>
> ALLAN PINKERTON

————— ·••◦◦◦•·• —————

ALLAN PINKERTON

★ 1819–1884 ★

DETECTIVE

————— ·••◦◦◦•·• —————

Born in Glasgow, Allan Pinkerton immigrated to America in 1842, eventually settling outside Chicago, where he opened a barrelmaking shop that also served as a station on the Underground Railroad. His career as America's pioneering detective began by happenstance when he discovered a ring of counterfeiters in the area. Their apprehension led to his eventual appointment as Chicago's first full-time detective. In 1850, he left that position to open his own detective agency, whose work was generally aimed at counterfeiters and train robbers. Pinkerton detectives also established extensive criminal dossiers and kept mug shots, groundbreaking procedures copied by municipal police departments.

In 1861, Pinkerton's investigations inadvertently exposed a plot to assassinate President-elect Lincoln as he traveled through Baltimore. Lincoln avoided disaster by changing his travel plans, and the Union later tapped Pinkerton to create a "secret service" that would ferret out Confederate military intentions. Pinkerton himself briefly went undercover and behind enemy lines in the South.

After the war, Pinkerton, back at the helm of his agency, expanded it to New York and Philadelphia and began writing true crime stories that gained widespread appreciation for the art of detecting. His agency's reputation was tarnished in a botched attempt in 1875 to apprehend Frank and Jesse James. It suffered further public opprobrium in the late 1800s when its agents became strikebreakers in labor disputes, but by then Pinkerton was dead. The Pinkerton logo—an all-seeing eye—led to the expression "private eye."

Allan Pinkerton He refined the art of detecting and during the Civil War headed the North's fledging "secret service." He poses here (far left) with northern dignitaries at Antietam, Maryland, around the time of the brutal battle.

RED CLOUD
★ 1822–1909 ★
OGLALA CHIEF

Oglala Lakota chief and warrior Mahpiua Luta (whose name translates as Red, or Scarlet, Cloud) was born on the Platte River in what is now north-central Nebraska. In the mid-1860s, he proved himself a natural leader, for two years resisting U.S. government encroachment on traditional buffalo hunting grounds. He harassed crews attempting to build the Bozeman Trail from Fort Laramie (southeastern Wyoming) along the Powder River to the newly discovered goldfields of Montana. Red Cloud's War, as it became known, ended with the Fort Laramie Treaty, which promised the Powder River Country to the Sioux; all the forts that had been erected along the Bozeman Trail were also abandoned. Red Cloud and his followers moved to the Red Cloud Agency established on the North Platte River in Wyoming as a supply point for his Oglala band as well as for Cheyenne and Arapaho.

Red Cloud's refusal to continue to fight white encroachment with force lost him a number of followers, including his son. But for the next two decades, Red Cloud pursued diplomatic means of protecting Native American rights and culture through lobbying and negotiations with federal agents and politicians. He made a number of trips to Washington and met with President Grant in an attempt to ward off more war. After the Great Sioux War of 1876 ended in the defeat of Crazy Horse, the Sioux ceded the Dakota Black Hills to the United States, and Red Cloud and his followers were relocated to the new Pine Ridge Agency in Dakota Territory. A few years before his death, he and his wife converted to Christianity.

Red Cloud After waging war to protect Indian lands, he used diplomacy instead.

WILLIAM SEWARD

★ 1801–1872 ★

STATESMAN

William Seward's boyhood was spent in rural New York, where his father was a physician. The family had three domestic slaves, and Seward early on espoused abolition. After graduating Phi Beta Kappa from Union College, he became a lawyer in Auburn, New York, and then began his political career. As Whig governor of the state from 1838 to 1840 he pushed through liberal causes such as greater funding for education, prison reform, and infrastructure projects. In 1849, he went on to the U.S. Senate as an outspoken opponent of slavery. In 1860, he expected to win the newly formed Republican

Philip Sheridan The general saved the day at the 1864 Battle of Cedar Creek, Virginia, when, returning from Washington, he rallied his troops. That fall he led the campaign to destroy farms in the Shenandoah Valley.

William Seward Lincoln's effective secretary of state

> *The President is the best of us, but he needs constant and assiduous cooperation.*
>
> **SECRETARY OF STATE**
> **WILLIAM SEWARD**

Party's nomination for president but narrowly lost to Abraham Lincoln.

When Lincoln was elected, he chose Seward as his secretary of state. The relationship had a rocky start, with Seward assuming that his own expertise and sophistication would allow him to run the administration of a weak president. But Lincoln soon disabused him of that misconception, and Seward was quick to see that although "executive skill and vigor are rare qualities," Lincoln had them. As the Civil War dragged at the

Union, he and Lincoln formed a strong partnership, with Seward executing a delicate diplomatic dance with other foreign powers that kept them from intervening in the American war. When senators passed an 1862 resolution expressing a lack of confidence in the secretary of state—owing in large part to Seward's high-handed arrogance—Lincoln masterfully fended off the attack.

Just as the Civil War was ending, Seward was involved in a carriage accident that left him bedridden. On the evening of April 14, as John Wilkes Booth was attacking Lincoln, his accomplice Lewis Powell (alias Payne) entered Seward's home on false pretenses and attacked him so viciously with a knife as he lay in bed that the wounds seemed fatal. Seward survived and continued as secretary of state under Andrew Johnson, who took Lincoln's place. During the short-lived Johnson Administration, Seward negotiated the purchase of Alaska from Russia, paying $7.2 million, or roughly two cents an acre. Though Seward considered it his greatest achievement, he understood that it would "take the country a generation to appreciate it." In his lifetime, Alaska remained known as "Seward's folly."

PHILIP SHERIDAN
★ 1831–1888 ★
UNION COMMANDER

A graduate of West Point, Philip Sheridan was an officer in the Army when the Civil War struck. He fought well in the western theater—at Booneville and Perryville, Kentucky, and in Tennessee at Stones River and Missionary Ridge. In the spring of 1864, Grant made him the cavalry commander in the Army of the Potomac, and he was with Grant in the early phases of the Wilderness Campaign. In early August, he was put in charge of the Army of the Shenandoah and ordered by Grant to "eat out Virginia clean and clear . . . so that crows flying over it for the balance of the season will have to carry their own provender with them." Sheridan's "Burning," as residents called it, laid waste to farms, livestock,

and fields in the north end of the Shenandoah Valley and had a crippling effect on southern morale. In March 1865, Sheridan rejoined Grant for the final push on Lee's army. He remained in the Army through the 1880s, posted to the Gulf Coast and to the West. He ended his career as general of the U.S. Army.

WILLIAM TECUMSEH SHERMAN
★ 1820–1891 ★
UNION COMMANDER

Though he had attended West Point, William Sherman, son of an Ohio Supreme Court justice, only briefly pursued a lackluster military career in his 20s. He was superintendent of the Louisiana Military Academy when the Civil War began, and he reenlisted, distinguishing himself at First Manassas. Moved to the western theater, he fought in major battles with Grant until 1864, when Grant was ordered east and given command of all Union armies; Sherman took his place as commander in the western theater. In early September, he

William Tecumseh Sherman His 1864–65 march through the South left destruction in its wake.

outflanked Johnston's southern army to capture Atlanta. Convinced that the only way to a victory was "total destruction . . . upon the civilian population in the path" of Union forces, Sherman waged total war as he left Atlanta and moved toward Savannah. His brutal March to the Sea laid waste to a 40- to 60-mile swath of Georgia. In late December, Sherman wired President Lincoln: "I beg to present you, as a Christmas gift, the city of Savannah."

From Savannah, Sherman marched into the Carolinas, leaving more destruction in his wake. Victorious at the Battle of Bentonville in North Carolina against Johnston's army, Sherman accepted the final southern surrender. He remained in the Army and served as its general in chief from 1869 to 1884.

This Army wagon served the Union during Sherman's southern campaign.

LELAND STANFORD
★ 1824–1893 ★
RAILROAD ENTREPRENEUR, POLITICIAN

New York–educated lawyer Leland Stanford had a practice in Wisconsin when, in 1852, a fire destroyed his office and convinced him to join his brothers in Sacramento, where the gold boom was ongoing. He prospered there, selling mine supplies and becoming head of the state's new Republican Party and in 1861, governor of the state. That same year, he and other members of the Big Four founded the Central Pacific Railroad and Stanford became president. He was accorded the honor of driving in the "golden spike" at Promontory Summit, Utah Territory, thus uniting his railroad with the Union Pacific to complete a transcontinental line. He went on to head the Southern Pacific and to serve in the U.S. Senate.

Like other Gilded Age barons, Stanford employed sometimes unscrupulous practices to further his own wealth and position, but he is also remembered

Edwin Stanton The bearded secretary of war (center) was a powerful figure in Lincoln's contentious Cabinet.

today for the university that bears the Stanford name. He and his wife, Jane, having lost their only son to typhoid fever at 16, determined that "the children of California shall be our children." Leland Stanford Junior University was founded in 1885 as a tuition-free institution. The Stanfords donated some $478 million (in today's dollars) to its establishment and running. However, at Stanford's death, his assets were frozen, due to loan repayments owed to the government for the building of the Central Pacific.

Not everyone knows, as I do, how close you stood to our lost leader, how he loved you and trusted you, and how vain were all the efforts to shake that trust and confidence, not lightly given and never withdrawn.

JOHN HAY, LINCOLN'S SECRETARY, TO EDWIN STANTON

Leland Stanford Stanford University's founder

EDWIN STANTON
★ 1814–1869 ★
SECRETARY OF WAR, CIVIL WAR

Edwin Stanton spent his boyhood in Steubenville, Ohio, and was largely self-educated. After studying law, he joined an Ohio practice and became a respected public figure, winning a case before the U.S. Supreme Court in 1849 and garnering a national reputation for his legal work. In 1860, James Buchanan appointed him U.S. attorney general, and in 1862, though he was a Democrat, he was chosen by Lincoln to serve as secretary of war after Simon Cameron resigned. Stanton, who had acted as a co-attorney with Lincoln in a case representing Cyrus McCormick, nonetheless initially doubted Lincoln's abilities, calling him "the original gorilla." Stanton himself was considered autocratic and irascible, yet during the ensuing years of civil war, Stanton and Lincoln became staunch admirers of one another, deeply bound by their commitment to preserve the Union. Stanton was one of Lincoln's closest advisers, and Lincoln spent many hours monitoring developments in the offices of the War Department. At Lincoln's deathbed, Stanton grieved openly and organized the pursuit and prosecution of Lincoln's assassins. He continued on as secretary of war under Lincoln's successor, Andrew Johnson, but Stanton was an ardent civil rights supporter and Johnson was not. Specifically to protect Stanton, Congress passed the Tenure of Office Act, requiring a president to have congressional approval before dismissing Cabinet members. Johnson's blatant disregard of the act in his 1867 removal of Stanton led to impeachment proceedings. When the Senate failed to convict the president, Stanton resigned his post.

President Grant appointed Stanton to the Supreme Court in 1869, but Stanton died before taking office.

J. E. B. Stuart The swashbuckling Confederate cavalry commander served as Lee's trusted eyes and ears.

J. E. B. STUART

★ 1833–1864 ★

CONFEDERATE COMMANDER

The Virginian who would become Robert E. Lee's eyes and ears—James Ewell Brown "Jeb" Stuart—was a West Point–educated Army officer who, in the 1850s, fought Native Americans and abolitionist militant John Brown in Kansas and at Harpers Ferry.

Joining the Confederate Army in 1861, he executed dazzling maneuvers in the Shenandoah and at First Manassas. In June 1862, with Union troops outside the Confederate capital, Stuart made his famous "Ride Around Richmond," reconnoitering the northern army and supplying Lee with vital intelligence that allowed Confederate forces to drive the Union into retreat. Stuart's exploits made him a popular hero—sometimes called "Beauty" because of his élan and vanity—and earned him a promotion to major general commanding all cavalry for the Army of Northern Virginia.

Throughout the rest of 1862 and early 1863, Stuart continued daring reconnaissance missions at Second Manassas, Antietam, and Chancellorsville. However, in June and July, Stuart lost his charmed momentum at Brandy Station and most important, at Gettysburg, where he was caught behind the Union Army and unable to supply Lee with the kind of intelligence that might have turned the tide of battle in the South's favor.

Stuart redeemed himself at the Battle of Spotsylvania Court House, Virginia, in the spring of 1864, but in the aftermath, he repulsed a Union force at Yellow Tavern and was mortally wounded and died a day later. He became enshrined as part of the South's "Holy Trinity," along with Lee and Jackson, in the years to come.

LOUIS SULLIVAN

★ 1856–1924 ★

ARCHITECT

Boston-born Louis Sullivan was the son of immigrants—an Irish father and Swiss mother. He spent two brief semesters studying architecture at the nearby Massachusetts Institute of Technology, but he dreamed of studying in Paris. Instead, he went to Chicago in 1873, because the Great Fire two years before had led to a flurry of rebuilding and a demand for architects. He worked for a while for the pioneering skyscraper designer William Le Baron Jenney before studying at the École des Beaux-Arts in Paris.

When Sullivan returned to Chicago, he eventually formed a partnership with Dankmar Adler, and the firm became a sought-after innovator of modern design in the Midwest. In all, Adler and Sullivan

> *Every building is like a person. Single and unrepeatable.*
>
> **LOUIS SULLIVAN**

were responsible for some 200 buildings, both commercial and residential. With the new technology of steel-beam construction, Sullivan celebrated the verticality of the skyscraper and embellished it with organic, natural motifs. Among his masterpieces were Chicago's Auditorium Building, Stock Exchange, and Carson, Pirie, Scott and Company Store; and St. Louis's Wainwright Building.

Sullivan was devoted to creating a distinctive American style of architecture, and he and his protégé, Frank Lloyd Wright, are considered the inspirational visionaries behind what became known as the Prairie school. Sullivan's famous dictum, "Form ever follows function," remains a byword of modern design.

CORNELIUS VANDERBILT

★ 1794–1877 ★

TRANSPORTATION MAGNATE

A Staten Island boy with little interest in schooling, Cornelius Vanderbilt bought a boat at 16 and began ferrying produce and passengers to New York City. That proved the modest beginnings of a vast American empire. Vanderbilt took advantage of the War of 1812 to expand his fleet and supply government posts in New York. After the war, he learned the steamship business and eventually monopolized river traffic on the Hudson. "Commodore" Vanderbilt continued to build his transportation interests for the remainder of his long career, capitalizing on the California gold rush, expanding his shipping interests, and founding the New York Central rail lines. In 1873, he established the first rail links between New York and Chicago.

The original Grand Central Depot built by Vanderbilt in New York in 1871 was replaced by this station in 1913.

Comrades Disunited

WEST POINT COMPADRES DIVIDED BY WAR

★ ★ ★

The U.S. Military Academy at West Point, New York, was only a few decades old when the men who would change the course of the nation flocked to its doors in the 1840s. As cadets, they trained and studied and pulled pranks together, and then most went on to fight as comrades in the Mexican-American War. Thirteen years later, they faced each other across battlefields. Just the class of 1846 alone claimed four brigadier generals (one Union, three Confederate), 14 major generals (nine Union, five Confederate), and a lieutenant general—the Confederacy's "Stonewall" Jackson. The Confederacy's other lieutenant general, A. P. Hill (class of 1847), had been Union commander George McClellan's roommate at West Point, though McClellan, too, was class of 1846. Ulysses S. Grant was a few years ahead, graduating in 1843.

Years after the war, in 1890, another 1846 graduate, Confederate veteran and former major general Cadmus Wilcox, served his country a final time with his death by natural causes. In a show of unity, four Union and four Confederate generals carried him to his grave.

West Point cadets in rank and file

His business dealings were generally ruthless, and his family relationships were often equally unsavory. "The contrast between heroism and meanness is constantly baffling in the study of his long career," wrote Louis Auchincloss, who chronicled New York elites and married into the Vanderbilt family. The Commodore did, however, endow what is now Vanderbilt University in Nashville, Tennessee.

WALT WHITMAN

★ 1819–1892 ★

POET

Brooklyn-raised Walt Whitman grew up in a large family with little money; by age 12, he was working in the printing business. Within the decade he was editing a daily newspaper and went on to become editor of the prestigious *Brooklyn Daily Eagle.* By mid-century, Whitman's free-soil beliefs had banished him from the newspaper business, and he began building houses and trying his hand at poetry. In 1855, he sold one of the houses to self-publish a slender volume, *Leaves of Grass,* whose 12 untitled poems heralded a new poetic style; Whitman followed it a year later with a second, longer edition. His reputation as a poet was growing when war refocused his, and the nation's, energies.

In 1862, Whitman left New York for Virginia, where his younger brother George had been wounded. Whitman continued in the war effort, tirelessly nursing the Union wounded in Washington. He often saw Lincoln's carriage pass by, and Lincoln's assassination inspired Whitman to write an elegy that became one of his most beloved poems, "O Captain! My Captain!"

Immediately after the war, Whitman was hired by the Interior Department but soon was fired as the poet of the notorious *Leaves of Grass.* Although American audiences frequently found his work prurient, it was acclaimed in England, Europe, and South America for its sense of the common man and celebration of homosexual love. Whitman wrote poetry until the end, revising and enlarging *Leaves of Grass* and publishing other volumes. Today, he is considered one of the nation's greatest poets.

Walt Whitman His genius ranks him among America's—and the world's—great poets.

Battles & Commanders
CIVIL WAR PITS BROTHER AGAINST BROTHER

Both North and South could claim a number of superior officers during the four savage years of war. But there were the poor commanders as well, and Lincoln grappled mightily with the failures of the various men he put in charge of the Army of the Potomac. Over and over, the Union lost battles in the eastern theater, but in the western theater, in Kentucky and Tennessee, the North's Gen. Ulysses S. Grant dominated the battlefield. By all measures, the North should have dominated the war. It fielded twice the number of troops than the far less populous South, and it had the industrial might to supply its men with arms, supplies, and uniforms. The South did not, yet feeling that their homeland had been invaded, Confederate forces persisted in waging their defensive war even when all hope was lost. The site of many of the great bloody battles are now enshrined as parks or preserves, and the names continue to ring ominously, even a century and a half later: Antietam, Chickamauga, Cold Harbor, Gettysburg, the bloodiest of them all. The Civil War pitted "brother against brother," all sides ultimately American.

A Union officer's kepi, sometimes called a McClellan cap after Gen. George McClellan

This flag hung from the window of a Fifth Avenue home when the Seventh Infantry Regiment marched through Manhattan on its way to war.

The gray, homespun cloth of a Confederate soldier's jacket soon grew brown with wear.

Well-worn leather cavalry boots of a Union sergeant

The fighting that raged in the farm fields along Antietam Creek, Maryland, on September 17, 1862, claimed more American casualties than any other single day of battle, before or since.

The LeMat black-powder revolver that belonged to Confederate general P. G. T. Beauregard

A Pennsylvania soldier is joined by his family at his encampment in northern Virginia. A family visit could make the waiting for action and the drudgery of camp routine far more tolerable.

The Confederacy's unassailable Stonewall Jackson was felled by his own men, mistakenly shot while reconnoitering at Chancellorsville, Virginia, 1863.

Soldiers often wrote letters home on paper and envelopes emblazoned with symbols of their cause.

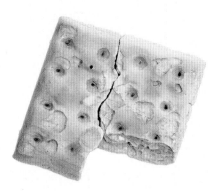

Hardtack, often full of weevils, was a staple food for soldiers on the march.

A POST–CIVIL WAR GOLDEN AGE

MODERN AMERICA BEGAN EMERGING AT THE TURN OF THE 20TH CENTURY. A nation that had been largely rural and small towns was becoming fully industrialized; by the time of World War I, the majority of Americans were urban. An America of accelerating technology was arising, as well as of mass media, consumerism, professional sports, movements for women's and civil rights, and the first national concerns about the environment.

The country had fulfilled its "Manifest Destiny," spreading from sea to sea, and began to look elsewhere. With the Philippines, Guam, Puerto Rico, and Hawaii acquired in 1898, Samoa in 1899, the Panama Canal Zone in 1903, and the Virgin Islands in 1917, America gradually emerged as a colonial empire.

Though it's hard to single out any one group of important American figures, the great age of American invention stands as representative of the best in America's can-do spirit. Among the inventors were Alexander Graham Bell, Thomas Edison, Nikola Tesla, George Westinghouse, Henry Ford, the Wright brothers, Leo Baekeland, and George Eastman.

American political life was changing as well. The 19th century had been the era of triumphant Jeffersonianism, idealizing small government and agrarian values. Early 20th-century politics would be dominated by a new political philosophy, Progressivism, which was oriented toward industrial and urban life.

(previous pages) The Wright brothers ushered in a new age of flight; here Wilbur soars above the Italian countryside in 1909.
(opposite) Alexander Graham Bell, one of the primary inventors of the telephone

Progressive leaders included journalists, educators, and ministers, as well as politicians for whom reform was a winning issue. They believed in efficiency, honesty, and applying practical knowledge to solve public issues, and they were intent on rousing the public against abuses. President Theodore Roosevelt called the progressive journalists who uncovered corruption and corporate malfeasance "muckrakers." He thought they often went too far, but the term became a badge of honor. Muckraking journalists wrote damning accounts of sweatshops, insurance and drug businesses, prostitution, and more.

Seldom was dishonesty in American public life more blatant than in the "Gilded Age" (a term coined by Mark Twain), nor did the gap open more widely between untaxed wealth and the modest incomes of working- and middle-class people. Wealthy families lived in a splendor unprecedented in America. The richest one percent of Americans held about 38 percent of national wealth. The most obvious participants in this Gilded Age wealth were the top industrialists and financiers, known as the robber barons, men such as Andrew Carnegie, John D. Rockefeller, Jay Gould, James Duke, J. P. Morgan, and Andrew Mellon. As though to atone for their materialism, these men also became some of the nation's greatest philanthropists. Their institutions, museums, and foundations continue to enrich American life today.

Before 1916 income tax did not exist; federal revenues came mainly from tariffs, excise taxes, and sale of public lands. Virtually every city had its political boss at the head of a crooked "machine," with New York City's notorious Tammany Hall machine and the Tweed Ring the most infamous. State legislatures were cesspools of corruption in which large corporations freely bought favors. Many congressmen were openly "on the take."

The federal government's powers were more limited than they would be in the century to come, and Congress was the chief initiator of policy, not the president. Gilded Age presidents were mostly earnest, bewhiskered men who could do little about the corruption of the day. James Garfield was assassinated in 1881 by a disappointed office seeker, a tragedy that helped push his successor, Chester Arthur, into signing the Pendleton Act in 1883, establishing the Civil Service system. Democrat Grover Cleveland made his reputation chiefly by vetoing more pension bills and special-interest legislation than all other Gilded Age presidents combined. These presidents saw their job as administrators, not as policymakers.

In the 1890s, corrupt city bosses and rich tycoons had more and more power; farmers and workingmen had less and less. Midwestern Populists advocated a return to the agrarian ideal. With modern farm machinery producing an oversupply of crops, prices dropped; high freight rates cut further into farm profits. Farmers were being

Serbian-born inventor Nikola Tesla demonstrates his magnifying transmitter in his Colorado Springs laboratory in 1899.

George Eastman's Brownie camera, introduced in 1900, made photography available to the masses.

1876	1879	1889	1895	1901
Telephone patented by Alexander Graham Bell	Thomas A. Edison invents electric lightbulb	Andrew Carnegie publishes "The Gospel of Wealth"	Atlanta Compromise speech by Booker T. Washington	Theodore Roosevelt becomes president

marginalized, left out of the new America. With the influential Farmers' Alliance and People's Party paving the way, the great orator William Jennings Bryan captured some of the Populists' imagination and ended up on the Democratic ticket for president in 1896. "The farmer who goes forth in the morning," he roared, "and toils all day . . . is as much of a businessman as the man who goes upon the Board of Trade and bets upon the price of grain."

Though Bryan lost races for the presidency three times, his voice was not lost. Progressives and Populists pushed for reform in politics, business, and other facets of American life. Laws were passed to break up trusts, to enact a graduated income tax, to provide referenda on state policies, to recall corrupt officials, to elect senators directly, to give women the vote, to close saloons, and to ensure hygiene in food and housing. Many of these became law by constitutional amendment; the amendment prohibiting the liquor trade was the only one repealed.

The Constitution had been written for an agrarian nation; the reformists tried to adapt it to urban, industrial society. With Teddy Roosevelt as president, real federal reform began. Stronger than any president since the Civil War, Roosevelt began the attempt to break Rockefeller's Standard Oil Company, Duke's tobacco trust, the railroad trust, and others. Known as a trustbuster, Roosevelt was, in fact, in favor of big business, just against bad business. His less forceful successor, William Howard Taft, actually brought more antitrust cases, but Roosevelt set the tone of presidential reform.

In other areas of reform, emerging women leaders such as Susan B. Anthony, Elizabeth Cady Stanton, Jane Addams, and Victoria Woodhull sought equality for their gender. African Americans Mary Ann Cary, Booker T. Washington, W. E. B. Du Bois, Paul Dunbar, Jack Johnson, and Carter G. Woodson represented a rising voice for racial equality among a minority population that had been in America since the beginning. Among Native Americans, Crazy Horse, Sitting Bull, Spotted Elk, Cochise, Geronimo, Black Elk, Sarah Winnemucca, and Zitkala-Sa fought for their people with both arrows and words.

American cultural life shifted as well during this period. Movies and radio, automobiles and airplanes reshaped the way people lived. Millions of Europeans, Asians, and southern blacks migrated to northern American cities. And Americans discovered and embraced jazz, modern art, and fundamentalism. Museums in the United States became institutional repositories of American life and lore. The International Exhibition of Modern Art, known as the Armory Show, held for several weeks in 1913 in New York City, was the country's first big showing of modern art.

Recruitment posters in 1917 called upon young men's patriotism prior to the World War I draft.

Henry Ford, age 37, demonstrates an early automobile in 1900; his inexpensive cars would soon populate the roads.

1903	**1903**	**1908**	**1917**	**1918**
Wright brothers test first successful plane at Kitty Hawk	W. E. B. Du Bois publishes *The Souls of Black Folk*	Henry Ford introduces Model T & assembly-line production	U.S. enters World War I	WWI ends; flu epidemic kills 600,000 Americans

BIOGRAPHIES

INVENTORS, REFORMERS & MONEYMAKERS 1877–1918

Having just emerged from Reconstruction, America entered a period of industrial growth. Westward expansion continued to open up opportunities, and 10 new states were created. An era of unprecedented wealth brought lavish living for some, while reforms in politics and commerce helped the poor. Still, those at the bottom were mired in poverty. Meanwhile, a surge of immigrants expanded the population, pumping new blood into America.

JANE ADDAMS
★ 1860–1935 ★
SOCIAL REFORMER, PEACE ACTIVIST

Poor health and a late start did not prevent Jane Addams from accomplishing so much in life that British labor leader John Burns called her "the only saint America has produced." That the social reformer, peace activist, and humanitarian did much of her work before women had the vote indicates how extraordinary was her gift to the world. Addams grew up, the eighth of nine children, in Cedarville, Illinois. Her father was a successful businessman and supporter of Abraham Lincoln. Addams's early life was marked by two important events. Her mother died when she was two; later, a bout of tuberculosis left her with a crooked spine.

Jane Addams She led the way in hands-on social work and reform.
Inset: Her 1910 book

Raised by a father and stepmother who believed in community involvement, Addams attended Rockford Female Seminary and was among the first women college graduates in the country. She quickly became known as a charismatic leader, serving as class president, president of the literary society, editor of the school magazine, and valedictorian.

Women at that time who wanted a career in community service were relegated to missionary work or teaching. Addams was uninterested in either of these, and even less so in the only other alternative—homemaking. She attended a woman's medical college for one term and then dropped out. Pain caused by her deformed spine left her bedridden for six months. Finally she underwent surgery, which was successful enough that she could begin to consider her options. Upon the death of her father, she inherited enough money to make a comfortable start.

Addams began traveling in Europe with close friend Ellen Gates Starr. In 1888, she visited Toynbee Hall, a community center in an impoverished London neighborhood. She decided to open a similar house in Chicago. She and Starr settled on a run-down mansion built by Charles Hull in the 1850s. Hull-House would become a model for hundreds of such houses across the United States.

Hull-House offered day care for working mothers, a kindergarten, and boys' club. Over time, it added a coffee shop, night courses, library, and meeting rooms. Addams began to see her mission not only as philanthropic but also as an agent of community empowerment. As

> *Of all the aspects of social misery nothing is so heartbreaking as unemployment.*
>
> **JANE ADDAMS**

such, she encouraged residents to lobby for local civic improvements—in sanitation, factory working conditions, the juvenile court system, and others.

From 1909 to 1915, her most productive years, Addams became a leader in many national women's organizations, advocated woman's suffrage, and authored six books. As a pacifist and president of the Women's International League for Peace and Freedom, she traveled in Europe and Asia, giving speeches

Horatio Alger, Jr. **His plucky heroes worked their way to the top of the capitalist heap.**

and meeting with civic leaders. In 1931, she became the first U.S. woman to win the Nobel Peace Prize, recognized for her "expression of an essentially American democracy of spirit."

HORATIO ALGER, JR.
★ 1832–1899 ★
WRITER

Harvard-trained minister Horatio Alger was the most popular American author in the last third of the 1800s. His first huge success, *Ragged Dick; or, Street Life in New York,* depicted the story of a boy who rose from rags to riches, and became a model for his type of hero—a man who through honesty, hard work, good attitude, and luck attains great financial and personal rewards. By the time of his death, Alger's formulaic stories had begun to go out of style; he had published more than 100 books.

The Age of Invention
DISCOVERIES SPUR EARLY TECHNOLOGY BUBBLE
★ ★ ★

The first "great" age of American technology—without which there would be no computers—occurred in the late 19th century. Scientists, inventors, and tinkerers were continually dreaming up new solutions to old problems and experimenting and testing until coming out with practical devices that altered the way people lived. Discoveries in the fields of electricity and electromagnetism helped spur this early technology bubble. Just as today, inventions often led to new industries, which in turn created enormous consumer demands and modern corporate giants.

The first telephone, patented in 1876 by Alexander Graham Bell, was one of many marvels on display at the American Centennial Exhibition in Philadelphia that same year. By 1900, there were nearly 600,000 phones in Bell's telephone system, American Telephone and Telegraph Company (AT&T), which had formed in 1885. Bell's rival, Thomas A. Edison, turned out a host of inventions. In 1877, Edison invented the phonograph. In 1879 came his electric incandescent lightbulb, and soon after, he won J. P. Morgan's financial backing to establish the Edison Electric Illuminating Company, which lit up New York

City's financial district. Competition with Edison goaded George Westinghouse to develop alternating current as a cheaper substitute for direct current. Edison merged with competitors in 1892 to incorporate the General Electric Company. Other late 1800s inventors include Henry Ford (early gasoline-powered car), George Eastman (Kodak camera), Francis and Freelan Stanley (Stanley Steamer automobile), and Guglielmo Marconi (first wireless telegraphy patent).

Edison phonograph

SUSAN B. ANTHONY
★ 1820–1906 ★
WOMEN'S RIGHTS ACTIVIST

Though an early champion of abolition and temperance, Susan B. Anthony is best known for her pioneering work for women's rights. She overcame her weakness as a public speaker to spread her message through hundreds of lectures and interviews. And as one of five women to appear on the back of the $10 bill (with suffragist Elizabeth Cady Stanton and others), Anthony continues to shine today as a brave and stubborn crusader.

Born into a family of Quakers in Adams, Massachusetts, Anthony became involved in the antislavery movement in the 1840s. In 1845, she moved with her

Members of the Manhattan delegation march in a Woman Suffrage Party parade in New York City in 1915. More than 25,000 people participated in the event.

family to a farm near Rochester, New York, where they held abolition meetings with the likes of Frederick Douglass and William Lloyd Garrison. Anthony was at this time a schoolteacher, a profession she followed from 1839 to 1849. But her real passion was for reform. She forged her mettle during these years, facing down threats and hostile mobs, and continuing to hand out leaflets, put up posters, and make antislavery speeches.

I declare to you that woman must not depend upon the protection of man, but must be taught to protect herself, and there I take my stand.

SUSAN B. ANTHONY

Susan B. Anthony She was an early and ardent proponent of women's suffrage.

While continuing her work for abolitionism, Anthony also became involved with both the temperance movement and educational reform. She was outraged that because she was a woman, she was not allowed to speak at an Albany temperance rally in 1853. That year, she formed the Women's State Temperance Society of New York. Soon after, at a state teachers' convention Anthony lobbied for better pay for women teachers and requested that women have a say at the convention. She would later speak out for equal education for both genders and all races.

Through her work with various causes, it became clear to Susan Anthony that one glaring overall issue demanded her complete attention: women's rights. In the early 1850s, she met and began working with Elizabeth Cady Stanton; together, with skills and personalities that complemented each other, they would begin expanding the women's rights movement into an unstoppable force. They worked together for voting rights, property rights, and educational opportunities. Anthony even pushed for dress reform, and for a while wore bloomers, which became a symbol of the movement.

After the Civil War, Anthony broke with the former abolitionists because of their support for the 15th Amendment, which gave voting rights to black men but not to women. In 1869, she and Stanton created the National Woman Suffrage Association. Its goal: an amendment to the U.S. Constitution giving women the right to vote.

During the 1870s and 1880s, Stanton kept up a busy round of speaking tours and petition gathering, and she co-edited with Stanton and Matilda Joslyn Gage a multivolume work entitled *History of Woman Suffrage.* She also published a weekly newspaper, *The Revolution,* whose motto was, "Men their rights, and nothing more; women their rights, and nothing less."

In her last speech, in 1906, she said, "I am here for a little time only, and then my place will be filled . . . The fight must not cease. You must see that it does not stop. Failure is impossible." Her death the next month was only a pause in the avalanche she had helped start. In 1920, Congress ratified the 19th Amendment, giving women the vote.

CHESTER A. ARTHUR
★ **1829–1886** ★
21ST U.S. PRESIDENT

The assassination of President James Garfield elevated Vice President Chester Arthur to a position the public was not ready for him to hold. An unpopular figure before his presidency, Arthur managed to calm the public with a steady hand, moderate political positions, and an inclusive administration.

I may be president of the United States, but my private life is nobody's damned business.

CHESTER A. ARTHUR

The oldest of nine children, Arthur grew up in villages in Vermont and upstate New York. In 1854, he became a partner in a New York City law firm and began taking civil rights cases. In 1855, he won blacks the right to ride on New York's streetcars.

During the Civil War, Arthur served as New York State's quartermaster general. Afterward, he worked his way up in the Republican Party, becoming its state chairman. He was also the customhouse collector, and because of a corruption investigation, he was asked by President Rutherford Hayes to resign. When the Republican National Convention of 1880 nominated James Garfield for president, Arthur was put up for the number two spot to appease New York's delegates.

Arthur became president on Garfield's death in 1881. Arthur's wife having died the year before, he installed his sister, Mary, as White House hostess. He vetoed a bill that would have halted Chinese immigration for 20 years, supported the reform-heavy Pendleton Civil Service Reform Act, and helped modernize the Navy. The tall, handsome leader had a kidney disease for most of his presidency; though it gave him pain, he kept it secret. He let his name be thrown into the 1884 presidential race, but lost the nomination.

Chester A. Arthur **Upon the assassination of President James Garfield, he became president and guided the nation for the next four years.** *Inset:* **An 1883 pin with the president's image**

ALEXANDER GRAHAM BELL

★ 1847–1922 ★

INVENTOR, EDUCATOR

Alexander Graham Bell was determined from an early age to make a name for himself. Bell was born in Edinburgh, Scotland, to a musician mother who was partially deaf and a father who taught the deaf to speak. From early on, Bell was a gifted musician who played by ear. But he would dedicate his life to the science of speech and sound, and the education of the deaf.

As a teenager, Bell began teaching music and speech in return for instruction in other subjects. With his two brothers he helped his father demonstrate visible speech, a system invented by his father to help those with deafness speak—symbols indicated the various position the lips, tongue, and throat had to assume to produce words.

By the late 1860s, Bell, living in London with his family, began doing experiments with acoustics, using electrically charged tuning forks to produce vowel sounds. Then, both of Bell's brothers died of tuberculosis. In 1870, looking for a

Alexander Graham Bell His telephone catapulted the communications industry into the future.

Queen Victoria's telephone, from 1877, was one of Bell's. She used it at Osborne House, Isle of Wight.

more salubrious climate, Bell's father moved what remained of the family to Brantford, Ontario, Canada. The family's fame as pioneers of deaf speech grew, and one year later a school in Boston requested a demonstration of visible speech. The elder Bell sent his son. Alexander soon opened a school in Boston for teachers of the deaf, and became a professor of vocal physiology at Boston University.

One of the many friends the affable, bright man made in Boston was a lawyer named Gardiner Greene Hubbard. Hubbard's daughter Mabel, deaf from scarlet fever at a young age, was one of Bell's students. When Hubbard found that Bell was conducting experiments with telegraphy,

Hubbard was impressed enough to offer him financial support, hoping that Bell might come up with something that could compete with Western Union. Bell was at that time trying to devise a way to send simultaneous messages over one wire, but he soon began envisioning a completely new method of communication—transmitting the spoken voice through a wire. He teamed up with an electrical instrument maker named Thomas A. Watson, and between 1874 and 1876, they created the telephone.

On March 10, 1876, three days after receiving a patent for his new, unproven device, Bell spoke into his transmitter: "Mr. Watson, come here. I want to see you." He had spilled battery acid on his clothes; he had also just uttered the first audible words through a telephone.

The following year, Bell Telephone Company was born, and two days later, on July 11, 1877, Bell married Mabel Hubbard. They set sail for England to introduce the telephone abroad. Returning the next year, they settled in Washington, D.C. Uninterested in the business side of telephony, Bell sold his stock early, having made enough to be set for life.

Bell continued to live a busy, productive life, developing a method for making phonograph records on wax disks, experimenting with genetics, conducting research into aviation, and succeeding his father-in-law as president of the National Geographic Society. In 1890, he founded the American Association to Promote the Teaching of Speech to the Deaf.

BLACK ELK
★ 1863–1950 ★
HOLY MAN

Sioux medicine man, veteran of Wounded Knee, and second cousin of Crazy Horse, Black Elk is known for his memoir *Black Elk Speaks,* which he dictated to ethnologist John G. Neihardt. During a serious illness as a child, Black Elk had a vision of being taken by Thunder Beings to a place where profound truths about the Earth and its people were revealed. The experience left a deep impression upon him, and, following a long-standing family tradition, he became a healer and holy man and continued to have important visions.

In 1887, he traveled to England with Buffalo Bill's Wild West show. Three years later he participated in the Sioux's final battle against the U.S. Army, at

> *Everything an Indian does is in a circle, and that is because the power of the world always works in circles.*
>
> **BLACK ELK**

Wounded Knee (in present-day South Dakota). He became a Catholic in 1904; as he later explained, "My children had to live in this world." As an old man he related the story of his life and outlined many sacred Sioux rituals. Mythologist Joseph Campbell is one of numerous scholars and writers influenced by Black Elk's story.

"And while I stood there," Black Elk said of his vision, "I saw more than I can tell and understood more than I saw; for I was seeing in a sacred manner the shapes of all things in the spirit, and the shape of all shapes as they must live together like one being. And I saw that the sacred hoop of my people was one of many hoops that made one circle, wide as daylight and as starlight."

Black Elk His stories, related to poet John Neihardt, became canonic Native American literature, vital as a counterweight to the industrial age.

WILLIAM JENNINGS BRYAN

★ 1860–1925 ★

ORATOR, STATESMAN

William Jennings Bryan was a brilliant orator and reform-minded politician who became a leader in the Democratic and Populist Parties and ran for president three times. He grew up in Illinois and, as a lawyer, moved to Lincoln, Nebraska, in 1887. He was elected to Congress in 1890 and built a reputation as a skilled debater who opposed the gold standard, which was supported by eastern bankers and industrialists.

After losing a bid for the Senate, Bryan became a newspaper editor and popular lecturer. Running for president in 1896, he won the Democratic nomination thanks to his stirring speech at the Democratic Convention in which he excoriated the gold standard opposition.

He gave 600 speeches in 27 states, but lost to the well-financed William McKinley. He again challenged McKinley in 1900, and lost. He ran a final time, in 1908, and lost to William Howard Taft. His political career was revived in 1913, when Bryan was appointed secretary of state by Woodrow Wilson. As a pacifist, however, he resigned in 1915 when Wilson took an aggressive stance toward Germany at the outset of World War I. Yet when the United States did get

> *You shall not press down upon the brow of labor this crown of thorns, you shall not crucify mankind upon a cross of gold.*
>
> **WILLIAM JENNINGS BRYAN**

involved, Bryan enthusiastically supported the effort.

In his final chapter, Bryan helped prosecute a Tennessee teacher for espousing Darwinism. Known as the Scopes trial, Bryan's religious fundamentalism won the day against modern science, but the orator paid a high price for the strain. Not long after the trial, he died.

ANDREW CARNEGIE

★ 1835–1919 ★

INDUSTRIALIST, PHILANTHROPIST

The leading steel manufacturer and one of the wealthiest individuals of his time, Andrew Carnegie ended up giving much of his money to educational, cultural, and scientific institutions. Born in Scotland, Carnegie moved with his family to Allegheny City, Pennsylvania, when he was 12. Mostly self-educated, he found work in a Pittsburgh telegraph office. During the Civil War, he assisted in the organization of the military telegraph system and began working for the Pennsylvania Railroad and investing in small iron mills and factories. Recognizing the importance of steel as a replacement for iron, he created a steel rail company in 1873.

Within three years, Carnegie's company was worth more than $1 million, and he kept expanding during an economic slump and pouring profits back into the company. A shrewd businessman, Carnegie bought the majority of H. C. Frick's coalfields and furnaces, which were vital to the making of steel. The conglomerate company, helmed by both Carnegie and Frick, was thus able to drive out competition and become the country's largest steelworks. During a violent strike at the Homestead steel plant in

William Jennings Bryan One of American's greatest orators delivers a campaign speech; he ran for president three times but never won.

Andrew Carnegie Almost as well known for his philanthropy as his industrial achievements

1892, Carnegie in absentia let Frick force the plant's reopening, thus apparently opposing organized labor. Carnegie outmuscled his competition for years; then he decided to sell out to the U.S. Steel Corporation in 1901 for nearly $500 million. He spent the rest of his life doling out hundreds of millions to build public libraries and technical schools, and to set up a number of charitable organizations.

MARY ANN SHADD CARY
★ 1823–1893 ★
ABOLITIONIST

The oldest child of free black parents, Mary Ann Shadd Cary was born in Wilmington, Delaware, and was sent to school in Pennsylvania, where education of blacks was legal. Cady moved to Ontario in 1851 after the United States passed the Fugitive Slave Act of 1850 and helped found a newspaper, *Provincial Freeman,* for blacks in Canada. There she assisted escaped slaves. After the war, she moved to Washington, D.C., taught school, became a lawyer, and worked for women's rights.

MARY CASSATT
★ 1844–1926 ★
ARTIST

Born into a wealthy Pennsylvania family, Mary Cassatt became a member of the French Impressionists. She moved to Paris in 1866 and, because the prestigious École des Beaux-Arts was closed to women, took private lessons. She later became a friend of painter Edgar Degas, whose informality of style had a strong influence on Cassatt's work. Adept at painting women, Cassatt employed bright colors and quick brushstrokes like the other Impressionists. In addition to painting, Cassatt influenced Americans to purchase Impressionist art. Failing eyesight forced her to give up painting for the last decade of her life.

Greater Good
THE GOLDEN AGE OF PHILANTHROPY
★★★

Although the robber barons of the late 19th and early 20th centuries enjoyed lavish living, they also used their wealth to establish important and enduring public institutions. Andrew Carnegie's thousands of libraries are but one example. Partner Henry Clay Frick, although not quite as charitable, bequeathed his New York City home (and a big endowment) to create one of the country's finest art museums. John Pierpont Morgan, who bought Carnegie's steel company, became a benefactor of the New York Public Library, the Metropolitan Museum of Art, the Cathedral of St. John the Divine, and many hospitals and institutions. John D. Rockefeller, head of Standard Oil, established the Rockefeller Institute for Medical Research, the General Education Board, the Rockefeller Foundation, and the Laura Spelman Rockefeller Memorial foundation. Railroad magnate Leland Stanford founded Stanford University.

Mary Cassatt was an artist and member of the French Impressionists. Shown here is her painting titled "Two Seated Women."

GROVER CLEVELAND

★ 1837–1908 ★

22ND & 24TH U.S. PRESIDENT

"Uncle Jumbo," as relatives called Grover Cleveland, was the only president to serve nonconsecutive terms. A portly, good-humored man, Cleveland led during a difficult period of financial upheaval and labor unrest. He won respect for taking positions that were prudent if not always popular; his unprecedented use of the veto strengthened executive power.

Born into a large family in northern New Jersey, Cleveland moved from one town to the next as the son of a minister. In 1858, he passed the New York bar exam and became a lawyer. He avoided fighting

Campaign medallions, like this one for Cleveland, were popular in the 1800s.

in the Civil War by paying a substitute to take his place; the practice was common at the time, but political opponents later criticized him for it. It didn't prevent him becoming district attorney, sheriff, mayor of Buffalo, and eventually governor of New York (1883–85).

During his first term as president (1885–89), Cleveland, the first Democrat to be elected since 1856, beefed up the Navy, helped clean up corruption in federal jobs, and tried to oppose tariff laws that favored big business. He was generally against imperialism, subsidies, and special interests. Time and again he battled a Republican Senate, resorting to the presidential veto 584 times.

In 1886, Cleveland became the only president to be married in the White House when he wed his 21-year-old ward, the daughter of a law partner. The press satirized the 27-year-age difference.

Cleveland's second term (1893–97) coincided with one of the worst economic depressions in the country's history. He and his party were blamed. His popularity, at a peak at the start of his term, plummeted. He retired to Princeton, New Jersey, where he served as a trustee and lecturer at Princeton University.

Grover Cleveland He was the only president to serve nonconsecutive terms and the first Democrat to be elected after the Civil War.

WILLIAM "BUFFALO BILL" CODY

★ 1846–1917 ★

SHOWMAN

William Cody grew up on the Great Plains and spent his teenage years in cattle drives and on wagon trains before trying his hand as a trapper, gold miner, Pony Express rider, and Army scout—all before the age of 26. By that point, he had a reputation as the western legend "Buffalo Bill," and he took that persona to the stage, starring in a Chicago play. His success led him to found his own troupe, along with Texas Jack and Wild Bill Hickok. Cody eventually created the Wild West show, an outdoor extravaganza that showcased the skills of actual

Buffalo Bill Cody He created the legendary Wild West show.

cowboys, cowgirls (including Annie Oakley), and Native Americans. In 1887, Cody's show constituted the featured American performance at Queen Victoria's Golden Jubilee in London. Duped by a Denver businessman, Cody was forced to auction off the Wild West show in 1913. He died four years later. At his request he was buried above Denver on Lookout Mountain.

CRAZY HORSE
★ CA 1842–1877 ★
SIOUX CHIEF

An Oglala Sioux chief, Crazy Horse was a leader in the Indian uprising against removal to a reservation in the Dakota Territory. He was one of the primary chiefs in the 1877 Battle of the Little Big Horn against U.S. troops.

My lands are where my dead lie buried.

CRAZY HORSE

Though no photos of Crazy Horse are confirmed to exist, accounts describe him as fairer of skin and hair than most of his people, which helped define his individuality. He became known for his bravery, tactical brilliance, and an ability to avoid death that seemed to imbue him with magical properties. His people called him "Strange One." Growing up in and around the Black Hills of present-day South Dakota, he became a young man at a time when U.S. settlers and gold prospectors were pushing into the region.

Crazy Horse This tintype may be the only photo of the Sioux chief; however, some question its authenticity.

In 1866, he helped lead an attack on Capt. William Fetterman and his 80 men, resulting in a massacre of U.S. troops. Then, in 1876, Gen. George Crook was sent to drive the Indians out of their encampments in the Montana Territory. Crazy Horse's surprise attack in the Rosebud Valley forced Crook out. The final big defense of his homeland took place on June 25, 1876, when Crazy Horse joined with Chief Sitting Bull on the Little Bighorn River. The combined army wiped out Lt. Col. George Custer's battalion.

He was relentlessly pursued afterward. With his tribe's numbers down from cold and hunger, Crazy Horse surrendered in Nebraska on May 6, 1877. He was killed while resisting a soldier's attempt to put him in jail.

James Buchanan Duke The magnate built a tobacco empire in North Carolina.

JAMES BUCHANAN DUKE
★ 1856–1925 ★
TOBACCO MAGNATE, PHILANTHROPIST

Born on a farm near Durham, North Carolina, James Duke became a powerhouse in the tobacco and cigarette industries. After studying business in New York, he returned home and began applying new production and marketing techniques to his father's tobacco factory. The acquisition of a cigarette-rolling machine in 1884 vastly sped up the manufacturing process. Duke promoted the family product by advertising on billboards and giving free cigarettes to immigrants. By 1889, he had merged his interests with other tobacco producers and controlled the vast majority of the market. A generous philanthropist, Duke was a major benefactor of Trinity College, which was renamed Duke University.

GEORGE DEWEY
★ 1837–1917 ★
ADMIRAL

A naval commander who defeated the Spanish at Manila Bay in the Philippines, George Dewey served in the Civil War and then rose in rank to commodore by 1896. Though not popular with his colleagues, he was also put in command of the Navy's Asiatic squadron in 1897. When war broke out between Spain and the United States in 1898, he sailed into Manila's harbor at midnight of May 1. His attack on the Spanish fleet began at dawn. By noon his six ships had beaten the enemy's 10, with no loss of American life. He was feted as a hero on his return to the United States.

PAUL LAURENCE DUNBAR
★ 1872–1906 ★
POET, WRITER

The son of former slaves, Paul Laurence Dunbar grew up in Dayton, Ohio, and was the only African American in his high school, where he was editor of the school newspaper. After graduation, Dunbar found work as an elevator operator and wrote in his spare time. In 1896, his poetry received favorable attention from novelist and critic William Dean Howells; he began giving public readings in the United States and Great Britain. The next year he took a job as a researcher in the Library of Congress in Washington, D.C. His later stories began to explore themes of racial inequality.

MARY BAKER EDDY
★ 1821–1910 ★
RELIGIOUS THINKER & LEADER

The founder of the First Church of Christ, Scientist, Mary Baker Eddy was raised on a New Hampshire farm. She was often ill as a child and young adult, and so she resorted to various cures, including homeopathy and mesmerism. Over time she became convinced that true healing was more of a spiritual than physical process. Her readings about Jesus' healing powers gave her proof. "The Bible was my textbook," according to Eddy. She began teaching and writing about the metaphysical nature of healing. She founded the First Church of Christ, Scientist in Boston in 1879 and the *Christian Science Monitor* newspaper in 1908.

Mary Baker Eddy The First Church of Christ, Scientist was founded by Eddy in Boston in 1879.

The Ghost Dance

A PROPHETIC VISION TO RESTORE HARMONY

★ ★ ★

The Ghost Dance ceremony originated in Nevada around 1870, soon faded, only to reemerge in its best known form in the late 1880s—largely out of anger and fear felt by American Indians regarding the onslaught of white settlers, military brutalization, and legislative oppression. Conditions were so severe that the Indians needed something to give them hope. The spiritual movement began with a dream by a Northern Paiute, Wovoka, during the solar eclipse on January 1, 1889. Wovoka claimed that he had entered the spirit world and seen the Earth open up to swallow all whites. At the same time, he saw all Indians rising up into the sky. Through repeated performance of the Ghost Dance, he claimed the dream, which promised harmony and freedom for Native Americans, would become a reality. Wovoka's message spread quickly throughout much of the Great Plains, developing an intensity that alarmed white settlers and the federal government. The movement reached its peak just before the Wounded Knee Massacre in December 1890, during which U.S. soldiers opened fire on the Sioux, killing more than 150 (some estimates put the number as high as 300). As news of the massacre spread, interest in the Ghost Dance and Wovoka's prophecies waned. What had started as a peaceful movement was brutally ended a year later by the military.

Native Americans partake in the Ghost Dance by forming a circle, chanting, and throwing dust over their heads. Paiute holy man Wovoka claimed that performing the dance would reunite the living with the dead, force white settlers to leave, and bring prosperity and peace to Indian peoples.

THOMAS ALVA EDISON

★ 1847–1931 ★

INVENTOR

The embodiment of America's inventive spirit, Thomas A. Edison produced more than a thousand inventions in a long life of hard work. Among his many inventions were an automatic telegraph repeater, quadruplex telegraph, printing telegraph, electric pen, mimeograph, carbon telephone transmitter, microphone, phonograph, Ediphone, incandescent electric lamp, electric valve, system of telegraphy for communicating with moving trains, kinetoscope, alkaline store battery, and talking motion pictures.

Thomas Alva Edison The man of a thousand inventions poses in his laboratory in 1906.

Edison moved with his family in 1854 from Ohio to Port Huron, Michigan, where he was a dreamy, unruly schoolboy. Working on a train as a newspaper seller at a young age, he experimented with chemicals in the baggage car, until the car caught fire. As a telegraph operator he blew up a telegraph station while tinkering with a battery.

> *There is
> no substitute
> for hard work.*
>
> **THOMAS EDISON**

Through his reading and tinkering, he derived his first patent, for an electric vote counter, in 1869. Failing to find a buyer, he formulated a rule: "Anything that won't sell, I don't want to invent."

By the mid-1870s, Edison's lab in Menlo Park, New Jersey, was buzzing with activity; he recruited scientists, technicians, and machinists to produce inventions to order. He also became a great promoter of his "invention factory." He once boasted "a minor invention every ten days and a big thing every six months or so." He kept his team working day and night, reviving them with food, drink, small talk, and organ music.

Edison's ability to transform one invention into another produced the phonograph, the incandescent light, motion-picture projector, and a microphone-like carbon transmitter that improved the telephone's audibility.

He thought it would take six weeks to come up with a safe, cheap electric light. It took more than a year. His team, arriving at a solution in 1879, had to rig up a system to provide houses with the marvel, so they created lamps, screw-in sockets, light switches, insulated wire, meters, fuses, and a central power station. When the Pearl Street station in lower Manhattan came into service in 1882, the world moved from the steam age into the electrical age.

In 1887, Edison set up a larger invention factory in nearby West Orange, his lab growing into a complex with 3,600 workers. Though they cranked out hundreds of patentable inventions over the next few decades, not everything was successful. Edison's storage battery to power an electric car, created after thousands of experiments, was swept aside by Henry Ford's gas buggies.

Soon after Edison's death on October 18, 1931, lights were dimmed at the White House and across the country in honor of the man who had lit the world.

MARSHALL FIELD

★ 1834–1906 ★

BUSINESSMAN

Born on a Massachusetts farm, Marshall Field brought innovations to retail merchandising. As a teen, Field honed his salesmanship working in a dry goods store. In 1856, he took a job in Chicago with a mercantile house, working his way up to partner. By 1881, Field had amassed a small fortune, enough to buy out a partner for $2.5 million and own a merchandising firm he called Marshall Field and Company. It built a reputation for honest customer relations, easy credit, and a return policy. Field's estate, worth $125 million, hugely supported the University of Chicago and the Columbian Museum, later the Field Museum of Natural History.

The Gilded Age

OPULENT LIFESTYLE OF AMERICA'S ROBBER BARONS

★ ★ ★

Opulent mansions, lavish parties, diamonds galore. These and other excesses of the rich came to denote the late 1800s, a period named for Mark Twain's satirical novel *The Gilded Age* (1873). With the rise in industry and consumerism following the Civil War, the time was ripe for savvy businessmen to make vast fortunes. These so-called robber barons seemed at times to compete with each other for the most conspicuous displays of materialism. Nowhere is their opulent lifestyle on greater show than in the fancy houses, quaintly termed "cottages," of Newport, Rhode Island.

Wealthy southern planters had been building fine homes in Newport since the 1830s to escape the summer heat. But the captains of industry added a new dimension to this bayside town. The largest and perhaps most extravagant home was railroad tycoon Cornelius Vanderbilt II's The Breakers, a 70-room cottage, completed in 1895. Its design by architect Richard Morris Hunt reflects the style of Italian Renaissance palaces. Cornelius's brother, William, also employed Hunt to build his 1892 extravaganza, a showplace of marble aptly named Marble House. At the turn of the century, Pennsylvania coal baron Edward J. Berwind modeled The Elms after an 18th-century Parisian château. Architect Stanford White built Rosecliff in 1902, with its tremendous ballroom, in imitation of the Grand Trianon at Versailles.

Maybe 30 men made up this elite club of the superwealthy, among them financier Jay Gould, financier Andrew Mellon, financier Henry Flagler, and industrialist Charles Schwab.

The Breakers, a 70-room cottage built by Cornelius Vanderbilt II and completed in 1895, exemplifies the opulence of the mansions of Newport, Rhode Island.

HENRY FORD
★ 1863–1947 ★
AUTOMOBILE MANUFACTURER

The largest maker of American automobiles in the early 1900s, Henry Ford revolutionized industry by innovating mass production, lowering costs to consumers, and raising employee salaries. By 1927, the Ford Motor Company had sold more than 15 million autos worldwide, half of all automobiles then sold. Ford's name for a while was synonymous with "car."

The oldest of six surviving children, Ford was born on a farm in Dearborn, Michigan. At 16, he went to Detroit and worked in machine shops for three years; he then returned home, married, worked a piece of land his father gave him, and tinkered in his garage. He built his first gas engine in 1893, and his first car, the Quadricycle, in 1896.

Ford was 40 before he finally hit on a formula for success. "The way to make automobiles," he told an investor, "is to make one automobile like another." Pulling together a group of backers, he

That man is best educated who knows the greatest number of things that are so, and who can do the greatest number of things to help and heal the world.

HENRY FORD

organized the Ford Motor Company in 1903 and produced an impressive 1,700 cars in 15 months. Cars were a luxury item not many people could afford. Ford's answer was to increase production by improving efficiency, and thereby lower prices. The first Model T rolled out in 1908. As orders for this no-nonsense car poured in, Ford introduced the first moving assembly line in 1913. When workers complained they were becoming slaves to machines, each laborer doing one repetitive job, Ford raised salaries to five dollars a day, 15 percent higher than the national average.

Such profit sharing allowed Ford to micromanage the behavior of his workers. The company's sociological department visited workers' homes and inquired about their diet, drinking habits, and savings accounts.

As Ford's power increased, he began integrating various facets of production, first manufacturing glass and steel, and then buying up iron and coal mines, a Brazilian rubber plantation, railway, and fleet of ships to

Henry Ford **The innovator (left) sold cars to the masses, especially his Model T (far left), millions of which rolled out of his Highland Park factory in Detroit, Michigan (top).**

ferry material to Dearborn. In control of one of the world's largest industrial empires, Ford was able to buy out his stockholders in 1919. The 1920s saw a decline in the Model T's popularity and a rise in the market share of competitor General Motors. Ford stubbornly refused to change the car, or its color—the only option was black. Finally, after selling more than 15 million Model T's, Ford came out with the Model A in 1927. In 1944, with the company losing money, Ford stepped aside and let his grandson Henry Ford II take over.

Ford's personality was complex and contradictory. An outspoken pacifist, he dedicated his factories to producing tanks and boats during World War I. He bought the *Dearborn Independent* and used it to deride liquor, Wall Street, the gold standard, monopolies, and the "International Jew." He promoted soybeans as a new crop for troubled farms, liked foot racing and folk dancing, and was a practical joker. He fired union organizers and hired thugs to control workers. His son Edsel founded the Ford Foundation, one of the world's largest benefactors of education, research, and development.

JAMES A. GARFIELD
★ 1831–1881 ★
20TH U.S. PRESIDENT

James A. Garfield, the second president to be assassinated, served less than six months before being shot. He lingered for 80 days before succumbing to his wound.

Garfield was born near Cleveland, Ohio, youngest of five children. He graduated from Williams College in Massachusetts in 1856. Athletic, handsome, and affable, Garfield became president of

James A. Garfield He was shot a few months after taking office by a disgruntled office seeker but remained alive for 80 days.

Western Reserve Eclectic Institute in Ohio at 26, after which he studied law and entered politics. In 1862, as a brigadier general in the Civil War, Garfield commanded a brigade at the Battle of Shiloh. The following year he was

A letter to Garfield's mother offers hope.

promoted to major general and later became a U.S. representative.

A Radical Republican during the war years, Garfield was in favor of Reconstruction measures, including confiscation of southern plantations and punishment of Confederate leaders. He was reelected to Congress eight times. In 1880, he took a middle ground between the factions of his party. In so doing, he ended up a dark horse candidate, narrowly winning the election.

Garfield began a reform of the spoils system, which doled out government offices to supporters, but was too late to suit one half-crazed office seeker. Charles Guiteau, passed over as consul in Paris, shot the president on July 2, 1881. The Constitution states that if a president is unable "to discharge the power and duties" of his office, the vice president shall step in. Because this had never happened in U.S. history and Garfield was at times lucid, Vice President Chester Arthur held back. A bullet, lodged near Garfield's spine, caused an infection, and on September 19, the president died.

GERONIMO
★ 1829–1909 ★
APACHE CHIEF

Born in the western part of present-day New Mexico, Geronimo grew up in the Mexican state of Chihuahua. He was a warrior of the Chiricahua Apache and became a symbol of the Indian way of life. From early on Geronimo's distrust of whites was deep—of Mexican soldiers for killing his wife and children, and of American settlers for taking his homelands. After the 1848 Treaty of Guadalupe Hidalgo, which gave the United States a large tract of Mexican land, Anglo-Americans began moving in to set up communities. The resulting disruption of the native population led to the establishment of an Apache reservation.

Confined to one area of Arizona in the mid-1870s, the Apache groups revolted. Geronimo and his followers escaped what they deemed prison and began fighting U.S. troops in the Southwest. For the next 10 years Geronimo's band lived free, hiding out in the countryside. He surrendered in early 1884, but broke out of prison again the following year. Finally, on September 4, 1886, he surrendered to Gen. Nelson Miles, who promised that his band would eventually be allowed to return to Arizona.

Geronimo and his followers were sent by train to Fort Pickens in Florida. In 1894, he was sent to Fort Sill in Oklahoma where he spent the last 14 years of his life. Though he never returned to Arizona, he was allowed to appear at expositions and sell photographs of himself.

> *Socialism holds nothing but unhappiness for the human race.*
>
> **SAMUEL GOMPERS**

Samuel Gompers The labor leader (center) founded the American Federation of Labor (AFL).

1886 established the AFL, an organization that strove for skilled workers' rights but opposed socialism and industrial unionism (organizing workers regardless of skill or trade), which some labor leaders such as Eugene V. Debs, founding member of the Industrial Workers of the World, sought. A powerful speaker and effective strike negotiator, the outgoing Gompers led the mainstream labor movement for 40 years.

SAMUEL GOMPERS
★ 1850–1924 ★
LABOR LEADER

Founder and first president of the American Federation of Labor, Samuel Gompers was born in England to a poor Dutch-Jewish family. They moved to the slums of New York when Gompers was 13, and he found work as a cigarmaker. The following year he and his father joined the local cigarmakers' union. Gompers became a union leader and by

JAY GOULD
★ 1836–1892 ★
FINANCIER, RAILROAD EXECUTIVE

Jay Gould was raised on a farm in Roxbury, New York, and moved to New York City in his early 20s. By the early 1860s, Gould was buying up stock in small rail lines, his goal to wrest control of the railroads from Cornelius Vanderbilt. To acquire the Erie Railroad, he issued stock illegally and then bribed legislators to make the move legal. Gould's next scheme

Geronimo The Apache leader and his band evaded capture by the Army for a decade.

America's Favorite Pastime

THE BEGINNINGS OF BASEBALL
★★★

Though popularized by Union soldiers during the Civil War, baseball was not invented by U.S. Army officer Abner Doubleday, as legend once said. The game evolved gradually, becoming firmly entrenched as "the national pastime" by the late 1800s. Professional baseball started in 1869 with the Cincinnati Red Stockings; by 1903, there were 16 teams in the two major leagues—the National and American. Early greats included Wee Willie Keeler, one of the game's best hitters; King Kelly, a notorious base stealer; Cap Anson, first player with more than 3,000 hits; and pitching legend Charlie "Old Hoss" Radbourn.

By the turn of the 20th century, many players were celebrities, Americans avidly following their careers at the ballpark or in the sports pages. Cy Young, who played from 1890 to 1911, remains the game's all-time leading winning pitcher (511 wins). Outfielder Ty Cobb still holds the highest lifetime batting average (.367). Other early stars include pitchers Christy Mathewson, Grover Cleveland Alexander, and Walter Johnson, and shortstop Honus Wagner.

Pin given to the New York Giants, winners of the second World Series, 1905

was to buy up gold, forcing prices higher, until a financial panic ensued known as Black Friday (September 24, 1869). In the 1870s, he bought major shares in western railroads, and in the 1880s, he gained control of Western Union.

RUTHERFORD B. HAYES
★ 1822–1893 ★
19TH U.S. PRESIDENT

Rutherford Hayes was born in central Ohio and became a lawyer in 1845. He fought admirably in the Civil War, being wounded four times. Hayes served in Congress from 1865 to 1867 and was governor of Ohio. Because of his political and war record and honest reputation, Hayes emerged as the nominee for president at the Republican National Convention of 1876.

An economic depression helped give Democratic candidate Samuel Tilden the edge in popular votes, although he remained one electoral vote short of victory, with four disputed states remaining. Hayes's campaign challenged votes in Florida, South Carolina, Louisiana, and Oregon. With both sides claiming victory, Congress set up a 15-man electoral commission to rule on the disputed votes. Three days before the scheduled inauguration day, the commission awarded all the disputed electoral votes to Hayes, giving him a one-vote victory. Although Democrats charged that Hayes had stolen the election, they were appeased when he called federal troops from the occupied South, ending Reconstruction.

During his presidential tenure, Hayes worked for reform of the civil service. He had vowed to serve only one term and led an active retirement, working for the education of southern blacks, prison reform, and veterans' affairs.

Nobody ever left the Presidency with less regret . . . than I do.

RUTHERFORD B. HAYES

Rutherford B. Hayes The Reconstruction-ending president strikes a Napoleonic pose.

William Randolph Hearst The publisher (left), with Chicago Mayor William Hale Thompson

WILLIAM RANDOLPH HEARST
★ 1863–1951 ★
PUBLISHER

William Randolph Hearst used his inherited wealth to create a publishing empire. He increased the circulation of his newspapers with sensational, often speculative, stories, a style of reporting called "yellow journalism." He left a print legacy of banner headlines, editorial crusades, and color comics.

Hearst was born in San Francisco, his father a U.S. senator and gold rush multimillionaire. He attended Harvard for two years but was expelled for a prank. In 1887, Hearst took the helm of his father's paper, the *San Francisco Examiner,* hired the best writers available, printed stories about crime and government corruption, and began making a mark in the industry.

Hearst's success enabled him to compete with New York publisher Joseph Pulitzer. Buying the *New York Journal* in 1895, Hearst cut the price of the paper, poached writers from Pulitzer, and

snagged more readers. His stories vilifying Spain's presence in Cuba may have helped cause the Spanish-American War in 1898.

Hearst set his sights on becoming U.S. president. He served New York in Congress from 1903 to 1907. He ran unsuccessfully for president, governor of New York, and mayor of New York (twice). He refocused all his energy on publishing, and by the 1930s owned more than 25 larges dailies. Besides a long-term mistress, his main interest was his baroque-style castle in San Simeon, California, which he filled with art treasures purchased on trips abroad. His five sons all continued in the media world.

MATTHEW HENSON
★ 1866–1955 ★
EXPLORER

The 1909 expedition of Matthew Henson and Robert E. Peary is recognized as being the first to reach the North Pole. Born in rural Maryland, Henson at 12 became a cabin boy on a ship based out of Baltimore. Joining with Peary, the black explorer began the first of several Arctic explorations, covering 9,000 miles on dogsleds between 1891 and 1902. In March 1909, the two explorers, accompanied by numerous Inuit and 133 dogs, set out from Ellesmere Island, Canada, to conquer the pole. Peary was given credit for first attaining the top of the world, and Henson's efforts were largely forgotten until he was reinterred in Arlington National Cemetery in 1988.

WINSLOW HOMER
★ 1836–1910 ★
ARTIST

One of the greatest 19th-century American painters, Winslow Homer grew up in the Boston area. He worked as a freelance illustrator in the late 1850s and then moved to New York and began working for *Harper's Weekly.* During the Civil War, the magazine hired him to illustrate battle scenes. After sojourns in Paris and

Matthew Henson Explored the Arctic with Robert Peary

Jack Johnson He was the first African-American heavyweight champion. *Inset:* 1931 boxing match poster

England, Homer returned home and in 1883 made his home in Prouts Neck on the coast of Maine. He became known for dramatic depictions of sea life, as well as rural scenes, often showing children. He honed his watercolor skills during this later part of his life, creating realistic, memorable images vivid with interplays of light and shadow.

> *To gain the kingdom of heaven is to hear what is not said, to see what cannot be seen, and to know the unknowable, and that is Aloha.*
>
> QUEEN LILIUOKALANI

JACK JOHNSON
★ 1878–1946 ★
BOXER

The son of former slaves, Jack Johnson became the first black heavyweight champion. He was born in Galveston, Texas, and worked as a laborer to help support his large family. Johnson started boxing as a teen. By his early 20s, he had established himself on the black boxing circuit and was eager to try for the world heavyweight title. At that time, white boxers refused to fight against blacks, but the outspoken Johnson became too well known to write off.

Breaking the color barrier, he took the title from Tommy Burns in 1908 in Australia. Many white fan and boxers were incensed and began looking for a "Great White Hope" who could defeat Johnson. Former champion James Jeffries came out of retirement for a match in 1910. Fifteen rounds later the "Fight of the Century" ended in Johnson's favor.

The champ dated and married across racial lines and lived a lavish lifestyle. This rankled some in the establishment, and in 1912, Johnson was convicted of violating the Mann Act, for transporting a woman across state lines for immoral purposes. Pretending to belong to a black baseball team, he fled to Canada and then to Europe, living as a fugitive for seven years. He lost in a title fight in Cuba in 1915. Five years later he returned to the United States and served 10 months in jail; then he continued fighting professionally until 1928. He later gave lectures and appeared in vaudeville acts.

QUEEN LILIUOKALANI
★ 1838–1917 ★
HAWAIIAN QUEEN

The first and last reigning queen of Hawaii, Queen Liliuokalani ruled the islands from 1891 to 1893. She was born in Honolulu and took the throne on the death of her brother. Attempting to shore up the monarchy and power of native Hawaiians through the Oni pa'a (Stand Firm) movement, she battled the powerful U.S. sugar industry, trying to frame a new constitution. Sugar plantation owners, led by Sanford Dole, requested that the queen abdicate. To avoid bloodshed, she ultimately stepped aside, though she asked President Cleveland to reinstate her. His efforts were blocked by Dole, she was imprisoned, and Hawaii was annexed by the United States in 1898.

Queen Liliuokalani The last queen of Hawaii reigned before the United States annexed the islands.

Juliette Gordon Low's hat

JULIETTE GORDON LOW

★ 1860–1927 ★

GIRL SCOUTS FOUNDER

Born in Savannah, Georgia, Juliette Gordon Low became founder of the Girl Scouts of the USA, an organization fostering individual growth, character, and self-sufficiency. After a failed marriage, Low met Sir Robert Baden-Powell, founder of the Boy Scouts, on a trip to England in 1911. She later told a cousin, "I've got something for the girls of Savannah, and all of America, and all the world, and we're going to start it tonight!" She began with a troop of 18 girls—known then as Girl Guides. Using natural fund-raising and public relations skills, she ensured that the organization would survive and thrive. Since Low's death, scouting has expanded to include millions of girls.

Juliette Gordon Low Founder (center) of the Girl Scouts of the USA poses with two young scouts.

WILLIAM MCKINLEY

★ 1843–1901 ★

25TH U.S. PRESIDENT

William McKinley was a popular, mainstream Republican during a period of economic prosperity. He was a proponent of the gold standard and tariff protectionism. A considerate, even-tempered man, he was devoted to an invalid wife, Ida, who mourned the loss of their two young daughters.

McKinley was born in Ohio and attended Allegheny College in Pennsylvania. In the Civil War he served with bravery as an aide-de-camp to Rutherford B. Hayes. Afterward he became a prosecuting attorney, and in 1877, he began the first of seven terms as a member of the U.S. House of Representatives. There he sponsored the McKinley Tariff Act, which put high taxes on imports. After serving as governor of Ohio from 1892 to 1896, McKinley was nominated for president. He defeated William Jennings Bryan, who supported the free coinage of silver, a Populist position.

When the U.S. battleship *Maine* exploded in Havana's harbor in Cuba, the press unleashed a barrage of articles persuading the country toward war with Spain, which owned the island nation. A brief war followed, giving the United

States control of the Philippines and other Spanish territories. Though some Republicans opposed what appeared to be an imperialist policy, McKinley did not waver in his expansionist decisions. McKinley won reelection in 1900. On September 5, 1901, he unveiled a free-trade policy at an exposition in Buffalo, New York. The next day an anarchist named Leon Czolgosz shot the president as he reached to shake his hand. Eight days later McKinley died, and Theodore Roosevelt became president.

ANDREW MELLON
★ 1855–1937 ★
FINANCIER

A financier and industrialist, Andrew Mellon served as secretary of the U.S. Treasury from 1921 to 1932. He was born in Pittsburgh to wealthy parents. After studying at the Western University of Pennsylvania (now the University of Pittsburgh), he helped start a lumber concern. On the retirement of his father in 1886, Mellon joined his Pittsburgh bank. He quickly became adept at discerning what start-up companies to finance with loans, and three years later, he established the Union Trust Company of Pittsburgh.

Mellon continued to increase his holdings in such large companies as Gulf Oil, American Locomotive, and Pittsburgh Coal, as well as in public utility, bridgebuilding, hydroelectric, steel, and insurance companies.

One of the richest men in the United States, Mellon became secretary of the treasury in 1921. He advised a reduction in income tax rates, a measure that Congress heeded. The post–World War I national debt then shrank from $24 million to about $16 million during the 1920s. From 1932 to 1933, Mellon served as ambassador to Great Britain.

Mellon's greatest philanthropic gift was the National Gallery of Art in Washington, D.C. He donated his $25 million collection—including numerous Rembrandts, Vermeers, and other great masterpieces—and gave $15 million for the building of the museum, though he did not live to see it open to the public in 1941. Mellon also gave $10 million for the founding of the Mellon Institute of Industrial Research in Pittsburgh (now Carnegie Mellon University).

The Spanish Flu
EPIDEMIC AT HOME AND ABROAD
★ ★ ★

As World War I was coming to an end in 1918, a new disaster struck. A global outbreak of influenza killed 50 million people, about 3 to 5 percent of the world's population. The deadly "Spanish flu" claimed more lives than the war. It was especially lethal to the young because of the overreaction of their immune systems. Some people died within hours.

The shipment of Chinese laborers across Canada to work behind British and French lines on the war's western front may have been the source of the contagion. More than 3,000 of the 25,000 workers transported across Canada starting in 1917 ended up in medical quarantine, many with flu-like symptoms. Wartime trenches, ridden with filth, disease, and death, were likely a breeding ground for the virus. Troops returning to such cities as Boston and Philadelphia helped spread the disease.

The scourge was the worst in American history; more than 25 percent of the U.S. population became sick and more than 600,000 died during the pandemic.

Red Cross volunteers help fight the deadly Spanish flu.

Andrew Mellon Secretary of the treasury and major art collector

J. P. MORGAN
★ 1837–1913 ★
FINANCIER

One of the leading financiers in United States history, John Pierpont Morgan was raised in Hartford, Connecticut, the son of well-to-do international banker Junius Spencer Morgan. J. P. Morgan was educated in Boston, Switzerland, and Germany, and in 1857, he went to work at his father's London bank. The next year he moved to New York. In 1871, Morgan became a partner in the financial firm of Drexel, Morgan and Company. He began investing in railroads and organizing mergers, creating International Harvester, General Electric, and U.S. Steel, the world's first billion-dollar corporation. Morgan became so powerful and influential that during a Wall Street panic in 1907, he calmed the marketplace by loaning money to banks and rallying other bankers and businessmen to join him in pledging their own assets during the crisis.

Given his power, it was not surprising that his methods would come under investigation. A U.S. House committee in 1912 looked into his operations and found no financial misconduct. He was widely reviled, however, as one of the craftiest and greediest of the robber barons. Biographers have discovered a more well rounded, brilliant, and, in fact, quite generous man. Owing to his privileged background, he was fluent in French and German, well versed in literature and the arts, and interested in the natural sciences. He started collecting art as a 19-year-old and later became the reason behind the prominence of the Metropolitan Museum of Art. He gave a large amount to the Harvard Medical School, founded the Lying-in Hospital in New York, helped build the Cathedral of St. John the Divine, and donated huge numbers of his valuable artworks and books to museums and libraries.

After Morgan's death, his son, John Pierpont Morgan, Jr., took over many of his father's positions and became chairman of U.S. Steel. He also extended credit to the Allies during World War I and, after the war, floated loans for European reconstruction.

JOHN MUIR
★ 1838–1914 ★
NATURALIST

Poet, tramp, explorer, and ardent and eloquent voice for wilderness, John Muir was largely responsible for the creation of Yosemite and Sequoia National Parks. He left his mark by convincing people of the value of forest conservation, helping persuade President Theodore Roosevelt to protect 148 million acres of forestlands. "In God's wildness lies the hope of the world," he wrote, echoing Thoreau, "the great fresh unblighted, unredeemed wilderness."

Muir was born in Scotland, moving with his family to Wisconsin when he was 11. He worked on his father's farm but found greater pleasure roaming the surrounding woods and fields. In 1867, he found employment in a carriage-parts factory in Indianapolis. An accident there left him blind for a month, an injury that changed his life; he gave up on mechanical engineering and devoted his life to nature. After a brief period of study in the natural sciences at the University of Wisconsin, he became a wanderer, his investigations taking him far and wide in the "University of Wilderness."

He sailed to Cuba, then Panama, and up the West Coast to San Francisco. After a week in Yosemite in 1868, he found work as a ranch hand and shepherd, and

J. P. Morgan The combative financier was famous for both shrewdness and generosity.

> *Climb the mountains and get their good tidings. Nature's peace will flow into you as sunshine into trees.*
>
> JOHN MUIR

he began sketching the mountain flora and fauna. Though he would continue to roam the world, he had found the place he would call home. He soon became known as a spokesman for Yosemite and in 1871 published his first article, on glacial erosion. With Muir's skill at befriending leaders in the literary and scientific fields, his reputation as a naturalist grew. His popularity and influence as a writer continued to grow as well.

In 1880, Muir married 32-year-old Louisa Strentzel, daughter of a fruit ranch owner. For a while he settled down, helping with the ranch and the raising of two daughters.

His wanderlust returning, Muir made a visit to Yosemite in 1889 and guided the editor of *Century Magazine* around Tuolumne Meadows to show him how sheep were destroying the landscape.

John Muir The naturalist (right) stands with President Teddy Roosevelt atop Glacier Point at Yosemite, which Muir helped preserve as a national park.

Muir's articles in the magazine led to the establishment of Yosemite National Park the following year.

Muir's extensive journeys took him to every continent except Antarctica, and his outpouring of words resulted in 10 books and 300 articles on travel and natural history. In addition to the parks in California, he helped set aside Mount Rainier, Petrified Forest, and Grand Canyon National Parks. In 1892, he and his supporters founded the Sierra Club to, as Muir put it, "do something for wildness and make the mountains glad." They launched a long and ultimately unsuccessful battle to stop the damming of the Hetch Hetchy Valley in Yosemite. Muir died a year after the dam became a reality, but his legacy as one of America's most important conservationists lives on.

The naturalist's journals were filled with his notes and sketches.

ROBERT PEARY
★ 1856–1920 ★
EXPLORER

Though it may never be possible to ascertain if Robert Peary actually reached the North Pole, as he claimed, his Arctic explorations increased the world's geographical knowledge while furthering the possibilities for travel in extreme conditions.

Raised in Maine, Peary attended Bowdoin College before joining the U.S. Navy as a civil engineer. He was assigned by the Navy to survey a canal route across Panama in 1886; he hired Matthew Henson, a black shipman, as an assistant.

A number of explorers at that time were bent on being the first to reach the pole. Their obstacles included frigid weather and shifting ice packs that could close up channels of water. On the ice, these intrepid explorers relied on dogs that pulled heavy sleds called sledges.

In 1886, Peary and Henson began the first of many expeditions to northern Greenland and Arctic Canada, each one giving them knowledge of the terrain and its hazards. They were aided in their

I have got the North Pole out of my system. After twenty-three years of effort, hard work, disappointments, privations, more or less suffering, and some risks.

ROBERT PEARY

travels by the local Inuit people. On a trip begun in 1905, with the support of President Theodore Roosevelt, Peary got to within 175 miles of the pole but was thwarted by melting sea ice. Finally, in 1909, Peary and a team of 24 men, 19 sledges, and 133 dogs made a heroic effort to reach the lofty goal. The final push included Peary, Henson, and four Inuit.

Before his return home, Peary heard that a rival, Frederick Cook, claimed to have made the pole the year before. At the time, his claim was discredited and Peary was given full honors for winning the polar race. Some experts have since questioned whether Peary's calculations were askew because of shifting ice floes.

Robert Peary used this compass when he traveled to the North Pole.

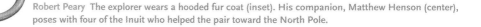

Robert Peary The explorer wears a hooded fur coat (inset). His companion, Matthew Henson (center), poses with four of the Inuit who helped the pair toward the North Pole.

JOSEPH PULITZER
★ 1847–1911 ★
NEWSPAPER PUBLISHER

Joseph Pulitzer came to America as a 17-year-old Hungarian immigrant and rose to become one of the most powerful newspaper publishers and editors in the country. His early plan was to become a soldier. After rejection by the Austrian, French, and British armies because of his weak eyes, he enlisted as a substitute for a draftee in the U.S. Union Army. After the war, he went to St. Louis and found jobs as a muleteer, baggage handler, and waiter.

Pulitzer next went to work as a reporter for a German-language newspaper. By 25, the rising star had become a publisher, and six years later he was owner of the newly merged *Post-Dispatch,* St. Louis's main evening paper. Within a few years this paper, with its populist slant, would make him a rich man.

> *There is not a crime, there is not a dodge, there is not a trick, there is not a swindle, there is not a vice which does not live by secrecy.*
>
> **JOSEPH PULITZER**

In 1883, Pulitzer bought the *New York World* and began turning it into the highest circulating newspaper in the nation. Articles exposed public and private corruption, often taking a sensationalistic tone to grab the attention of readers. Almost completely blind and in poor health after 1887, Pulitzer quit the newsroom and directed his papers from home. He became depressed and extremely sensitive to noise, and went abroad in search of medical help.

Joseph Pulitzer **His newspapers exposed corruption; his bequest founded the Pulitzer Prizes.**

Pulitzer left $2 million to establish a school of journalism at Columbia University; the annual Pulitzer Prizes for excellence in journalism, literature, drama, and music were started with some of this bequest.

The Plight of the Needy
SOCIAL WELFARE AND REFORM IN AMERICA
★ ★ ★

Up until the early 1900s, public government welfare in the United States consisted mainly of benefits to veterans and their families. Privately funded concerns such as Jane Addams's Hull-House and charitable gifts from some of the robber barons attempted to fill an increasingly large need for social relief. In the early 20th century, welfare programs began shifting from the local to the state level, with benefits aimed at needy children and the elderly.

Prodding the nation to open its eyes to the plight of the needy, journalists such as Danish-American social reformer Jacob Riis (1849–1914) delved into the filth of America's slums and tenements, digging up dirt readers could smell and feel. Riis's articles and photographs about New York's underbelly exposed the ugly truths of substandard housing, education, and child labor. His *How the Other Half Lives* (1890) got the attention of Theodore Roosevelt, then a civil service commissioner, who responded, "I have read your book, and I have come to help." The result was an improved water supply, playgrounds, and child labor laws.

Muckraking journalist and political philosopher Lincoln Steffens (1866–1936) penned articles and lectured on crooked leaders in government, business, and labor. In *The Shame of the Cities* (1904) and other books, he took aim at those who profited at the expense of the working poor. Another reform leader, Jacob Coxey (1854–1951) attracted national attention not through writing but by organizing a massive march on Washington to agitate for government jobs during the depression of the 1890s. Though he was arrested for walking on the Capitol lawn, his 500-man army helped prick the conscience of a nation.

Jacob Riis's book helped improve conditions in slums.

JOHN D. ROCKEFELLER
★ 1839–1937 ★
INDUSTRIALIST, PHILANTHROPIST

Though criticized as a monopolist, John D. Rockefeller dominated the U.S. oil industry and became known as much for his philanthropy as his business empire. He was born the son of a peddler in upstate New York, moving with his family to Cleveland in 1853. He first found work as a produce clerk, and by 19, he was a merchant in a grain commission house. When the first oil wells started up in nearby Pennsylvania, he saw the future gushing and built an oil refinery in 1863.

Within two years Rockefeller had the largest refinery in Cleveland. Now he had to secure his position in a highly competitive field. Bringing efficiency to every level of his business, and partnering with Henry Flagler and others, he survived and created the Standard Oil Company in 1870. To control distribution, Rockefeller built pipelines and railroad tank cars, he negotiated special rates with railroads, and bought ships, docks, and warehouses. By the end of the decade, Standard Oil had gone from 10 percent of American refining to 90 percent.

By putting Standard Oil stock into a trust, Rockefeller was able to continue to expand and dominate. When the Ohio Supreme Court ordered him to dissolve the trust in 1892, he cunningly "dissolved the trust" and moved the holdings to a new company in a different state

(New Jersey). Not until 1911 was the U.S. Supreme Court able to break up his monopolistic grip of the oil market.

By 1897, Rockefeller had shifted his entire concern to philanthropy. He donated more than half a billion dollars in his lifetime, mostly through foundations he created for the benefit of

education, medicine, conservation, and other concerns. His only son, John D. Rockefeller, Jr. (1874–1960), continued the charitable work, much of it through the Rockefeller Foundation, established in 1913 to fight hunger, improve health, and address overpopulation and environmental degradation.

John D. Rockefeller The RCA Building (now the Comcast Building), circa 1945, was completed in 1933 and was the centerpiece of Rockefeller Plaza and locus of the Rockefeller empire. *Inset:* A portrait of the philanthropist.

Roosevelt's ivory-handled
Colt revolver

THEODORE ROOSEVELT

★ 1858–1919 ★

26TH U.S. PRESIDENT

Theodore "Teddy" Roosevelt still looms large as one of America's great characters. The youngest person to become president, he engineered the acquisition of the Panama Canal Zone and began construction of the Panama Canal, helped break up Standard Oil and other trusts, preserved vast amounts of land, and won the Nobel Peace Prize for helping end the Russo-Japanese War.

Born into an old Dutch family in New York City, Roosevelt early on proved himself an able scholar and athlete, even though he was small as a child, asthmatic, and nearsighted. At 18, he entered Harvard College, and in 1881, he became a politician, winning three one-year terms to the New York State Assembly and becoming known as a reformer.

Roosevelt's wife and mother both died on the same day, February 14, 1884. The upheaval led Roosevelt to go out to the Dakota Territory, where for two years he operated a cattle ranch, hunted, and became a lover of the great outdoors. The vigorous life helped strengthen the young man into a tough and enthusiastic leader.

Returning to the political world, Roosevelt was appointed by President Harrison to the Civil Service Commission in 1888. Proving himself capable, Roosevelt became head of the Police Department of New York City in 1895. Two years later he was assistant secretary of the Navy. When war broke out against Spain in Cuba, Roosevelt resigned so he could form a cavalry regiment. The reported triumph of his Rough Riders won him widespread fame.

> *The nation behaves well if it treats its natural resources as assets which it must turn over to the next generation increased and not impaired in value.*
>
> **THEODORE ROOSEVELT**

In 1898, Roosevelt became governor of New York. Two years later he was chosen as McKinley's running mate on the Republican ticket. With the assassination of McKinley in 1901, Roosevelt became president of the United States. An impassioned orator and committed reformer, Roosevelt set about becoming a trustbuster, helping to break up business monopolies that exploited workers and consumers. He added an unprecedented 150 million acres to the national forests and established many national parks and monuments. In foreign policy, he believed that America should "speak softly and carry a big stick."

Accordingly, he increased funding to the Navy and sent ships on a world tour, flexing America's military muscle. To easily move the fleet between oceans, he supported revolutionaries in Panama (then part of Colombia); the new Republic of Panama gave the United States the right to build the Panama Canal.

The popular president won reelection in 1904 by a landslide, and continued to expand American influence abroad. He declined, as pledged, to run for another term, but in 1912 he decided to run again. Roosevelt and the Progressive Party, known as the "Bull Moose Party" after Roosevelt received its nomination, only siphoned off votes of progressive Republicans, giving the election to the Democrat Woodrow Wilson. Roosevelt continued to maintain an active life, going on an expedition to the Brazilian jungle in 1913–14. He died at 60 of a blood clot in his heart.

Theodore Roosevelt An 1898 portrait of Roosevelt as commander of a volunteer cavalry unit during the Spanish-American War

UPTON SINCLAIR
★ 1878-1968 ★
WRITER

A muckraking journalist, Upton Sinclair became a best-selling novelist with *The Jungle* (1906), his self-published exposé of the meatpacking industry. He was born in Baltimore, Maryland, and began writing and selling stories as a teenager. After several failed novels, Sinclair began working on an undercover assignment for a socialist newspaper. His investigation of Chicago's meatpacking plants revealed squalid conditions and animal cruelty, which had never been described. The publication of the vivid, realistic *The Jungle* caused Sinclair's literary status to soar and helped bring food industry reform. Considered an uneven stylist, he wrote some 90 books, including the Pulitzer-winning novel *Dragon's Teeth* (1942).

Sitting Bull The Sioux leader, an outspoken critic of white settlers, guided his people in their last years on the free and open plains.

SITTING BULL
★ CA 1831-1890 ★
SIOUX CHIEF

Hunkpapa Sioux Chief Sitting Bull (Tatanka Iyotake) was born in the Dakota Territory near Grand River. During his lifetime, he was to witness the demise of the Sioux Nation while serving as one of its greatest spiritual leaders.

In 1863, he participated in a skirmish with federal troops; a year later he was fighting again at the Battle of Killdeer Mountain, in which Gen. Alfred Sully's 2,200 troops dispersed a Sioux encampment of some 6,000 warriors in retaliation for an uprising in Minnesota. By the time gold was discovered in the Black Hills in 1874, Sitting Bull had become an outspoken and articulate critic of the white settlers, who were now flocking to the region in violation of an 1868 treaty.

When the Sioux were ordered onto reservations in 1875, Sitting Bull refused. In a vision during a Sun Dance he saw soldiers falling like grasshoppers. Soon after, Lt. Col. George Custer and 210 cavalrymen were annihilated by a larger Sioux encampment on the Little Bighorn River in southeastern Montana. Though some national sympathy was aroused for the Indians, the general tide was against them. The Army's new tactic was to gradually wear down the Indians and starve them out. The near extinction of the buffalo drove many to surrender.

"We kill buffaloes as we kill other animals, for food and clothing, and to make our lodges warm," said Sitting Bull. "They kill buffaloes—for what?" In May 1877, he and his dwindling band decamped for

> *I never taught my people to trust the Americans. I have told them the truth—that the Americans are great liars. I have never dealt with the Americans. Why should I? The land belonged to my people.*

SITTING BULL

Canada. Four years later Sitting Bull and his followers, tired and famished, returned to the Dakota Territory and surrendered at Fort Buford. In 1833, he moved to the Standing Rock Reservation, where he continued to speak against the selling of Sioux land. For a while he traveled with Buffalo Bill Cody's Wild West show, signing autographs for

Upton Sinclair His work exposed poor working conditions in industry.

50 cents apiece. When the Ghost Dance movement—predicting the demise of the whites and the return of the buffalo—came to the Dakotas in 1890, Indian police were sent to arrest Sitting Bull as a precaution. He was living again near the Grand River on the Standing Rock Reservation. A struggle broke out, and Sitting Bull was shot and killed. In a jarringly comic note, his show horse, cued by the gunfire, began doing tricks.

SPOTTED ELK

★ CA 1826–1890 ★
SIOUX CHIEF

A leader of the Miniconjou band of the Teton Lakota (Sioux), Spotted Elk ("Big Foot") was the son of Lakota chief Lone Horn. He and his three brothers would all become tribal leaders, Spotted Elk in 1877 after the death of his father.

After the battles of the Sioux and Army in 1875–76, the Miniconjou surrendered and were moved to the Cheyenne River Indian Reservation in present-day South Dakota. Spotted Elk encouraged his people to settle down to raising corn, building schools, and accepting a new way of life. Conditions on the reservation were often worse than what the nomadic tribe had previously known. Finding themselves poor and hungry, they latched on to the promise of the Ghost Dance movement, which swept the region like a religious revival in 1890. Paiute holy man Wovoka prophesied that the white people would leave and buffalo return if the Indians performed the Ghost Dance day and night in "bulletproof" muslin shirts until they dropped with exhaustion with visions of dead relatives and a world without whites.

Settlers living near the reservations became nervous; the Army sent troops to quell what they considered an uprising.

In December 1890, Spotted Elk and his band headed south to the Pine Ridge Reservation, hoping to join forces with Chief Red Cloud. A detachment of the U.S. Cavalry met up with the ragged band of 350 Indians and escorted them to an encampment along Wounded Knee Creek. In the morning, the Indians were ordered to give up their weapons. During a tent search, a shot was fired, and in the ensuing melee more than 300 Indian men, women, and children were killed, including Spotted Elk. The massacre was the final episode in the Indian-white wars.

Spotted Elk The Sioux chief was killed at the 1890 Wounded Knee Massacre in South Dakota, the final "battle" waged by the U.S. Army against the Indians.

ELIZABETH CADY STANTON

★ 1815–1902 ★

WOMEN'S RIGHTS LEADER

An early leader for women's suffrage and equality, Elizabeth Cady Stanton was born near Albany, New York, and graduated from the Troy Female Seminary. Through reading law books belonging to her father, a U.S. congressman, she learned of women's second-class legal status. In 1840, she married lawyer and abolitionist Henry Brewster Stanton. A honeymoon trip to London included the World's Anti-Slavery Convention, which did not allow women delegates. There she met Quaker preacher Lucretia Mott, and thus began a long association. In 1848 Stanton and Mott organized a women's rights convention, which was held in Seneca Falls, New York. Stanton penned a "Declaration of Sentiments," echoing the Declaration of Independence: "We hold these truths to be self-evident, that all men and women are created equal."

Elizabeth Cady Stanton She helped organize the first women's rights convention.

Levi Strauss His sturdy blue jeans, depicted in this advertisement, remain popular and fashionable today.

In 1851, she began working with suffragist Susan B. Anthony. Stanton wrote many of Anthony's speeches as well as articles on divorce, property rights, and temperance. Like Anthony, she broke away from former abolitionists after the Civil War because of their support for a 15th Amendment that gave voting rights to black men but not women. Stanton and Anthony founded the National Woman Suffrage Association in 1869, Stanton serving as its president until 1890. At Stanton's urging, a women's voting amendment was introduced in the U.S. Senate in 1878. It was reintroduced every year for 41 years, finally passing in 1919.

LEVI STRAUSS

★ 1829–1902 ★

CLOTHING MANUFACTURER

Born in Germany, Levi Strauss immigrated to America in 1847. He started out working in his brothers' dry goods business in New York City. Following the gold rush trend to move West, Strauss went to San Francisco in 1853 and began selling wholesale to the mining trade. He sold fabrics and other goods, and in 1872, he jointly patented with Jacob Davis a new kind of sturdy work pants made of tent canvas, with metal rivets at the pockets.

Strauss called them "waist overalls," though they later, after a change from canvas to denim, became known as blue jeans or Levi's. The pants made Strauss rich, and his company continues to thrive.

WILLIAM HOWARD TAFT
★ 1857–1930 ★
27TH U.S. PRESIDENT

William Howard Taft was the only person to serve as president and Supreme Court justice. A reluctant politician, Taft was far happier as a jurist; when he became Chief Justice, he considered it the highlight of his career.

Taft was born in Cincinnati, Ohio. His father served as President Grant's secretary of war and attorney general, and as an ambassador for President Arthur. After graduating from Yale, Taft studied law at the University of Cincinnati and was admitted to the bar in 1880.

In 1886, he married Helen "Nellie" Herron, daughter of a former law partner of President Hayes. Nellie's ambition and Taft's family connections precipitated Taft's slide toward politics. President Harrison appointed him U.S. solicitor general in 1890, and two years later a U.S. circuit judge. In 1900, he was appointed the first governor of the Philippines, a new U.S. possession.

After serving as Theodore Roosevelt's secretary of war, Taft was persuaded by his wife and Roosevelt to run for president. He cruised to victory on Roosevelt's coattails. And though the portly new president worked hard, Taft was never comfortable in the role. He was reluctant to push the limits of executive power and to try to unify the conservative and progressive factions of the Republican Party. But he did enforce antitrust legislation and established a corporate income tax.

Progressive Republicans became disenchanted with Taft and backed Roosevelt in the 1912 election, leading to an all-out war between the two wings of the party and between Taft and Roosevelt. Woodrow Wilson tallied 435 electoral votes to Roosevelt's 88 and Taft's 8. After serving in various capacities, Taft was appointed Chief Justice by President Harding in 1921.

"Separate but Equal"
THE JIM CROW LAWS
★★★

With the end of Reconstruction in 1870s, southern state legislatures as well as local jurisdictions began writing Jim Crow laws to keep blacks and whites separate. Named for a character in blackface minstrelsy from the 1820s, these laws were also designed to keep blacks from voting. With the Supreme Court ruling in *Plessy* v. *Ferguson* (1896) that allowed for "separate but equal" facilities for the two races, segregation became firmly condoned and entrenched.

Legalized discrimination against blacks in nearly all public and private enterprise helped lead to a massive movement of African Americans, known as the "Great Migration," out of the rural South during World War I. Between 1917 and 1918, millions left to work in war industries in cities such as Los Angeles, Chicago, and New York, where blacks could vote and were more safe from lynch mobs. Not until the 1950s did Jim Crow begin dying out, starting with the Supreme Court's decision in *Brown* v. *Board of Education* ruling school segregation unconstitutional.

Anti–Jim Crow button

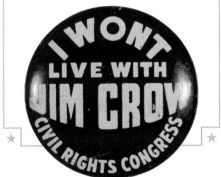

William Howard Taft The president rides with his wife, Helen. After his one term, he became a Supreme Court justice, the position he had always wanted.

IDA TARBELL
★ 1857–1944 ★
JOURNALIST

A muckraking journalist who exposed the anticompetitive practices of large corporations, Ida Tarbell was born in Erie County, Pennsylvania, her father a petroleum producer who was financially hurt by Rockefeller's monopoly. She began writing for *McClure's Magazine* in 1894 and wrote several popular biographies, including a two-volume *Life of Abraham Lincoln* (1900). She is best known for her two-volume *History of the Standard Oil Company* (1904), which was first published as a series of articles. In it she interviewed former employees, thereby revealing corruption and giving impetus to antitrust legislation.

NIKOLA TESLA
★ 1856–1943 ★
INVENTOR

Nikola Tesla Best known for designing AC electricity supply systems, he was an eccentric and wide-ranging inventor and futurist.

With his invention of an alternating current system that made long-distance power transmission possible, Nikola Tesla helped open up the age of electric light. He beat Guglielmo Marconi in demonstrating the wireless. In 1898, he exhibited radio-controlled model boats and torpedoes. His experiments also anticipated radar, x-rays, solar power, and the atom smasher.

A Serb born in Croatia (then part of the Austrian Empire), Tesla was blessed with a photographic memory. After studying in Prague, he went to work in 1881 for the Budapest telegraph company. Walking through a park, he had a vision of an alternating current motor. He moved to America in 1884 and, after a stint with Thomas Edison, formed his own company. George Westinghouse bought his patents and used the AC system to illuminate the 1893 World's Columbian Exposition in Chicago. The event marked the victory of Tesla's AC over Edison's DC.

A few years later Tesla's generators harnessed the power of Niagara Falls. To generate extremely high voltages, he invented the Tesla coil, important to most early radio and TV sets. Tesla's brilliance and compelling personality made him a social success among New York's millionaires, whom he cultivated as patrons. He received backing in 1900 or 1901 from J. P. Morgan for a "world wireless" plant on Long Island, part of a system that would transmit messages freely, known today as broadcasting. A financial panic came along and the backing ended.

After a nervous breakdown, the genius engineer grew increasingly eccentric, spending his time feeding pigeons and doting on one that was almost pure white. He had become a U.S. citizen in 1891.

MARK TWAIN
★ 1835–1910 ★
WRITER

Born Samuel Langhorne Clemens, Mark Twain was a novelist and humorist who captured American diction and coined the term "Gilded Age" to describe the excesses of his time.

Twain grew up in Hannibal, Missouri, along the Mississippi River. His father died young, and Twain went to work as a store clerk and delivery boy, and then as an apprentice to local printers. In 1857, he set out in a steamboat, intending to go to South America to seek his fortune;

> *Always do right.*
> *This will gratify*
> *some people and*
> *astonish the rest.*
>
> **MARK TWAIN**

instead, he ended up learning to pilot a riverboat and stayed on the Mississippi until the start of the Civil War in 1861.

After serving for two weeks with a company of Confederate volunteers, Twain headed west with his brother and landed in Carson City, Nevada, where he became a prospector and newspaper reporter. He continued west, ending up for a while in San Francisco. His first nationally popular story, "The Celebrated Jumping Frog of Calaveras County," appeared in a New York paper in 1865.

Twain then became a traveling correspondent in Hawaii, his reports gaining him widespread recognition and providing him with funding for travels to Europe and the Holy Land. In *The Innocents*

Mark Twain His combination of humor, satire, and vernacular dialogue created a new American style.

Abroad (1869) he lampooned American tourists as well as the sights they took in. *Roughing It* (1872) recalled his adventures in Nevada and other places.

His literary career established, Twain married in 1870 and soon moved to Hartford, Connecticut, where he would live for 20 years. His first novel, *The Gilded Age* (1873), co-written with Charles Dudley Warner, was followed three years later by the highly successful *The Adventures of Tom Sawyer,* in which he first made extensive use of his childhood memories.

Other books followed, including *Life on the Mississippi* (1883), a vivid memoir and account of regional lore.

In *Adventures of Huckleberry Finn* (1885), Twain employed humor and dialect to probe the complexities of race, the underclass, and the nature of freedom in a tale of two runaways—a boy and a slave. Since its publication the book has been banned many times, in many places, for its loose grammar, portrayal of immorality, questionable racial attitudes, and bad language. But it remains an American classic.

After going bankrupt from bad investments, Twain was forced to recoup his losses on a worldwide lecture circuit in the mid-1890s. He continued to write into his final years, though his outlook became more caustic and gloomy, particularly after the death of his wife in 1904.

Mark Twain's classic tale, *Adventures of Huckleberry Finn,* at right in its first edition

The author portrayed life on the Mississippi, shown here in a Currier and Ives lithograph.

WILLIAM "BOSS" TWEED
★ 1823–1878 ★
POLITICIAN

A quintessentially powerful and corrupt politician, "Boss" Tweed, born in New York City, became head of Tammany Hall, New York's Democratic Party organization. By controlling party nominations and having influence with wealthy industrialists, he was able to illegally profit from city contracts. His Tweed Ring included the city chamberlain, comptroller, and mayor. The group siphoned off more than $30 million into their own pockets. Cartoons by Thomas Nast inflamed public outrage, and Tweed was imprisoned for forgery and larceny in 1873. He was released, rearrested, and escaped to Cuba and then Spain. Extradited in 1876 to the United States, he died in prison.

BOOKER T. WASHINGTON
★ 1856–1915 ★
EDUCATOR, REFORMER

One of the most important black American leaders and educators of his time, Booker T. Washington founded the Tuskegee Normal and Industrial Institute (now Tuskegee University) in Alabama. Born a slave on a farm near Roanoke, Virginia, Washington worked in a salt furnace and then a coal mine after the Civil War. In 1872, he walked 500 miles to Hampton, Virginia, and enrolled in the Hampton Institute, an agricultural school for blacks. After several years as a teacher, Washington was tapped in 1881 to head a new school for blacks in Tuskegee, Alabama. With his guidance the school grew from two small buildings to 100 buildings, 1,500 students, 200 teachers, and a $2 million endowment.

Washington proved himself not only an able instructor and administrator but also an effective fund-raiser. He traveled about the state, ensuring potential donors that his school was no threat to white political rule and that his students would not compete for jobs with whites. His idea was to instruct blacks to better themselves by working hard at agricultural and industrial pursuits and improving their manners, morals, and characters. He believed that thrift and patience were the road to financial independence and thus to respect by the white community. Political and civil rights would eventually follow.

Booker T. Washington He championed the idea of black progress through hard work, thrift, and patience. His ideas were challenged by black intellectuals who disagreed with this approach.

Thomas E. Watson **The Populist politician, a progressive, became a white supremacist.**

Washington advanced his beliefs in a pivotal speech at the Atlanta Exposition in 1895. "In all things that are purely social," he said, "we can be separate as the five fingers, yet one as the hand in all things essential to mutual progress." Called the "Atlanta Compromise," Washington's premise came under attack by African-American intellectuals such as W. E. B. Du Bois, a Massachusetts-born professor, who argued that such a philosophy would keep blacks from higher education and achievement. But to Washington, vocational training made much more sense, especially in the impoverished South.

Washington served as an adviser on racial issues to Presidents Theodore Roosevelt and William Howard Taft. Though he was not openly supportive of the equal rights agenda of progressive blacks, he quietly funded lawsuits that opposed segregation and supported voting and jury rights. A controversial figure during and after his lifetime, Washington trod a delicate path between conservative whites and liberal blacks.

THOMAS E. WATSON
★ 1856–1922 ★
POLITICIAN

A progressive turned white supremacist, Thomas Watson was born in Georgia to a wealthy family. His father's postwar poverty made him angry at outside political forces. Watson was elected to Congress in 1890 as a Democrat and then became the Populist 1896 candidate for vice president (running with William Jennings Bryan) and for president in 1904. Called a "strange and vivid character" by the *New York Times,* he promoted a mixed agenda of farmers' rights, racial and religious bigotry, nonintervention in World War I, and rejection of the League of Nations. Watson was also a lawyer, publisher, author, and senator.

GEORGE WESTINGHOUSE
★ 1846–1914 ★
INVENTOR, MANUFACTURER

The man who put U.S. electric power on alternating current, George Westinghouse was born in Central Bridge, New York. He served in both the Union Army and Navy in the Civil War and received his first patent in 1865, for a rotary steam engine. Four years later he organized the Westinghouse Air Brake Company, his inventions boosting railroad safety and efficiency. The Westinghouse Electric Company, started in 1886, shifted early American power transmission from direct to alternating current. During the 1880s, his stream of inventions earned him about one patent per month, including the friction gear, geared turbine, and air springs.

SARAH WINNEMUCCA
★ CA 1844–1891 ★
EDUCATOR, WRITER

Renowned for her open criticism of government policy regarding the Paiute, Winnemucca was born in what would later be western Nevada. From 1866 to 1878, she worked as an interpreter and guide for the military and then at the Malheur Reservation in Oregon. In the late 1870s, she began lecturing in the West on the mistreatment of her people, who had been attacked and whose land had been confiscated. In 1880, she brought the Paiute case to President Hayes in Washington, D.C. She later gave some 300 lectures in East Coast cities, founded an Indian school, and wrote an autobiography, *Life Among the Piutes: Their Wrongs and Claims* (1883).

Sarah Winnemucca **The educator was the first Native American woman to publish in English.**

VICTORIA CLAFLIN WOODHULL

★ 1838–1927 ★

REFORMER

Raised poor in Ohio, Victoria Woodhull performed in family medicine shows and advocated women's suffrage, free love, and mystical socialism. She married a doctor at 14, had two children and then left him. She and her sister Tennie traveled, performing acts of spiritualism and mesmerism. Though accused of fraud and moral turpitude, they kept drawing audiences. They moved to New York and charmed Cornelius Vanderbilt, who helped them set up a brokerage firm. The sisters also started a newspaper, espousing legalized prostitution and sexual equality. In 1872, Woodhull, representing the Equal Rights Party, ran for president. Five years later the sisters moved to England, married wealthy men, and became involved in charity and women's suffrage.

Victoria Claflin Woodhull She scandalized the nation.

Carter G. Woodson His books were among the first to document the experience and history of black Americans.

CARTER G. WOODSON

★ 1875–1950 ★

HISTORIAN

Born to former slaves in central Virginia, Carter Woodson became the premier writer of black history in his day. To help support his family, he worked as a sharecropper and miner, earning enough to enroll in high school by 20, which he completed in two years. He attended Berea College in Kentucky and then worked in the Philippines as an educator. After studying at the University of Chicago, Woodson became in 1912 the second African American to earn a doctorate from Harvard (after W. E. B. Du Bois). His field was the neglected subject of black American history. In 1915, he founded the Association for the Study of Negro Life and History to foster scholarly pursuit of the discipline. The following year he started the *Journal of Negro History*. Of his 16 books, the most well known is *The Negro in Our History* (1922). He is considered the father of black history studies and Black History Month.

WILBUR AND ORVILLE WRIGHT

★ WILBUR, 1867–1912 ★
★ ORVILLE, 1871–1948 ★

AVIATION PIONEERS

The Wright brothers achieved the first powered flight in a heavier-than-air machine. In so doing, they inaugurated the era of aviation.

Born near Millville, Indiana, Wilbur became a tall, serious young man, the perfect complement to his dapper, enthusiastic brother, Orville, who was born in Dayton, Ohio. The two became an inseparable pair, interested in all things mechanical, and enjoyed arguing with each other, often switching ideas in the middle of an argument. Neither finished high school, but both were avid readers, their clergyman father's library lined with books. They ran a print shop for a while and then opened a bicycle shop, riding the new craze for bikes. Here they learned how to transmit power by a chain and sprockets, how to make precision parts, how to control a bicycle not just around its vertical axis, as in steering, but also around its fore-and-aft axis, to keep it from falling.

There was plenty of information about aerodynamics at the time; the problem was that much of it was wrong. They began conducting extensive experiments and recording the results in

The Wright brothers achieved the first successful flight in a motor-powered airplane, changing the world; further experiments added knowledge to the field.

> If I were giving
> a young man advice
> as to how he might
> succeed in life,
> I would say to him,
> pick out a good father
> and mother, and
> begin life in Ohio.
>
> **WILBUR WRIGHT**

detail. To test wing designs, they mounted sections of wing on a bicycle. They built a wind tunnel and came up with data so accurate that modern instruments can add only minor refinements. As their ideas took shape in kites and gliders, the Wrights sought out the winds and slopes near Kitty Hawk, North Carolina, for flight tests.

On December 17, 1903, they were ready to fly the world's first airplane. Four men and a boy came to watch; there were no reporters. By a coin toss, Wilbur went first: He overcontrolled and slammed into the ground. Orville took a turn. He flew 12 seconds into a stiff headwind before jolting onto the sand 120 feet away. Three more flights that day stretched the distance to 852 feet, in 59 seconds. Sustained, controlled flight had begun.

The brothers were as methodical after Kitty Hawk as before. Their plan was to refine the invention into a practical flying machine, protect it with patents, and then sell airplanes. With little press interest in what seemed an impractical invention, they were free to work unbothered until receiving their first patent in 1906. Their new airplane company became a success. In 1912, Wilbur died of typhoid, and three years later, Orville sold the company, his heart no longer in it. He returned to experimental work. Neither brother ever married.

ZITKALA-SA
★ 1876–1938 ★
WRITER, REFORMER

Daughter of a Yankton Sioux woman and Euro-American man, Zitkala-Sa ("Red Bird") was born Gertrude Simmons in South Dakota. As a teen, Simmons took on her Indian name. She attended Earlham College in Indiana and began teaching at the Carlisle Indian Industrial School in Carlisle, Pennsylvania, in 1897. Here she published numerous short stories and essays in the *Atlantic Monthly* and *Harper's New Monthly* about her struggles with cultural identity. In 1902, Zitkala-Sa married and moved to a reservation in Utah. Later she was a liaison to the Bureau of Indian Affairs in Washington, D.C., editor of *American Indian Magazine,* and founder of the National Council of American Indians.

Zitkala-Sa **She founded the National Council of American Indians.**

Coming to America

A NEW WAVE OF IMMIGRATION

he two decades on either side of the turning century saw a massive wave of immigration to America's shores. It was even bigger than an earlier wave that had helped build the growing nation. From 1880 to 1924 (when severe immigration restrictions were enacted), some 26 million newcomers arrived—the largest migration in world history. They ballooned a population that in 1880 stood at only 50 million. Whereas the earlier wave was mostly German, Irish, and other western and northern Europeans, the second wave was primarily from eastern and southern Europe. Large numbers of Italians came during this period, as well as Jews fleeing persecution in Russia, Poland, and Hungary. Standing up for the immigrant poor were people like Lawrence Veiller (1872–1959), whose work on various New York committees helped bring some housing reforms. Many discovered that America was not all they'd been dreaming of. But often it was better than what they had left behind.

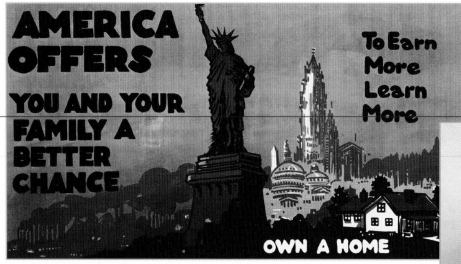

A poster geared toward immigrants shows what the United States had to offer. Immigrants constituted the overwhelming majority of the northern urban poor between 1880 and 1924.

En route to Ellis Island, immigrants view the Statue of Liberty in New York Harbor. The peak years for Ellis Island were between 1903 and 1914, when the facility processed about 2,000 immigrants a day.

A group of Jewish immigrants dines at a converted hangar in Southampton, England, on the way to a better life in the United States in 1924.

Immigrants rest on a deck of an ocean liner sailing from Antwerp to New York. Many had relatives in America; others were just hoping to start a new life.

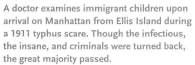

A doctor examines immigrant children upon arrival on Manhattan from Ellis Island during a 1911 typhus scare. Though the infectious, the insane, and criminals were turned back, the great majority passed.

There is a mysterious cycle in human events.
To some generations much is given.
Of other generations much is expected.
This generation of Americans has a rendezvous with destiny.

FRANKLIN DELANO ROOSEVELT

THE REBIRTH OF AMERICA

AMERICA AFTER WORLD WAR I WAS HURTLING INTO THE MODERN AGE. BETWEEN 1910 and 1920, the United States went from a nation of less than half a million cars to more than eight million. A system of good roads stitched the land, skyscrapers shot up in cities, machinery altered farm life, and the electric industry revolutionized homes and businesses. In that same decade, urban dwellers began outnumbering those in small towns and rural areas. Movies and jazz reflected more relaxed cultural attitudes.

One of the most noteworthy cultural and political events of the immediate postwar years was the addition of the 19th Amendment to the Constitution. Ratified in 1920, the amendment gave women a constitutional right to vote. The measure had been decades in the making, and though it was a breakthrough for women, it did not significantly change voting patterns. Women voted along party lines much the way that men did. But it was a sign of the times that many women were no longer simply handmaidens for their husbands. Short skirts, bobbed hair, open talk about sex, and drinking in speakeasies during Prohibition (1920–1933) were a few of the ways women expressed their growing independence.

Working-class women lived much as they always had—they were overworked and underpaid. Middle-class white women could buy vacuum cleaners and washing machines, and often learned to drive automobiles. Black women frequently worked as domestics at low wages.

(previous pages) Perched on a beam 800 feet above ground, workers break for lunch during the 1932 construction of New York's RCA Building.
(opposite) With women getting the constitutional right to vote in 1920, suffragettes encouraged them to use their new power.

New York City policemen dump liquor down a sewer after a raid. The failed Prohibition experiment began in 1920 and ran until its repeal in 1933.

The return of peace and prosperity in the early 1920s sparked a new wave of transatlantic immigration. As it had during previous waves, Congress severely cut down the allowed number of immigrants, this time from 350,000 in 1921 to less than half that number three years later, with quotas by place of origin favoring western Europeans.

With the onset of Prohibition by act of Congress in 1920, the manufacture, sale, transportation, and importation of intoxicating beverages were forbidden, and a great and doomed social experiment was afoot. The law said nothing about the drinking of such beverages, and Americans were determined to get their liquor. The federal government ended up losing taxes that legal alcohol would have generated, while spending on often futile law enforcement. Defying the law became a mark of sophistication. Though some liquor was "home brew" and "bathtub gin," much was supplied by organized crime. Prohibition gave a boost to the underworld, which reached into middle-class American life, where the demand for illegal alcohol seemed insatiable. Ruthless gangsters like Chicago's Al Capone flourished.

As much as anything, the 1920s were, for many, an exciting decade of revolt against old-time values, especially by urban Americans who considered themselves sophisticated. These older values were sometimes referred to as Puritanism, which social and literary critic H. L. Mencken defined as "the haunting fear that someone, somewhere, may be happy."

The 1920s were noted for Republican presidents (Harding, Coolidge, and Hoover), the popularity of baseball (thanks in part to Babe Ruth), the craze for aviation (driven by Charles Lindbergh), the rise of jazz (performed by the likes of Jelly Roll Morton, Louis Armstrong, and Duke Ellington), and the temporary reemergence of the Ku Klux Klan in the rural South, Midwest, and parts of the rest of the nation. Writers included F. Scott Fitzgerald, Ernest Hemingway, Sinclair Lewis, and Langston Hughes; their subjects, in order, were New York, expatriate, midwestern, and black American experiences.

The Roaring Twenties ended with the Wall Street crash of 1929. It shattered illusions of constant economic growth, shook faith in democratic capitalism, and ushered in the Great Depression, the worst economic downturn in U.S. history. With no safety net to help check the collapse, the Depression was widespread, deep, and long. Because President Hoover and a Republican Congress were unable to stop the bleeding, America voted in a Democratic Congress and president, Franklin D. Roosevelt. The winter of 1932–33 saw unemployment peak at 25 percent and bank failures proliferate.

By the 1920s, baseball had become firmly entrenched as America's pastime and most widely followed sport.

Roosevelt came to the presidency with no concrete plan except to shore up American capitalism and preserve liberties. He was determined to put people back to work, stabilize the financial system, and construct some sort of social safety net. Soon an "alphabet soup" of agencies began pouring from Congress, among them the National Recovery Administration (NRA), Agricultural Adjustment Act (AAA), Public Works Administration (PWA), Civilian Conservation Corps (CCC), Federal Housing Administration (FHA), Rural Electrification Administration (REA), Tennessee Valley Authority (TVA), and the Securities and Exchange Commission (SEC).

Roosevelt sometimes pursued seemingly contradictory policies, juggling results into something that he could reassure the public was working. The panic stopped, and gradually

1920	1925	1926	1927	1929
Prohibition begins; women get right to vote	F. Scott Fitzgerald publishes *The Great Gatsby*	NBC, first national radio network, created	Charles Lindbergh's solo transatlantic flight	Wall Street crash begins Great Depression

Americans got back to work and began to feel that hope *was* possible. The president helped save the capitalist system by cleaning up Wall Street, insuring bank accounts, encouraging workers to organize, and creating Social Security. Economic stabilizers such as pensions and unemployment insurance helped prevent future depressions.

But Roosevelt's New Deal policies, like his optimism and glowing radio voice, were not enough. Unemployment still soared, and a lingering drought gripped the Great Plains, forcing many to flee west, as recounted in John Steinbeck's 1939 novel, *The Grapes of Wrath*. Not until after the rise of military industries in World War II and four long years of war did privation turn to prosperity.

In January 1941, Roosevelt persuaded Congress to allow the government to "lend or lease" war matériel to countries resisting Nazi Germany. Hitler had already taken Austria, Czechoslovakia, Denmark, Norway, the Low Countries, and France. Britain was out of money and desperate for help. The American defense industry began gearing up. By 1945, 17 million jobs would be created by the war. By December 1941, after the Japanese attack on Pearl Harbor, the United States and remnants of the democratic world were fighting for survival against murderous tyrannies. America and Britain had to find common cause with Joseph Stalin, who had no more respect for liberal democracy than did Hitler. War finally ended the Great Depression, and unemployment almost disappeared. About 16 million men served in the military; in addition, 400,000 women volunteered for the medical corps and women's units.

More than three brutal years later, on April 30, 1945, Hitler committed suicide; one week after that, Germany surrendered unconditionally. The war in the Pacific continued until the world's first atom bombs destroyed Hiroshima and Nagasaki on August 6 and 9. Five days later Japan announced its surrender. In all, 400,000 Americans had lost their lives (second only to the Civil War), and more than a million were seriously wounded. The war was over; the atomic age had begun.

A movie poster advertises the release of *New Orleans*, a drama starring jazz greats Louis Armstrong, Billie Holiday, Woody Herman, and Kid Ory.

African-American soldiers stand in formation at Fort Bragg, North Carolina; as late as World War II, segregated units were still the rule.

1932
FDR is elected president, first of four terms

1933
Roosevelt's New Deal begins; Prohibition ends

1936
Jesse Owens wins four gold medals at Berlin Olympics

1940
Richard Wright publishes *Native Son*

1945
Germany & Japan surrender, ending World War II

BIOGRAPHIES

FIGHTERS FOR FREEDOM
& CHANGE 1919-1945

The end of World War I initiated a period of relative peace and prosperity in the United States. Radio and motion pictures began to unite Americans in a shared culture that featured jazz, baseball, and the beginnings of "modern" consumerism. Although the 1920s were a time of high living for some, the Great Depression brought hardship to many. Gearing up for and fighting in World War II gave the nation a renewed unity and purpose.

MARIAN ANDERSON
★ 1897-1993 ★
SINGER

THOMAS HART BENTON
★ 1889-1975 ★
PAINTER

MARY MCLEOD BETHUNE
★ 1875-1955 ★
EDUCATOR

Born in Philadelphia to poor African-American parents, Marian Anderson became one of the world's leading contraltos. She started singing in church choirs and then took private lessons, for which her church raised money. Concert tours at home and in Europe in the late 1920s and early 1930s cemented her reputation. Anderson struggled with racial discrimination, most famously in 1939 when she was barred from singing at Constitution Hall in Washington, D.C. She later became the first African American to sing in the White House and in the Metropolitan Opera. Conductor Arturo Toscanini declared "a voice like hers occurs once in a hundred years."

Hailing from Missouri, Thomas Hart Benton helped advance the American regionalism style of art. Though he experimented with modernism in Paris, he returned to the United States and began working in a more direct style, painting scenes of working and family life. His work was distinguished by its bold color, sculptural quality, and a powerful flowing element that he felt conveyed the energy of the American experience. Many of his paintings and murals depict U.S. history and folklore. The movement he and others (including Grant Wood and John Steuart Curry) created flourished from the 1920s to the 1940s.

Mary McLeod Bethune rose from humble origins—born to former slaves in South Carolina—to become one of the

Mary McLeod Bethune The activist founded Bethune-Cookman University.

Margaret Bourke-White The photojournalist perches on a gargoyle on New York's Chrysler Building.

foremost black leaders of her time. In 1904, she opened the Daytona Educational and Industrial Training School for Negro Girls in Daytona Beach, Florida, and it grew to include a farm, high school, and nursing school. By 1923, it had become a coed institution, later known as Bethune-Cookman University.

In 1935, Bethune founded the National Council of Negro Women (NCNW). From then until 1944, she served as President Franklin Roosevelt's special adviser on minority affairs. She was also appointed to government positions by Presidents Coolidge, Hoover, and Truman. As director of Negro Affairs in the National Youth Administration (1936–1944), she helped find employment for young people and funding for black graduate students.

A monument to Bethune was erected in the nation's capital in 1974. Twenty years later, the Mary McLeod Bethune Council House, at the first headquarters of the NCNW, opened as a national historic site in Washington, D.C.

MARGARET BOURKE-WHITE
★ 1906–1971 ★
PHOTOJOURNALIST

A pioneer in the use of the photo essay, Margaret Bourke-White was born in New York City. In 1929, she became a photographer for *Fortune* magazine, shooting pictures of machinery, factories, and industrial workers. Seven years later she joined the staff of *Life* magazine. During World War II, Bourke-White took her talents to Europe's battlefields. Surviving the torpedoing of a transport ship, she went on to cover the war in Italy and Moscow. Her 1945 pictures of Holocaust victims shocked readers around the globe. In later assignments she captured India's fight for independence, racial and labor unrest in South Africa, and the Korean War.

OMAR BRADLEY
★ 1893–1981 ★
ARMY GENERAL

Born in Missouri, Omar Bradley graduated from the U.S. Military Academy in 1915 and became a major during World War I. In World War II, as a major general, he commanded the II Corps in helping capture Tunisia. Later that year he successfully invaded Sicily. In 1944, his forces took part in the Normandy invasion and the liberation of France. After the war, Bradley served as administrator of veteran affairs, Army chief of staff, and in 1949 as the first chairman of the Joint Chiefs of Staff. In 1950, he was honored with the rank of five-star general, the fifth in American history.

Un-American Activities
ROOTING OUT "COMMUNIST" INFILTRATION
★ ★ ★

By 1938, Nazism had been imported by radical groups in the United States, their uniforms, marches, and anti-Semitic blather causing a minor stir. Texas congressman Martin Dies began to investigate such "un-American" activities. Dies was a Democrat who, with other southern politicians, had turned against Franklin D. Roosevelt in his second term and sided with conservative Republicans. Their target was not homegrown Nazis, but Communists. Convinced that Reds had infiltrated FDR's New Deal agencies, they were eager to root out these "threats" to the American way of life. Dies and other House members became notorious for badgering witnesses and assuming guilt by association. With threats of jail and ruined reputations, they set their sights on such groups as labor unions, the Federal Writer's Project, and film industry leaders, including Humphrey Bogart. Dies and his committee became a model for the postwar anticommunist witch hunts of Joseph McCarthy and others.

Actor Humphrey Bogart was targeted as "un-American."

PEARL S. BUCK
★ 1892–1973 ★
WRITER

Born in West Virginia, Pearl Buck grew up in China, the daughter of missionaries. After attending college in the United States, she returned to China and began publishing articles and stories in 1922 about Chinese life. Her best known work, *The Good Earth,* appeared in 1931; it portrays the efforts of a Chinese peasant and his slave wife to gain land. The novel won the Pulitzer Prize. In 1935, she moved to the United States, and three years later she was awarded the Nobel Prize for literature. Her total output included more than 65 books and hundreds of stories and essays.

AL CAPONE
★ 1899–1947 ★
GANGSTER

One of the most notorious gangsters in American history, Al Capone was born in Brooklyn, New York, to Italian immigrants. Dropping out of school after the sixth grade, he joined Johnny Torrio's James Street Boys. During a fracas in a saloon, he received a knife wound and nickname, "Scarface." In 1919, Capone moved to Chicago to help run Torrio's brothel concern. With the start of Prohibition in 1920 a bustling new market in illegal liquor opened new opportunities for organized crime. Through murder and witness intimidation, Torrio and Capone began to control much of the bootlegging market. With Torrio's retirement to Italy, Capone became Chicago's leading gangster, expanding his business to include

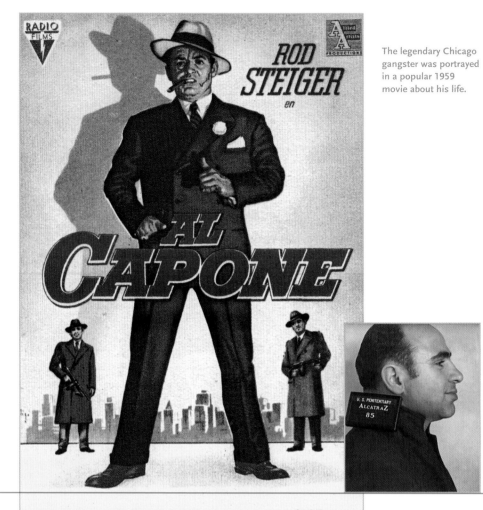

The legendary Chicago gangster was portrayed in a popular 1959 movie about his life.

RADIO FILMS — ROD STEIGER en AL CAPONE

FAY SPAIN · JAMES GREGORY · NEHEMIAH PERSOFF
DIRECTOR : RICHARD WILSON

Al Capone Seen here in a mug shot at Alcatraz federal penitentiary in 1934

gambling and other illegal activities. Considered a celebrity, he rode to events in an armored limousine. His operation bribed politicians and police, and fought rivals with submachine guns. Though his henchmen were believed responsible for the killing of seven members of the Bugs Moran gang in the St. Valentine's Day Massacre of 1929, nothing was ever proved.

In 1931, Capone was indicted for income tax evasion and sentenced to 11 years in prison and $80,000. He served eight, first in Atlanta and then at the new Alcatraz facility in San Francisco Bay. He retired to his estate near Miami, Florida, and died from complications of syphilis.

GEORGE WASHINGTON CARVER
★ CA 1864–1943 ★
SCIENTIST

Born a slave on a Missouri farm, George Washington Carver became an internationally famous agricultural researcher, his investigations into the uses of peanuts and other crops helping the South shift from the dominant cotton monoculture to other options.

Shortly after Carver's birth, his father was killed in an accident and his mother was kidnapped by slave raiders. Former owners, the Carvers, taught him to read and write, and at about age 11 he moved to nearby Neosho to attend a school for blacks. Making money from cooking, laundering, and homesteading, he enrolled in Simpson College in Iowa in 1890. Six years later he earned a master's degree in agriculture at Iowa State University and accepted a position as head of the agriculture department at the Tuskegee Institute in Alabama.

Carver began doing extensive research into ways that farmers, especially blacks, could get more production out of the local soil. For decades, cotton, which heavily depleted the soil, had been the main cash crop. Carver's experiments with peanuts, sweet potatoes, and cow peas showed the variety of ways these crops could be used.

After 1914, Carver focused mostly on peanuts, deriving more than 300 peanut-based products, including ink, soap, face powder, and a milk substitute.

George Washington Carver The experimental scientist from Missouri promoted crop diversification in the South.

Though most of his products proved unmarketable, his emphasis on sustainable agriculture was prescient, and his engaging personality helped promote black achievement.

CALVIN COOLIDGE
★ 1872–1933 ★
30TH U.S. PRESIDENT

Born on July 4 in Vermont, Calvin Coolidge graduated from Amherst College in Massachusetts and opened a law firm in 1898. Working his way up in the Republican Party in Massachusetts, he became mayor of Northampton, state senator, and governor (1918). In 1921, he became vice president under Warren

The chief business of the American people is business.

CALVIN COOLIDGE

Harding and was the first in that office to attend Cabinet meetings. He became known as "Silent Cal" for his reserved, modest temperament. Harding's death in 1923 propelled Coolidge into the presidency; the following year he won a full term. Coolidge's policies were generally pro-business, antiregulatory, and isolationist; he also promoted civil rights. He declined to run for a second term.

Calvin Coolidge The 30th U.S. president served a full term after the death of Harding.

COUNTEE CULLEN
★ 1903–1946 ★
WRITER

Raised by his grandmother, Countee Cullen began writing in high school. By the time he graduated from New York University in 1925, he had published his first volume of poetry, *Color*. A year later he earned his master's from Harvard. Subsequent books established him as a key figure in the Harlem Renaissance literary movement. His poetry used European forms and traditions, particularly from Keats and Shelley, to explore themes of the black American experience. In 1928, he married Yolande Du Bois, daughter of intellectual and Niagara Movement leader W. E. B. Du Bois, but the marriage lasted only two years. He also penned plays and children's books.

Clarence Darrow The defense attorney reads his mail during the 1925 Scopes trial.

CLARENCE DARROW
★ 1857–1938 ★
LAWYER

Born in Ohio, Clarence Darrow became the most renowned American lawyer of the early 20th century, reputed particularly for criminal defense work.

After studying at Allegheny College and the University of Michigan Law School, Darrow became a member of the Ohio bar in 1878. He practiced law in small Ohio towns until 1887, when he and his wife and son moved to Chicago, where he became friends with influential Judge John Altgeld. When Altgeld became governor, he appointed Darrow to be a legal counsel for the city. Darrow began specializing in labor law. Among his early important cases were efforts to free political activists convicted of murder in the 1886 Haymarket riot and his defense of union leader Eugene V. Debs for contempt of court. Though he lost the Debs case, he had begun building a solid reputation.

In 1902, President Theodore Roosevelt appointed Darrow arbitrator of the Pennsylvania anthracite coal strike. Five years later Darrow mounted a successful defense of William Haywood, leader of the Industrial Workers of the World, charged with plotting to murder the former governor of Idaho.

Darrow's most high-profile cases came late in his life. In the 1924 Leopold-Loeb case, he defended two young men who pleaded guilty to kidnapping and murdering a 14-young-old boy. His opposition to the death penalty gave him impetus to try a bold new strategy, arguing that the young men were psychologically stunted and thus, although guilty, they did not deserve to die for their crimes. He won the case. In the 1925 Scopes trial, Darrow defended the right of John T. Scopes to teach evolution. Representing Tennessee, orator William Jennings Bryan prevailed, but Darrow's incisive arguments highlighted the problems inherit in laws based on religious belief instead of scientific knowledge.

BENJAMIN O. DAVIS, SR.
★ 1877–1970 ★
U.S. ARMY GENERAL

Born in Washington, D.C., Benjamin Davis rose to prominence as the first African-American general. After volunteering to serve in the Spanish-American War in 1898, he became a career military man. His sterling reputation and leadership skills helped him advance in a racially biased institution, and in 1940, he was made brigadier general. Davis taught military science at Ohio's Wilberforce University and the Tuskegee Institute in Alabama. His tours of duty included the Philippines and Liberia. During World War II, he served, among other things, as an adviser on black soldiers, pushing for full integration of the armed forces. His awards included the Bronze Star and the Distinguished Service Medal.

DOROTHY DAY
★ 1897–1980 ★
JOURNALIST

A journalist and reformer, Dorothy Day was born in New York City and joined the Socialist Party in college. During the Depression, she and French-born philosopher Peter Maurin set up more than 30 hospitality houses for the poor and homeless in a number of U.S. cities. She and Maurin founded the Catholic Worker Movement, a group supporting charity, peace, and nonviolent social reform, and in 1933, they began publishing *The Catholic Worker,* a monthly newspaper. Day published her autobiography, *The Long Loneliness,* in 1952.

The Manhattan Project

BIRTH OF THE ATOMIC BOMB

★ ★ ★

World War II spurred sudden growth in science and technology. The most potentially dangerous and world-changing of technologies occurred as a result of a massive effort code-named the Manhattan Project. Launched in 1942, the project was based upon the use of nuclear fission—splitting the nucleus of a uranium atom—to create a new weapon of unprecedented power.

The secret project was given top priority to compete with German scientists who appeared to be investigating the same technology. Some of the world's top physicists, including Hungarian-born Edward Teller, were brought under the leadership of American physicist J. Robert Oppenheimer, who coordinated the research at three facilities—Los Alamos, New Mexico; Hanford, Washington; and Oak Ridge, Tennessee. The $2 billion project was known to few people, including President Roosevelt. Vice President Harry Truman did not know until he became president after Roosevelt's death.

Physicist Enrico Fermi, having fled fascist Italy, proved that a self-sustaining chain reaction of nuclear particles would release enormous amounts of energy. New findings in hand, scientists and engineers at Los Alamos began assembling the world's first atom bomb. Using plutonium (another radioactive element) instead of uranium, they exploded the device in the desert on July 16, 1945. The blast was brighter than the sun, producing temperatures as high as 7,000 degrees Fahrenheit, and leaving a towering column of smoke with a mushroom-shaped head. A month later, an atom bomb was dropped on Hiroshima, Japan. Another fell on Nagasaki a few days later. Both cities were destroyed—including about 140,000 people, who were vaporized, burned, or irradiated. The bombs brought about the surrender of Japan, thus ending the war.

The first atomic test creates a searing image against an early morning sky. The bomb was detonated at Alamogordo, New Mexico, on July 16, 1945.

CECIL B. DEMILLE

★ 1881–1959 ★

FILMMAKER

A titan of the motion-picture industry, Cecil B. DeMille was a director, producer, screenwriter, and actor who specialized in the epic drama during the glory days of Hollywood.

DeMille was born in the small town of Ashfield, Massachusetts, to a playwright father and a mother who became an acting teacher. After graduating from Pennsylvania Military College in 1898, he attended the American Academy of Dramatic Arts in New York and began acting on the stage.

In the first decade of the 1900s, he teamed up with Jesse Lasky and Samuel Goldwyn to create a silent-movie company that would later become Paramount Pictures. His first film, *The Squaw Man* (1914), was shot in a Hollywood barn and is considered the first feature-length movie. Over the next two years, DeMille would direct more than 20 films and bring important innovations to editing, lighting, and storytelling.

After World War I, DeMille presented movies exhibiting a new moral freedom, but audience backlash made him turn to biblical themes. His 140-minute epic *The Ten Commandments* (1923) was the first to have a budget topping $1 million. By the 1930s, with talking pictures established, he was also making Westerns and romantic adventure movies, including *The Plainsman* (1936), starring Gary Cooper as Wild Bill Hickok, and *Union Pacific* (1939).

Among hits in the 1940s were *Reap the Wild Wind* (1942), with John Wayne; *Unconquered* (1947), a colonial adventure with Gary Cooper; and *Samson and Delilah* (1949), starring Hedy Lamarr. And in 1949, he was presented with a special Academy Award for his lasting achievements in movie entertainment. In 1952, he brought out the extravagant circus spectacle *The Greatest Show on Earth*, which won the Oscar for best picture. DeMille's last picture was a remake. Released in 1956, *The Ten Commandments,* with Charlton Heston and a cast of thousands, is an enduring classic of large-scale moviemaking.

On the set, DeMille could be known as an egotistical tyrant, barking orders through a megaphone and a loudspeaker system. But his unfailing devotion to pleasing the public paid off in big profits for Paramount and the film industry as a whole. His box-office grosses, when adjusted for inflation, total $30 billion. He died of heart failure at 77 in Hollywood, California, the place where his dreams became the stuff of movie magic to be shared with millions.

Cecil B. DeMille Starting as an actor and playwright, he went on to produce and direct many of Hollywood's early extravagant features, including the 1934 hit *Cleopatra*.

WALT DISNEY

★ 1901–1966 ★

MOTION-PICTURE PRODUCER

Creator of many cartoon characters adored around the world, Walt Disney pioneered the art of studio animation and became a legendary maker of feature-length cartoon movies.

Disney was born in Chicago but moved with his family at a young age to a Missouri farm. They moved again to Kansas City, Missouri, where as a young man he began studying cartooning. In World War I, he drove a truck for the American Red Cross in Germany and France.

Returning to Kansas City, Disney began making one- and two-minute animated shorts for a film advertisement company. In 1923, he went to Los Angeles to try to become a producer or director. Not finding work, he rented space in the back of a real estate office and set up a cartoon studio. His first hit came in 1928 with a cartoon called *Steamboat Willie* that introduced a character named Mickey Mouse. The next year he brought out the "Silly Symphonies," a series that would in time feature such characters as Donald Duck, Minnie Mouse, and dogs Goofy and Pluto. These early efforts, with their escapism, color, and jaunty music, were highly appealing to the public during the Depression years.

Walt Disney He pioneered motion-picture cartoons, such as "The Whoopee Party" (above); his name remains synonymous with big-budget animated and family features.

Disney's foray into full-length movies came in 1937 with his release of *Snow White and the Seven Dwarfs*. It captivated audiences, becoming one of the world's most popular movies. A string of animated hits based on fairy tales and children's stories would follow: *Pinocchio* (1940), *Fantasia* (1940), *Dumbo* (1941), *Bambi* (1942), *Cinderella* (1950), *Alice in*

> *I've never called this art. It's show business.*
>
> **WALT DISNEY**

Wonderland (1951), *Peter Pan* (1953), *Lady and the Tramp* (1955), *Sleeping Beauty* (1959), *101 Dalmatians* (1961), and *The Jungle Book* (1967).

After commercial success with animated features, Disney began making movies about wild animals and movies with human actors, including *The Parent Trap* and *The Absent-Minded Professor*, both 1961, and the highly popular *Mary Poppins* (1964), which employed some animation. His nature films, edited to create an adventure story, were not true documentaries, but they were in keeping with his brand. With the rise in popularity of television, Disney smartly capitalized on this new medium and hosted a weekly show that presented made-for-TV films. His company is today a multinational media and entertainment conglomerate.

Further success followed with the opening of the Disneyland theme park in Anaheim, California, in 1955. Disney was still planning and designing the tremendous Walt Disney World in Florida at the time of his death.

W. E. B. DU BOIS
★ 1868-1963 ★
HISTORIAN, SOCIOLOGIST

The leading African-American intellectual in the early 20th century, W. E. B. Du Bois became a leader of the growing protest movement that swept the country as blacks sought to gain civil rights equivalent to those of their white countrymen.

Du Bois was born in Massachusetts and graduated from Fisk University, a black college in Nashville, in 1888. Seven years later he became the first African American to earn a Ph.D. from Harvard. In 1897, he began teaching at Atlanta University, where he remained for the next 13 years. Here, he published a

> *It is a peculiar sensation, this double-consciousness, this sense of always looking at one's self through the eyes of others.*
>
> W. E. B. DU BOIS

number of important papers on the conditions of black Americans, and he began moving away from the idea that scholarship could change the country's racial problems. He began to believe that only through higher education, protest, and agitation could blacks get past repressive working conditions, disenfranchisement, discriminatory laws, and lynchings.

Du Bois's philosophy was in stark contrast with that of Booker T. Washington, a former Virginia slave, educator, and founder of the Tuskegee Institute, who thought that reserved striving, especially in agriculture and the vocations, would eventually improve the lot of blacks, not direct confrontation with whites. Du Bois argued in *The Souls of Black Folk* (1903) that Washington's approach would only put off the time when blacks could emerge from oppression. The two divergent camps characterized black intellectual thought in the early 1900s.

In 1909, Du Bois helped found the National Association for the Advancement of Colored People (NAACP), and from 1910 to 1934 he edited the NAACP magazine, *The Crisis.* In his writings, Du Bois espoused a black nationalism, especially the doctrine of Pan-Africanism, a belief that all people of African descent should work together to overcome societal prejudice. Disenchanted with what he believed was the NAACP's focus on elite blacks instead of the poor, Du Bois resigned from the organization and began to move away from American capitalism and more toward Marxism as the solution for the masses. He spent the next 10 years back at Atlanta University, teaching and writing. Then, in 1944, he returned to the NAACP, taking a research position for four years. A second and final split hurled him ever toward the left end of the political spectrum. He joined the Communist Party in 1961 and moved to Ghana, where he died two years later at 95.

W. E. B. Du Bois The scholar espoused a philosophy of agitation and protest to accomplish social change.

Amelia Earhart The aviator (below) after becoming the first woman to fly solo across the Atlantic in 1932; *inset:* Earhart's goggles. At left, she stands next to the Lockheed Electra in which she disappeared in 1937.

AMELIA EARHART
★ 1897–1939 ★
AVIATOR

The first woman to fly across the Atlantic Ocean, Amelia Earhart was born and raised in Kansas. In 1915, she and her mother and sister moved to Chicago to escape an unstable, alcoholic father. Following World War I, Earhart volunteered as a nurse's aide with the Red Cross and came in contact with several wounded pilots. Thus began her interest in aviation.

In 1920, after a 10-minute airplane ride at a California air show, Earhart was hooked. She took flying lessons from Neta Snook, one of the few female pilots at that time. In 1921, she bought a second-hand yellow biplane and the following year set an altitude record for women of 14,000 feet. For the next few years Earhart continued to work on her aviation skills, living on an inheritance from her grandmother. When the money ran out, she sold her plane, headed east, briefly studied at Columbia University, and then dropped out and found work as a teacher

Courage is the price that life exacts for granting peace.

AMELIA EARHART

and social worker. She continued to fly when she could and began making a name for herself in aviation circles.

After Charles Lindbergh's solo flight across the Atlantic in 1927, the idea of a woman flying across the ocean took hold. In 1928, Earhart was asked to participate in a transatlantic flight as a passenger. She eagerly agreed, and so on June 17, 1928, she flew with a pilot and co-pilot in a Fokker from Newfoundland to South Wales, the flight lasting 20 hours and 40 minutes. Earhart soon became a celebrity,

thanks in part to one of the flight's promoters, publisher George Putnam, whom she married.

She proved herself a worthy pilot in a successful flight across North America, and in 1931, she became the first president of the Ninety-Nines, an organization of female pilots. The next year she became the first woman to fly solo across the Atlantic and was awarded the Distinguished Flying Cross from Congress.

Continuing to set records with various feats of aviation, Earhart set her sights on an unprecedented circumnavigation of the globe. After flying from Oakland to Miami, she took off from Miami with navigator Frederick Noonan on June 1, 1937. They flew to Puerto Rico and then New Guinea, having covered 20,000 miles in all, about three-quarters of the planned journey. On July 2, they took off for what would be the longest leg, a 2,600-mile flight to Howland Island in the central Pacific. Radio messages picked up by the U.S. Navy indicated their plane was low on fuel. The plane and crew were never found. The most likely of many theories is that after making navigation errors, they ran out of fuel and crashed into the ocean.

Earhart's leather jacket. Her disappearance during an attempted round-the-world flight in 1937 remains a mystery.

Albert Einstein Ranking with Isaac Newton and Charles Darwin among the most important scientists of all time, he opened up the world of quantum physics.

ALBERT EINSTEIN
★ 1879–1955 ★
PHYSICIST

Albert Einstein was one of the most important scientists in history, fundamentally altering the way we view the world. He was awarded the 1921 Nobel Prize in physics.

Einstein was born in Ulm, Germany. Moves to Munich and Italy followed during his school years. He went to Zurich to study mathematics and physics at the Swiss Federal Polytechnic Institute, from which he graduated in 1900. He became a technical assistant in the Swiss Patent Office, where he worked until 1909.

> *Our defense is not in armaments, nor in science, nor in going underground. Our defense is in law and order.*
>
> **ALBERT EINSTEIN**

Einstein earned his doctoral degree in 1905. That was also the year he wrote three papers, each of which would become the basis for a new subdiscipline of physics. The first paper opened up the theory of quantum mechanics by proposing that light is a stream of particles

Within the Barbed Wire
JAPANESE-AMERICAN INTERNMENT
★ ★ ★

Anti-ethnic hysteria was low in World War II compared with World War I. The glaring exception was aimed at the Japanese. Legitimate fears of a Japanese attack on the West Coast morphed into discrimination against Japanese Americans. Fearing saboteurs and spies, politicians and the military convinced FDR to order the removal of Japanese residents of the western states. Foreign-born Japanese-American residents and U.S.-born Japanese-American citizens had to sell their property, generally at a loss, and move to one of 10 internment camps. Many locals of European descent were happy to see successful Japanese farmers and business owners go. Some 120,000 people, two-thirds of whom were U.S. citizens, were herded off to bleak camps in isolated areas. Privacy was minimal, food inadequate, and humiliations frequent. In 1988, the U.S. apologized, giving surviving internees $20,000 each.

A wooden puzzle made by an interned Japanese American

that together have wavelike properties. The second paper, for which he is most famous, introduced the special theory of relativity, in which he presented his famous equation for subatomic matter,

$E = mc^2$, or energy is equivalent to mass times the speed of light squared. The third paper dealt with Brownian motion, which confirmed the atomic theory. All this groundbreaking work was accomplished when Einstein was 26.

In 1909, he became a professor of theoretical physics at the University of Zurich. Seven years later, now teaching in Berlin, he published his general theory of relativity, which included gravity in the theory of relativity and thus allowed all branches of physics to be expressed with the same kinds of mathematical equations. But it did not bring all the branches into one grand unified theory, and this problem continued to occupy him for the rest of this life. It has never been adequately solved.

Einstein's house was seized by the Nazis in 1933. He moved to Princeton, New Jersey, where he worked and taught for the rest of his life (becoming an American citizen in 1940). He also played classical violin, music being one of his greatest joys.

DWIGHT D. EISENHOWER
★ 1890–1969 ★
34TH U.S. PRESIDENT

Born in Texas to a modest family, Dwight D. Eisenhower became leader of the Allied forces in Europe in World War II, commander of NATO, and president of the United States.

Eisenhower graduated from the U.S. Military Academy at West Point in 1915 and married Mamie Doud the next year. Though he'd been a middling student at West Point, he was at the top of his class at the

Army's Command and General Staff College in 1926. He eventually served under General MacArthur in the Philippines.

At the outbreak of World War II, Eisenhower was made chief of the Army's War Plans Division; in 1942, he became commander of the U.S. forces in Europe, promoted for his leadership over many senior officers. He led the invasion of North Africa in 1942 and the invasion of western Europe from Normandy in 1944.

Hugely popular after the war, Eisenhower served as president of Columbia University and in 1950 as commander of NATO. The famous general was courted by both Democrats and Republicans, and after President Truman decided not to run for reelection, Eisenhower declared his candidacy for president on the Republican ticket. He swept to victory.

A strong, likable leader, Eisenhower often took a centrist position. He favored big business and small government but

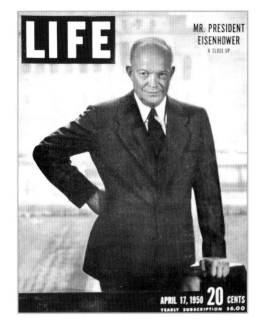

Eisenhower as president of Columbia University in 1950, three years before becoming U.S. president

also supported Social Security, the minimum wage, and creation of the Department of Health, Education, and Welfare. He sent federal troops to Arkansas to enforce federal court decisions and made resistance to such laws a federal offense in 1960. His victory in the 1956 election was even larger than in 1952. His second term was marked by the inauguration of the U.S. space program after the launching of a Soviet satellite in 1957 and an eventual break with Cuba when Fidel Castro took power in a revolution against American-backed dictator Fulgencio Batista. After leaving office in 1961, Eisenhower retired to his cattle farm in Gettysburg, Pennsylvania, where he wrote three memoirs.

Dwight D. Eisenhower The popular two-term president was the first soldier to hold the office since Ulysses S. Grant.

I LIKE IKE

DUKE ELLINGTON
★ 1899–1974 ★
BANDLEADER, COMPOSER

One of the most important figures in jazz, Duke Ellington played piano, pioneered big band music, and wrote thousands of songs, many of which became jazz standards.

Ellington was born in Washington, D.C., to musically gifted, middle-class parents. He started studying piano at 7, and began playing professionally at 17. He married high school sweetheart Edna Thompson at 19; they had one son.

Ellington moved to New York in 1923 to play in a jazz ensemble and soon became its leader. The Ellington band, which eventually included 12 members,

> *Music is how I live, why I live, and how I will be remembered.*
>
> DUKE ELLINGTON

played at the Cotton Club in Harlem from 1927 to 1932. Their blend of smooth melody, unexpected rhythmic accents, and rich harmonies was affectionately called "jungle music." Ellington's orchestrations mixed seamlessly with band members' solos to create an organic improvisatory effect, both warm and driving.

Among Ellington's hit songs were "Mood Indigo," "It Don't Mean a Thing (If It Ain't Got That Swing)," "Sophisticated Lady," "In a Sentimental Mood," "Prelude to a Kiss," and "Satin Doll." The mid-1930s to mid-1940s were Ellington's most creative years, when he presented such large-scale compositions as "Concerto for Cootie" and "Ko-Ko."

In 1939, composer and arranger Billy Strayhorn joined Ellington's band. His "Take the A Train" became the band's theme song. Other key figures in the band

included saxophonists Johnny Hodges, Harry Carney, and Ben Webster; trombonists Joe Nanton and Lawrence Brown; trumpeters Cootie Williams and Rex Stewart; and bassist Jimmy Blanton.

Ellington enjoyed a long creative and collaborative life. In the 1960s, he began writing film scores and sacred music, and recorded with up-and-coming musicians such as John Coltrane and Charles Mingus. His autobiography, *Music Is My Mistress,* was published in 1973. Ellington earned 13 Grammy Awards, three of them posthumously.

F. SCOTT FITZGERALD
★ 1896–1940 ★
WRITER

Preeminent chronicler of the excesses of the Roaring Twenties, F. Scott Fitzgerald was born in St. Paul, Minnesota. As a student at Princeton University, he wrote musicals and acted in the prestigious Triangle Club. His first novel, *This Side of Paradise* (1920), was started during this time. He continued writing about the cynicism and moral lapses of what he called the "Jazz Age" in *The Beautiful and Damned* (1922). The Jazz Age was, he wrote in his first novel, "a generation grown up to find all Gods dead, all wars fought, all faiths in man shaken." His masterpiece, *The Great Gatsby* (1925), was a short novel far less popular than his previous works but of much greater depth.

His marriage to the flamboyant Zelda Sayre, of Montgomery, Alabama, was the source of much joy and sorrow to Fitzgerald. Their escapades were the stuff of tabloid fodder, but she ultimately had to retire to a mental asylum. Some of

Duke Ellington The jazz composer and conductor poses before his first European tour. Below, he jams with Cab Calloway (on piano) at a private party.

became the minister at First Baptist Church in Montclair, New Jersey.

As a pastor, professor, and author, he spent his considerable energy discussing the conflict between religion and modern life. Arguing for the inclusion of science in religious thought and practice, he spoke out against fundamentalism. At the outset of World War I, he was one of the few ministers to advocate American involvement, a position he backed up by volunteering as a YMCA chaplain in France. During this time he also worked with the YMCA in England and Belgium.

In a key 1922 sermon, "Shall the Fundamentalists Win?" he explained that the Bible was not the literal "word of God" but a living document of God's will. Christian history, in his view, progressed and changed over the centuries, along with advances in other areas of human thought. His outspoken views put him in a pitched battle against Protestant conservatives, a battle that played out throughout the 20th century and beyond.

Fosdick served as pastor in various New York City churches: the First Presbyterian Church, Park Avenue Baptist Church, and the nondenominational Riverside Church. Riverside's most famous member and benefactor was financier John D. Rockefeller, Jr. From 1908 to 1946, Fosdick also taught at Union Theological Seminary. His sermons were aired on the National Vespers nationwide radio program. Among his many books are *The Meaning of Prayer, The Manhood of the Master, The Modern Use of the Bible, On Being a Real Person,* and his autobiography, *The Living of These Days.*

> *So we beat on, boats against the current, borne back ceaselessly into the past.*
>
> F. SCOTT FITZGERALD

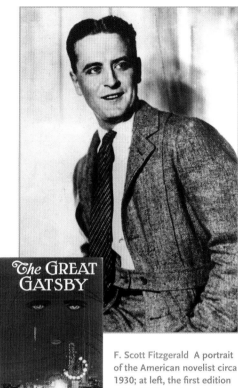

F. Scott Fitzgerald A portrait of the American novelist circa 1930; at left, the first edition of his 1925 masterpiece, *The Great Gatsby*

Fitzgerald's finest writing occurs in *Tender Is the Night* (1934), about a psychiatrist who falls in love with and marries one of his patients. Fame, high living, and alcohol abuse may have thinned Fitzgerald's literary output, but the novels and stories he wrote in his short life continue to entertain and instruct.

HARRY EMERSON FOSDICK

★ 1878–1969 ★

PREACHER

One of the most influential liberal Protestant ministers of his time, Harry Emerson Fosdick was born in Buffalo, New York. He graduated from Colgate University in 1900 and Union Theological Seminary in 1904. That same year he

Harry Emerson Fosdick The Protestant theologian is shown in the pulpit of the Park Avenue Baptist Church in New York City.

Woody Guthrie The father of American folk music wrote more than 1,000 songs.

WOODY GUTHRIE

★ 1912–1967 ★

SINGER-SONGWRITER

Legendary songwriter Woody Guthrie was born in Okemah, Oklahoma, to a musically gifted mother who taught him folk songs. He was soon playing them on guitar and harmonica. Early tragedies— the accidental death of a sister, a fire that destroyed the house, his father's financial downfall, and his mother's battle with Huntington's disease—would become the

emotional grist of his work.

As a teenager, Guthrie began playing in the streets for money, developing his skills as a performer. Moving to Texas to be with his father, he married his first wife at age 19. During the Depression of the 1930s, he migrated west away from the hard conditions created by the Dust Bowl; his experiences hitchhiking, riding freight trains, and singing in hobo camps deepened his connection with the poor working class.

In 1940, Guthrie landed in New York City, where he began associating with Pete Seeger and other folk musicians. He formed a group called the Almanac Singers, which began garnering him widespread fame. His marriage ended in 1943, the same year he published his autobiography, *Bound for Glory*. The next year he wrote his most famous song, "This Land Is Your Land." Joining the merchant marines during World War II, Guthrie turned toward political themes, with antifascist songs. He remarried and, after the war, moved to Coney Island, New York. In the late 1940s, he developed symptoms of Huntington's, the nerve disease that killed his mother. He took off for California, married a third time, and eventually moved back to New York, spending his last years in a hospital. His second wife visited him regularly, as did his most famous protégé, Bob Dylan. He is the father of 1960s singer Arlo Guthrie.

WARREN G. HARDING

★ 1865–1923 ★

29TH U.S. PRESIDENT

Born on a farm in Ohio, Warren Harding became a newspaper publisher in Marion in his 20s and soon allied with Republican state politicians. By 1915, he had worked his way up to U.S. senator. At the 1920 presidential convention, Harding was nominated as a compromise candidate. A conservative against international involvement, he won easily in the post–World War I climate. In office, he helped pass a protective tariff and legislation restricting immigration. In 1923, his secretary of the interior Albert Fall was accused of leasing federal oil reserves to his own business associates. Before the sensational Teapot Dome scandal could erupt, Harding, on a tour out West, died of unknown causes.

Warren G. Harding He died before the Teapot Dome scandal erupted.

ERNEST HEMINGWAY

★ 1899–1961 ★

WRITER

Born in Cicero (now Oak Park), Illinois, Ernest Hemingway became one of the most well known and respected writers of his time. He served a short stint reporting for the *Kansas City Star* before going to Italy to work as an ambulance driver during World War I. He was wounded and then hospitalized in Milan, early experiences of violence and bravery that became themes in his writing.

After the war Hemingway returned home, worked odd jobs, and married Hadley Richardson. He then headed to Paris as a foreign correspondent for the *Toronto Star*. He became friends with a group of expatriate writers—among them F. Scott Fitzgerald, Gertrude Stein, and Ezra Pound—their postwar disillusionment earning them the nickname the "lost generation." After publishing two books of stories and poems, he achieved early success with his first novel, *The Sun Also Rises* (1926), about a group of expatriate artists in France and Spain. His tragic love story *A Farewell to Arms* (1929) furthered his growing reputation. His rambling life of fishing, hunting, skiing, drinking, and attending bullfights was worked into his writing and became part of his public persona.

Returning to the United States in 1928, Hemingway continued to write short stories, two books of which contain some of his finest and most enduring stories: "A Clean, Well-Lighted Place," "The Short Happy Life of Francis Macomber," and "The Snows of Kilimanjaro." Hemingway employed a terse style, with a pared-down vocabulary to achieve subtle and precise effects, both emotional and visceral. His male characters are known for their courage and virility in the face of loss and danger—in his words, their "grace under pressure."

Covering the Spanish Civil War as a reporter in the late 1930s, Hemingway gleaned the material for one of his greatest novels, *For Whom the Bell Tolls* (1940). A worldwide celebrity by the 1940s, he was as well known for his manly exploits, his adventurous life, and his four wives as for his writing. His short novel *The Old Man and the Sea* (1952) again explored the idea of a man of courage accepting fate; it won the Pulitzer Prize. He won the Nobel Prize for literature in 1954. Seven years later, suffering from illness and depression, he committed suicide.

Hemingway drew on real people to write his greatest works, two of which are shown here.

The world breaks everyone and afterward many are strong in the broken places.

ERNEST HEMINGWAY

Ernest Hemingway The author writes on a portable table during a big game hunt in Kenya in 1952.

Langston Hughes A 1954 portrait of the author.
He is best known for poems praising black identity.

LANGSTON HUGHES
★ 1902–1967 ★
WRITER

African-American author Langston Hughes was born in Joplin, Missouri, to parents who separated when he was young. He early on had a love for reading and was deeply influenced by his storyteller grandmother. Though he moved often in his younger years, he was voted class poet and editor of his high school yearbook. He published his first poem at 19. After attending Columbia University from 1921 to 1922, he took a job on a freight ship to Africa and tramped around Europe.

In 1926, working as a busboy in Washington, D.C., he left some of his poems beside the plate of poet Vachel Lindsay. Lindsay's "discovery" of the budding

*What happens to
a dream deferred?
Does it dry up like a
raisin in the sun? . . .
Or does it explode?*

LANGSTON HUGHES

black poet helped advance Hughes's career. Hughes received a scholarship to Lincoln University in Pennsylvania. Before his graduation in 1929, he had published two books.

Hughes is best known for his poems about black pride and hope, many of which use rhythms imitative of jazz. An influential member of the Harlem Renaissance black cultural movement, he often wrote poetry in blues clubs. He wrote or edited more than 50 books, including works of poetry, short stories, and autobiography; he also wrote for the stage and for children. "It is the duty of the younger Negro artist," he wrote, ". . . to change through the force of his art that old whispering 'I want to be white,' hidden in the aspirations of his people, to 'Why should I want to be white? I am a Negro—and beautiful!'"

ZORA NEALE HURSTON
★ 1891–1960 ★
WRITER

Zora Neale Hurston was born the fifth of eight children in the town of Notasulga, Alabama, her father a carpenter, sharecropper, and preacher. A year later they moved to Eatonville, Florida, a town founded by African Americans. A few

years after the death of her mother when Hurston was 13, she joined a traveling theater company and found work as a maid, waitress, and manicurist.

Hurston attended Howard University for four years, during which she began writing. She went to New York City in 1925 and studied anthropology under Franz Boas at Barnard College. In the late 1920s, she began publishing short stories, thereby gaining the financial support of wealthy New York patrons. Of her four novels, her most famous is *Their Eyes Were Watching God* (1937), about a black woman's growing sense of her identity. Her writing shows her interest in black Southern culture, colorful use of metaphor, poignant sense of humor, and talent for storytelling. She wrote two works of folklore and one of autobiography, *Dust Tracks on a Road* (1942).

After traveling to the Caribbean and immersing herself in local folklore, she continued writing but with less success. About 1950 she returned to Florida, where she worked a number of jobs—housecleaning, teaching, library work, and newspaper reporting. She died in poverty and was buried in an unmarked grave in Fort Pierce.

Zora Neale Hurston The writer at a NYC book fair circa 1937

The Harlem Renaissance

THE BLACK CULTURAL MOVEMENT OF THE 1920S AND 1930S

★ ★ ★

A flowering of African-American artistic, literary, and intellectual energy, the Harlem Renaissance enriched American life by fostering some of the best talent of the 1920s through the mid-1930s. This cultural ferment centered on the New York neighborhood of Harlem and moved black literature from often weak imitations of Anglo writers to vigorous new forms of creativity that expressed uniquely black themes.

Writers Langston Hughes, Jean Toomer, Nella Larsen, Wallace Thurman, Arna Bontemps, Countee Cullen, Zora Neale Hurston, and others anchored the movement, mentored by older writers such as critic Alain Locke, sociologists W. E. B. Du Bois and Charles S. Johnson, and writers James Weldon Johnson and Claude McKay. James Johnson's early novel *Autobiography of an Ex-Coloured Man* (1912) broke new ground in the black genre, while Wallace Thurman's satirical novel *The Blacker the Berry* (1929) poked fun at some of the new black intelligentsia. Given support by white interest in black culture, the movement was aesthetic instead of political, intent mainly upon, as Hughes stated, the "expression of our individual dark-skinned selves."

A parallel movement in music occurred at the same time in Harlem, with the rise in popularity of jazz. Bandleaders Duke Ellington, Count Basie, and Cab Calloway played regularly at Harlem nightclubs. Jazz singer Billie Holiday and blues singer Bessie Smith made appearances in many of the same venues. Although not technically part of the Harlem Renaissance, the music of this period was a vital element in the cross-fertilization of the arts.

After giving distinctive voice to African Americans, the Harlem Renaissance faded during the Depression of the 1930s as many of its stars drifted away to find whatever work they could. With the advent of the civil rights movement, the movement acquired wider recognition.

Louis Armstrong plays at a recording rehearsal. The Harlem Renaissance of black literature helped cross-fertilize other arts.

Helen Keller A circa 1910 portrait of the deaf and blind author and educator

HELEN KELLER

★ 1880–1968 ★

EDUCATOR, POLITICAL ACTIVIST

Stricken at less than two years old with a disease that left her blind and deaf, Helen Keller became one of the world's premier humanitarians and a co-founder of the American Civil Liberties Union.

Keller was born in Tuscumbia, Alabama, and though extremely intelligent was a wild child, locked in her own world, until age six when her parents, on the advice of Alexander Graham Bell, hired teacher Anne Sullivan from Boston. At first Sullivan made no progress; then in a dramatic breakthrough, the determined teacher spelled the word "water" into Keller's hand while water poured over it. Now with the gift of language, Keller could connect objects with words, and she learned voraciously.

Within three years, Keller was reading and writing in Braille. She began taking lessons in speech and was able to finish school and attend Radcliffe College; Sullivan remained with her as an interpreter. In 1904, Keller graduated with honors and began working for various organizations for the blind. She also wrote articles, spoke before legislatures, and initiated the Helen Keller Endowment Fund.

Keller soon began traveling overseas, lecturing on behalf of the blind in developing and war-torn nations. She visited more than 25 countries, giving hope to untold numbers of disabled people. Among her many books were *The Story of My Life* (1903), *Out of the Dark* (1913), and *Teacher* (1955).

> *There are some who can live without wild things, and some who cannot.*
>
> **ALDO LEOPOLD**

ALDO LEOPOLD

★ 1887–1948 ★

NATURALIST

Born in Burlington, Iowa, Aldo Leopold became a wildlife biologist and conservationist who worked to merge the field of ecology with proper wildlife management. He graduated from Yale University in 1908 and earned a master's in forestry. From 1909 to 1928, he was employed by the U.S. Forest Service; he taught at the University of Wisconsin from 1933 until his death. His *A Sand County Almanac* (1949) remains a classic of insightful nature writing. Other works include the textbook *Game Management* (1933) and *Round River* (1953), a book of essays.

Organized Labor

WORKERS GAIN BENEFITS

★ ★ ★

By the 1930s, labor union membership had declined from about five million a decade earlier to three million. Most members belonged to skilled craft unions. Yet to be represented were the laborers in the growing automobile, steel, mining, and textile industries, in which mass production required little skill. During the hard years of the Depression, national sentiment shifted from business executives to workers. New Deal policies resulted in a number of gains for labor. The National Industrial Recovery Act (1933) mandated a minimum wage and allowed for collective bargaining; the National Labor Relations Act (1935) guaranteed good faith bargaining between business and unions. The Congress of Industrial Organizations, helmed by John L. Lewis, separated from the American Federation of Labor and promoted unions and strikes by "unskilled" industrial workers. During World War II, labor leaders and unions pledged not to strike. But with prosperity returning after the war, organized labor again took its share of business profits by winning wage increases and other benefits.

A worker circa 1935 punches his time card.

JOHN L. LEWIS
★ 1880–1969 ★
LABOR LEADER

A dominant figure in the labor movement, John Lewis was president of the United Mine Workers of America from 1920 to 1960 and founder of the Congress of Industrial Organizations. He early on proved himself a shrewd analyst and negotiator, and helped win wage increases for miners. Working for collective bargaining power for mass-production workers, he allied with the powerful American Federation of Labor. He and his unions broke away, formed the Congress of Industrial Organizations in 1938, and negotiated contracts with General Motors and U.S. Steel. His fiery oratory and rough-and-tumble style helped gain medical and pension benefits for miners.

His next novel, *Babbitt* (1922), is perhaps his best. Another satirical look at midwestern values, the story centers on the changing values of George Babbitt, a businessman and father whose civic pride and earnestness begin to seem hollow, inescapable barriers to a life of depth and passion. An idealistic young doctor confronts corruption and prejudice in Lewis's next novel, *Arrowsmith* (1925), for which he was awarded the Pulitzer Prize. He refused the prize, declaring that it was not awarded on the basis of literary merit. *Elmer Gantry* (1927) targets religious hypocrisy and ignorance. In *Dodsworth* (1929), a wealthy manufacturer goes to Europe and deals with marriage problems.

Lewis wrote another half dozen novels after 1930, but none of them had the sharpness of vision and energetic wit of his earlier works. His fame gone, he died alone and unhappy in Italy.

Lewis's 1935 semi-satirical political novel was adapted for the stage in 1936.

SINCLAIR LEWIS
★ 1885–1951 ★
WRITER

Born in Minnesota, Sinclair Lewis became in 1930 the first American to win a Nobel Prize for literature. Praised more for his incisive observations than artistic originality, his books remain noteworthy documents of their time and place.

Lewis graduated from Yale University in 1908 and spent the next several years traveling around the country doing editorial work. He published four apprentice novels before achieving popular success with *Main Street* (1920), about a provincial midwestern town. The book's carefully rendered local speech and social customs made Lewis a sudden figure in the literary landscape.

Sinclair Lewis A 1935 photograph of the writer. He received the Nobel Prize in literature in 1930 "for his . . . ability to create, with wit and humour, new types of characters."

CHARLES LINDBERGH
★ 1902–1974 ★
AVIATOR

Born in Detroit, Michigan, to a father who became a U.S. congressman, Charles Lindbergh made the first nonstop solo flight across the Atlantic Ocean. He instantly rose to unwanted heights of fame.

An only child, Lindbergh spent much of his youth alone. For a while he studied mechanical engineering at the University of Wisconsin, but his interests lay more with cars, motorcycles, and airplanes. He moved to Lincoln, Nebraska, in 1922 and learned to fly. Four years later he enrolled in the U.S. Air Service Reserve; in 1926, he became an airmail pilot.

The young aviator began soliciting funds from St. Louis businessmen so that he could compete for a $25,000 prize for making a New York-to-Paris flight. Soon he was off to New York (from St. Louis), completing the flight in the *Spirit of St. Louis* in a record 14.5 hours. On May 20, 1927, Lindbergh embarked on his historic journey across the Atlantic. He made the 2,610-mile trip in 33.5 hours, for which he received the Medal of Honor and widespread acclaim.

In the early 1930s, Lindbergh and his wife, Anne Morrow, mapped a number of air routes around the world. Then, in 1932, their infant son was kidnapped and murdered. To escape the publicity, the Lindberghs moved to Europe in 1936, where they remained until the early 1940s. Criticized for speaking out against American involvement in World War II, Lindbergh later supported the war effort as an adviser to aircraft companies. Though the dashing hero's reputation had fallen, his books helped restore it. *The Spirit of St. Louis* (1953) won the Pulitzer Prize for biography.

Huey Long Powerful governor of Louisiana

HUEY LONG
★ 1893–1935 ★
GOVERNOR

Born near Winnfield, Louisiana, Huey Long became a controversial populist politician, his slogan "Every Man a King" indicating his anti–big business, pro-worker position. Nicknamed the "Kingfish," Long wielded formidable power when he became Louisiana's governor in 1928. After embarking on an ambitious program of public works and welfare, he was impeached for misuse of state funds and then acquitted. He was elected to the U.S. Senate in 1930 and became a Democratic presidential candidate in 1935. That same year, he was assassinated in the state capitol in Baton Rouge. A brother, Earl Long, was also a governor, and a son, Russell Long, served as U.S. senator.

Charles Lindbergh The aviator in flying gear before leaving New York on his 1927 transatlantic flight; and a view of his plane, the *Spirit of St. Louis*, upon landing in Paris on May 20.

DOUGLAS MACARTHUR

★ 1880–1964 ★

ARMY GENERAL

Known for his commanding and at times imperious leadership, and devotion to the Army and the United States, Douglas MacArthur served with distinction in World War I and was commander of Allied forces in the Southwest Pacific during World War II.

MacArthur was born in Little Rock, Arkansas, to a father who had served as an officer in the Civil War (Union Army) and the Spanish-American War. MacArthur graduated from the U.S. Military Academy at West Point in 1903 with highest honors and took a commission as a junior officer in the Army Corps of Engineers. During World War I, he proved himself an effective combat leader; twice wounded, he was decorated for bravery. By 1918, he had risen to the rank of brigadier general.

After serving in a number of posts, MacArthur was sent by President Roosevelt to the Philippines as a military adviser in 1935, even though he had been widely criticized for sending troops to disperse protesting veterans in Washington, D.C. Two years later he retired from active duty. In July 1941, MacArthur returned as commander of Army forces in the Far East. He was caught off guard when the Japanese attacked the Philippines shortly after striking Pearl Harbor on December 7, 1941, but regrouped and mounted a spirited defense of the islands that lasted until March 1942. For his actions he received the Medal of Honor, the nation's highest military award.

MacArthur then began an offensive move against Japan, and in 1943, he gradually pushed their forces from New Guinea and surrounding islands, seizing or isolating strategic centers. At the same time, his forces were advancing northward in the Pacific to neutralize key Japanese-held bases. In October 1944, he was able, as promised, to return to the Philippines, which his troops liberated.

After the war ended in 1945, MacArthur was put in charge of the occupation and rebuilding of Japan. In 1950, he was made commander of the new United Nations forces in an effort to push the North Korean Army out of South Korea. Retreating in the face of a counteroffensive by Chinese forces, he was frustrated by his orders to conduct limited warfare.

For his outspoken insubordination, President Truman relieved him of duty in 1951. He returned to the United States a popular hero. He served as chairman of the board of the Remington Rand Corporation in New York City, wrote his memoirs, and advised Presidents Eisenhower, Kennedy, and Johnson.

It is fatal to enter any war without the will to win it.

DOUGLAS MACARTHUR

Douglas MacArthur A 1945 portrait of the tough-minded, controversial general

MACARTHUR, MASTER OF THE MIKADO

even though he had never been a field commander. He went straight to work building up the size and strength of the Army, trying to match the Germans' tremendous fighting force. In under four years, U.S. forces swelled from under 200,000 to 8,300,000 equipped and trained troops. Marshall especially excelled at coordinating efforts between branches of the military, between civilian and military leaders, and between Allied fighting forces.

After the war, President Truman appointed Marshall to a special posting in China. Though he failed to negotiate an end to the civil war there, he gained diplomatic experience and in 1947 became Truman's secretary of state. With the Cold War now on, Marshall saw that economic recovery of Europe was crucial to preventing the spread of communism. He persuaded Congress to provide funding for what became known as the Marshall Plan, a rebuilding effort to which the United States donated $13 billion. His European negotiations also helped establish West Germany and the North Atlantic Treaty Organization (NATO), both seen as crucial in containing communist influence in Western Europe.

Marshall retired because of poor health in 1949, but a year later Truman persuaded him to serve as secretary of defense. He helped increase United

George Marshall Author of the Marshall Plan, the general mapped out a way toward peace after World War II.

GEORGE MARSHALL
★ 1880–1959 ★
SOLDIER, STATESMAN

One of the most admired soldier-statesmen in U.S. history, George Marshall was the Army's chief of staff during World War II and then secretary of state and secretary of defense. For his work in the reconstruction of Europe after the war, he became in 1953 the first military professional to win the Nobel Peace Prize.

Marshall was born in Uniontown, Pennsylvania, his father a coke and coal merchant who fell on hard times. Educated at the Virginia Military Institute, Marshall earned his commission in 1902 and began serving in the Philippines. As a young leader he was known for his quiet confidence and his ability to persuade and inspire. He was married to Elizabeth Carter Coles for 25 years until her death in 1927; three years later, he married a widow named Katherine Brown who had three children.

In World War I, Marshall worked as a staff officer helping plan offensives in France. Then, when the Second World War broke out, he was made chief of staff,

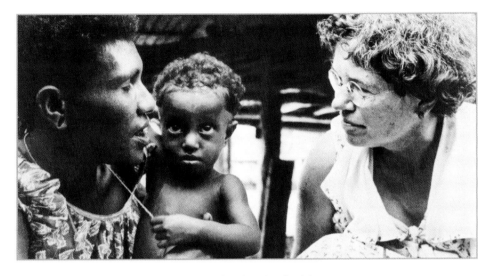

Margaret Mead The anthropologist on a visit to the Admiralty Islands in 1953

Nations troop strength in Korea, and resigned in 1951. Shortly before his resignation, Senator Joseph McCarthy slandered him as a tool of the Communists. Though the accusations cast a shadow over Marshall's final years, his supporters remained loyal, and such charges have been repudiated by historians.

MARGARET MEAD

★ 1901–1978 ★
ANTHROPOLOGIST

Margaret Mead helped pioneer the field of cultural anthropology, her extensive fieldwork investigating the influence of cultural conditioning upon personality. Born in Philadelphia, she graduated from Barnard College and earned a Ph.D. from Columbia University. In 1925, she went to Samoa in the Pacific to research the lives and customs of adolescent girls in a premodern society. She made several trips to other islands, including New Guinea and Bali. In more than a dozen books, she established herself as a leading intellectual and helped popularize anthropology and the idea of women with careers. From 1926 to 1969, she served as a curator of ethnology at the American Museum of Natural History in New York City.

H. L. MENCKEN
★ 1880–1956 ★
JOURNALIST, CRITIC

Using acerbic wit and precise language, H. L. Mencken was the most important influence on American literature and culture from around 1910 to 1940.

Henry Louis Mencken was born in Baltimore, and he began reporting for the *Baltimore Morning Herald* at 18. Four years later, the young man was managing editor of the sister paper, the *Baltimore Evening Herald.* When the paper folded in 1906, he went to work for the *Baltimore Sun,* where he stayed for the rest of his career. He also wrote some 2,000 book reviews for *Smart Set,* which he edited with George Jean Nathan from 1914 to 1923. And he helped found the *American Mercury,* a magazine of humor and politics. These two journals became key leaders of American taste and culture. Using literature as a jumping-off point, Mencken left no facet of American life untouched. His barbed critiques jabbed at the weaknesses and hypocrisies of organized religion, big business, and middle-class tastes. He observed that Americans were "the most timorous, sniveling, poltroonish, ignominious mob of serfs and goose-steppers ever gathered under one flag in Christendom since the end of the Middle Ages."

He used his savage pen to undermine the work of writers he considered successful hacks while promoting emerging authors such as Theodore Dreiser and Sinclair Lewis. Among his books are *The American Language* (1919), the six-volume *Prejudices* (1919–1927), and three autobiographies. He retired after suffering a stroke in 1948.

Conscience is the inner voice that warns us somebody may be looking.

H. L. MENCKEN

H. L. Mencken The journalist covers a political convention in Philadelphia.

JELLY ROLL MORTON

★ 1890–1941 ★

PIANIST, SONGWRITER

Born Ferdinand Joseph Lamothe to Creole parents in New Orleans, Jelly Roll Morton became one of the first creators of jazz. He learned piano at an early age and began playing in bordellos, mixing ragtime with blues and improvisation. As a teenager he traveled around the country, making a living as a musician, vaudevillian, and gambler. From 1926 to 1930, his band, the Red Hot Peppers, made recordings now considered jazz repertory classics. His claims that he invented jazz were dismissed as hyperbole by his contemporaries, and his popularity faded. In 1938, folklorist Alan Lomax recorded interviews with Morton and examples of his playing, ensuring his legacy in jazz history.

Edward R. Murrow The pioneering broadcast journalist in a photograph circa 1954

The front cover of a 1915 publication of the "Jelly Roll Blues," a Jelly Roll Morton hit

EDWARD R. MURROW

★ 1908–1965 ★

BROADCAST JOURNALIST

Born near Greensboro, North Carolina, Edward R. Murrow became one of the preeminent radio and television journalists, setting a standard for serious, balanced news reporting.

After graduating from Washington State University in 1930, Murrow led the National Student Federation. He joined the Columbia Broadcasting System (CBS) in 1935 as director of Talks and Education. Two years later he went to London as head of the network's European bureau. His emphasis soon shifted from cultural programming to covering Nazi aggression, starting with Austria and the Anschluss in 1938. With air raid sirens and bursting bombs in the background, Murrow calmly reported on the German attacks on Britain.

After the war, Murrow returned to the United States and became the vice president of news, education, and discussion programs at CBS. But within two years he was back to broadcasting, presenting a one-hour weekly program. In 1950, the journalist reported on the Korean War, and in 1954, his reporting on Senator Joseph McCarthy helped defang the ringleader of the Red Scare, which had unjustly impugned many Americans for supposed leftist leanings. Murrow's important 1960 documentary *Harvest of Shame* detailed the hard life of migratory farm workers.

In 1961, President Kennedy appointed Murrow director of the U.S. Information Agency; he resigned in 1964 because of lung cancer. A heavy smoker, he died in 1965.

REINHOLD NIEBUHR
★ 1892–1971 ★
THEOLOGIAN, ETHICIST

Born in Missouri to an immigrant German minister, Reinhold Niebuhr became one of the leading proponents of the neoorthodox Protestant movement, which started in the 1920s.

After receiving his master's in divinity from Yale in 1915, Niebuhr served as pastor of a small Detroit church for 13 years. During this time, he saw the dispiriting effects of assembly-line production upon low-wage workers and began to question capitalism. In 1928, Niebuhr moved to New York City and joined the faculty of Union Theological Seminary, remaining there until 1960. With the arrival of the Depression, he began embracing socialism, while his theology turned to a more conservative form of Christianity. His 1932 book, *Moral Man and Immoral Society,* assailed the failures of liberal Protestantism. In this and other works, his systematic critiques of social problems stressed Christian faith as the best way of understanding and overcoming modern dilemmas of society and self. A profound and influential thinker, he spread his message by preaching on college campuses and writing articles and essays. His brother, H. Richard Niebuhr, was also an important Christian theological ethicist.

Niebuhr's Marxist and pacifist positions evaporated with the rise of Nazism and the outbreak of World War II. Above all a pragmatist, he advocated restraint in America's postwar involvement in Southeast Asia, much as he had criticized Communist advances in Europe. A stroke in 1952 forced him to curtail much of his activity.

CHESTER NIMITZ
★ 1885–1966 ★
ADMIRAL

Commander of the Pacific Fleet during World War II, Chester Nimitz undertook the rebuilding of the U.S. Navy after the Japanese attack on Pearl Harbor on December 7, 1941. Directing the Navy and the Marines in the Pacific, he launched a campaign of island-hopping, gaining one outpost after another, including major victories at Midway, Iwo Jima, and Okinawa. With a supply line stretched across the Pacific, he led the United States to the gateway of Japan. After the war he served, among other duties, as chief of naval operations. Nimitz was born in Texas and graduated from the U.S. Naval Academy in 1905.

Reinhold Niebuhr A profound thinker, the theologian's Christian realism addressed the failings of liberal Protestantism.

Rosie the Riveter
WOMEN FILL IN THE GAP
★★★

With 16 million men off fighting in World War II, women had to fill the vacuum left in the American workforce. The "Rosie the Riveter" campaign encouraged women to step up as their patriotic duty. The iconic image of Rosie, displayed on posters and advertisements throughout the land, was of a bandanna-wearing woman, flexing her bicep, and saying, "We Can Do It."

Defense-contractor employers, particularly in munitions and aviation, were in need of women in skilled and unskilled positions to supply the war effort overseas. During the war years, millions of women worked outside the home, swelling women's participation in the workforce from 25 to 37 percent. Besides factory work, women joined the armed services in unprecedented numbers. About 350,000 women served at home and abroad. The Women's Army Corps (WAC) began recruiting women in 1942; other service branches followed suit. The Women Airforce Service Pilots (WASP) transported supplies and tested and ferried planes, thus freeing up male pilots for combat duty.

A World War II poster circa 1942

J. Robert Oppenheimer He oversaw the creation of the first atom bomb.

J. ROBERT OPPENHEIMER
★ 1904–1967 ★
PHYSICIST

Known as the father of the atomic bomb, J. Robert Oppenheimer was the technical director of the Manhattan Project, which built the world's first nuclear weapons during World War II.

Oppenheimer was born in New York City, his father a successful German textile importer. He graduated from Harvard summa cum laude in 1925, studying physics, chemistry, Latin, Greek, and Oriental philosophy. He went to Cambridge University in England and to the University of Göttingen in Germany. There, he met Niels Bohr and other eminent physicists working on quantum theory. From 1928 to 1940, he shuttled back and forth between the University of California, Berkeley and the California

I am become death, the destroyer of worlds.

J. ROBERT OPPENHEIMER, QUOTING THE BHAGAVAD GITA AFTER WITNESSING THE FIRST ATOMIC EXPLOSION

Institute of Technology. He rapidly became one of the country's leading researchers on subatomic particles and was known for his leadership qualities.

In June 1942, Oppenheimer was appointed scientific director of the Manhattan Project, a secret mission to try to harness nuclear energy to create a bomb. He assembled a think-and-create tank of more than 3,000 people and managed a steady stream of theoretical and mechanical problems. On July 16, 1945, at Alamogordo, New Mexico, he and his team of top scientists observed the first nuclear explosion.

After the war Oppenheimer served as chair of the General Advisory Committee to the Atomic Energy Commission from 1947 to 1952. In 1953, he was accused of communist sympathies and of opposing the development of the hydrogen bomb. Only the latter was true, but his security clearance was revoked and his reputation unfairly damaged. Until 1966, he was director of Princeton's Institute for Advanced Study.

Dorothy Parker The writer was known for her savage wit.

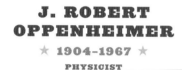

DOROTHY PARKER
★ 1893–1967 ★
WRITER

As famous for her sparkling wit and literary criticism as for her poetry and short stories, Dorothy Parker was a member of the Algonquin Round Table, a renowned salon of writers who met regularly at the Algonquin Hotel in New York City. Parker was born in West End, New Jersey, and began writing for *Vanity Fair* and in 1925 for the *New Yorker*. Her first collection of poems appeared in 1926, her first book of short stories in 1930. Using crisp dialogue and precise observation, she showed sympathy for her characters while delineating the hypocrisy and cruelty of their urban surroundings.

GEORGE PATTON
★ 1885–1945 ★
ARMY GENERAL

An expert in tank warfare tactics, George Patton was one of the most successful and revered generals in World War II. His brash, tough manner inspired loyalty in his troops—who called him "Old Blood and Guts"—and fear in his enemies.

Born in San Gabriel, California, Patton was descended from a Virginia family with a strong military tradition. He graduated from the U.S. Military Academy in 1909 and placed fifth in the pentathlon at the 1912 Olympics. During World War I, he was assigned to the U.S. tank corps in France. He won the Distinguished Service Cross for his outstanding leadership.

George Patton The general (left) arrives in Great Britain during World War II. The flamboyant officer (above) was the subject of the 1970 biopic *Patton*.

In World War II, he was part of the North African campaign in 1942, and the following year his Seventh Army successfully invaded Sicily. Shortly afterward, his temper flared when he slapped two hospitalized soldiers suffering from battle fatigue. He was reprimanded by General Eisenhower, and his promotion to major general was delayed.

Back in action in 1944, Patton began a bold and rapid roll across German-held France. His forces captured one town after another, at times moving far in advance of their supplies. In command of the Third Army, he helped win the decisive Battle of the Bulge near Bastogne, Belgium, in December 1944 and then swept across Germany and into Czechoslovakia and Austria.

Stationed in Germany after the war, Patton was injured in a car accident near Mannheim and died 12 days later.

FRANCES PERKINS
★ 1880–1965 ★
SECRETARY OF LABOR

The first woman Cabinet member, Frances Perkins became secretary of labor under Franklin Roosevelt. She was born in Boston and graduated from Mount Holyoke College in 1902; she earned her master's from Columbia University in 1910. After volunteering at Jane Addams's Hull-House, she became a labor and reform activist, lobbying for worker safety, minimum wages, maximum hours, and child labor laws. She became New York's industrial commissioner in 1929; she was secretary of labor from 1933 to 1945 and then served on the U.S. Civil Service Commission until 1953. She later taught at Cornell University's School of Industrial and Labor Relations.

EMILY POST
★ 1872/73–1960 ★
WRITER

Maven of manners, Emily Post wrote books and newspaper columns on etiquette, informing the public how to behave in social situations. She was born the only daughter of a wealthy architect in Baltimore. After a divorce in 1906, she began writing novels and short stories, but it was the publication of *Etiquette* in 1922 that brought her huge success. Her commonsense approach to manners, stressing consideration for making others feel at ease, won her a wide audience. She appeared for eight years on a radio program and updated her advice to accommodate changing social attitudes.

Emily Post She wrote the bible on manners and social etiquette.

A. Philip Randolph The black leader (front row, right) was instrumental in directing the 1963 March on Washington.

A. PHILIP RANDOLPH
★ 1889–1979 ★
CIVIL RIGHTS LEADER

A major voice in the labor and civil rights movements, A. Philip Randolph was born in Florida and attended the City College of New York. In 1917, he helped found *The Messenger* (later *Black Worker*) magazine and began running for political positions as a socialist.

Randolph turned to fighting the Pullman Company by organizing the Brotherhood of Sleeping Car Porters, the first successful black trade union. In 1925, he became the union's first president; in 1937, the union negotiated its first contract with Pullman, Randolph helping the porters gain pay increases and shorter hours. The next year, he took the union out of the American Federation of Labor (AFL) because of its weaknesses in battling discrimination. Instead, he joined the new Congress of Industrial Organizations (CIO).

Now a force to be reckoned with in the overlapping fields of labor and black activism, Randolph threatened a march on Washington in 1941 to protest discrimination against blacks in federal agencies and in businesses with federal contracts. The move helped convince President Franklin Roosevelt to issue an executive order banning discrimination in government and the defense industry. Randolph became vice president of the combined AFL-CIO in 1955 and a director of the March on Washington for Jobs and Freedom in 1963.

RINGLING BROTHERS
★ ALBERT, 1852–1916 ★
★ OTTO, 1858–1911 ★
★ ALFRED, 1861–1919 ★
★ CHARLES, 1863–1926 ★
★ JOHN, 1866–1936 ★
CIRCUS IMPRESARIOS

Creators of one of the world's most successful circus companies, the Ringling Brothers were sons of German harness-maker August Rüngeling. Albert was born in Chicago, Otto in Baraboo, Wisconsin, and the others in McGregor, Iowa. After touring for two seasons with a variety show—juggling, dancing, and performing skits—the brothers organized their own circus, which presented

Ringling Brothers The famous family, who transformed their touring company into a world-renowned circus

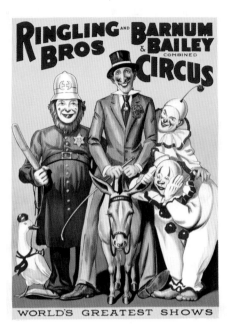

A circa 1938 Ringling Bros. and Barnum & Bailey Circus show poster

its first show in Baraboo on May 19, 1884. The brothers themselves, along with about 20 hired hands, made and pitched the tent, sold tickets, played in the band, and performed in the show.

They began traveling from one town to another, the circus moving in horse-drawn wagons. Two other brothers, August and Henry, joined them on occasion. By 1890, they were transporting their show by train and competing with the much larger Barnum & Bailey circus. With their business acumen, division of labor, and sense of entertainment, the Ringling Brothers were able, upon the death of James Bailey, to buy Barnum & Bailey in 1907. The two circuses continued to travel separately until merging in 1919 to form the largest circus in the United States.

The John and Mable Ringling Museum of Art stands on an estate in Sarasota, Florida, the land originally purchased by John Ringling in 1911. The Ringling family sold the circus in 1967.

BILL "BOJANGLES" ROBINSON
★ 1878–1949 ★
DANCER, ACTOR

Known for his elegant tap dancing and affable manner, Bill Robinson began performing on the streets of Richmond, his birthplace. By 1891, he had joined a traveling company and performed in nightclubs and vaudeville acts, almost always for black audiences. After serving in World War I, he starred in a popular musical revue on Broadway in 1928. His success led to appearances in 14 motion pictures, most famously opposite child star Shirley Temple in several musicals. Robinson was married three times. He co-founded the New York Black Yankees baseball team in Harlem. Earning millions, he gave away much of his wealth and died in poverty.

WILL ROGERS
★ 1879–1935 ★
HUMORIST

Famous for his gentle social criticism and homespun humor, Will Rogers was born in Oologah, Indian Territory (now Oklahoma). He dropped out of school in 10th grade to become a cowboy and later traveled to South Africa as a trick roper with a Wild West show. After a circus stint in Australia and New Zealand, he returned to the United States and became a vaudevillian. He began talking while doing lasso tricks, his topics ranging from business to government to people. He acted in movies, appeared on the radio, wrote a newspaper column, and authored six books. Rogers died in a plane crash in Alaska.

The Glory Years
HOLLYWOOD AT ITS PEAK
★★★

Hollywood emerged as an American icon in the 1920s, a place where glamorous people lived and made larger-than-life dreams. The movie industry was created by a group of Polish-Jewish entrepreneurs with roots in prewar vaudeville and old-country Yiddish theater. Men like Samuel Goldwyn and Harry and Jack Warner were fascinated with the energy, dazzle, and opportunity that America represented to enterprising immigrants, and their vision of American life became projected onto screens around the country. They also invented the famed—and exploitative—studio system, in which movie stars and writers, directors, and cameramen "belonged" to their producers. Paramount Pictures, 20th Century Fox, Metro-Goldwyn-Mayer, Columbia, Warner Brothers, and other studios kept tight control over every facet of their productions. Part of the Southern California metropolis centered on Los Angeles, Hollywood came to embody the promise of America. Featuring stars such as Gary Cooper, Greta Garbo, John Barrymore, Claudette Colbert, and Joan Crawford, movies sold to worldwide audiences a vision of America that was upwardly mobile, witty, fun, and sexy.

Hollywood screen star Marlene Dietrich

The typewriter used
by Eleanor Roosevelt

ELEANOR ROOSEVELT
★ 1884–1962 ★
FIRST LADY

Widely respected and admired, Eleanor Roosevelt was the wife of President Franklin D. Roosevelt, a United Nations diplomat, and a humanitarian with a distinguished record of service to a number of causes.

Roosevelt was born in New York City, the niece of Theodore Roosevelt. She attended school in England, returned to America, and, in 1905, married Franklin D. Roosevelt, a distant cousin. Her married years were spent raising five children and serving as a hostess for her husband's early political friends. After FDR was stricken with polio in 1921, she became more of a public figure, helping to inspire him to continue in politics. From 1924 to 1928, she served as financial chair of the women's committee of the state Democratic Party. She also joined the Women's Trade Union League, co-founded a non-profit factory near Hyde Park, New York, and bought and ran a private school.

Thus it was not surprising that she continued with a busy roster of activities and liberal causes after her husband became president in 1933. The breadth of her involvement was unprecedented for a first lady and, for some, unseemly. Unfazed by criticism, she soldiered on. She made extensive research trips for the president, reporting back on various programs and living conditions; she instituted White House press conferences for women reporters; she wrote a daily column; and she gave radio broadcasts.

During World War II, Roosevelt traveled to England and the South Pacific, helping to boost morale among the troops and strengthen ties with U.S. allies. After the death of her husband on April 12, 1945, she continued leading a breathtakingly busy life, advancing the causes of minorities, the poor, and the disadvantaged. Appointed by President Truman to the United Nations General Assembly, she served as chair of the Human Rights Commission and helped draft the Universal Declaration of Human

> *You must do the thing you think you cannot do.*
>
> **ELEANOR ROOSEVELT**

Rights. President Kennedy appointed her to the National Advisory Committee of the Peace Corps. She remained a popular lecturer, wrote several books, and kept promoting humanitarian ideals. Her life of work served as an inspiration for a generation of women.

Eleanor Roosevelt The first lady (right) on the way to the White House with Queen Elizabeth in 1939.

FRANKLIN D. ROOSEVELT

★ 1882–1945 ★

32ND U.S. PRESIDENT

The only president to be reelected three times, Franklin D. Roosevelt shepherded the United States through the Great Depression and World War II. His confident leadership, outgoing personality, firm belief in helping the underprivileged, and undaunted energy during war (despite failing health) earned him a place in the pantheon of the most extraordinary Americans.

Roosevelt was born the only child of wealthy parents in Hyde Park, New York. He graduated from Harvard University in 1903 and then studied at Columbia University Law School, passing the bar in 1907. He began practicing with a firm in New York City and soon became active in politics. In 1910, he ran for the New York Senate as a Democrat in a Republican district and won.

Three years later Roosevelt was appointed assistant secretary of the Navy by President Woodrow Wilson. For the next seven years Roosevelt served with able efficiency, his rising popularity such that he was nominated for vice president in 1920. With the Democrats' loss to Warren Harding, Roosevelt went back to private life, the head of a family that included five children.

In 1921, Roosevelt contracted polio, leaving him without the use of his legs. Encouraged by his wife and others, he decided to get back into politics and was elected governor of New York in 1928. With the onset of a widespread economic depression, Republican President Hoover fell from favor, and Roosevelt was elected president in 1932.

Roosevelt took office while the U.S. banking system was collapsing, farms were foreclosing, factories were shutting down, and unemployment was out of control. The president acted quickly to reassure a panicking public. He began pushing legislation through Congress to establish federal insurance for bank deposits, regulate the stock market, and set up the Civilian Conservation Corps and, eventually, other agencies to provide jobs and relief, and build a solid American infrastructure. He also started a series of "fireside chats," radio broadcasts to inform the public what was being done. Though he was sometimes assailed for overreaching, his New Deal policies began paying dividends, and FDR handily won reelection in 1936.

With the outbreak of World War II in 1939, Roosevelt urged American aid to

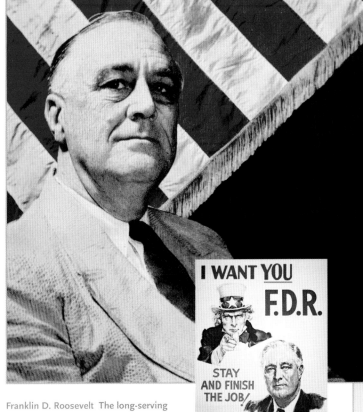

Franklin D. Roosevelt The long-serving president in a portrait circa 1941; *inset:* A campaign poster

Britain, France, and China. A reluctant public began changing its mind after the fall of France. With the attack on Pearl Harbor in December 7, 1941, America was at war, and FDR took a strong role in guiding the U.S. armed forces.

In the meantime, he had won an unprecedented third term in office in 1940. The physical and mental strain on the president contributed to heart and circulatory problems that led to his death a few months after being elected to a fourth term and a few months before the end of the war.

> *True individual freedom cannot exist without economic security and independence . . . People who are hungry and out of a job are the stuff of which dictatorships are made.*
>
> **FRANKLIN D. ROOSEVELT**

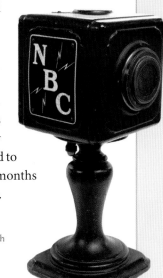

FDR's radio microphone on which he broadcast his fireside chats

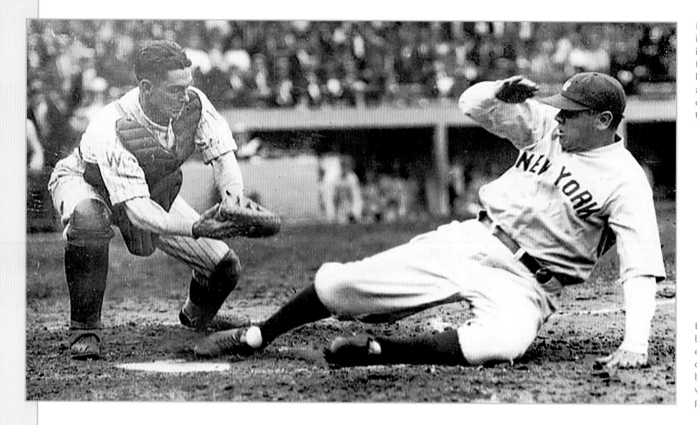

Babe Ruth The baseball icon slides into home, in a 1920s game. The Babe provided a bright light to millions of fans as they coped with the devastating impact of the Great Depression.

Below, the slugger's bat and a signed ball are examples of the kinds of collectors' items that became popular and valuable with the rising prominence of baseball.

BABE RUTH
★ 1895–1948 ★
BASEBALL PLAYER

Baseball legend Babe Ruth was born George Herman Ruth in a poor section of Baltimore. His baseball skills were first developed at the St. Mary's Industrial School for Boys. In 1914, he began playing for the Baltimore Orioles, then a minor league team; he earned his nickname because he was only 19. Later that year Ruth began his major league career as a pitcher for the Boston Red Sox. In his career with the Red Sox, he accrued an impressive record of 89 wins to 46 losses.

By this time, Ruth had also displayed phenomenal prowess as a hitter. In 1919, he was sold to the New York Yankees,

where he became an outfielder. He quickly began to change the nature of the game; high scores and home runs became much more common, adding to baseball's excitement. In 1920, Ruth blasted 54 home runs, a new record that smashed his nearest competitor that year by 35 homers. In 1927, he hit 60, a record that lasted 34 years. The "Sultan of Swat" became a celebrity, his flashy swagger a symbol of the Roaring Twenties. His growing fame helped sell so many tickets that the new Yankee Stadium was called "The House That Ruth Built."

On his retirement in 1935, Ruth held 56 major league records, including a lifetime home run total of 714, not topped until 1974 by Hank Aaron. Ruth helped the previously unheralded Yankees win seven American League pennants and four World Series. After his

> *Baseball was, is and always will be to me the best game in the world.*
>
> **BABE RUTH**

death from cancer, his body lay in repose in Yankee Stadium; more than 100,000 people came to pay their respects.

NICOLA SACCO & BARTOLOMEO VANZETTI

★ SACCO, 1891–1927 ★

★ VANZETTI, 1888–1927 ★

ANARCHISTS

Defendants in a controversial murder trial, Nicola Sacco and Bartolomeo Vanzetti were political anarchists who came to the United States from Italy. Sacco was born in the small southern Italian town of Torremaggiore. He immigrated to the United States in 1908 with his brother and found work in construction and at a textile company in Milford, Massachusetts. From 1910 to 1917, he worked as a shoe trimmer at the Milford Shoe Company. He married Rosina Zambelli in 1912; they had two children.

In 1913, Sacco began going to weekly meetings of Circolo di Studi Sociali, a group of 25 anarchists, and he began writing for an anarchist newspaper. He met Vanzetti in 1917; they and others moved to Mexico to avoid the draft for World War I. A few months later he returned to the United States and settled in Stoughton, Massachusetts.

Vanzetti, from Villafalletto in northern Italy, also arrived in 1908 and began working in a New York kitchen. He left the city the following year, drifted about finding odd jobs, and eventually ended up as a pick-and-shovel worker in Springfield, Massachusetts, in 1912. A loner, he spent much of his time reading books on political philosophy and began to gravitate toward anarchism.

After leaving Mexico in 1917, Vanzetti made his way back to Massachusetts and became a fish peddler so that he could spend his days outside. In 1920, he and Sacco were arrested for murdering a factory paymaster and a guard during a robbery in Braintree, Massachusetts. They were found guilty the following year; a series of appeals followed, and they were executed in 1927.

America on Trial
THE SACCO-VANZETTI AFFAIR
★ ★ ★

The 1921 capital murder trial of Italian immigrants Nicola Sacco and Bartolomeo Vanzetti is noted for its controversial mix of politics and jurisprudence. Sacco and Vanzetti were arrested in April 1920 for the robbery and murder of a payroll master and guard at a shoe factory in Braintree, Massachusetts. Avowed anarchists, Sacco and Vanzetti were spotted returning to their car near the scene of the crime; they were armed. Their six-week trial ended on July 14, 1921, with a guilty verdict.

The assassination of President McKinley in 1901 by an anarchist resulted in a law banning anarchists from entering the country. A fringe political system advocating the abolition of government, anarchism was on the wane around the world but was still feared in the post–World War I United States. Bolsheviks and radicals were being deported to Soviet Russia.

After the trial, the presiding judge, Webster Thayer, admitted that the duo's political leanings helped convince him of their guilt. A public outcry arose about the trial's fairness, with many people claiming there was too little evidence to convict and pointing to evidence that an anarchist gang was responsible.

The appeals process lasted six years. On August 23, 1927, Sacco and Vanzetti were executed by electric chair. Protests far and wide condemned the whole process. Outside the place of execution, Boston's old Charlestown prison, tens of thousands of protesters gathered to decry what they claimed was a travesty of justice. In 1977, Massachusetts governor Michael Dukakis signed a proclamation declaring the trial improper. Some historians believe that only Sacco was guilty.

Protesters rally in London against the death sentence of Sacco and Vanzetti in the United States.

Margaret Sanger The activist opened the first birth-control clinic in the United States in 1916.

MARGARET SANGER
★ 1883–1966 ★
WOMEN'S RIGHTS ACTIVIST

A pioneering feminist, Margaret Sanger advocated the need for birth control, a term she coined. She was born in Corning, New York, one of 11 children in a poor Catholic Irish-American family. She became convinced that her mother's many pregnancies, as well as miscarriages, helped cause her early death.

Sanger worked briefly as a teacher and became a nurse in New York City's Lower East Side, where she observed the relationship between high rates of fertility and poverty, illegal abortion, and infant mortality. She and her architect husband, William Sanger, also immersed themselves in the bohemian culture of Greenwich Village, socializing with reformist writers like Upton Sinclair.

In 1912, Sanger began to devote herself to educating women about sex. She started writing a newspaper column and two years later began publishing a magazine called *The Woman Rebel,* which

No woman can call herself free until she can choose consciously whether she will or will not be a mother.

MARGARET SANGER

promoted voluntary motherhood, or, as she called it, "birth control." She was indicted for mailing "obscene and immoral materials" under the Comstock Act of 1873, which prohibited publishing information about contraception.

To avoid prison, Sanger fled to England, returning in 1915 to face the charges; they were eventually dropped. The following year she opened the first birth-control clinic in the United States. Again arrested, this time as a "public nuisance," she spent 30 days in jail. In 1921, she founded the American Birth Control League, which became a forerunner of the Planned Parenthood Federation of America. She continued to work for women's

rights her whole life. In addition to pushing legalization of birth control, she helped raise funding in the early 1950s to support research into the creation of a "magic pill." The first oral contraceptive appeared on the market in 1960.

BESSIE SMITH
★ 1894–1937 ★
SINGER

Born into a poor family in Tennessee, soulful blues singer Bessie Smith left home as a teenager to tour with a minstrel show. Championed by blues artist "Ma" Rainey, Smith sang in southern saloons and theaters. In 1923, she began recording with Columbia Records. Among jazz musicians she recorded with were Louis Armstrong, Fletcher Henderson, and Benny Goodman. Her popularity declined in the 1930s as musical tastes began to

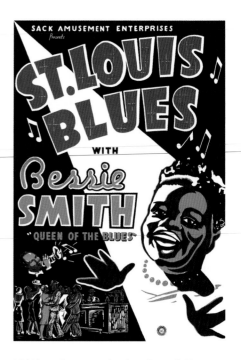

A 1929 movie poster advertises *St. Louis Blues,* starring Bessie Smith.

change, and though black audiences bought millions of her records, she was little known to white audiences for most of her life. She died from injuries suffered during a car crash in Mississippi.

JOHN STEINBECK
★ 1902–1968 ★
WRITER

Born in Salinas, California, John Steinbeck portrayed in vivid, lyrical prose the struggles and triumphs of the working class and the conflicts between man and nature. He worked as a farm laborer while studying at Stanford University. Not until his third novel (fourth book), *Tortilla Flat* (1935), did he win critical and popular success. Other important works include the short novel *Of Mice and Men* (1937), about two migrant workers; Pulitzer-winning *The Grapes of Wrath* (1939), concerning a Depression-era family and considered his greatest work; and *East of Eden* (1952), a multigenerational saga. Steinbeck won the Nobel Prize for literature in 1962.

JOHN WAYNE
★ 1907–1979 ★
ACTOR

Born Marion Robert Morrison in Winterset, Iowa, John Wayne became a symbol of the macho American male, whether cowboy, sports hero, sailor, or marine. The burly, slow-talking actor made his first leading-role appearance in *The Big Trail* (1930), a box-office flop. After many years in B movies, "Duke" finally broke through with John Ford's popular

Western *Stagecoach* (1939). Other classic John Wayne movies include *The Long Voyage Home* (1940), *The Spoilers* (1942), *Red River* (1948), *Sands of Iwo Jima* (1949), *Rio Grande* (1950), *Rio Bravo* (1959), and *True Grit* (1969), for which he won an Academy Award for best actor.

IDA B. WELLS
★ 1862–1931 ★
CIVIL RIGHTS ACTIVIST

Crusader against lynching and black oppression, Ida Wells was born into slavery in Holly Springs, Mississippi, to politically active parents. She became a teacher in Memphis and co-owner and editor of a black newspaper, *The Free Speech and Headlight.* Her editorials blasted disenfranchisement, violence against blacks, substandard schools, and black indifference. After the lynching of a store owner friend, she encouraged blacks to leave town. Her newspaper office was wrecked

Ida B. Wells The black activist documented the use of lynching as a means of oppressing blacks.

by a mob, and she was warned to stay away. She retreated to England and continued publishing antilynching material. In 1895, she married Chicago lawyer Ferdinand Barnett. The following year she helped form the National Association of Colored Women.

John Wayne Known as Duke, the popular actor (center) appeared in nearly 250 films.

Woodrow Wilson The president and First Lady Edith Bolling Wilson, who played a strong behind-the-scenes role

WOODROW WILSON

★ 1856–1924 ★

28TH U.S. PRESIDENT

America's only Ph.D. president, Thomas Woodrow Wilson was an educator and reform politician before becoming the president who guided America through World War I. After the war he continued working for world peace and democracy, his proposed League of Nations a forerunner to the United Nations.

Wilson was born in Staunton, Virginia, son of a Presbyterian minister. He graduated from the College of New Jersey (now Princeton) in 1879 and earned his Ph.D. from Johns Hopkins University in 1886. In 1902, he became president of Princeton. Known as a brilliant speaker and high-minded idealist, Wilson was asked by the Democrats to run for governor of New Jersey in 1910. He won easily and launched a successful batch of social reforms. Wilson's quick rise to prominence catapulted him into a run for president in 1912; with Republicans split between President Taft and Theodore Roosevelt, Wilson won. He set about helping small businesses, approving the Federal Reserve Act, and supporting labor unions.

Sometimes people call me an idealist. Well, that is the way I know I am an American . . . America is the only idealistic nation in the world.

WOODROW WILSON

Wilson won a second term in part because of the slogan "He kept us out of war." Yet when Germany continued sinking American ships, he asked Congress to declare war. U.S. entry into World War I in 1917 helped bring that conflict to an end the following year. Wilson set forth his "Fourteen Points" at the Versailles peace conference. His plan for a lasting worldwide peace included establishment of a League of Nations. Though Europe adopted the plan, the U.S. Congress was loath to commit to a binding foreign obligation and refused.

While touring the country to drum up support for the treaty, Wilson had a paralytic stroke in October 1919. It wasn't his first stroke, but it left him an invalid, and the treaty failed in the Senate. He was awarded the Nobel Peace Prize in 1919.

FRANK LLOYD WRIGHT

★ 1867–1959 ★

ARCHITECT

Perhaps America's most famous architect, Frank Lloyd Wright was born in Richland Center, Wisconsin. He briefly attended the University of Wisconsin before moving in 1887 to Chicago, where he became a draftsman. That same year he joined the architectural firm of Dankmar Adler and Louis Sullivan. Six years later he created his own firm. From Sullivan, father of modern functionalism, Wright learned about adapting form to function. His early significant designs were in what became known as the Prairie style. These low structures emphasized horizontal lines to fit in with their surroundings. The use of wood and other natural materials helped achieve a harmonious blend of building and setting. Many of Wright's early 1900s buildings were built in and around Chicago. In the 1920s, he designed homes in Southern California using precast concrete blocks. His Imperial Hotel in Tokyo was among the few surviving buildings of a 1923 earthquake. New York's Guggenheim Museum is an example of his later work.

Frank Lloyd Wright The innovative architect was known for human-centered design.

Master Houses

THE ARCHITECTURE OF FRANK LLOYD WRIGHT

★ ★ ★

By 1900, the Prairie school of architecture had taken hold in the Midwest, and 33-year-old Frank Lloyd Wright was its chief proponent. Designs for Prairie-style houses called for mass-produced materials, earth tones, and roomy living spaces; walls were simple and few, allowing flow from one large room to another. The idea was to achieve comfort and convenience at reasonable cost. The aesthetic appeal was in the horizontal elements, making the house feel part *of* the low-lying prairie, not set *on* it. Wright even designed furniture to complement his organic designs. In the first decade of the 20th century, he designed 50 such homes. Robie House (1910) on the campus of the University of Chicago is one of his finest Prairie houses.

In the 1930s, Wright developed a new kind of inexpensive, elegantly simple house. The "Usonian" design had a flat roof and consisted of one story on a heated concrete foundation. Examples include the Jacobs House near Madison, Wisconsin, and the Goetsch-Winckler House in Okemos, Michigan.

Wright's masterpiece house was built between 1936 and 1937 on a wooded hillside near Uniontown, Pennsylvania. Fallingwater was designed for Pittsburgh millionaire Edgar Kaufmann. Jutting out over a small waterfall in a creek, the house seems to grow from the rock cliff it rests against. Descending rectangles of native stone and glass mimic the ledges of the waterfall and blend the building into the scenery. The intimate interior forces the eye outside to the natural surroundings. The *New York Times* called the house Wright's "most sublime integration of man and nature." Wright's own homes, Taliesin and Taliesin West, preserve his legacy and his principles of organic architecture.

One of the best known works of American architecture, Fallingwater, located in Pennsylvania, employs local stone and other materials to fit into the natural landscape. *Inset:* A chair designed by the architect

The Hungry Years
AMERICA IN THE GREAT DEPRESSION

The Roaring Twenties came to a screeching halt on October 24, 1929, the day Wall Street crashed. The 1930s were known for the worst economic crisis in the country's history. During the Great Depression, the hardest hit were the low-wage earners and industrial and farm workers. With no safety nets such as pensions and unemployment and bank deposit insurance, a bad situation grew worse. Runs on banks became common as panicky savers tried to close their accounts and banks tried to call in loans. Soup kitchens sprang up everywhere, local governments and churches doing what they could to help. A lingering drought gripped the Great Plains region, causing prairie soil, mistreated for half a century, to turn into the Dust Bowl. Refugees fled to California's farm-labor camps. President Franklin Roosevelt's New Deal, initiated in 1933, was a program of government reforms that helped ease the effects of the Depression.

Dorothea Lange's iconic 1936 photo of the Great Depression depicts migrant worker Florence Owens Thompson, mother of seven.

Migrant workers' earnings ranged from 75 cents to $1.25 a day, based on the quantity of product picked.

The Civilian Conservation Corps (CCC) was launched with the aim of restoring forests in the United States. Tree planting, trail clearing, and firefighting also provided desperately needed jobs.

Life was difficult for migrant workers. An orange pickers' camp in California in 1938 shows the minimal living conditions under which the pickers lived.

A CCC reforestation project helps shore up eroded hillsides and plants windbreaks. The work-creation program was part of President Franklin D. Roosevelt's New Deal policies.

And so, my fellow Americans: ask not what your country
can do for you—ask what you can do for your country.
My fellow citizens of the world: ask not what America will do for you,
but what together we can do for the freedom of man.

JOHN F. KENNEDY

LEADER OF THE FREE WORLD

THE UNITED STATES EMERGED FROM WORLD WAR II AS THE WORLD'S ECONOMIC and military leader. If there were debates about the ensuing Cold War, the often tense standoff that developed between the United States and Communist U.S.S.R., they focused on how, not whether, to check the threat of communism, a one-party system of government, with all property held by the state. To assist a Europe wrecked by war and thereby strengthen it against possible Soviet aggression, President Truman and Congress approved the Marshall Plan, created by Secretary of State George Marshall. The four-year program channeled some $13 billion in aid to Western Europe.

On the domestic front, the Servicemen's Readjustment Act (known as the GI Bill of Rights) helped nearly eight million veterans finish college, buy homes, and reintegrate into the workforce. A new era of prosperity was at hand, and the accompanying rise in births created the "baby boom" generation (approximately 1946 to 1964).

But the shadow of communism spread real fear across the country. With the establishment of the People's Republic of China in 1949, about one-third of the world now lived under communism. The testing of a Soviet atom bomb, a war to contain communist North Korea, and the conviction of Julius and Ethel Rosenberg and others for sending information to the Soviets sent shock waves through the American public. Legitimate concerns about communist infiltration gave way to hysteria with Senator Joseph McCarthy's

(*previous pages*) **Apollo 11 astronaut Edwin "Buzz" Aldrin on the moon during the first manned lunar mission in 1969**
(*opposite*) **Dr. Martin Luther King, Jr., waves to the crowd during the 1963 March on Washington for Jobs and Freedom.**

Begun in the mid-1950s, the interstate highway system soon linked the country.

Rock bands like the Grateful Dead, reflecting a nonconformist lifestyle, began proliferating in the 1960s. A poster advertises a Deadhead concert.

investigations of suspected communists in high-ranking positions from 1950 to 1954, when he was excoriated by the Senate for unfounded accusations.

In 1952, America elected popular World War II hero Dwight D. "Ike" Eisenhower president. He launched the interstate highway system, the greatest public works project in American history, and kept Roosevelt's New Deal policies intact, including Social Security and programs that increased American infrastructure while creating jobs. He also continued Truman's buildup of nuclear weapons, to match the Russians' growing arsenal, creating the effective but risky doctrine of mutual assured destruction, whereby a nuclear strike by one country guaranteed all-out retaliation by the other.

Americans received another shock from the Soviet Union when their Sputnik satellite, the world's first, arced across the night sky like a warning. The space race was on. The U.S.S.R. appeared to have more competitive drive, and many observers claimed there was a missile gap between the two countries. Eisenhower could not reveal the truth—that there was no gap—without giving away secret surveillance of the U.S.S.R. by U-2 spy planes. In 1960, a Soviet missile shot one down deep inside Russia; the pilot, Francis Gary Powers, parachuted to the ground. He was convicted of espionage and jailed but released in an exchange in 1962.

The 1950s had been a decade of affluence and upward mobility for white middle-class America. A time of faith in God, country, and science. The calm, however, belied a boiling discontent. African Americans would soon foment a movement to force the United States to make good on its promise of equality for all. Women were still considered domestic workers for the most part, giving up jobs they had held during the war to return to being housewives. But evidence of disquiet was uncovered in Betty Friedan's *The Feminine Mystique*. Disillusionment, boredom, stress, and alcoholism indicated that all was not perfect in the 1950s household. In questioning the moral compass of an affluent society, Americans came face-to-face with the expanding civil rights movement. The Supreme Court's epochal decision in the

1947	1950	1951	1960	1963
Truman Doctrine and Marshall Plan begin	Joseph McCarthy ignites anticommunist hysteria	MacArthur is relieved of command in Korea	Harper Lee publishes *To Kill a Mockingbird*	Martin Luther King gives "I Have a Dream" speech

1954 *Brown* v. *Board of Education* case ruled that segregation in public schools was unconstitutional. But enforcement of the ruling would take many years, and public schools were but one entity that discriminated against blacks. In a carefully planned strategy, the National Association for the Advancement of Colored People (NAACP) began a program of massive protest, starting with Rosa Parks refusing to give up her seat on a bus in Montgomery, Alabama. In part led and inspired by the eloquence of the Reverend Dr. Martin Luther King, Jr., the revolution spread to cities across the South and beyond. The bus boycott worked, as blacks walked or shared rides, thus draining a municipal system dependent upon black riders.

King had studied the civil disobedience ideas of Russian novelist Leo Tolstoy and India's Mohandas Gandhi. He combined these with the Christian gospels to create a forceful challenge to America: Throw off racism, embrace the cause of justice, and realize the inclusive American dream of equal opportunity. "We must use the weapon of love," he preached. Defenders of segregation, shown in ugly brutality on television, lost moral authority, and the tide began to turn toward acceptance of an integrated society. Important civil rights bills were finally signed in the early and mid-1960s by Presidents John F. Kennedy and Lyndon Johnson.

Remembering all too clearly the "loss" of China to communism, President Johnson wanted to prevent South Vietnam from falling to communist forces from the north. Military advisers sent by Eisenhower and Kennedy were already in place. In 1964, Johnson extracted from Congress a resolution empowering him to protect American lives in Vietnam. Then he and the Pentagon planned a massive bombing campaign that began in 1965. A long and costly war was set in motion. It was not long before antiwar protests sprung up on campuses across the country, raising the chant "Hell not, we won't go!" The Vietnam War cost more than 58,000 American military lives and $138.9 billion, not ending until 1975 with South Vietnam falling to North Vietnam.

The Vietnam War, a long and deadly conflict, grew increasingly unpopular in the United States. The conflict ended in 1975 with the fall of Saigon.

Johnson's Great Society program, establishing safety nets for the elderly and poor, helped raise many above the poverty line, but the welfare and urban renewal projects often created more problems than they fixed (squalid public housing, cycle of dependency, decline of public schools). Numerous urban areas exploded into uprisings in the summers of the 1960s. This unrest combined with the growing antiwar movement reached a boiling point in 1968. The assassination of Martin Luther King, Jr., in April was followed by rioting and burning in major cities. In June, Senator Robert Kennedy, brother of President John Kennedy, and a man many believed could bridge the gap between races and ages, was assassinated while campaigning for president. With his death, the country seemed to lose its former sense of God-given purpose; hope was replaced with cynicism and distrust. President Nixon's tumultuous fall from grace in 1974 during the Watergate scandal—the country's worst political corruption episode—marked the nadir of public trust in its high elected officials.

But a culture that valued personal freedoms was developing in the 1960s and '70s. In 1973, the Supreme Court established a woman's right to an abortion in *Roe* v. *Wade*. Former activists of the 1970s sought fulfillment in Eastern spirituality, New Age cults, recreational drugs, sex, and career building. Balancing these left-leaning trends was a new rise in evangelical Protestantism. Ever more multicultural, America was still struggling to define itself.

1963	**1968**	**1969**	**1974**	**1976**
President Kennedy is assassinated	MLK, Robert Kennedy are assassinated	American astronauts walk on the moon	Nixon resigns under threat of impeachment	Jimmy Carter is elected president

BIOGRAPHIES

EXPLORERS, ACTIVISTS & ENTERTAINERS 1946-1979

After World War II, the United States and U.S.S.R. were the world's superpowers. Both began huge buildups of nuclear arsenals, and America attempted to stop the spread of communism. The civil rights, antiwar, and countercultural movements marked the 1960s. This turbulent time was followed by post-Vietnam and post-Watergate distrust in government and uncertainty of American clout caused by the taking of hostages in Iran in 1979.

BUZZ ALDRIN
★ 1930– ★
ASTRONAUT

Born in Montclair, New Jersey, Edwin Eugene "Buzz" Aldrin, Jr., was the second person to walk on the moon, during the 1969 Apollo 11 mission.

Buzz Aldrin He piloted the lunar module during the moon landing.

Aldrin graduated from the U.S. Military Academy at West Point, New York, in 1951. He became an Air Force pilot and flew 66 combat missions in Korea. In 1963, he earned his doctorate in astronautics from the Massachusetts Institute of Technology, writing his dissertation on orbital mechanics. That same year, he became an astronaut.

On the Gemini 12 flight into space, November 11, 1966, Aldrin completed a record-breaking space walk, his 5.5-hour extravehicular activity marking a new achievement in space travel. On July 20, 1969, he followed Neil Armstrong in stepping upon the lunar surface. The historic event was viewed by more than 500 million people, a record television audience. The astronauts spent about two hours setting up data-collecting equipment, collecting nearly 50 pounds of rocks, and taking photographs.

After returning to Earth, Aldrin was awarded the Presidential Medal of Freedom. He has remained an active proponent of space exploration, in particular of manned missions to Mars. Aldrin is the author of nine books, including a best-selling autobiography, *Magnificent Desolation* (2009), and *No Dream Is Too High* (2016).

NEIL ARMSTRONG
★ 1930-2012 ★
ASTRONAUT

The first person to set foot on the moon, Neil Armstrong was born in western Ohio. He interrupted his college studies in 1951 to fight in the Korean War; as a Navy pilot he flew 78 combat missions. Armstrong graduated from Purdue

> *That's one small step for a man, one giant leap for mankind.*
>
> NEIL ARMSTRONG

University in 1955, and spent the next 17 years as an engineer, test pilot, astronaut, and administrator for the National Advisory Committee for Aeronautics and its succeeding agency, the National Aeronautics and Space Administration (NASA).

Armstrong became an astronaut in 1962. In 1966, he commanded the Gemini 8 mission, during which he and David Scott completed the first ever docking of two space vehicles. Later complications forced the astronauts to abort the mission and splash down in the Pacific Ocean.

On July 16, 1969, Armstrong, Buzz Aldrin, and Michael Collins blasted off with Apollo 11. Four days later Aldrin piloted the lunar module to the surface of the moon, where he and Armstrong made the first lunar walk. Less than 24 hours later, the lunar module lifted off, docked with the orbiting command module, and returned to Earth. Among many awards, Armstrong was presented with the Presidential Medal of Freedom.

Armstrong left NASA in 1971 and became a professor of aerospace engineering at the University of Cincinnati. From 1982 to 1992, he served as chairman of Computing Technologies for Aviation, and in 1986, he was vice chairman of the Presidential Commission on the tragic space shuttle *Challenger* explosion. Though he avoided publicity, Armstrong remained an advocate for a well-funded U.S. space program until his death.

Neil Armstrong The astronaut, shown here in a 1969 portrait, commanded the Apollo 11 lunar landing mission in July of that year.

Racing the Soviets
AMERICA'S EARLY FORAYS INTO SPACE

★ ★ ★

When the Soviet Union launched the first man-made satellite into space in October 1957, a race began between the U.S.S.R. and the United States to place the first man in space. The Soviets won when cosmonaut Yuri Gagarin orbited the Earth in April 1961. A month later, President Kennedy challenged the nation to achieve the goal, before the decade was out, "of landing a man on the moon and returning him safely to Earth." The competitive nature of the early American space program helped fuel federal funding. The National Aeronautics and Space Administration was created in 1958. Then, on May 5, 1961, Alan B. Shepard, Jr., became the first American in space with a 15-minute suborbital flight. On February 20, 1962, John Glenn became a national hero as the first American to orbit Earth.

No space program has generated more excitement than Project Apollo. At a cost of $25.4 billion over 10 years, the Apollo program was one of the largest nonmilitary technological enterprises the United States had ever undertaken, with the possible exception of the Panama Canal. A fire in 1967 killed three astronauts in a capsule on the ground. But the program persevered, and on July 20, 1969, Neil Armstrong and Buzz Aldrin became the first people to walk on another planetary body. Six more moon missions, ending in 1972, continued the program's success. When an Apollo 13 fuel tank burst, the mission became one of survival. The resourcefulness of the crew and ground control brought the craft safely back to Earth. In 1975, Apollo and Soyuz spacecraft docked together, celebrating a thaw in U.S.-Soviet relations.

Apollo 11 blasts off on July 16, 1969.

ELLA BAKER
★ 1903–1986 ★
CIVIL RIGHTS ACTIVIST

Born in Norfolk, Virginia, Ella Baker became one of the foremost leaders of the civil rights movement of the 1950s and '60s. Growing up in rural North Carolina, she listened to the stories of her grandmother, a former slave who had been whipped by an owner. Baker graduated from Shaw University in Raleigh in 1927 and then moved to New York City. By about 1940, Baker was traveling for the National Association for the Advancement of Colored People (NAACP), raising money and recruiting new members. In 1958, she accepted Dr. Martin Luther King's request to become acting director of the Southern Christian Leadership Conference (SCLC). Three years later she left the SCLC and became involved with the Student Nonviolent Coordinating Committee, a group whose creation she encouraged. For the rest of her life she kept a hand in protest organization and political activism, constantly working for equal rights for African Americans.

JAMES BALDWIN
★ 1924–1987 ★
WRITER

Born in Harlem in New York City, James Baldwin was an African-American novelist, essayist, and playwright whose work explores racial relations in the United States. After high school, he spent several years studying and working at low-paying jobs. In 1948, he moved to Paris, where he was based for the next eight years. His

James Baldwin He decried an American society that accepted racial discrimination.

first novel, *Go Tell It on the Mountain* (1953), draws from his teen years as a preacher. *Giovanni's Room* (1956) examines themes of homosexuality. His first book of essays, *Notes of a Native Son* (1955), established him as a major voice in black American literature.

LUCILLE BALL
★ 1911–1989 ★
ACTRESS

One of the most popular comedians in television history, Lucille Ball was born near Jamestown, New York. A hard early life was marked by the death of her father when she was three years old; for a while she lived with her impoverished step-grandparents.

At age 15 she attended a New York City drama school, but shyness forced

Lucille Ball The beloved comedian pioneered the role of the funny yet smart woman on TV. She is best known for her popular *I Love Lucy* show.

Children have never been very good at listening to their elders, but they have never failed to imitate them.

JAMES BALDWIN

her to drop out. She then became a model, and in the early 1930s, she moved to Hollywood, where she began getting small parts in musical and comedy movies. After marrying Cuban bandleader Desi Arnaz in 1940, she continued trying to break though as a film star. Turning to radio, she found success with a comedy program called *My Favorite Husband*.

With Arnaz, Ball formed Desilu Productions and received a contract for a television show called *I Love Lucy*. First airing in October 1951, the sitcom was an immediate hit. Episodes dealt with the zaniness of family life and working women. For four of the six-season run, the show was the highest ranked in the nation.

After 1957, Desilu Productions came out with a number of other successes, including *The Dick Van Dyke Show, Star Trek,* and *Mission: Impossible.* Ball and Arnaz divorced in 1960, and a year later Ball married comedian Gary Morton. She bought out Arnaz, thus becoming the first woman to operate a major TV production studio. She continued playing comic roles in *The Lucy Show* (1962–68) and *Here's Lucy* (1968–1974).

LINDA BROWN
★ 1942– ★
CIVIL RIGHTS ACTIVIST

Linda Brown was a child of 13 when a landmark civil rights case bearing her last name was heard by the Supreme Court. She was born in Topeka, Kansas, some seven blocks from a public grade school. Because she was black, she had to walk to a black school farther from home.

My father pondered "Why? Why should my child walk four miles when there is a school only four blocks away?"

LINDA BROWN

A Supreme Court ruling from 1896, *Plessy* v. *Ferguson,* upheld state laws permitting segregated public facilities as long as they were considered equivalent. This "separate but equal" principle applied to schools, parks, buses, railroad cars, restrooms, and even drinking fountains.

Linda Brown The youngster (left), shown here with sister Terry, was at the center of a landmark civil rights case.

States' Jim Crow laws, discriminating against blacks, especially in the South, and backed by the Supreme Court, could thus maintain a racially segregated society. But by 1950, blacks had begun organizing in an effort to challenge a system that in fact allowed for unequal and inferior facilities and opportunities.

The National Association for the Advancement of Colored People (NAACP) urged parents such as Oliver Brown, father of Linda Brown, to try to enroll their children in all-white schools. As expected, she was denied entry to the third grade at her nearby school. The NAACP filed a lawsuit on her behalf, along with suits from some other states.

The plaintiffs' chief lawyer, future Supreme Court justice Thurgood Marshall, argued the case that became known as *Brown* v. *Board of Education.* The Court ruled unanimously in the plaintiffs' favor, agreeing that racial segregation in public schools was unconstitutional. The case set a precedent for other challenges to racially divided public places. Linda Brown herself continued working for desegregation in the Topeka school system.

RALPH BUNCHE

★ 1903/04–1971 ★

STATESMAN

One of the founders and high-ranking diplomats of the United Nations (UN), Ralph Bunche won the Nobel Peace Prize for negotiating an important Arab-Israeli truce, becoming the first African American thus honored.

Bunche was born to poor parents in Detroit, Michigan. After their deaths when he was 13, he moved to Los Angeles to live with his grandmother. He worked odd jobs and graduated from the University of California, Los Angeles in 1927. Seven years later he had earned his Ph.D. in government and international relations from Harvard. He began teaching at Howard University in 1928, and he did postdoctoral research in London and in Africa.

> There are no warlike people—just warlike leaders.
>
> RALPH BUNCHE

An expert on colonialism, Bunche worked during World War II in the U.S. Office of Strategic Services as an analyst on Africa and the Far East. In 1944, he joined the U.S. State Department and began helping plan the creation of the UN. In 1948, when he was at work on a tough negotiation between warring Israelis and Palestinian Arabs, he had to step up into the lead role when the UN's chief negotiator was assassinated. His work paid off the following year, when an armistice was agreed upon. For his diplomatic skill in the conflict he was awarded the Nobel Peace Prize in 1950.

Bunche also worked for the U.S. civil rights movement, serving on the board of the National Association for the Advancement of Colored People and participating in marches in Alabama. He continued working with the UN nearly until his death in 1971.

Ralph Bunche The diplomat won a Nobel Prize for brokering peace in the Mideast.

RACHEL CARSON

★ 1907–1964 ★

ENVIRONMENTALIST

A writer and biologist, Rachel Carson was born and raised in the Allegheny River town of Springdale, Pennsylvania. She graduated from Pennsylvania College for Women (now Chatham University) in 1929 and received her master's in zoology from Johns Hopkins University in 1932.

The U.S. Bureau of Fisheries hired Carson to write radio scripts, and she also began writing newspaper articles on natural history. She eventually became editor in chief for the U.S. Fish and Wildlife Service, resigning in 1952 to write full time.

Her book *The Sea Around Us* (1951) details in lyrical prose the history and science of the sea; it won the National Book Award. Other books and articles continued to describe various natural environments and their interrelation with people.

With the publication of *Silent Spring* in 1962, Carson launched contemporary American environmentalism. The book outlines the disastrous ecological effects of the insecticide DDT (dichloro-diphenyl-tricholorethane). The chemical

Preserving America

THE ENVIRONMENTAL MOVEMENT TAKES OFF

★ ★ ★

The modern environmental movement dates from the publication of Rachel Carson's landmark 1962 book *Silent Spring,* which examined the pervasiveness of DDT in the food chain. The resulting public outcry eventually led to governmental action. By the end of the 1960s, environmentalism had become a cause on college campuses and a hot political issue. Idealists expanded their agendas to include concern for the Earth and all its creatures. Among environmental concerns were pollution, harmful chemicals, and destruction of natural habitats. In 1970, the first Earth Day was celebrated in the United States. That same year the National Environmental Policy Act was signed into law to help achieve important legislation to protect the land, water, and air as well as plants and animals. Some species near the brink of extinction began making impressive comebacks. Also in 1970, Congress and President Nixon established the Environmental Protection Agency to investigate environmental hazards, make environmental impact reports, and ban dangerous substances and clean up contamination.

By the early 1970s, concern began growing over the depletion of nonrenewable resources, particularly petroleum. With a goal of energy independence as well as less pollution, President Carter signed into law the bill that established the Department of Energy to encourage fuel conservation and research on alternative energy sources.

In the mid-1970s, scientists had evidence that man-made chemical compounds called chlorofluorocarbons (CFCs) were contributing to the breakdown of the protective ozone layer of the atmosphere. In 1978, the United States banned the use of CFCs in aerosol cans. They continued to be produced for refrigerants and insulation until the mid-1990s.

The first Earth Day, April 22, 1970, New York City

industry waged a publicity campaign against the popular book, but its carefully delineated argument reached a wide audience and people began to question the long-term effects of man-made chemicals on the natural world. In a wider sense, Carson's writings underscored the idea that humans are part of an ecosystem, yet have a unique ability to alter it on a massive scale, not always for the good of man or nature.

In 1963, Carson testified before Congress, appealing for legislation to protect both the environment and human health. Her work helped curb the use of pesticides that were poisoning the human food supply as well as the habitats of birds, fish, and other animals.

Rachel Carson The author of *Silent Spring* helped start the modern environmental movement.

Jimmy Carter The Georgia native served in the nation's highest office from 1977 to 1981.

JIMMY CARTER
★ 1924- ★
39TH U.S. PRESIDENT

Serving as president for one term, James Earl (Jimmy) Carter occupied the White House during a difficult time marked by inflation, an energy crisis, and hostage taking in Iran. His steadfast idealism was rejected by voters when he ran for a second term, but as an elder statesman he has been widely respected.

Carter was born in Plains, Georgia, and was raised in a family farmhouse with no indoor plumbing or electricity. He graduated from the U.S. Naval Academy in 1946 and began serving on the Navy's first nuclear submarine under Capt. Hyman Rickover.

In 1953, he and his wife, Rosalynn, returned to Georgia to save the family peanut farm after the death of his father. He was elected to the state senate and became known for cleaning up waste in government and helping repeal discriminatory voting laws. Losing a bid for governor in 1966 against segregationist Lester Maddox, he ran again in 1970 and won. Though he had courted segregationists, he announced upon becoming governor that segregation in Georgia was over.

In 1974, Carter announced his intention to run on the Democratic ticket for president. He was virtually unknown nationally, and with no widespread political base, he began building a coalition of blue-collar workers, rural residents, blacks, and liberals. Flashing a big, toothy smile, he greeted audiences, saying, "My name is Jimmy Carter, and I'm running for president." With Senator Walter Mondale of Minnesota for a running mate, he narrowly defeated President Ford in November 1976.

In the wake of the Watergate scandal, Carter wanted to make the presidency more transparent and informal. He often wore jeans in public to appear a man of the people, and he eschewed the pomp of high office. On his first day in office he issued a pardon to those who had evaded the draft during the Vietnam War. His lack of dealmaking experience quickly became apparent when Congress defeated his consumer protection bill. He also advocated independence from foreign oil and the development of alternative energy sources. A price-fixing scheme by the Organization of Petroleum Exporting Countries (OPEC) led to massive inflation and a national recession.

In foreign affairs Carter's goal of human rights met with mixed success. He was criticized for pulling the United States from the Olympics and stopping the sale of wheat to Russia in protest over Russia's war in Afghanistan. He also met resistance in his plan to give control of the Panama Canal Zone to Panama (the plan went into effect in 1999). The high point of Carter's term was the 1978 Camp David Accords, a peace agreement between Egypt and Israel.

The most troubling event of Carter's presidency occurred in Iran in 1979 after the United States gave sanctuary to the deposed shah. Ayatollah Khomeini seized control in the spring, and in the fall, militants took more than 50 Ameri-

> *America did not invent human rights. In a very real sense . . . human rights invented America.*
>
> **JIMMY CARTER**

can hostages from the U.S. Embassy. Held for more than a year, the blindfolded hostages were shown on television and became a symbol of American weakness. A rescue attempt failed, but Carter negotiated the hostages' release before leaving office.

Perceived as a poor leader of both foreign and domestic affairs, Carter was easily beaten by Ronald Reagan in 1980. Since then he has remained active as a freelance ambassador, an adviser on the Middle East, and a promoter of international human rights. He has authored numerous books.

In 2002, he won the Nobel Peace Prize. In 2015, the 91-year-old former president was diagnosed with metastatic cancer but recovered enough to continue working.

CESAR CHAVEZ

★ 1927–1993 ★

LABOR LEADER

Born near Yuma, Arizona, Cesar Chavez became a union leader and labor organizer dedicated to improving the lives of farmworkers. He spent his early years toiling the fields as a migrant worker. After serving for two years in the Navy following World War II, he joined the National Agricultural Workers' Union.

In 1952, Chavez began working for California's Community Service Organization. Ten years later he resigned and formed the National Farm Workers Association. In 1965, he organized a strike against California grape growers. Though wine grape growers agreed to the terms of the strike, table grape growers held out. Chavez, as president of the newly formed United Farm Workers

You are never strong enough that you don't need help.

CESAR CHAVEZ

Organizing Committee (UFWOC), led a national boycott of California's table grapes, and by 1970, most growers had accepted the union's terms of improved pay and working conditions. A strike later that year against lettuce growers without union contracts met with less success.

In 1971, the UFWOC became the United Farm Workers of America. With many grape growers not renewing union contracts, Chavez continued to lead boycotts and marches. Among his nonviolent techniques was the hunger strike, which may have contributed to his death. His slogan was "¡Viva la huelga! [Long live the strike!]" His work and legacy continue to inspire movements for the rights of Mexican-American and Latino workers.

Cesar Chavez The union leader worked for the rights of farm laborers in the West.

WALTER CRONKITE
★ 1916–2009 ★
JOURNALIST

Known as "the most trusted man in America," Walter Cronkite gained wide fame as a steady-handed newscaster who helped pioneer television journalism.

Cronkite was born in St. Joseph, Missouri, moving with his family in 1927 to Houston. At the University of Texas (1933–35) he studied journalism. He earned money on the side writing for the *Houston Post* and then left college to work full time there. From 1939 to 1948, he worked for United Press (now United Press International). During World War II he served as one of the agency's overseas war correspondents, reporting from the North Atlantic, London, and North Africa. He flew with bombing missions over Germany and reported on the D-Day invasion of Normandy, France. After the war, he covered the Nürnberg (Nuremberg) trials and then was UP's bureau chief in Moscow.

In 1950, Cronkite was hired by CBS as a TV correspondent and anchor in Washington, D.C. During the 1950s, he hosted *You Are There, The Morning Show,* and a documentary series called *The Twentieth Century.* In political news shows and events such as presidential conventions, he proved an affable, even-tempered host and reporter, with a talent for ad-lib commentary.

In 1962, Cronkite became anchorman of the *CBS Evening News,* and for the next 19 years he was beamed into millions of American living rooms every evening. Shortly after he joined CBS, the news broadcast was expanded from 15 minutes to 30. His emotional but steady reports on the assassination of President

Shirley Chisholm The U.S. representative was the first African-American woman in Congress. Here, she announces her entry for the Democratic nomination for president in 1972.

SHIRLEY CHISHOLM
★ 1924–2005 ★
POLITICIAN

The first black woman to serve in Congress, Shirley Chisholm was born in New York City, her father a factory worker and her mother a seamstress. From 1929 to 1934, she lived with her grandmother on the Caribbean island of Barbados, where she acquired a West Indian accent. She graduated cum laude from Brooklyn College in 1946 and earned her master's from Columbia University in 1952. After teaching in nursery school and directing day care centers, she became in 1959 an educational consultant for New York City's Bureau of Child Welfare.

From 1965 to 1968, Chisholm served as a Democratic representative to the New York State Assembly, and in 1968, she ran for the U.S. House of Representatives from New York's 12th district. Having recently been redrawn, the district was expected to elect an African American; Chisholm defeated two other black candidates to become the first black woman in Congress. During her 14 years in the House, Chisholm worked for political reform. Assigned to the House Agricultural Committee, she took the unusual step of objecting and was later put on the Veterans' Affairs Committee and finally the Education and Labor Committee, where she felt she could be of most use to her constituents. In 1971, she was one of the founding members of the Congressional Black Caucus. She ran for president in 1972 but failed to win the Democratic nomination. Chisholm authored two books, *Unbought and Unbossed* (1970) and *The Good Fight* (1973).

> *When morality comes up against profit, it is seldom that profit loses.*
>
> SHIRLEY CHISHOLM

proclaimed that America's war on drugs was a failure and he favored a strengthened United Nations.

ANGELA DAVIS
★ 1944- ★
ACTIVIST

An activist for civil and women's rights, Angela Davis was born in Birmingham, Alabama, to schoolteacher parents. She did graduate work in philosophy at the University of California, San Diego. There she became a member of the militant Black Panthers group and joined the Communist Party. Her teaching position at UCLA was terminated in 1970 due to her political opinions. In 1970, she was accused of kidnapping, murder, and conspiracy for allegedly helping a prisoner on trial escape. After spending 18 months in jail, she was acquitted. She eventually became a professor at the University of California, Santa Cruz, and author of numerous books. She continues to lecture widely.

Walter Cronkite The wise, evenhanded, avuncular presence in American living rooms, via the *CBS Evening News*

Angela Davis The radical and activist after being fired from UCLA

Kennedy and the Apollo 11 moon landing have become part of the history of those events. After reporting from Vietnam in 1968 in the wake of the Tet Offensive, Cronkite editorialized that "we are mired in stalemate" and that a negotiated settlement was the only reasonable way out of the war. President Johnson told his staff, "If I've lost Cronkite, I've lost Middle America." Johnson's choice not to run for reelection was likely linked to Cronkite's reportage.

In the 1970s, Cronkite lent his trusted voice to the Watergate scandal, the resignation of President Nixon, and the American spaceflight program. He resigned from his position of anchor of the *CBS Evening News* in 1981 but continued to work on special assignments, including hosting documentaries for the Public Broadcasting Service and cable television. Cronkite's autobiography, *A Reporter's Life,* was published in 1996. Winner of several Emmy and Peabody Awards, he was in 1981 honored by President Carter with the Presidential Medal of Freedom, the highest civilian award in the United States.

In addition to his TV appearances, Cronkite remained politically active well into his 80s, criticizing in a syndicated column the 2003 invasion of Iraq. He

Miles Davis The innovative jazz musician was known for "cool jazz" style.

MILES DAVIS
★ 1926–1991 ★
MUSICIAN

Born in Alton, Illinois, Miles Davis became one of the leading jazz trumpeters and bandleaders. He studied at the Juilliard School in New York City and began performing with saxophonist Charlie Parker and others, helping to create bebop, a fast and harmonically complex style of jazz. Recordings in 1949 and 1950 initiated "cool jazz," a restrained, yet rich and melodic small-orchestra sound. In the 1950s, he recorded the influential *Miles Ahead* and *Porgy and Bess,* orchestrated by Gil Evans, and performed with saxophonist John Coltrane, bassist Ron Carter, and pianists Bill Evans and Herbie Hancock. Davis later began experimenting with rock and jazz fusion.

MARJORY STONEMAN DOUGLAS
★ 1890–1998 ★
ENVIRONMENTALIST

Defender of the Everglades, Marjory Stoneman Douglas was born in Minneapolis, Minnesota, and graduated from Wellesley College with the honorific "Class Orator." In 1915, she began writing for the *Miami Herald,* eventually editorializing about feminism, racial justice, and conservation. Her 1947 book *The Everglades: River of Grass* is considered the definitive work on the southern Florida ecosystem she fought to protect. In 1969, she founded the Friends of the Everglades to help in her battle against agriculture and real estate interests that siphon off precious water, lifeblood of the Everglades. Almost until the time of her death at 108, she continued working for the Everglades' health.

RALPH ELLISON
★ 1914–1994 ★
WRITER

Born in Oklahoma City, Ralph Ellison grappled with questions of black American identity. After studying music at the Tuskegee Institute, he moved to New York City and began publishing short stories, reviews, and essays. During World War II, he worked as a cook for the merchant marines and

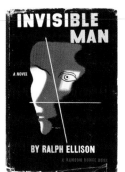

A first edition copy of Ralph Ellison's masterpiece

began writing *Invisible Man* after the war. The autobiographical novel relates the life of a southern black man who moves to New York, fights white oppression, and ends up ignored and misunderstood. It won the National Book Award. He later published two collections of essays; a collection of stories and an unfinished novel—*Other Stories* and *Juneteenth*— were published posthumously.

> *I am invisible, understand, simply because people refuse to see me.*
> RALPH ELLISON

JERRY FALWELL
★ 1933–2007 ★
MINISTER

Born in Lynchburg, Virginia, to a Christian mother and atheist father, televangelist Jerry Falwell graduated from Baptist Bible College in Springfield, Missouri, and in 1956 founded the Thomas Road Baptist Church in Lynchburg. Its congregation would swell to 20,000. Falwell began airing his sermons on TV, gaining an international audience of more than 50 million. In 1971, he founded what would become Liberty University, a fundamentalist Christian institution. Opposed to abortion, feminism, and gay rights, he formed a conservative political organization called the Moral Majority in 1979. That group ended in 1989, but Falwell remained a major force in conservative activism.

Woodstock

THE PARTY THAT DEFINED A GENERATION

★★★

 four-day music festival in August 1969, Woodstock came to symbolize the growing countercultural movement of the 1960s, as many young people revolted against American societal norms, mass consumerism, and the Vietnam War. For many left-leaning citizens, as well as others, authority stood for oppression, and open attitudes to sex and drugs represented freedom.

The festival was to be held in Woodstock, New York, but after locals objected, it was moved 60 miles west to a farm near Bethel. Some 400,000 students, hippies, war protesters, and lovers of rock music showed up for an event promoted as "Three Days of Peace and Music." Despite downpours, traffic jams, and shortages of food and water, festival celebrants maintained a spirit of community and harmony.

Concert headliners included Jimi Hendrix, Janis Joplin, the Grateful Dead, Jefferson Airplane, Santana, The Who, and Crosby, Stills, Nash, and Young. A documentary film, *Woodstock* (1970), helped further the appeal of many artists who had not broken into the mainstream of Top 40 radio.

Jimi Hendrix on a 1968 album cover

William Faulkner The author writing on a glass-topped table in his Mississippi home

WILLIAM FAULKNER

★ 1897–1962 ★

WRITER

•••◦●◦•••

A novelist and short story writer of great power and originality, William Faulkner brought the post–Civil War South to vivid life, sparking a birth of southern artistic endeavor and influencing writers for decades to come.

Faulkner was born in New Albany, Mississippi, and spent most of his life in nearby Oxford. He dropped out of high school and later spent a year at the University of Mississippi. Following a collection of poems published in 1924, he brought out his first novel, *Soldiers' Pay,* two years later. By 1927, he had finished writing his third novel, *Sartoris* (published 1929). Also published in 1929, *The Sound and the Fury* borrowed James Joyce's stream of consciousness technique to tell of the dissolution of a family through multiple points of view. Later that year he married Estelle Oldham and wrote *As I Lay Dying* (1930).

Several major works explored the themes of miscegenation and the southern consciousness, including *Light in August* (1932), *Absalom, Absalom!* (1936), and *Go Down, Moses* (1942). Though Faulkner's novels were usually tragic, they were almost always leavened with a comedic verve inherited from Mark Twain. Much of his work was set in Yoknapatawpha County, a fictional version of his own Lafayette County. For the universality of his characters' struggles with violence, love, pride, and sacrifice, he won the Nobel Prize for literature in 1949.

Reagan in the primaries, and he was narrowly defeated in the general election by Jimmy Carter. In retirement, he stayed politically involved and served on several corporate boards. His mixed record was tempered by the perceived restoration of honesty to the office of the president.

BETTY FRIEDAN
★ 1921–2006 ★
WOMEN'S RIGHTS ACTIVIST

Feminist and writer Betty Friedan was born in Peoria, Illinois, and graduated from Smith College in 1942 with a degree in psychology. In the mid-1940s, she became a reporter in New York City. With her second child on the way, she was frustrated as a homemaker and began surveying other Smith graduates to see if they felt the same. Her research was incorporated into her book *The Feminine Mystique* (1963), which described women's limited roles at the time and the societal pressures to stay at home rather than find fulfilling careers.

The book's huge popularity thrust Friedan into the limelight and kicked off a wave of women's rights activism and feminism. By examining women's economic and social dependency upon their husbands, she hit a nerve with readers in the United States and abroad. The myth of the cheerful housewife was explored and exposed, and she postulated that women's subservience made them victims of discrimination.

In 1966, Friedan co-founded the National Organization for Women (NOW) and served as its first president. Pushing for abortion rights, she started the National Association for the Repeal of Abortion Laws in 1969. That year she

Gerald Ford He married dancer and model Betty Bloomer in 1948; they had four children.

GERALD FORD
★ 1913–2006 ★
38TH U.S. PRESIDENT

With the resignation of President Nixon on August 9, 1974, Vice President Gerald Ford became president, inheriting a position tarnished by his predecessor. Born in Omaha, Nebraska, Ford grew up in Grand Rapids, Michigan. He graduated from the University of Michigan (1935), where he was a football star, and earned a law degree from Yale in 1941. During World War II, he joined the Navy and served on an aircraft carrier in the Pacific. After the war, Ford practiced law, and in 1948, he was elected to the U.S. House of Representatives as a Republican. A likable leader and shrewd dealmaker, he became in 1965 the House minority leader. An expert on budget and appropriations, he led opposition to President Johnson's Great Society legislation.

With the resignation of Vice President Spiro Agnew in 1973, President Nixon nominated Ford for vice president. Approved by Congress, Ford began his new job as Nixon was falling ever deeper into trouble with the Watergate scandal. Eight months after becoming vice president, Ford became president when Nixon was forced to resign. Ford thus became the first person unelected as president or vice president to assume the highest office.

Ford's simple, honest style was not enough to turn the economy around; his battles with Congress made him appear ineffective. His pardon of Nixon shortly after assuming the presidency was very unpopular. Running for reelection in 1976, Ford faced a tough challenge by Ronald

also divorced Carl Friedan, father of her three children. Two years later she helped establish the National Women's Political Caucus with other key activists, including Gloria Steinem and Bella Abzug.

Friedan espoused a wider version of feminism that included the entire family

> *Man is not the enemy here, but the fellow victim. The real enemy is women's denigration of themselves.*
>
> **BETTY FRIEDAN**

Betty Friedan The feminist and author in a 1960 photo. She co-founded NOW.

in her 1981 book, *The Second Stage,* and she delineated issues older women face in *The Fountain of Age* (1993). A memoir, *Life So Far,* appeared in 2000.

JOHN GLENN
★ 1921–2016 ★
ASTRONAUT, U.S. SENATOR

John Glenn became a national hero as the first American to orbit the Earth in 1962. Born in Cambridge, Ohio, he grew up in nearby New Concord and attended the local Muskingum College. He married high school sweetheart Anna Castor in 1943 and became a pilot in the Marine Corps. He flew 59 missions over the Pacific in World War II; during the Korean War, he flew 90 missions and shot down three planes. The highly decorated veteran next became a test pilot.

In 1959, Glenn joined the Gemini program. In April 1961, Soviet cosmonaut Yuri Gagarin became not only the first man in space but also the first to orbit the Earth. Less than a year later, Americans felt pride and relief when Glenn made three orbits of the Earth, a nearly five-hour flight, on February 20, 1962. The returning astronaut met with President Kennedy and was honored with a ticker-tape parade in New York City.

John Glenn The astronaut poses beside a Mercury capsule in 1962. He became a U.S. senator in 1974.

Glenn resigned from the space program in 1963 and from the Marines in 1965. He then became a consultant to NASA and a businessman. After a previous run for the U.S. Senate, he won election as an Ohio Democrat in 1974. He co-sponsored the Nuclear Nonproliferation Act of 1978, helping to prevent the spread of nuclear weapons to nonnuclear nations. Glenn was reelected to the Senate three times and then, in 1998, did not run again. He was briefly a presidential candidate in 1984. In 1998, Glenn became at 77 the oldest man in space when he flew on a mission with the space shuttle *Discovery.* He continued to promote the U.S. space program until his death in 2016.

BILLY GRAHAM
★ 1918- ★
EVANGELIST

A popular Christian evangelist at large-scale revival services, William Franklin (Billy) Graham was born near Charlotte, North Carolina, and raised on the family dairy farm. When he was 16, he went to revival meetings presented by a traveling preacher named Mordecai Ham. Inspired, he enrolled in Bob Jones College in Tennessee but, finding it too conservative, transferred to Florida Bible Institute; he was ordained in a Southern Baptist Convention church in 1939. After earning his bachelor's in theology, he continued his studies at Wheaton College, Illinois, where he met his wife, Ruth McCue Bell.

In the 1940s, Graham was a pastor in Illinois, a member of Youth for Christ missionary group, and president of a group of Minnesota Christian schools. He became known for his emotion-stirring gospel sermons and his charisma, and in 1949, he was invited to preach at a revival in Los Angeles.

> *When wealth is lost,*
> *nothing is lost;*
> *when health is lost,*
> *something is lost;*
> *when character is*
> *lost, all is lost.*
>
> **BILLY GRAHAM**

A radio appearance by Graham helped publicize the event, which ended up being extended five weeks. William Randolph Hearst's newspaper syndicate gave extensive coverage to the revival. Graham's career as a preacher to mass audiences was launched.

In the post–World War II climate, Graham's stand against communism, and the underlying threat of nuclear war, was readily accepted. He soon began hosting a weekly radio program, *Hour of Decision,* carried across the country by ABC. The program moved to television, thus gaining an audience of millions around the world. His sermons—via TV, radio, and print—have likely reached a greater number of listeners than those of any preacher in history. His live revivals, carried on television, featured him preaching about evil, sin, and the salvation of Christ; his simple message and commanding voice, softened by a mountain North Carolina accent, galvanized untold numbers to try to change their lives.

Though sometimes criticized by both the left and the right, he has maintained a reputation for sincerity and integrity that sets him apart from many modern televangelists. Throughout his

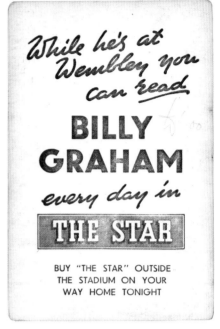

The preacher's name was used to advertise this newspaper and promote sales.

more than 40-year career he met with and ministered to several presidents and was many times ranked by Gallup as one of the 10 most admired men in the world. He retired in 2005. His son Franklin Graham (born 1952) continues some of his father's ministries, but has been criticized for his more conservative positions.

RICHARD HOFSTADTER
★ 1916–1970 ★
HISTORIAN

Born in Buffalo, New York, Richard Hofstadter graduated from the University of Buffalo in 1937 and earned his Ph.D. from Columbia University in 1942. After teaching for two years at the University of Maryland, he taught at Columbia for the rest of his career. His books, several of them best sellers, limned American political, social, and intellectual thought. He won Pulitzer Prizes for *The Age of Reform* (1955) and *Anti-Intellectualism in*

Billy Graham The influential evangelist, seen here preaching in 1966, has advised multiple presidents.

American Life (1963). In the latter book he argued that egalitarian democracy, dating from Andrew Jackson, has created a mainstream distrust of intellectuals.

J. EDGAR HOOVER
★ 1895–1972 ★
FBI DIRECTOR

Director of the Federal Bureau of Investigation (FBI) for 48 years, J. Edgar Hoover made the agency one of the greatest law enforcement organizations in the world; his controversial techniques came under scrutiny late in his career.

Born in Washington, D.C., Hoover was a student cadet corps leader, star debater, and Presbyterian Sunday school teacher. He earned a master's in law from George Washington University in 1917 and went to work with the Department of Justice's Alien Enemy Bureau. In 1919, Hoover was placed in charge in investigating those people considered dangerous radicals. After displaying a talent for organizing raids and making massive arrests, he was promoted in 1924 to director of the FBI.

The bureau at that time had a reputation for corruption and incompetence. Hoover instituted quick changes, firing many employees and introducing strict standards of conduct. Building up the FBI's credibility, he also claimed for it more and more power. Until 1934, agents could not carry firearms or make arrests, unlike state agencies. Hoover created a fingerprint file that became the largest in the world, and he established a crime laboratory and training academy. His FBI gradually became a top-flight crime-fighting organization. By tracking down high-profile criminals and

J. Edgar Hoover The legendary and controversial crime stopper was director of the FBI.

publicizing his agency's successes, Hoover made the FBI a prestigious institution that became mythicized in movies, books, and comics.

Always on the lookout for public enemies, real and imagined, Hoover helped break up foreign spy rings in World War II and then turned his sights on Communists, Black Panthers, and civil rights leaders including Martin Luther King, Jr., and Attorney General Robert Kennedy. His methods included illegal wiretapping, microphone surveillance, and intimidation. Though he came under increasing criticism for authoritarian overreach, so entrenched was he that no president fired him. He died in office at age 77. Revelations of his abuses of civil rights, furthering his political agenda, have since damaged his reputation.

LYNDON B. JOHNSON
★ 1908–1973 ★
36TH U.S. PRESIDENT

Assuming the presidency upon President Kennedy's assassination in 1963, Lyndon B. Johnson made strides in civil rights, but his escalation of the Vietnam War undermined his effectiveness and he did not run for a second full term.

Born in Johnson City, Texas, Johnson struggled in school after his father lost the family farm. He taught for a while and moved into politics, serving as an aide to a Texas congressman in 1931. Seven years later, at 28, he became a congressman. An ally of President Roosevelt and natural politician, he represented his district for the next 10 years. In 1934, he met and married Claudia "Lady Bird" Taylor.

Johnson won a seat in the Senate in 1948. In 1951, he became the Senate whip and in 1955 the majority leader. A senator for 12 years, Johnson was instrumental in the passage of civil rights bills in 1957 and 1960. He ran against John Kennedy for the 1960 Democratic nomination, but after Kennedy was nominated, he accepted the offer of running for vice president. Their narrow victory in the general election owed much to Johnson's delivery of southern votes.

Johnson was in the Dallas motorcade in which President Kennedy was killed and was sworn in as president on Air Force One later that day. He began vigorously pushing Kennedy's proposed tax cuts, civil rights legislation, antipoverty programs, and conservation measures. In the 1964 election against Barry Goldwater, he won by the largest popular vote majority in history; he then put forward his Great Society plan of social reforms,

Edward Kennedy The senator celebrates the 90th birthday of his mother, Rose (left), in 1980.

including Medicare for the elderly, urban development, education programs, and housing for the poor. The Vietnam War was meanwhile heating up. Johnson introduced ground troops in 1965 and built up troop strength from 100,000 to 500,000-plus in three years. Despite the expense of money and lives, the United States was no closer to victory in 1968. A growing antiwar movement sank Johnson's approval rating to less than 30 percent. He decided not to run for reelection and retired to his ranch in Texas.

EDWARD KENNEDY
★ 1932–2009 ★
U.S. SENATOR

Called the "Lion of the Senate," Edward "Teddy" Kennedy was the youngest of the four Kennedy brothers. A senator for 47 years, he pursued a liberal agenda of progressive reforms. Kennedy was born in Boston, graduated from Harvard in 1956, and earned his law degree from the University of Virginia in 1959. Two years after campaigning for his brother John F. Kennedy in 1960, he won a seat in the Senate as a Massachusetts Democrat at 30, minimum age for a senator. A year later his brother, the president, was assassinated. In 1969, Kennedy drove off a bridge on Chappaquiddick Island, Massachusetts. His passenger, Mary Jo Kopechne, drowned. This event, along with rumors of a playboy lifestyle, made the American public distrustful of his judgment, but his home state continued to support him.

In the Senate, Kennedy at first supported the Vietnam War but then began to oppose it. In domestic policy, he favored support for minorities and the disadvantaged, and he worked for arms control, strict antitrust laws, and national health insurance. He served as the Democratic whip from 1969 to 1971, was chairman of the Senate Judiciary Committee from 1977 to 1981, and chairman of the Labor and Human Resources Committee from 1987 to 1995. He ran for president in 1980 but was beaten in the primaries by Jimmy Carter. At his death, Kennedy was seen as a champion of liberal issues and titan of the Senate.

The Rise of the Suburbs

HOW LEVITTOWN INSPIRED MODERN LIVING

★ ★ ★

The spread of suburbs owes much to William Jaird Levitt (1907–1994). After World War II, the builder realized that returning veterans would need affordable housing, and so he began mass-producing homes on a 1,200-acre tract of land on Long Island in New York. His company, Levitt & Sons, Inc., built more than 17,000 houses there between 1947 and 1951. On what were once potato fields and small farms, Levittown became a checkerboard of similar-looking houses, growing to a population of more than 60,000 by the late 1950s. Community centers, swimming pools, and schools enhanced the appeal of life beyond the big city. Two other Levittowns were built, one in Pennsylvania (1951–1956) and one in New Jersey (1958, now Willingboro).

Levitt's philosophy was simple: "We believe," he is reputed to have said, "that every family in the United States is entitled to decent shelter." However, African Americans were initially banned from buying homes, per Levitt's dictates. The one-story houses had radiant heat, a carport, washing machine, and stove. At first there were two basic styles, built alternately along a street; residents sometimes got confused about the location of their own homes.

With the postwar increase in automobiles, families were willing to live farther from the city. They moved to escape crime, crowding, pollution, and racial tension. Businesses began moving farther out as well in the 1950s, '60s, and '70s, leaving many inner-city neighborhoods destitute of decent-paying blue-collar jobs.

A 1957 view of Levittown on Long Island, New York, depicts the beginnings of homogeneous housing developments and the rise of the suburbs in the United States.

Jackie Kennedy Seated beside then Senator John F. Kennedy, Jackie reads to their daughter, Caroline, at their summer home on Cape Cod.

JACKIE KENNEDY (ONASSIS)
★ 1929–1994 ★
FIRST LADY

Wife of President Kennedy, Jackie Kennedy was one of the most popular first ladies in history, appreciated for bringing elegance to the White House and dignity to the funeral of her husband. Five years after the president's death, she remarried and became Jacqueline Kennedy Onassis.

Jackie was born Jacqueline Lee Bouvier in Southampton, New York, daughter of a stock speculator. She learned to ride horses, write, and paint; attended boarding school; and enrolled in Vassar College. Spending her junior year in France, she polished her sense of style with a French overlay. After graduating from George Washington University in 1951, she was hired as a photographer-reporter for the *Washington Times-Herald.* At a dinner party in 1952, she met John F. Kennedy, then a congressman from Massachusetts. A year later they were married. In 1960, then-Senator Kennedy announced that he was running for president.

The new first lady began turning the executive mansion into a showcase of American history and culture, overseeing the acquisition of artwork and furniture that had been owned by previous presidents. She gave a tour of the restored White House on television, a show watched by a record 56 million viewers. She also began inviting intellectuals, musicians, and actors, in addition to the diplomats and statesmen they were expected to entertain.

Kennedy's beauty, grace, and fashion sense won hearts at home and abroad. She often traveled with the president and spoke fluent French, Italian, and Spanish. During their 1961 tour of France, the president referred to himself as "the man who accompanied Jacqueline Kennedy to Paris."

On November 22, 1963, Kennedy was sitting beside the president when he was shot in an open car motorcade in Dallas, Texas. The image of her standing a short time later in her bloodstained pink suit as Vice President Johnson took the oath of office was seared upon the American consciousness. She went about planning the funeral with composure, copying details from the funeral of Abraham Lincoln.

In 1968, Kennedy married Greek shipping magnate Aristotle Onassis, one of the world's richest men. He died seven years later. She returned to New York City and became a book editor. Kennedy Onassis died of cancer at age 64. Her son, John, died in an airplane crash in 1999; her daughter, Caroline, became ambassador to Japan in 2013.

JOHN F. KENNEDY
★ 1917–1963 ★
35TH U.S. PRESIDENT

John F. Kennedy was the first president born in the 1900s, the first Roman Catholic to be president, and the youngest person elected president (Teddy Roosevelt was a year younger when he became president on the death of McKinley). Upon his assassination by Lee Harvey Oswald, Kennedy became the youngest to leave office. President for only two years and 10 months, he left an enduring legacy of youth, hope, and dreams unrealized.

Kennedy was born into a life of wealth in Brookline, Massachusetts, son of Joe Kennedy, a well-connected businessman. After studying at Harvard University, he joined the Navy in 1941 and became captain of a Patrol Torpedo boat. During World War II, when the boat was torpedoed by the Japanese, he helped

If more politicians knew poetry, and more poets knew politics, I am convinced the world would be a little better place in which to live.

JOHN F. KENNEDY

save fellow crewmen and was awarded for his heroism.

Kennedy's father had urged his oldest son, Joe, to enter politics, but with Joe's death in the war, John Kennedy took up the mantle and ran for Congress in 1946. He won as a moderately conservative Democrat. Reelected twice, he then won a Senate seat in 1952, upsetting Senator Henry Cabot Lodge, Jr. Two years later, while recovering from back surgery, Kennedy began writing a best-selling, Pulitzer Prize–winning book, *Profiles in Courage*, about the lives of congressional leaders.

After a failed bid for the Democratic vice presidential nomination in 1956, Kennedy began campaigning for the presidency. He used his youth (thought by some an obstacle), good looks, charm, and intelligence to outdo Vice President Nixon in the first televised presidential debates and then went on to win the election by a slim margin.

In office, Kennedy had to repeatedly confront the Soviets, most notably in Cuba. His attempt in April 1961 to invade the island at the Bay of Pigs and overthrow dictator Fidel Castro failed. He met two months later with Soviet leader Nikita Khrushchev about the division of Berlin. In 1962, he blocked Khrushchev's attempts to put nuclear

missiles on Cuba during a nervous two weeks called the Cuban Missile Crisis. In 1963, he negotiated a nuclear test ban treaty. He continued sending military advisers to Vietnam in 1961 to stop the spread of communism, starting a long and costly war.

At home, Kennedy initiated the Peace Corps, proposed a comprehensive civil rights bill, and furthered American commitment to space exploration. His death in November 1963 was mourned throughout the world. Though stories of infidelity and connection to organized crime have since hurt his image, Kennedy remains one of the most popular presidents.

CHICAGO DAILY NEWS

PRESIDENT IS KILLED
Texas Sniper Escapes; Johnson Sworn In

John F. Kennedy His promising term as president was cut short by an assassin on November 22, 1963. *Inset:* Headlines across the country proclaimed the tragedy.

Democrat. He became a formidable presence in the Senate, outspoken critic of the escalating Vietnam War, and advocate for the rights of minorities and expansion of antipoverty programs. By 1968, he was stumping for president to continue his brother's unfinished work. With wins in five out of six primaries over Senator Eugene McCarthy, Kennedy made a victory speech on June 4 at the Ambassador Hotel in Los Angeles. On his way out he was fatally shot by Sirhan Sirhan, a Jordanian-born Arab. He was buried near his brother in Arlington National Cemetery.

MARTIN LUTHER KING, JR.
★ 1929–1968 ★
CIVIL RIGHTS LEADER

A black Baptist minister with an extraordinary gift for speaking and a prophetic vision, Martin Luther King, Jr., emerged as a major leader of the civil rights movement in the United States. For his tenet of nonviolent resistance to effect change, modeled after that of Mahatma Gandhi, he won the Nobel Peace Prize in 1964.

King was born the son of a pastor in Atlanta, Georgia. At age 15, he enrolled in Morehouse College and received his B.A. in 1948. He then studied for three years at Crozer Theological Seminary in Pennsylvania and in 1955 earned his Ph.D. in theology from Boston University. In Boston, he met and married Coretta Scott.

In 1954, King became pastor of the Dexter Avenue Baptist Church in Montgomery, Alabama. From this pulpit he would help escalate a movement that would spread across the country. When Rosa Parks was arrested in 1955 for

Robert Kennedy Kennedy campaigns for the presidency in 1968. Like his brother, President Kennedy, Bobby was assassinated. *Inset:* The cover of *Life* features the slain politician.

ROBERT F. KENNEDY
★ 1925–1968 ★
ATTORNEY GENERAL, U.S. SENATOR

Robert "Bobby" Kennedy served as attorney general in the administration of his older brother, President John Kennedy, and later became a U.S. senator. He was assassinated in June 1968 while running for president. Born in Brookline, Massachusetts, Kennedy was one of seven children born into the wealthy family of Joseph and Rose Kennedy. He left Harvard University to join the Navy during World War II; he later graduated from Harvard in 1948 and from the University of Virginia School of Law three years later. That same year, he married Ethel Skakel, his sister's roommate.

In 1951, Kennedy began working for the Criminal Division in the U.S. Department of Justice but resigned to manage his brother John's run for senator. From 1953 to 1955, he was a legal counsel for the Senate Subcommittee on Investigations, and in the late 1950s, he led an investigation of labor and management activities. Kennedy served as campaign manager in his brother's successful bid for the presidency in 1960. The new president appointed him U.S. attorney general, in which position he supported the civil rights movement and fought organized crime, his efforts leading to the conviction of teamster's union leader Jimmy Hoffa. In the months following his brother's assassination in 1963, he struggled with grief.

Kennedy resigned his position as attorney general in 1964, and later that year he ran for U.S. senator as a New York

refusing to give up her seat on a Montgomery public bus, King led a boycott of the bus system. King's home was bombed and he was arrested, but just over a year later the Supreme Court ruled bus segregation unconstitutional.

Recognized as a dynamic and inspiring young leader, King helped organize the Southern Christian Leadership Conference to spread the movement for racial equality across the South and beyond. The organization aimed to end discrimination in public facilities, including schools, hotels, and restaurants, as well as to ensure voting rights.

In 1960, King moved his base of operations to Atlanta and continued to push for civil rights. He traveled throughout the country and abroad, gave more than 2,500 speeches from 1957 to 1968, and wrote five books. He

If a man hasn't discovered something that he will die for, he isn't fit to live.

MARTIN LUTHER KING, JR.

engineered a large protest in Birmingham, Alabama, which received national press as policemen used dogs and fire hoses to try to drive away protesters. The attention helped convince President Kennedy that he should propose a comprehensive civil rights bill. In his "Letter From a Birmingham Jail," King wrote, "Injustice anywhere is a threat to justice everywhere."

The largest civil rights rally of the 1960s was the March on Washington for Jobs and Freedom on August 28, 1963. More than 200,000 protesters converged on the National Mall to encourage Congress to pass Kennedy's bill and call attention to black unemployment. As one of the leaders, King delivered his eloquent "I Have a Dream" speech. He led successful protests in Selma, Alabama, and Chicago in 1965 and 1966 and began crusading for federal assistance for the poor. On April 4, 1968, King was killed by escaped convict James Earl Ray in Memphis, Tennessee, where he was planning to lead a march to support striking garbage workers. Riots broke out in cities across the country. In 1983, Congress and President Reagan honored him by creating a federal holiday celebrating his life, the second American (after George Washington) so recognized.

Martin Luther King, Jr. Shown here leading the March on Washington in 1963, King remains long after his death an inspiration for racial equality.

HENRY KISSINGER

★ 1923- ★

SECRETARY OF STATE

Diplomat Henry Kissinger had a major influence on U.S. foreign affairs from 1969 to 1977. He won the Nobel Peace Prize in 1973 for negotiating a ceasefire in Vietnam. Though Kissinger's tactics have been called ruthless and even harmful, his intelligence and skill as a statesman shaped the present world order and helped the United States achieve better relations with China, Russia, and other countries.

Born in Fürth, Germany, Kissinger came to the United States with his family in 1938 to escape Nazi persecution of Jews. A quiet, serious student, Kissinger studied accounting in the City College of New York. After becoming a U.S. citizen in 1943, he was drafted into the Army and sent to fight in Germany. During this time, he shifted his field of interest to political history. Kissinger finished earning his degree at Harvard in 1950. He stayed on another four years to earn his Ph.D. and then joined the Harvard faculty, where he remained until 1969, teaching courses on government and international relations.

Kissinger's 1957 book, *Nuclear Weapons and Foreign Policy,* brought him acclaim as an expert on strategic policy. He argued against Eisenhower's stance of threatening massive retaliation, instead believing that a flexible response of conventional weapons and tactical nukes was a more realistic way to fight Soviet aggression. In *The Necessity for Choice* (1960), he moderated his approach to conventional weapons only, yet warned of a missile gap between the Cold War powers.

During the 1960s, while still a professor, he served as a special adviser to Presidents Kennedy and Johnson. In 1969, he became President Nixon's national security affairs adviser and began negotiating secretly with North Vietnam to end the conflict there, although Kissinger and Nixon also escalated the war by secretly bombing and invading Cambodia. The costly war had become hugely unpopular at home, and Kissinger was looking for a face-saving settlement. Though he and diplomat Le Duc Tho of North Vietnam signed a ceasefire agreement in 1973, the war continued another two years.

Secretary of state from 1973 to 1977, Kissinger worked on achieving peace between Israel and its Arab neighbors. In 1983, President Reagan named him chair of a commission on Central America. From 1984 to 1990 (under Reagan and Bush), he served on the President's Foreign Intelligence Advisory Board. He has advised a number of high-ranking officials, including Hillary Clinton.

MALCOLM X

★ 1925–1965 ★

AFRICAN-AMERICAN LEADER

An ardent leader of the black nationalist movement, Malcolm X was a minister and key spokesman for the Nation of Islam. He was born Malcolm Little in Omaha, Nebraska, his father a follower of black leader Marcus Garvey. The family moved to Lansing, Michigan, and when Malcolm was 12 years old, his father was killed by a streetcar; Malcolm believed it was a crime committed by white racists. The impoverished family

Henry Kissinger The controversial statesman won the Nobel Peace Prize in 1973.

struggled to survive. After Malcolm's mother was put in a mental hospital, he lived in various foster homes.

Malcolm X dropped out of school and then left the Michigan State Detention Home and moved in with a half sister in Boston. He became a petty criminal, drug dealer, and gang leader in Boston's Roxbury section and in Harlem, New York City. From 1946 to 1952, he was put in prison for robbery. There he became a member of the Nation of Islam (Black Muslims), a black American movement based upon Islam and black nationalism or separatism. He read voraciously, gave up smoking and gambling, and changed his last name to X, a Nation of Islam tradition that equated surnames with those of slave owners.

Power in defense of freedom is greater than power in behalf of tyranny and oppression because power, real power, comes from our conviction which produces action.

MALCOLM X

Malcolm X The revolutionary advocated black nationalism. *Inset:* Poster for a 1972 documentary

Released from prison, he became an articulate, fiery orator for the rights of blacks "by any means necessary." The black nationalist, or black pride, movement was often portrayed in contrast to the nonviolent movement led by Martin Luther King, Jr. The Nation of Islam went a step further than merely seeking freedom from oppression, for it equated whites with devils and espoused the notion of black superiority. Malcolm founded a Nation of Islam temple in Boston and later became minister in a Harlem temple, the largest outside of the Chicago headquarters.

Speeches at Harvard, Oxford, and other places gave Malcolm a platform for his ideas on aggressive civil disobedience and black identity and independence. Through his influence the Nation of Islam swelled to some 500,000 members. Disenchanted with the organization's lack of political initiative, Malcolm eventually broke with it. In 1964, he traveled to Mecca and began to believe that orthodox Islam was a better solution to black Americans' problems. In 1965, he founded the Organization of Afro-American Unity to promote civil and human rights. While lecturing in Harlem on February 21, 1965, Malcolm was assassinated. Three Nation of Islam members were convicted of the murder. His *Autobiography of Malcolm X* was published later that year.

THURGOOD MARSHALL

★ 1908–1993 ★

SUPREME COURT JUSTICE

The nation's first black Supreme Court justice, Thurgood Marshall was born in Baltimore, Maryland, the grandson of a slave. He attended Lincoln University in Pennsylvania; among his classmates were author Langston Hughes and musician Cab Calloway. After graduating, he applied to the University of Maryland Law School but was denied admission because of his race. The rejection stung, but, determined to further his education, he attended the law school at Howard University, graduating in 1933 at the top of his class.

That same year Marshall prosecuted his first case, a successful suit against the University of Maryland to force the admission of a black law student. From 1938 to 1950, he was the chief counsel for the National Association for the Advancement of Colored People (NAACP). He presented 32 NAACP cases before the Supreme Court, winning 29. During this time, he was also asked by the United Nations and the United Kingdom to assist in drafting constitutions for the new nations of Ghana and what is now Tanzania.

> ## Sometimes history takes things into its own hands.
>
> ### THURGOOD MARSHALL

Marshall's most important case was a challenge to the 1896 Supreme Court ruling in *Plessy* v. *Ferguson,* which resulted in the "separate but equal" doctrine. Marshall's law school mentor had encouraged his students to overturn this ruling. In 1952 and again in 1953, Marshall argued the *Brown* v. *Board of Education of Topeka* case before the Supreme Court; the ruling in his favor marked the beginning of desegregation of U.S. public schools. Other important wins included constitutional challenges to the exclusion of black voters and to discriminatory housing covenants.

In 1961, President Kennedy appointed Marshall to the U.S. Court of Appeals; after several months, the Senate confirmed the appointment. Four years later President Johnson appointed him U.S. solicitor general, and in 1967 to the Supreme Court. He served there until retiring in 1991, taking liberal positions on such issues as affirmative action, the rights of welfare recipients, capital punishment, and free speech.

Thurgood Marshall The lawyer prosecuted important civil rights cases and then joined the Supreme Court as its first African-American justice.

Joseph McCarthy The senator from Wisconsin was the face of anticommunist witch hunts.

JOSEPH MCCARTHY
★ 1908–1957 ★
U.S. SENATOR

Praised and then vilified, Senator Joseph McCarthy led investigations into possible communist infiltration of the U.S. government. His aggressive pursuit of so-called communists resulted in the term "McCarthyism"—publicized allegations of subversion based on unsubstantiated evidence.

Born in Grand Chute, Wisconsin, McCarthy graduated from Marquette University, earning his law degree in 1935. From 1940 to 1942, he was a circuit court judge; he then enlisted in the Marines and became a first lieutenant. In 1946, he won a hard-fought campaign for a seat in the U.S. Senate as a Republican.

The youngest senator then serving, McCarthy worked on low-profile issues until 1950 when he began working for the Permanent Subcommittee on Investigations; three years later he was chairman. There he led the charge that 205 communists had worked their way into the State Department. Reelected in 1952, he continued his crusade, questioning officials and insinuating, though never proving, that many were "card-carrying Communists." His accusations even included the Eisenhower Administration.

Though supporters at first considered McCarthy patriotic, the tide turned in 1954 after his interrogations of Army and civilian officials, a 36-day nationally televised spectacle. Many of the accused lost jobs and reputations. At one point an attorney for the Army asked McCarthy, "Have you no sense of decency, sir, at long last?"

Later that year the Senate took the unusual step of censuring their colleague for "contemptuous" conduct and "conduct contrary to Senate traditions." He was also relieved of his chairmanship. He died a few years later from complications of alcoholism at the age of 48.

Hunting Pinkos
MCCARTHYISM AND THE RED SCARE
★ ★ ★

With the communist victory in China in 1949, the 1950 invasion of Korea by communists, and the conviction of several Americans as Soviet spies, fear of communism in the United States reached a peak. The time was ripe for the rise of Joseph McCarthy, the senator who led investigations of communism in high U.S. government circles. Established committees had been investigating "disloyal" Americans with ties to the left. But McCarthy's five-year pursuit of high-ranking communists, later termed "a witch hunt," spun off mini-McCarthys across the nation. Careers of academicians and public officials were ruined, families were torn apart, and suicides were caused by the whisper of communist taint. Hollywood was not immune to the cleansing. Screen Actors Guild president Ronald Reagan advocated naming names of those suspected of communist leanings. The paranoia began to die down after the Senate officially censured McCarthy in 1954. He had been unable to substantiate a single charge of communist treachery. The self-aggrandizing senator had caused enough harm—civil liberties had given way to personal attacks and character assassinations.

Anticommunist rally in California

MARILYN MONROE

★ 1926–1962 ★
ACTRESS

Film star and sex symbol, Marilyn Monroe was born Norma Jeane Mortenson in Los Angeles. She made her film debut in 1948, gaining recognition two years later for parts in *The Asphalt Jungle* and *All About Eve*. She starred in light comedies such as *Gentlemen Prefer Blondes* (1953), moving beyond the dumb blonde role with more substantial turns in *Bus Stop* (1956) and *The Misfits* (1961). She married baseball star Joe DiMaggio in 1954, divorcing him the same year. From 1956 to 1961, she was married to playwright Arthur Miller. The stresses of stardom led to her overdose on sleeping pills at 36.

Paul Newman The popular actor played tough but lovable heroes. He is also known for his charitable contributions.

> *Give a girl the right shoes, and she can conquer the world.*
>
> MARILYN MONROE

Marilyn Monroe She played sexy and glamorous roles as well as smart ones.

PAUL NEWMAN

★ 1925–2008 ★
ACTOR

Born in Cleveland, Ohio, Paul Newman studied acting at Kenyon College, Yale, and the Actors Studio in New York City. He worked in television and made his Broadway debut with *Picnic* in 1953. Leaving for Hollywood, Newman became a success with *Somebody Up There Likes Me* (1956). He played numerous roles as outsiders or rebels, notably in *The Hustler* (1961), *Cool Hand Luke* (1967), *Butch Cassidy and the Sundance Kid* (1969), and *The Sting* (1973). Nominated eight times for a best actor Academy Award, he won for *The Color of Money* (1986). His Newman's Own food company has raised more than $250 million for charities around the globe.

RICHARD NIXON

★ 1913–1994 ★
37TH U.S. PRESIDENT

The only American president to resign office, Richard M. Nixon enjoyed a rapid rise in politics and suffered an equally rapid fall. His tenure weakened Americans' trust in government.

Born in Yorba Linda, California, Nixon graduated from California's Whittier College in 1934 and from the law school at Duke University in 1937. He served in the Navy during World War II. After the war he entered politics, winning a seat in the U.S. House of Representatives in 1946; he was reelected two years later.

Nixon's strong anticommunist position helped him win election to the U.S. Senate as a Republican in 1950. Two years later Dwight Eisenhower chose him as his running mate for the presidential election. The team won and Nixon served as vice president for the next eight years.

In 1960, Nixon ran for president but was narrowly defeated by John Kennedy. Two years later he lost a bid for governor of California and then announced he was retiring from politics. Despite that promise, he began to angle for a reentry, campaigning for Barry Goldwater, who lost to Lyndon Johnson in 1964. Owing in large part to Southern Democrats

becoming Republicans after the civil rights initiatives of the 1960s, Nixon defeated Hubert Humphrey in the 1968 presidential race. In 1972, Nixon paid a momentous visit to communist China, reopening relations for the first time in 21 years. In domestic policy, he put controls on wages and prices to manage inflation, and he reaffirmed his strong support for the Equal Rights Amendment in 1972.

Nixon won reelection against Senator George McGovern in 1972 by one of the largest margins in U.S. history. Yet his

own history had taught him not to take anything for granted. His covert unit had bugged the Democratic headquarters in Washington's Watergate complex. Congress opened inquiries in early 1973. Facing impeachment, Nixon resigned on August 9, 1974. He was pardoned a month later by President Ford.

Nixon spent his remaining years traveling and writing books on foreign policy. He lost his wife, Pat, to lung cancer in 1993. He suffered a stroke and died in April 1994.

Nixon's Folly

THE WATERGATE SCANDAL

★ ★ ★

The unraveling of Richard Nixon's presidency was caused by his involvement in the worst political scandal in U.S. history. In 1971, Nixon created a special unit known as "the Plumbers" to plug White House "leaks." Their methods included burglary and wiretapping. In 1972, under the direction of the Committee for the Re-Election of the President (CRP), they bugged the Democratic National Committee headquarters at the Watergate complex in Washington.

Washington Post reporters Bob Woodward and Carl Bernstein began receiving information about the break-in and subsequent cover-up from a source known only as "Deep Throat." Not until 2005 was he revealed as FBI associate director William Mark Felt. By early 1973, there was evidence that the White House had tried to use the CIA and FBI to cover up the crimes. An active FBI investigation into the possible administration misdeeds was also under way. In May of that year, the Senate began the so-called Watergate hearings, chaired by North Carolina Senator Sam J. Ervin, Jr. Former presidential counsel John Dean testified that he had helped with the cover-up and that Nixon knew about it.

In July 1973, Congress learned of Nixon's secret Oval Office tapes and asked the president to surrender them. He refused. Backed into a

Flanked by son-in-law David Eisenhower, Richard Nixon says goodbye after resigning in August 1974.

corner, he asked Attorney General Elliot Richardson to fire special prosecutor Archibald Cox, but Richardson resigned. Nixon finally released edited versions of the tapes. In the meantime, several White House officials were indicted on conspiracy charges. Finally, in July 1974, the

Supreme Court forced Nixon to give up the original tapes. They contained the "smoking gun," evidence that he conspired to cover up the Watergate break-in. With the House drawing up articles of impeachment and the president's support eroding, he resigned in August.

LEE HARVEY OSWALD

★ 1939–1963 ★

ALLEGED ASSASSIN

Accused of shooting President John F. Kennedy, Lee Harvey Oswald was born in New Orleans shortly after the death of his father. An emotionally detached youth, he became a marksman in the Marines and was court-martialed twice for illegal weapons and violence. In 1959, he defected to the Soviet Union, but three years later, married and with a daughter, he returned to the United States. He bought firearms and tried to visit Cuba via Mexico; then he found work in the Texas School Book Depository in Dallas.

On November 22, 1963, Oswald was seen carrying a long package into the book depository. Another witness saw a man with a rifle on the building's sixth floor. At 12:30 p.m. that day, three shots hit the motorcade of the president, who was in Dallas to rally support for his reelection. Two struck the president; one wounded Texas governor John Connally. Kennedy died a short time later. Oswald was spotted leaving the area and shot and killed police officer J. D. Tippit. Apprehended at a suburban movie theater 90 minutes after the Kennedy shooting, Oswald was taken into custody. Two days later, while being transferred to the county jail, he was shot and killed by club owner Jack Ruby, who had mob ties.

A 1964 commission headed by Chief Justice Earl Warren determined that Oswald had acted alone. A congressional committee in 1979 disputed that finding; some conspiracy theorists believed a Soviet spy had assumed Oswald's identity. In 1981, he was disinterred; medical experts declared the body was Oswald's.

Jesse Owens The black athlete triumphed at the Olympic Games in Berlin, Germany, in 1936, becoming the first American track-and-field athlete to win four gold medals in a single Olympiad.

JESSE OWENS

★ 1913–1980 ★

TRACK-AND-FIELD STAR

A standout athlete, Jesse Owens made history at the 1936 Olympics in Berlin, winning four gold medals and embarrassing host Adolf Hitler, who hoped the games would showcase the supremacy of the German and "Aryan" people.

Owens was born in Oakville, Alabama, moving with his family to Cleveland, Ohio, when he was nine. He worked odd jobs and in high school began to excel as a runner. He continued to work on his track skills as a student at Ohio State University from 1933 to 1936. When traveling with the team, he had to sleep and eat in "blacks-only" hotels and restaurants. At a meet in Michigan in 1935, he broke three world records and tied a fourth. His record in the long jump would last for 25 years.

At the 1936 Summer Olympics, Owens won the 100- and 200-meter races and the broad jump (long jump); he also was on the winning 400-meter relay team. The relay and the 200 were Olympic records. In his lifetime, Owens set seven world records.

After the Olympics, Owens worked in public relations, was involved in youth work, traveled to India and the Far East as a goodwill ambassador, and served as secretary of the Illinois State Athletic Commission. A heavy smoker, he died of lung cancer.

CHARLIE PARKER

★ 1920–1955 ★

SAXOPHONIST

Flashing like a meteor onto the jazz scene, Charlie "Yardbird" Parker was born in Kansas City, Kansas, and began playing alto saxophone at 13. At around 20 years old, he headed to New York City and began developing an original, driving,

Oh! I just have lots of ideas, and throw away the bad ones.

LINUS PAULING

angular style that would help create bebop jazz. Playing first with Earl Hines and then with Dizzy Gillespie, Miles Davis, and others, Parker lit up the clubs on 52nd Street. But real attention came only when he toured Europe. His genius was not fully recognized at home until after his early death from years of alcohol and drug abuse.

ROSA PARKS

★ 1913–2005 ★

CIVIL RIGHTS ACTIVIST

When Rosa Parks refused to give up her seat to a white person on a bus in Montgomery, Alabama, she helped touch off a revolution. Parks was born in Tuskegee, Alabama, and attended the Alabama State Teachers College. She was a civil rights organizer, serving as secretary for the NAACP in 1955 when she was arrested for not yielding her seat. Martin Luther King, Jr., led a successful boycott of the bus system, which precipitated other similar protests. Because of the boycott, Parks lost her seamstress job and moved to Detroit. From 1965 to 1988, she worked for Michigan congressman

Charlie Parker The American saxophonist and jazz composer is pictured playing his favorite instrument in 1947.

Rosa Parks Receives the Congressional Gold Medal in 1999

John Conyers, Jr. Her autobiography, *Rosa Parks: My Story,* appeared in 1992.

LINUS PAULING

★ 1901–1994 ★

CHEMIST

Theoretical physical chemist Linus Pauling was born in Portland, Oregon, and earned his Ph.D. at the California Institute of Technology in 1925. Applying quantum mechanics to structural chemistry and studying the diffraction of x-rays through crystals, he explained the atomic nature of chemical bonds, thereby ushering in the age of modern chemistry and molecular biology. He was awarded the 1954 Nobel Prize in chemistry. For working to ban the testing of aboveground nuclear weapons, he received the 1962 Nobel Peace Prize on the day the Nuclear Test Ban Treaty went into effect. More than 11,000 scientists from 49 countries signed his UN petition.

ADAM CLAYTON POWELL, JR.
★ 1908–1972 ★
PREACHER, ACTIVIST

Born in New Haven, Connecticut, Adam Clayton Powell, Jr., grew up in New York City and earned a master's in religious education from Columbia University in 1932. He became pastor of a Harlem church and used his position to advocate for fair employment and housing opportunities. In 1944, he was elected to the U.S. House of Representatives, becoming one of only two blacks in Congress (with Illinois's William Dawson). In 1961, he became chairman of the House Committee on Education and Labor. Charges of misuse of public funds, a slander case, and his absenteeism led to a decline in his popularity; Powell was defeated in the Democratic primary in 1970.

ELVIS PRESLEY
★ 1935–1977 ★
MUSICIAN

Rock-and-roll singer Elvis Presley was born in Tupelo, Mississippi. Presley made his first recordings in Memphis while working as a truck driver. Blending country and western with rhythm and blues, he became a rock sensation with such hits as "That's All Right," "Heartbreak Hotel," "Love Me Tender," and "All Shook Up." In addition to his singing, he was famous for his hip gyrations. Appearances on TV and in movies spread his name far and wide, but drug use compromised his health. At the time of his death from a heart attack, he had the most popular show in Las Vegas.

PAUL ROBESON
★ 1898–1976 ★
SINGER, ACTOR

Born in Princeton, New Jersey, to a father who was a former slave, Paul Robeson was a star athlete and graduate of Rutgers before attending Columbia University Law School. By 1925, the talented graduate was earning rave reviews on stages in London and New York. He starred in many plays, with roles in *Show Boat, The Emperor Jones,* and *Othello.* He also made numerous movies and records. With an international reputation, Robeson spoke out against racism and segregation. For his views and visits to the Soviet Union, his passport was revoked, and his popularity in the United States declined. From 1958 to 1963, he lived in Europe.

As an artist I come to sing, but as a citizen, I will always speak for peace, and no one can silence me in this.

PAUL ROBESON

JACKIE ROBINSON
★ 1919–1972 ★
BASEBALL PLAYER

The first African American to play in the major leagues, Jackie Robinson was born in Cairo, Georgia. He was a four-sport athlete at the University of California, Los Angeles, excelling in baseball, football, basketball, and track. Joining the Army during World War II, he was court-martialed for refusing to yield his seat on a segregated bus. The intervention of the press and NAACP helped him receive an honorable discharge.

Elvis Presley The big American pop star performs in Hawaii in 1973. His pinkie ring (below) is symbolic of his glittering sense of style.

In 1945, Robinson began playing on a Negro American League team. The Brooklyn Dodgers signed him in October 1945, and he spent 1946 with their top minor league team, the Montreal Royals. In 1947, he was called up to play for the Dodgers, breaking the color barrier. During one barrage of harassment, team captain Pee Wee Reese put his arm around Robinson, creating an iconic moment of solidarity. Robinson quickly earned respect, becoming "rookie of the year." His prowess at second base, batting, and base stealing earned him the honor of the league's most valuable player in 1949. He retired in 1957, went into business, served on the board of the NAACP, and became the first black inducted into the Baseball Hall of Fame in 1962.

Norman Rockwell's vision of good old-fashioned American fun

NORMAN ROCKWELL
★ 1894–1978 ★
ILLUSTRATOR

Born in New York City, Norman Rockwell became one of America's most well known magazine artists. He dropped out of high school to study at the National Academy of Design in New York. After graduating, he was employed as an illustrator for *Boys' Life*. In 1916, he painted the first of his 322 covers for the *Saturday Evening Post*. Rockwell's detailed, realistic paintings told stories of classic American scenes, including Charles Lindbergh's crossing of the Atlantic and Neil Armstrong's stepping on the moon. Whereas his earlier paintings were often sentimental and idealized, after he began painting for *Look* magazine in 1963, his work was more issue-oriented, covering such topics as the Vietnam War, race relations, and poverty.

Jackie Robinson He broke baseball's color barrier in 1947, defying insults from fans of opposing teams.

American Music
FROM JAZZ TO DYLAN
★ ★ ★

Jazz, America's indigenous classical music, was continuing to evolve in exciting new ways in the 1940s and '50s. Quartets helmed by the likes of saxophonist Gerry Mulligan and pianists Dave Brubeck and John Lewis were pushing the form beyond the harmonic structures of bebop into scale-based harmonies. By 1961, saxophonist Ornette Coleman was breaking out of all structure with his almost totally improvised record *Free Jazz*.

Meanwhile, another new American musical form was developing that would eclipse the popularity of jazz. Combining blues and country, rock-and-roll was born in the early 1950s with such artists as Chuck Berry and Little Richard.

Among American originals, few have had greater influence than Bob Dylan (born 1941), winner of the 2016 Nobel Prize for literature. Author of dozens of classic songs, the folk artist turned rock icon—with his scratchy voice, jangling harmonica, and poetic lyrics—gave voice to 1960s protest in "The Times They Are a-Changin'" and "Blowin' in the Wind," as well as to youth and freedom—"Rainy Day Women #12 & 35," "It Ain't Me Babe," "Mr. Tambourine Man," and others.

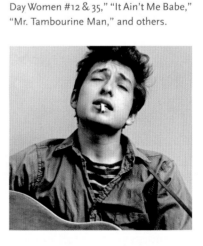

Bob Dylan, New York City, 1961

Julius and Ethel Rosenberg The couple was convicted of passing data on nuclear weapons to Soviet agents.

coded messages, they traced the leak to Julius Rosenberg. Ethel reputedly typed up Greenglass's notes for the Soviets.

Julius was arrested on July 17, 1950, and Ethel a few weeks later. The trial the following year led to conviction and a sentence of death. Despite worldwide pleas for mercy, they were executed in 1953 by electric chair at Sing Sing prison in New York. The key witness, Greenglass testified against his brother-in-law and sister in exchange for a 15-year prison sentence; he was released in 1960. He claimed after his release that he had lied about his sister's involvement. Two other conspirators—a courier named Harry Gold and a college friend of Julius's, Morton Sobell—drew 30 years; Gold served 16, Sobell 18. In 2008, Sobell admitted he had been a spy and gave telling details of his association with Julius, noting that Ethel played "no active role."

JULIUS & ETHEL ROSENBERG

★ JULIUS, 1918–1953 ★
★ ETHEL, 1915–1953 ★

SPIES

The first U.S. citizens executed for spying, Julius and Ethel Rosenberg were accused of working for the Soviet Union during World War II. Both Rosenbergs were born and raised in New York City's Lower East Side. Her father a Russian immigrant, Ethel was the oldest child of Barney and Tessie Greenglass. After high school she began working for the National New York Packing and Shipping Company and met Julius at a union event. His parents were from Russia, and he had attended the same school as Ethel. He joined the Young Communist League as a teen, and in 1939 graduated from City College with a degree in electrical engineering. That same year he and Ethel were married.

The following year Julius joined the U.S. Army Signal Corps. In 1945, he was dismissed for lying about being a Communist Party member. By then, he had already been funneling U.S. military secrets to the Soviets. He was aided by Ethel's brother, David Greenglass, who worked as a machinist on the atom bomb project in Los Alamos, New Mexico. When the Soviet Union tested its first nuclear bomb, U.S. officials scrambled to discover how they had procured information to build the device. Deciphering

JACK RUBY

★ 1911–1967 ★

NIGHTCLUB OWNER, MURDERER

The man who shot and killed Lee Harvey Oswald, alleged assassin of President Kennedy, Jack Ruby was born in Chicago. As a nightclub and dance hall manager in Dallas, he was acquainted with a number of organized crime figures and was arrested eight times for misdemeanors. In November 1963, two days after the Kennedy shooting, he went to the Dallas police headquarters, emerged from a crowd of reporters, and shot Oswald in the abdomen with a revolver. He originally claimed connection with a larger conspiracy, but a few weeks before his death from a pulmonary embolism in 1967, he declared he had acted alone.

JONAS SALK

★ 1914–1995 ★

SCIENTIST

Jack Ruby He assassinated Kennedy's assassin, Lee Harvey Oswald, with this revolver, a .38 Colt Cobra.

Developer of the first effective polio vaccine, Jonas Salk was born in New York City and graduated from the New York University School of Medicine in 1939. Until 1942, he worked at New York's Mount Sinai Hospital, doing research on viruses. He then went to the University of Michigan, where he became a professor of epidemiology, moving to the University of Pittsburgh in 1947.

At Pittsburgh Salk began doing research on a vaccine for poliomyelitis. Using a killed polio virus, he inoculated himself, his wife, and his three sons. The test proved safe and after further tests, the vaccine was administered in a mass trial of 1.8 million schoolchildren in 1954. Sponsored by the National Foundation for Infantile Paralysis (later called the March of Dimes), it was deemed safe and effective in 1955. An oral vaccine developed by Albert Sabin in the late 1950s proved safer and longer lasting. The use of both vaccines has practically eradicated polio.

Salk also helped create a vaccine for influenza and made great strides in the areas of bacteriology and immunology. In 1963, he founded the Salk Institute for Biological Studies in La Jolla, California. There, he and his colleagues investigated, among other things, the body's autoimmune response, which plays a key role in diseases and in the rejection of transplanted organs.

BAYARD RUSTIN

★ 1910–1987 ★

CIVIL RIGHTS LEADER

Organizer of the 1963 March on Washington for Jobs and Freedom, Bayard Rustin was born in West Chester, Pennsylvania, and attended the City College of New York. From 1941 to 1953, he worked for the nondenominational Fellowship of Reconciliation. A believer in pacifist agitation for racial justice, he was the primary organizer of the Southern Christian Leadership Conference. In 1965, he helped found the A. Philip Randolph Institute to continue Randolph's work for economic and social reforms. He published *Down the Line* (1971) and *Strategies for Freedom* (1976) and lectured widely on civil and gay rights. In 2013, Rustin was posthumously awarded the Presidential Medal of Freedom.

Jonas Salk One of the leading scientists in the fight against polio and other diseases

BOBBY SEALE
★ 1936– ★
POLITICAL ACTIVIST

Co-founder of the Black Panther Party, Bobby Seale was born in Dallas, Texas, and joined the Air Force at 18. Three years later he was given a bad conduct discharge. He initially planned to study engineering at Merritt College in California, where he met Huey Newton. In 1966, he and Newton founded the Black Panthers, a militant organization that sought to empower blacks to seek better jobs, housing, education, justice, and self-respect. Their uniforms included military-style leather jackets and berets, and they often carried firearms. They also established after-school and free meal programs as well as medical clinics.

Seale and seven other activists were arrested for inciting a riot outside the

Susan Sontag The writer was a leading intellect, novelist, and social and art critic.

1968 Democratic National Convention in Chicago. After trying to represent himself in court, he was sentenced to four years for contempt. He was released from jail in 1972 and returned to Oakland. By then, the Black Panthers had factionalized into disarray, a process helped along by the FBI. Seale ran for mayor of Oakland in 1973 but lost in a runoff. His autobiography, *A Lonely Rage,* was published in 1978. Some of the proceeds from his cookbook, *Barbeque'n With Bobby Seale: Hickory & Mesquite Recipes* (1988), go to various social organizations. He has lectured at hundreds of colleges on community organizing, racial justice, and his life as a Black Panther.

Bobby Seale Co-founder of the radical Black Panthers

SUSAN SONTAG
★ 1933–2004 ★
WRITER

Essayist and novelist Susan Sontag was born in New York City. A precocious reader, she graduated from high school at age 15 and went to the University of California, Berkeley. She later transferred to the University of Chicago and then earned her master's in philosophy at Harvard. After studying abroad, she returned to the United States in the late 1950s and began writing essays for *The Nation,* the *New York Review of Books,* and the *Partisan Review.*

Sontag's first novel, *The Benefactor* (1963), was an experimental work expanding on her theories on art and culture. She gained widespread acclaim with her 1964 essay "Notes on Camp," examining the way high and low art affect each other; it was included in the collection *Against Interpretation* (1966), which argues for the acceptance of emotional reaction to art over intellectual criticism. Other collections include *On Photography* (1977) and *Illness as Metaphor* (1978). Later novels were published in 1992, *The Volcano Lover,* and 2000, *In America,* which won the National Book Award. She also wrote and directed four films and penned several plays.

She herself received severe criticism for her response to the 9/11 attacks, viewing them as a consequence of American actions and attitudes.

GLORIA STEINEM

★ 1934- ★

WOMEN'S RIGHTS ACTIVIST

Writer and lecturer Gloria Steinem has been an advocate for women's causes since the late 1960s. Born in Toledo, Ohio, she helped care for her mother who suffered from mental illness for several years after her parents divorced. She attended Smith College, graduating with a degree in government in 1956. After studying on a fellowship in India, she became a freelance journalist, writing articles on feminism and women's issues. She went undercover as a scantily clad waitress at New York's Playboy Club to write an exposé for *Show* magazine in 1963.

In the late 1960s, Steinem became one of the founding editors of *New York* magazine and wrote a regular column on politics. She teamed up with other leaders in the women's movement, including

Bella Abzug and Betty Friedan, to form the National Women's Political Caucus in 1971 to campaign for women's rights in the workplace and social life. The following year she published the first issue of *Ms.* magazine, a feminist periodical that took on such issues as domestic violence and abortion rights.

A woman without a man is like a fish without a bicycle.

GLORIA STEINEM

We Shall overcome

Gloria Steinem The feminist helped found the National Women's Political Caucus.

Steinem's collection of essays *Outrageous Acts and Everyday Rebellions* (1983) covered topics as varied as the importance of work and the politics of food. *Marilyn,* a biography of Marilyn Monroe, appeared in 1986. Her 1992 book, *Revolution from Within: A Book of Self-Esteem,* came under fire from feminist circles for being too much like personal self-help instead of her usual call to action. But she defended the work as "the most political thing" she'd written: "I was saying that many institutions are designed to undermine our self-authority in order to get us to obey their authority." Another collection, *Moving Beyond Words: Age, Rage, Sex, Power, Money, Muscles: Breaking Boundaries of Gender,* was published in 1994.

Steinem was diagnosed with breast cancer in 1986 but survived the disease. In 2000, she married environmental and animal rights activist David Bale (father of actor Christian Bale). He died three years later. In the 2008 presidential election, she endorsed Hillary Clinton, claiming gender, not race, was "the most restricting force in American life."

helped draw up the arrangement for Germany's unconditional surrender in May. In July, he went to Potsdam, Germany, for a summit meeting with British prime minister Winston Churchill and Soviet premier Joseph Stalin.

Truman was faced with the daunting task of ending the war with Japan. After learning from advisers that an invasion of Japan could cost half a million American lives, he gave approval for dropping two atom bombs in early August, the first practical use of man-made nuclear energy. A few days after the bombing, Japan agreed to give up.

> *The responsibility of great states is to serve and not to dominate the world.*
>
> **HARRY S. TRUMAN**

Harry S. Truman As president, he authorized the use of atomic weapons to end World War II.

HARRY S. TRUMAN
★ 1884–1972 ★
33RD U.S. PRESIDENT

A plainspoken politician, Harry Truman became president after only 83 days as vice president. When President Roosevelt died, Truman stepped up to lead the country at the end of World War II, making the grave decision to drop atomic bombs on Japan. Though critics considered him inadequate for the land's highest office, he became one of the nation's strongest presidents, helping shape the future nation and world.

Truman was born in Lamar, Missouri, and graduated from high school in 1901.

His family did not have the money to send him to college, so he became a bank clerk in Kansas City and in 1906 returned home to run the family farm. After a couple of business failures, he served with valor as an Army captain in World War I. In 1919, he married childhood friend Bess Wallace.

Earning a reputation for his honesty and efficiency, he won a seat in the U.S. Senate in 1934. He won reelection in 1940 and became prominent as chairman of a committee overseeing prices charged by defense contractors.

During the 1944 presidential race, Truman was a compromise candidate for vice president, becoming president upon Roosevelt's death in April 1945. Truman

With the war over, Truman worked hard to establish a lasting peace. The Marshall Plan was set up to restore the economies of Western Europe and check possible Soviet advances. The North Atlantic Treaty Organization pact of 1949 created a military alliance of non-communist European countries. By this time, Truman had won reelection by a narrow margin over Thomas Dewey. In 1950, Truman ordered troops to South Korea to push back a communist invasion from the north. At home, he established a committee on civil rights.

Rather than seek reelection in 1952, he retired to his home in Independence, Missouri. He had, as he put it, admiringly quoting another man's headstone, "done his damnedest."

Saving Europe
THE MARSHALL PLAN
★ ★ ★

The United States believed that the devastation of World War II left Europe vulnerable to communist Soviet influence and aggression. To counter this seeming threat to democracy, President Truman in March 1947 announced that the United States intended to provide financial assistance for the rehabilitation of Western Europe. Named for the plan's architect, Secretary of State George Marshall, the "Marshall Plan" was officially known as the European Recovery Program. Between 1948 and 1952, the United States sent some $13 billion in food, machinery, and goods to Europe to create financial stability, widen trade, and restore agricultural and industrial production. The Marshall Plan worked so well that Truman extended the plan to developing nations around the world; it evolved in 1961 into the Organisation for Economic Co-operation and Development. In his memoirs, President Truman wrote, "the Marshall Plan will go down in history as one of America's greatest contributions to the peace of the world."

Symbolic decals adorned aid packages sent to Europe after World War II.

WERNHER VON BRAUN
★ 1912–1977 ★
ROCKET SCIENTIST

One of the pioneers of rocketry and space flight, Wernher von Braun was born in Wirsitz, Germany (now Wyrzysk, Poland). He became fascinated with the idea of space travel and in 1932 began working on missiles for the German Army. In the meantime, he earned his Ph.D. in physics in 1934.

> *I have learned to use the word impossible with the greatest caution.*
>
> **WERNHER VON BRAUN**

During World War II, Von Braun was a key figure in the creation of the V-2 rockets that Germany used to bomb Allied cities. The V-2 was a 46-foot missile weighing 13.5 tons; flying at 3,500 miles an hour, it could deliver a 2.2-ton warhead to a target 500 miles away. In 1945, Von Braun organized the surrender of 500 German rocket scientists, as well as their rocket designs. He, along with other leading engineers, was sent to the United States to work on guided missile systems.

For the next 15 years Von Braun worked for the U.S. Army, first in New Mexico and then at the Redstone Arsenal in Huntsville, Alabama. At Redstone, he and his team built the four-stage Jupiter rockets that would launch the first U.S. satellites and send an astronaut into space.

In 1960, the team began working for the newly created U.S. space program (NASA) to build the giant Saturn rockets that would propel the first astronauts to land on the moon. Von Braun became a U.S. citizen in 1955 and a leading spokesman for the U.S. space program. He retired from NASA in 1972 to work for Fairchild Industries, an aerospace company.

The scientist is featured with a model of one of his moon rockets on the cover of *Life*, 1957.

Wernher von Braun He stands beside one of his Saturn V rocket engines at the Marshall Space Flight Center in Huntsville, Alabama.

GEORGE WALLACE
★ 1919-1998 ★
POLITICIAN

Best known as a segregationist politician, George Wallace was born in Clio, Alabama, the son of a farmer, and graduated from the University of Alabama Law School in 1942. He served three years in the Army Air Forces, making bombing raids over Japan. He was an assistant state's attorney in 1946 and was elected twice to the Alabama state legislature. From 1953 to 1959, he served as a circuit court judge.

A Democrat, Wallace ran for governor of Alabama in 1958 and lost. In 1962,

Segregation now, segregation tomorrow, segregation forever.

GEORGE WALLACE

he ran on a platform of the economy and of opposing federal enforcement of racial integration of schools; he won the race. In 1963, he tried to block enrollment of two black students at the University of Alabama. President Kennedy federalized the National Guard to allow the students to matriculate. Other attempts to prevent integration—at Birmingham, Huntsville, Mobile, and Tuskegee—made him the

national face of stubborn resistance to racial change.

The state not then allowing consecutive terms as governor, Wallace's wife, Lurleen, ran for and won the position in 1966. Wallace was reelected in 1970, 1974, and 1982, becoming the first four-term governor of the state. He ran for president as an Independent in 1968 and as a Democrat in 1972. During the latter campaign, he was shot and wounded, leaving him paralyzed below the waist. He ran again as a Democrat in 1976. In 1978, he began to apologize for his opposition to integration, and during his successful run for governor in 1982, he received heavy black support.

EARL WARREN
★ 1891-1974 ★
CHIEF JUSTICE OF
THE UNITED STATES

Earl Warren served as Chief Justice of the United States from 1953 to 1969, a period of landmark changes in laws regarding racial desegregation, legislative apportionment, and criminal procedure.

Born in Los Angeles, Warren studied law at the University of California, Berkeley. He served as a district attorney from 1925 to 1939 and as California's attorney general from 1939 to 1943. In 1943, he became governor of California, a position he held for 10 years until President Eisenhower nominated him as Chief Justice of the United States. His only defeat came in 1948 when he ran as

George Wallace The segregationist governor changed his stance in later life. *Inset:* Campaign pin, 1968

a Republican for vice president under Thomas Dewey.

Warren's most significant case was in 1954, when he led the court in its unanimous ruling in the 1954 *Brown v. Board of Education.* The decision overturned a 58-year-old court ruling by declaring that racial segregation in public schools was unconstitutional. In other majority opinions, he also took liberal stances, including a 1964 ruling that state legislatures must apportion representatives by population rather than area ("legislators represent people, not trees or acres"). A 1966 ruling in *Miranda* v. *Arizona* held that police must inform suspects of their rights. Other cases protected the rights of protesters, of publications, and of individuals refusing to testify before a congressional committee (limiting the power of 1950s communist witch hunts).

Separate educational facilities are inherently unequal.

EARL WARREN

ROY WILKINS
★ 1901–1981 ★
CIVIL RIGHTS LEADER

Born in St. Louis, Missouri, Roy Wilkins became a leader of the National Association for the Advancement of Colored People (NAACP). After graduating from the University of Minnesota with a degree in sociology, he worked for a black newspaper. In 1931, he joined the NAACP staff and from 1934 to 1949 was

Roy Wilkins The activist directed the NAACP and supported nonviolent protest.

editor of its publication, *Crisis.* Wilkins was named executive secretary (later executive director) of the NAACP in 1955. He met with five presidents, participated in important civil rights marches, and helped win numerous legislative victories. Opposing the black separatist movement, he believed strongly in integration and nonviolent protest. He retired from the NAACP in 1977.

RICHARD WRIGHT
★ 1908–1960 ★
WRITER

One of the leading African-American writers of his time, Richard Wright was born near Natchez, Mississippi, the son of a sharecropper. He worked at various odd jobs, graduated valedictorian of his high school, and migrated to Chicago by 1927. He eventually became a writer with the Federal Writers' Project and joined the Communist Party.

In the early 1930s, Wright published a number of poems, but national attention came with the publication of his first novel, *Uncle Tom's Children* (1938). The book's quartet of long stories deal with southern black males victimized by racial violence. By now, Wright was living in New York City and working as an editor for the communist *Daily Worker.* His next novel, *Native Son* (1940), relates the story of a young black man who accidentally kills a white girl, and by fighting his prosecution and death sentence, he becomes aware of his place in a racially unjust world. The book became a best seller and was adapted into a successful Broadway play staged by Orson Welles. In 1944, Wright dropped ties with the Communist Party, and the following year, he published an autobiography, *Black Boy,* a powerful and moving account of his years in Mississippi and Tennessee. He later concentrated on essays and existential fiction, most of it not as critically acclaimed as his earlier work.

Richard Wright His writing detailed the plight of blacks in the United States.

A Generation on Fire
SOCIAL MOVEMENTS OF THE 1960S AND 1970S

The 1960s and '70s were marked by mass demonstrations and rallies in support of a number of causes. Many Americans began realizing the effectiveness of organized protest to create change within the legislative and court systems. The civil rights movement, gaining momentum in the 1950s, focused attention on voting rights and the integration of schools and other public facilities. Blacks and whites joined in sit-ins and marches, especially in the South. At the same time, protests against the Vietnam War began heating up. A wide variety of people, with students often in the vanguard, called for an end of U.S. involvement in Vietnam. The modern women's movement eventually emerged and saw the founding of the National Organization for Women, which fought for nondiscrimination in education and the workplace, equal pay, and reproductive freedom. On June 28, 1969, the gay rights movement essentially began at the Stonewall Inn in New York City when hundreds fought back against police oppression.

Activist Marty Robinson rallies a crowd of 200 in preparation for the first mass march for gay rights in New York City on July 27, 1969.

Vietnam War protesters hold up a large peace symbol. The symbol, designed in 1958 for nuclear disarmament, was widely used during antiwar demonstrations in the 1960s.

Thousands march for civil rights in New York City on March 15, 1965. Their banner supports the Selma march in Alabama, which brought greater awareness to the difficulty faced by blacks in the South.

Protesting the conflict in Vietnam, students march with antiwar placards on the campus of the University of California, Berkeley in 1969.

Women's rights activist Alice Paul, founder of the National Woman's Party, poses in front of a suffrage banner in Washington, D.C., in 1969.

National Guardsmen block protesters as they take to Memphis streets on March 29, 1968, six days before the assassination of Martin Luther King, Jr., in the same city.

CHAPTER 8

1980–PRESENT

The poet called Miss Liberty's torch "the lamp beside the golden door" . . . And through that golden door our children can walk into tomorrow with the knowledge that no one can be denied the promise that is America.

RONALD REAGAN

INTO A NEW MILLENNIUM

I N 1980, RONALD REAGAN WON THE PRESIDENCY—HIS ELECTION SIGNIFYING TO many a major societal shift in America. "Family values" became a catchword, and conservatives took political control—a reaction against perceived excesses of the previous two decades. Reagan soon launched programs to reform the economy, revamp foreign policy, and rebuild America's self-confidence. His personality and doctrine came to be known as the Reagan Revolution.

Thus began the decade of the 1980s, a period from then until now that has been tumultuous at times and fraught with terrorism at home and abroad, financial swings, environmental disasters natural and man-made, and growing evidence of human-caused climate change. Technology entered Americans' lives in ways never imagined, and the global and national political landscape shifted in new and unexpected directions.

Domestic and foreign terrorism increased during the 1990s and into the next millennium. The year 1995 saw the bombing of the Murrah Federal Building in Oklahoma City by Timothy McVeigh, followed the next year by a bomb explosion, orchestrated by an antiabortion zealot at the Atlanta Olympics. Al Qaeda terrorists used three hijacked airliners to attack the twin towers in New York City and the Pentagon near Washington, D.C., on the fateful day of September 11, 2001; another hijacked airliner in all likelihood was forced by American citizens to crash in Pennsylvania. These actions galvanized the nation into

(previous pages) On election night 2016, jubilant supporters in New York City celebrate the news of Donald Trump's election as the 45th U.S. president. *(opposite)* Ronald Reagan cavorts with wife Nancy and son Ronald, Jr., at their California ranch in the mid-1960s.

Steve Jobs debuts the iPad tablet in San Francisco in January 2010. His development of the Apple computer helped pave the way for today's electronic age.

Barack Obama takes the oath of office in January 2009, with wife Michelle and daughters Sasha and Malia at his side.

George W. Bush's so-called War on Terror and included passage of the Patriot Act and creation of the Department of Homeland Security.

Generally, the American economy grew steadily through the 1980s and 1990s. But early in 2000, the so-called dot-com bubble burst in the stock market negatively impacted many technology companies. Then, beginning in December 2007, a major global recession caused primarily by dubious financial decisions by major banking institutions hamstrung the United States and world for several years. A slow recovery resulted in the Dow Jones Industrial Average surpassing the 20,000 mark for the first time in January 2017.

Natural disasters plagued the country. On May 18, 1980, the volcanic eruption of Mount St. Helens in Washington sent a plume 80,000 feet into the air and deposited ash in 11 states. Persistent drought has impacted much of the western United States since the mid-1990s, affecting agriculture and causing devastating wildfires in many states. Hurricane Katrina struck the Louisiana coast in 2005, killing more than a thousand and flooding up to 80 percent of New Orleans. In 2012, Hurricane Sandy rampaged the East Coast—particularly New Jersey—causing an estimated $67.6 billion in damages. Tornadoes also caused damage.

A February 2008 outbreak of 87 tornadoes struck the southern states and Ohio Valley, and on May 22, 2011, a massive tornado tore through Joplin, Missouri, with winds in excess of 200 miles an hour.

Natural disasters were only part of the story. On March 24, 1989, oil tanker *Exxon Valdez* struck a reef in Prince William Sound, Alaska, releasing nearly 11 million gallons of crude oil into a rich marine habitat. Captain Joseph Hazelwood was not at the helm, and Exxon blamed him for the accident. Eventually more than 1,100 miles of coastline and 11,000 square miles of ocean were affected. On April 20, 2010, the explosion and sinking of the *Deepwater Horizon* oil rig about 40 miles off the coast of Louisiana in the Gulf of Mexico resulted in oil gushing from the seafloor for 87 days until the well was capped—perhaps as much as 3.19 million barrels total—creating an oil slick that washed up on about 1,000 miles of coastline.

1980	1986	1989	1991	1995
Ronald Reagan is elected as the 40th president	Space Shuttle *Challenger* explodes on takeoff	Introduction of the World Wide Web	Operation Desert Storm	Oklahoma City bombing by Timothy McVeigh

In the 1980s, climate scientists, led by James Hansen, began warning about increasing global warming caused by human activities. Although the argument over the validity of this thesis continues, multiple studies published in peer-reviewed scientific journals show that "97 percent or more of actively publishing climate scientists agree: Climate-warming trends over the past century are very likely due to human activities." Evidence of this increasing problem: A dramatic rise in carbon dioxide and other gases in the atmosphere, a rise in the global average sea level of 6.7 inches in the last century, warming oceans, shrinking continental ice sheets, and retreating mountain glaciers.

Burgeoning technology saw huge mainframe computers yielding to the advent of personal computing: desktop computers, laptops, tablets, smartphones. Development of the World Wide Web in 1989 opened massive new opportunities for computer-based information gathering, sources of news, and eventually the explosion of online merchandising. Communications—previously limited to landline telephones, TV, radio, and handwriting—gave way to fax machines, cell phones, e-mail, and texting. Social media, propelled by Mark Zuckerberg with the 2004 launch of Facebook, has expanded wildly over the years. Powerful new imaging systems revolutionized medicine, including sequencing the human genome; technical advances in weaponry, including drones, enhanced military operations; and the launch of the Hubble Space Telescope in 1990 largely transformed exploration of the universe.

The Hubble Space Telescope peers deeply into space and time from its orbit about 350 miles above Earth. Its high-resolution images help shed light on the mysteries of the universe.

The global political landscape changed dramatically with the fall of the Berlin Wall in November 1989, followed a couple years later by the dissolution of the Soviet Union and end of the Cold War; many Americans saw these actions as an affirmation of democracy as a form of government and of capitalism over communism. Heightening tensions soon focused on the Middle East, as Iraq's Saddam Hussein invaded Kuwait, precipitating international military intervention with the U.S.-led Operation Desert Storm in 1991. Operation Iraqi Freedom was launched in 2003 based on information—later shown to be erroneous—that Hussein had stockpiles of weapons of mass destruction.

Adding to the unrest, the global response to the spreading of U.S.-style democracy and consumerism began to sow seeds of discord that would result in a growth of anti-American extremism. Following the 9/11 al Qaeda attacks on the United States, U.S. and British forces invaded Afghanistan in 2001 in an attempt to unseat the ruling Taliban, shatter al Qaeda, and most importantly capture its leader, Osama bin Laden. Navy Seals eventually killed bin Laden in May 2011, in Pakistan.

At home, Geraldine Ferraro was the first woman to run for national office on a major party ticket as vice president in 1984, Barack Obama was elected as the 44th president and the first African American to hold that office, same-sex marriage was legalized in all 50 states, political conservatism expanded, and Donald J. Trump was elected president in 2016, after a highly contentious race.

2001
Al Qaeda attacks on the twin towers and Pentagon

2005
Hurricane Katrina strikes the Gulf of Mexico coast

2007
Great Recession begins

2008
Barack Obama is elected as first black president

2016
Donald J. Trump is elected as 45th president

BIOGRAPHIES
LEADERS, LEGENDS, THINKERS & ENTREPRENEURS 1980–PRESENT

areening into the 21st century, the United States has confronted an era of political divisiveness, breathtaking advancements in technology, burgeoning growth in the businesses of sports and entertainment, terrorism at home and abroad, and leadership in a truly global world. The following is a sampling of key Americans whose distinguished contributions have impacted the lives of Americans and shaped today's world from 1980 to the present.

MADELEINE K. ALBRIGHT
★ 1937– ★
DIPLOMAT, SECRETARY OF STATE

First woman to serve as U.S. secretary of state, Madeleine Albright was born in Prague, Czechoslovakia, in 1937; escaping the Nazi invasion, she and her family eventually settled in Denver, Colorado. She became an American citizen in 1957. Albright served as chief legislative assistant to Maine senator Edmund Muskie from 1976 to 1978. In 1978, National Security Adviser Zbigniew Brzezinski—a former professor—sought her out to serve on the National Security Council during the Carter Administration.

In 1993, President Clinton appointed Albright as U.S. ambassador to the United Nations. Under Clinton, she was

Women have to be active listeners and interrupters— but when you interrupt, you have to know what you are talking about.

MADELEINE K. ALBRIGHT

unanimously confirmed in January 1997 as the 64th secretary of state—the highest-ranking woman in the history of U.S. government up to that time. During Albright's tenure, she worked to stabilize relations with China and Vietnam, brokered negotiations between Israel and neighboring Arab countries, spoke out for global human rights, and sought to halt the spread of nuclear weapons. In

2001, she resigned as secretary of state. Barack Obama awarded her the Presidential Medal of Freedom in 2012.

SHERMAN ALEXIE
★ 1966– ★
POET, NOVELIST, FILMMAKER

A preeminent Native American writer, Sherman Alexie is a member of the Spokane/Coeur d'Alene tribe. His work reflects the realities of contemporary Native American life and focuses on the poverty, despair, and substance abuse that plagues reservation life. Despite this focus, he writes with irony and humor, and many of his characters have a quiet nobility. An early work of fiction, *The Lone Ranger and Tonto Fistfight in Heaven,* formed the basis of *Smoke*

Signals, a film for which Alexie wrote the screenplay. In 1996, Alexie won the American Book Award for his novel *Reservation Blues.*

MUHAMMAD ALI

★ 1942–2016 ★
HEAVYWEIGHT BOXER, PHILANTHROPIST

Born Cassius Clay in segregated Louisville, Kentucky, Muhammad Ali began boxing at 12, an interest that propelled him to a gold medal in the 1960 Rome Olympics. He turned professional and in 1964 won his first world heavyweight title with a technical knockout of Sonny Liston. Outspoken and colorful, Ali proclaimed himself "The Greatest." Also in 1964, he joined the black Muslim group the Nation of Islam. Drafted to serve in Vietnam in 1967, Ali refused based on religious beliefs. Convicted of draft evasion, he was stripped of his heavyweight title, but on appeal the Supreme Court overturned the conviction in 1971.

Ali lost the heavyweight title to Joe Frazier in 1971, regaining it in 1974 with a knockout of George Foreman. Four years later he lost the title to Leon Spinks, regaining it from Spinks later that year. Ali is the only boxer in history to have won the heavyweight title three times. He retired from the ring in 1981 to devote his life to philanthropy. In 1984, it was revealed that he had Parkinson's disease, possibly caused by head trauma from his boxing career.

Ali is widely regarded as one of the greatest boxers of all time and was named the "Sportsman of the Century" by *Sports Illustrated.* He died from septic shock on June 3, 2016.

WOODY ALLEN

★ 1935– ★
FILM DIRECTOR, SCREENWRITER, ACTOR

Called "a treasure of the cinema" by critic Roger Ebert, Woody Allen has been a mainstay in the world of film since the 1950s. He has directed more than 40 movies and won four Academy Awards, one for best director (*Annie Hall,* 1977) and three for best original screenplay (*Annie Hall,* 1977; *Hannah and Her Sisters,* 1986; *Midnight in Paris,* 2011). Inspiration for much of his work derives from his New York Jewish upbringing. Despite his professional successes, Allen has led a tumultuous personal life, including allegations of child molestation, which were later dismissed.

Woody Allen A controversial filmmaker and actor

Muhammad Ali Heavyweight champion, he was perhaps the greatest boxer ever.

Breaking the Glass Ceiling
WOMEN IN POWER
★★★

Building on the feminist movement of the 1960s and '70s, women of the 1980s and onward have increasingly moved into positions of influence in politics, business, and other arenas. Sandra Day O'Connor was the first woman to serve on the Supreme Court; Geraldine Ferraro was the first woman to run for national office, as vice president; Nancy Pelosi is the first woman to serve as speaker of the House of Representatives; Janet Yellen is the first female chair of the Federal Reserve. Marissa Mayer (Yahoo), Mary T. Barra (General Motors), Ursula M. Burns (Xerox), and Meg Whitman (Hewlett Packard), among others, are CEOs of major U.S. corporations. Barbara Walters became the first female co-anchor of a major network news program at *ABC Evening News* and later was co-executive director and co-host of *The View.* Oprah Winfrey—the only U.S. African-American billionaire—has dominated the entertainment industry for more than two decades.

Maya Angelou Stately and gracious, she was a deeply respected African-American writer and poet.

MAYA ANGELOU
★ 1928-2014 ★
POET, AUTOBIOGRAPHER, ACTIVIST

One of the most influential contemporary female African-American writers, Maya Angelou wrote six best-selling autobiographies, focusing on the struggles and triumphs of a young black woman growing up in the mid-1900s. The first—and most popular—was *I Know Why the Caged Bird Sings.* Her several books of poetry explored racial and gender issues, the strength of the human spirit, and need for social justice. In 1993, President Clinton asked her to write and read a poem for his first inauguration; "On the Pulse of Morning" called for peace, racial and religious harmony, justice, and understanding. Angelou was deeply inspired by Martin Luther King, Jr.

ARTHUR ASHE
★ 1943-1993 ★
TENNIS PRO, ACTIVIST

Arthur Ashe was the first and only African-American male tennis player to win the U.S. Open (1968) and Wimbledon (1975); he was also the first African American to be ranked number one in the world (1975). Although slight of build, he was known for his aggressive game. Heart problems forced him to retire in 1979; during the second of two bypass surgeries, Ashe contracted the AIDS virus from an infected blood transfusion. He spent his final years as an activist raising awareness about the disease. He was also an activist for black equality, particularly for black athletes. He died at 49 and received the Presidential Medal of Freedom posthumously from President Bill Clinton in 1993.

Arthur Ashe With his 1975 Wimbledon trophy

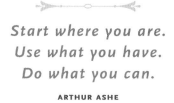

Start where you are.
Use what you have.
Do what you can.

ARTHUR ASHE

JOSEPH BIDEN
★ 1942- ★
U.S. SENATOR, VICE PRESIDENT

For 36 years, Joe Biden served as U.S. senator from Delaware, first elected in 1972 at the age of 29—the sixth youngest senator in history. He was widely respected for his knowledge of foreign relations and criminal justice issues; he served for 12 years as the chairman or ranking member of the Senate Foreign Relations Committee. Biden was elected as the 47th vice president of the United States, with President Barack Obama as president in 2008, and served two terms in that position. As vice president, Biden focused on gun control, women's rights, and foreign policy, among other issues.

WARREN BUFFETT
★ 1930- ★
BUSINESSMAN, INVESTOR,
PHILANTHROPIST

One of the wealthiest and most respected businessmen in the world, Warren Buffett assumed control of Berkshire Hathaway—a multinational conglomerate holding company—in 1965 and drove it to global financial prominence; the company has investments in media, insurance, energy, and food and beverage industries. Buffett is famous for

Warren Buffett One of the world's wealthiest people

pinpointing undervalued companies and making them wildly successful. In 2006, the Nebraskan announced that he would donate the bulk of his fortune (85 percent) to charity. As of October 2016, at age 86, he had a net worth of $64.5 billion, the third richest American behind Bill Gates (#1) and Jeff Bezos (#2).

GEORGE HERBERT WALKER BUSH
★ 1924– ★
41ST U.S. PRESIDENT

Born into a family that valued public service, George H. W. Bush followed in the footsteps of his father, Prescott Bush, a senator from Connecticut. On his 18th birthday, Bush enlisted in the military and became one of the youngest fighter pilots in the Navy; he flew some 58 combat missions during World War II.

After graduating from Yale, he moved to Texas to work in the oil business but soon entered the political arena. He served as a congressman from Texas for two terms starting in 1967. Later, in 1971, Bush was appointed by President Nixon as American ambassador to the United Nations and in 1976 by President Ford as

director of the Central Intelligence Agency. In 1980, he aspired to be the Republican candidate for the presidency but lost the nomination to Ronald Reagan, who offered Bush the vice presidency. During two terms as vice president, Bush focused on antidrug programs and helping to formulate foreign policy.

In 1988, he became the Republican candidate for president and won the election over Michael Dukakis. As he assumed office, Bush affirmed traditional American values and sought to establish "a kinder and gentler nation." But he was faced with a dramatically changing world; early in his administration the Berlin Wall fell and the Soviet Union dissolved. In 1991, following Iraq strongman Saddam Hussein's invasion of Kuwait, Bush authorized a U.S.-led coalition invasion of Kuwait. Operation Desert Storm succeeded in routing Iraqi forces in just 100 hours of action.

On the home front, Bush signed into law the Americans with Disabilities Act but soon faced growing economic pressures. During the Republican Convention before his election, Bush had famously stated, "Read my lips; no new taxes." But he was forced by a growing budget deficit and Democratic pressure to agree to raising taxes. This cost him public support and contributed to his losing the 1992 election to Bill Clinton.

Bush and his wife, Barbara, retired to their home in Houston, Texas; both were active in the campaign for the presidency of their son George W. Bush, who became the 43rd president in 2001.

Read my lips; no new taxes.

GEORGE H. W. BUSH

George Herbert Walker Bush A dedicated public servant, he served as vice president and as the 41st president.

GEORGE WALKER BUSH

★ 1946– ★

43RD U.S. PRESIDENT

George W. Bush is only the second son of a former president to become president—the other was John Quincy Adams. During the Vietnam War, Bush enlisted in the Texas Air National Guard, ensuring no overseas service, and afterward went into the oil business in Texas. Once known for his partying ways, he became a born-again evangelical Christian under the tutelage of Billy Graham. In 1994, he won a hard-fought battle to become governor of Texas, where he developed his theme of "compassionate conservatism."

Bush gained the Republican presidential nomination in 2000. His close battle with Al Gore resulted in a virtual tie. Ballot irregularities in Florida put that state's electoral votes in question; the Supreme Court eventually decided the election, ruling in Bush's favor and declaring him the winner with a 271–266 electoral vote margin. Just eight months into office, al Qaeda conducted attacks on New York and Washington on September 11, 2001. Bush responded by launching what he called the War on Terror. He authorized military action in Afghanistan that unseated the Taliban but did not crush al Qaeda or lead to the capture of Osama bin Laden. In 2003, a U.S.-led coalition launched Operation Iraqi Freedom, a mission based on what proved to be inaccurate intelligence that Saddam Hussein was hiding weapons of mass destruction; the operation ceased after six weeks, but troops remained in Iraq through Bush's presidency and beyond.

Bush won a second term but faced growing discontent within the nation, which was enduring two wars, surging national debt, the Hurricane Katrina disaster, and a credit crisis that resulted in a plunging stock market. He left office in 2009 with one of the lowest approval ratings ever for an American president.

George Walker Bush As 43rd president, he confronted terrorist attacks and severe economic difficulties.

HILLARY RODHAM CLINTON

★ 1947– ★

FIRST LADY, SECRETARY OF STATE, PRESIDENTIAL CANDIDATE

Born to a middle-class, Republican family, Hillary Rodham Clinton was educated at Wellesley College and Yale Law School, where she met her future husband, Bill Clinton. They married in 1975. When Bill Clinton was Arkansas governor during

> *The worst thing that can happen in a democracy—as well as an individual's life—is to become cynical about the future and lose hope.*
>
> **HILLARY RODHAM CLINTON**

the late 1970s and early 1980s, Hillary served as first lady of the state, taught and practiced law, and began raising the couple's daughter, Chelsea, born in 1980. When Bill Clinton was elected president in 1992, she became a proactive first lady, focusing on health reform and family issues, and acting as an adviser to her husband. Her efforts at health care reform met bitter defeat, but she did manage to assure passage of the Children's Health Insurance Program. Following her husband's two terms, Clinton successfully ran for the U.S. Senate from New York, the first first lady in history to be elected to public office. As a Democratic senator she supported President Bush's international initiatives—particularly the wars in Afghanistan and Iraq—but opposed many of his conservative domestic initiatives.

In 2008, Clinton declared herself a presidential candidate for the Democratic nomination, the first woman ever to seek the highest office. She was defeated in the primary by Barack Obama but accepted his appointment as secretary of state after his election. She served in this role from 2009 to 2013, focusing on women's rights and human rights, leading diplomatic efforts during the Arab Spring in the Middle East, but

The Clintons Hillary and Bill Clinton with daughter Chelsea campaign for Hillary's presidential bid in 2016.

facing controversy over the attack on the U.S. diplomatic post in Benghazi, Libya.

In 2015, she again announced her candidacy for president. She won the Democratic nomination, defeating Vermont senator Bernie Sanders. In a contentious and negative presidential race with Republican Donald J. Trump, Clinton was a solid front-runner according to the polls going into Election Day. In a stunning upset, she was defeated by Trump in the electoral college (while winning the popular vote) and conceded the victory to him on election night.

> There is nothing wrong with America that cannot be cured by what is right with America.
>
> **BILL CLINTON**

WILLIAM JEFFERSON CLINTON

★ 1946– ★

42ND U.S. PRESIDENT

William "Bill" Clinton credits his devotion to public service to an inspirational meeting with President Kennedy at the White House when he was a boy. Arkansas-born, Clinton became governor of that state in 1979. In 1992, he became the Democratic nominee for president. He won that election over incumbent George H. W. Bush and assumed office as the third youngest president and first from the baby boomer generation.

Early in his first term, he faced a resounding defeat when his wife Hillary Clinton's plan for health care reform failed to reach Congress. He was more successful with legislation to upgrade education, restrict handgun sales, and strengthen environmental regulations.

After defeating Bob Dole in 1996, Clinton succeeded with legislation for modified health care reform. He later authorized bombing Iraq after Saddam Hussein refused United Nations inspection for nuclear, chemical, and biological weapons.

In 1998, Clinton was involved in a sex scandal with White House intern Monica Lewinsky and was impeached for perjury and obstruction of justice by the House of Representatives. The Senate found him not guilty in 1999, and his apology as well as the support of his wife helped him regain much of the public's support.

Overall, the Clinton years were ones of peace and economic prosperity with a low unemployment rate, a balanced budget, low inflation, the highest rate of home ownership in history, and reduced welfare rolls. Following his presidency, Clinton has been active in humanitarian causes, in combating climate change, and in supporting his wife's candidacy for the presidency in 2008 and 2016.

FRANCIS COLLINS
★ 1950– ★
PHYSICIAN, GENETICIST

Francis Collins, M.D., Ph.D., was director of the National Human Genome Research Institute from 1993 to 2008 and the leader of the Human Genome Project that resulted in mapping and understanding the sequence of human DNA in 2003. The success of this project led medical researchers to help diagnose thousands of illnesses and diseases caused by genetic disorders, including cancer. A born-again Christian, Collins founded the BioLogos Foundation, which explores the intersection of science and religion. In 2006, he published *The Language of God: A Scientist Presents Evidence for Belief,* in which he discusses his personal faith and how he sees religion interfacing with many sciences. He was also concerned about the ethics of genetic research, advocating strongly for the privacy of genetic information.

In 2007, President George W. Bush awarded Collins the Presidential Medal of Freedom. In 2009, President Obama nominated him for the position of director of the National Institutes of Health, the largest biomedical research agency in the world. Collins was instrumental in placing a new emphasis on research into the brain and Alzheimer's disease.

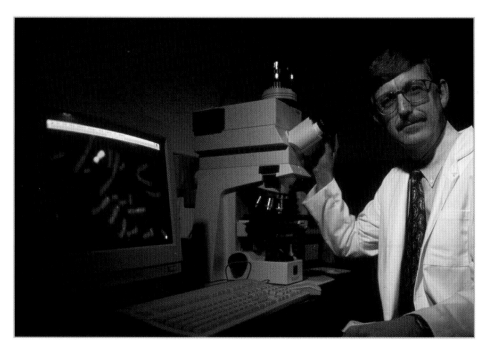

Francis Collins A prominent and respected researcher into genetic and brain disorders

> *I find it oddly anachronistic that in today's culture there seems to be a widespread presumption that scientific and spiritual views are incompatible.*
>
> **FRANCIS COLLINS**

JARED DIAMOND
★ 1937– ★
GEOGRAPHER, AUTHOR

One of the most comprehensive thinkers writing today, Jared Diamond—a geography professor at UCLA—brings together history and a variety of sciences to address big-picture ideas of human evolution and society. One of his main themes is that societies fail not because of politics, warfare, or outside influences, but because they mismanage the environment in which they live. He explores this concept in his award-winning book *Collapse: How Societies Choose to Fail or Succeed,* citing such societies as the Polynesians of Easter Island and the ancestral Puebloans of the American Southwest. He won the Pulitzer Prize for his book *Guns, Germs, and Steel: The Fates of Human Societies,* which discusses the environmental factors that propelled Western societies to dominate the globe. A recipient of the MacArthur Foundation Fellowship "genius grant," Diamond speaks 12 languages and has

Jared Diamond A penetrating writer and thinker

The Rise of the Internet

A REVOLUTION IN COMMUNICATIONS AND INFORMATION SHARING

★ ★ ★

The development of the Internet—a vast computer-based network—was made possible by the invention of the digital computer. In 1962, MIT scientist J. C. R. Licklider theorized that computers could share information in an "intergalactic network." Over the next few years other researchers moved this theory to actuality. Leonard Kleinrock developed a way of sending information from computer to computer by breaking data into units or packets of information. Robert Taylor and colleagues developed ARPANET, the first network of computers. The growth of ARPANET and other networks in the 1970s posed a different problem—how do they all communicate? Vint Cerf solved the question with the development of the Transmission Control Protocol, which allowed computers on different networks to communicate.

In 1989, another leap forward came with the introduction of the World Wide Web by Tim Berners-Lee; this created a vast body of information that people could actually retrieve, instead of just share from one computer to another. Further development produced ways to access that information, and in 1992, the first browser, called Mosaic, later renamed Netscape, was developed. It was a user-friendly method of obtaining information from the Internet.

Development of the personal computer allowed individuals to access information, communicate by e-mail, and even shop. Jeff Bezos, founder and CEO of Amazon.com, is credited as one of the earliest developers of e-commerce. He started by selling books online but quickly expanded to other products. Today, virtually every business and organization has a website to sell products or provide information. With the technology explosion, ways to access the Internet expanded—from desktops to laptops to tablets to smartphones and wearable devices.

A person selects Internet content from a computer's optical touch display in 2010.

---

pursued his evolutionary studies with more than 25 expeditions to New Guinea and other nearby islands to explore ecology and the evolution of birds.

GERALDINE FERRARO

★ 1935–2011 ★

MEMBER OF THE HOUSE OF REPRESENTATIVES

New York Democrat Geraldine Ferraro was elected to the House of Representatives in 1978 on a platform that portrayed her as tough on crime and as a proponent of the working class. She served three terms and was a strong advocate for the Equal Rights Amendment. She vocally opposed many of Ronald Reagan's policies, especially his economic ones. In 1984, she was selected by Democratic presidential candidate Walter Mondale to be his running mate, the first woman to run for vice president on a major party ticket. She

> *You don't have to have fought in a war to love peace.*
>
> **GERALDINE FERRARO**

proved to be a feisty campaigner who drew large crowds, but her focus was soon deflected by questions about her and her husband's finances. This proved to be an ongoing issue in the campaign, and eventually the Mondale-Ferraro ticket lost in a landslide to the Reagan-Bush ticket.

Geraldine Ferraro In 1984, she became the first woman to run for the office of vice president for a major party, alongside Walter Mondale.

BILL GATES

★ 1955– ★

ENTREPRENEUR, PHILANTHROPIST

Bill Gates is known as a brilliant and innovative businessman, a crafty marketing genius, but also a ruthless competitor with a confrontational management style. He founded Microsoft, the world's largest computer software business, with boyhood friend Paul Allen.

Gates began to show interest in computer programming at 13, and this continued at Lakeside School in Seattle, where he met Allen; the two would spend hours in the school's computer lab. While Gates was enrolled at Harvard and Allen was working at Honeywell in Boston, the two became involved in developing software for an early computer hardware company, MITS, based in Albuquerque, New Mexico. They moved to Albuquerque, licensed their software to MITS and other computer companies, and in 1975 founded their own new company, Micro-Soft, later Microsoft.

In 1979, Gates and Allen moved the growing enterprise to Bellevue, Washington, and that year the company grossed $2.5 million. With companies like Apple, IBM, and Intel developing hardware, Gates aggressively began touting the quality and functionality of Microsoft's software. In 1980, IBM was looking for an operating system for its new personal computer; Gates met with IBM executives and reached an agreement to provide the software; he licensed an existing operating system and adapted it for IBM and later for other computer firms. He called it MS-DOS.

In 1981, Microsoft incorporated with Gates as CEO, and in 1983, it went international, opening offices in Japan and Great Britain. That year, Paul Allen was diagnosed with Hodgkin's disease and resigned from the company. In November 1985, Gates launched Windows, a user-friendly operating system that used a mouse instead of keyboard commands.

> *Your most unhappy customers are your greatest source of learning.*
>
> **BILL GATES**

Gates decided to take Microsoft public in 1986 with an initial public offering of $21 per share; because he owned 45 percent of the 24.7 million shares, he became an overnight multimillionaire at 31. That same year, Gates became a billionaire after the stock increased in value and split several times. During the 1990s, Microsoft was investigated by the Federal Trade Commission for unfair business practices and charged with antitrust violations; after years of hearings the suit resulted in a settlement.

On January 1, 1994, Gates married Melinda French, an innovative Microsoft executive. Her influence combined with the death of his mother, an active civic leader, convinced Gates that he had an obligation to others. The couple established the William H. Gates Foundation in 1994, later consolidated as the Bill and Melinda Gates Foundation, which supports education and world health, among other causes.

In 2000, Gates stepped down as CEO of Microsoft, and in 2014 as chairman of the board, to devote more time to his foundation. He is currently the wealthiest man in the world with a 2016 net worth of $87.4 billion.

Bill Gates The computer software pioneer and his wife, Melinda, through the Bill and Melinda Gates Foundation, support many causes.

ROBERT GATES

★ 1943– ★

DIRECTOR OF THE CIA, SECRETARY OF DEFENSE

For nearly 27 years, Robert Gates held positions in the CIA and the National Security Council. In 1987, President Reagan nominated him as director of the CIA, but Gates withdrew the nomination because of his possible involvement with the Iran-Contra political scandal. Four years later, President George H. W. Bush again nominated him and he was confirmed as director and served until early 1993. In 2006, President George W. Bush nominated Gates to be secretary of defense, a position he held until his retirement in 2011 under President Obama. As secretary of defense, Gates oversaw the conflict in Iraq, including the beginning of the withdrawal of U.S. troops from Iraq.

Al Gore Vice president under Bill Clinton for eight years, Gore is a strong advocate for the reality of global climate change.

Robert Gates Secretary of defense from 2006 to 2011, Gates managed the U.S. military operation in Iraq.

ALBERT GORE, JR.

★ 1948– ★

SENATOR, VICE PRESIDENT

Son of longtime Tennessee senator Albert Gore, Sr., Al Gore served as an elected national official for 24 years. In 1976, he ran for the House of Representatives and was elected as a Tennessee Democrat to four consecutive terms. He ran for the Senate and was first elected in 1985. While in Congress, Gore was known as a moderate and much of his focus was on environmental and technology issues.

In 1992, Democratic presidential nominee Bill Clinton selected Gore as his running mate. The so-called Baby Boomer Ticket won two elections; one of Gore's objectives as vice president was to cut back federal bureaucracy. In 2000, Gore ran for president but was defeated by George W. Bush in a hotly contested campaign that was finally resolved by the Supreme Court—although Gore won the popular vote, Bush won the electoral vote and became president.

Gore became a vocal critic of the Bush Administration but turned his attention to the threat of global warming. The 2006 documentary film *An Inconvenient Truth,* which Gore narrated, focused on the aspects and dangers of human-caused climate change; it won an Academy Award for best documentary. On December 10, 2007, Gore received a Nobel Prize for his body of work on global warming.

The climate crisis offers us the chance to experience what very few generations in history have had the privilege of knowing: a generational mission.

AL GORE

JAMES HANSEN
★ 1941– ★
CLIMATE SCIENTIST, ACTIVIST

Called the "Paul Revere of the climate-change movement," James Hansen was one of the first scientists to study the effects of global warming and warn about its impact. His 1988 congressional testimony on climate change not only raised awareness regarding the subject but also pointed out the threats to future generations. From 1981 to 2013, Hansen served as director of NASA's Goddard Institute for Space Studies; in 2000, his research, along with the research of other scientists, pointed out that the significant rise in global temperatures has been caused by the increase in greenhouse gases over the past hundred years. His disappointment at the lack of governmental action in addressing the problems of climate change led him to become an outspoken advocate on the issue. He currently directs the Program on Climate Science, Awareness, and Solutions at Columbia University's Earth Institute.

Steve Jobs The developmental genius under whose influence Apple pioneered a series of revolutionary technologies, including smartphones, tablets, pads, watches, and others

STEVE JOBS
★ 1955–2011 ★
INVENTOR, ENTREPRENEUR

Steve Jobs, co-founder and CEO of Apple Computer, grew up in the area of California south of San Francisco later known as Silicon Valley. As a boy, he showed an interest in electronics and mechanics, and in 1973, worked for a year at Atari as a video game designer before traveling to India for nine months.

Returning to the Bay Area, he and Steve Wozniak—a high school friend with whom he shared a keen interest in electronics and computers—founded Apple Computer to sell Wozniak's innovative Apple I computer. Jobs worked out of his father's garage marketing the Apple I and later the Apple II, which was released in 1977; within three years, the company made $139 million from sales of the Apple II. In 1980, Apple

James Hansen He was among the first climate scientists to warn about the effects of human-caused global warming.

The innovative iPhone, first launched in 2007, is a popular choice of smartphone.

went public and had a market value of $1.2 billion by the end of the first day of trading. Fierce competition with IBM's PC, which had cornered the business market, led Apple in 1984 to develop the Macintosh computer with its intuitive operating system and mouse-driven graphical user interface.

Strong differences in strategic direction within Apple's management led Jobs to resign in 1985; he founded NeXT, Inc., a hardware and software company focused on the education market, and the following year bought an animation company from George Lucas that he renamed Pixar. This successful company produced such animated megahits as *Toy Story* and *Finding Nemo* and has netted billions in profits. Disney later bought Pixar.

In 1996, Apple bought NeXT, and Jobs eventually returned as CEO to the company he had co-founded. A new spirit of innovation at Apple soon resulted in the introduction of the iMac followed by the MacBook, iPod, and iPhone. In 2003, Apple introduced iTunes, which in 2010 became the largest music vendor in the world. The iPad tablet computer was released that same year.

In his role as a corporate executive, Jobs demanded excellence in his employees. In his personal life, he was private and didn't publicly acknowledge that he had been battling pancreatic cancer since 2003; he died of complications from the disease in 2011.

MICHAEL JORDAN
★ 1963– ★
PROFESSIONAL BASKETBALL PLAYER, BUSINESSMAN

Lauded by many as the greatest basketball player of all time, Michael Jordan dominated the sport from the mid-1980s to the late 1990s. A graduate of the University of North Carolina, where he was named NCAA Player of the Year twice, Jordan was drafted by the Chicago Bulls in 1984 and quickly showed his dominance as a scorer and defensive player. He won six NBA championships with the Bulls, the first in 1991, and was the league's Most Valuable Player five times. He also won gold medals at the 1984 and 1992 Olympics.

Following his third championship in 1993 and the murder of his father, Jordan retired from basketball to pursue baseball. After a full year in the minor leagues, though, he returned to the Bulls and won three more championships. He retired in 1999 and became part owner and president of basketball operations for the Washington Wizards; in 2001, the lure of the game drew him back to the court as a player for two more years. He ended

his playing days with the all-time best scoring average of 30.12 points. In 2006, he became part owner of the Charlotte Bobcats (later the Hornets) and in 2010 became majority owner and chairman of the team.

In addition to his basketball success, Jordan is one of the most prolifically marketed individuals; his Nike Air Jordan sneakers, first introduced in 1985, became and remain globally desired. He has marketing relationships with many other major companies, including Coca-Cola, Gatorade, and Hanes, and has earned an estimated $100 million a year in endorsements. In 2014, he became the first NBA player to be a billionaire.

Michael Jordan Winner of six NBA championships and two Olympic gold medals, Jordan is regarded as perhaps the greatest basketball player of all time.

Billie Jean King Founder of the Women's Tennis Association

BILLIE JEAN KING
★ 1943– ★
PROFESSIONAL TENNIS PLAYER

Billie Jean King was a force not only on the tennis court but also for gender equality in her sport. Born into a family of athletes, King in 1961 was part of the youngest team to win a Wimbledon women's doubles championship. She won her first Wimbledon singles championship in 1966. In 1971, she was the first woman in any sport to earn more than $100,000 in a year, but she was disheartened by the inequality in pay between male and female champions. In 1973, she formed the Women's Tennis Association

Victory is fleeting, losing is forever.

BILLIE JEAN KING

and that year forced the U.S. Open to have equal pay for all participants.

That same year, the so-called Battle of the Sexes occurred, following the taunting of women tennis players by 55-year-old Bobby Riggs, the 1939 Wimbledon champion. He challenged King to a match, and on September 20, 1973, King defeated Riggs in straight sets before an estimated 50 million television viewers.

In all, King won 39 major singles, doubles, and mixed doubles championships and was elected to the International Tennis Hall of Fame in 1987. The tennis center at Flushing Meadows—home of the U.S. Open—is named for her. King was the first prominent female athlete to announce her homosexuality, in 1981.

CHARLES G. & DAVID H. KOCH
★ CHARLES, 1935– ★
★ DAVID, 1940– ★
INDUSTRIALISTS, POLITICAL ACTIVISTS

Koch Industries, a massive energy and chemical conglomerate, is the second largest privately owned company in the United States with annual revenues of $115 billion. Charles G. Koch is chairman and CEO of the company and David H. Koch is executive vice president; each has a personal net worth of more than $40 billion. The Koch brothers are well known for actively supporting conservative organizations and political candidates, earmarking hundreds of millions of dollars for such donations. Likewise, they philanthropically support hospitals and medical research, education, the arts, underprivileged populations, and other charities.

JOHN MCCAIN
★ 1936– ★
U.S. SENATOR

Son of a four-star admiral, John McCain graduated from the Naval Academy in 1958 and served in Vietnam as a fighter pilot; he was shot down in 1967 and tortured as a prisoner of war until 1973. After leaving the Navy in 1981, McCain was elected to the House of Representatives in 1982 and in 1984. He ran successfully for the Senate in 1986 and has been reelected several times. As a congressman, McCain is known as a straight-talking conservative who supported military actions and campaign financing reforms. In 2000, he lost the Republican nomination for president to George W. Bush. He gained the nomination in 2008, but he and running mate Sarah Palin lost the election to Barack Obama. McCain remains an active member of the Senate and was a vocal opponent of President Obama's foreign policies.

John McCain U.S. senator from Arizona

Evangelicals & Politics
THE RISE OF THE RELIGIOUS RIGHT
★ ★ ★

The so-called religious right, a coalition of mostly white conservative evangelicals and fundamentalists with the backing of what Richard Nixon styled as the "silent majority" and Jerry Falwell repackaged as the "Moral Majority," began gaining political sway in the late 1970s and 1980s. Falwell; Pat Robertson, leader of the Christian Coalition of America; and other right-wing Christian political factions voiced concerns over what they perceived as a declining moral state in the United States, with increasing divorce rates, drug use, teen sexuality, and homosexuality. Borrowing grassroots organizing techniques from the civil rights movement and the New Left, they supported conservative social policies regarding evolution, abortion, school prayer, stem-cell research, homosexuality, contraception, and pornography.

The 1980 Republican platform adopted several of these policies, including dropping support for the Equal Rights Amendment, supporting the restoration of school prayer, and opposing abortion. In 1980 and 1984, Republican presidential candidate Ronald Reagan received a large majority of the vote of people who identified themselves as born-again Christians. George W. Bush, who spoke of his Christian faith, received 68 percent of the white evangelical vote in 2000 and 78 percent in 2004.

John McCain, 2008 Republican presidential candidate, selected Sarah Palin as his running mate partly because of her popularity with the religious right. After the election, Palin vocally supported the newly forming Tea Party movement. Although not overtly aligned with the conservative religious right, Tea Party members—according to a 2012 CBS News survey—identified themselves as 89 percent white, nearly 75 percent conservative, and 39 percent evangelical. Not as strong as it was in the 1980s, the religious right still influences contemporary American politics.

War is wretched beyond description, and only a fool or a fraud could sentimentalize its cruel reality.

JOHN MCCAIN

TIMOTHY MCVEIGH
★ 1968–2001 ★
DOMESTIC TERRORIST

On April 19, 1995, Timothy McVeigh, working with Terry Nichols, parked a truck loaded with 4,000 pounds of homemade explosives next to the Alfred P. Murrah Federal Building in Oklahoma City and set a two-minute detonator. The resulting explosion killed 168 people, including 19 children, and injured hundreds more. Later that day, McVeigh was arrested on unrelated vehicle and gun charges; he was identified two days later as the bomber. He was convicted on 11 counts, including conspiracy and murder, and executed by lethal injection in 2001. Nichols was sentenced to a record-setting 161 consecutive life sentences. McVeigh claimed he was motivated by a federal government he perceived as tyrannical and against which he needed to make a statement. The bombing is considered the most significant act by a domestic terrorist in U.S. history.

The ruins of the Murrah Federal Building in Oklahoma City after being bombed by Timothy McVeigh and Terry Nichols

BARACK OBAMA

★ 1961– ★

44TH U.S. PRESIDENT

Born in Hawaii of a father from Kenya and a mother from Kansas, Barack Obama in 2009 became the first African-American president in the history of the United States. After receiving his law degree from Harvard in 1991, he settled in Chicago, working as a civil rights lawyer and teaching constitutional law at the University of Chicago Law School. Obama married Michelle Robinson in 1992. In 1996, he was elected to the Illinois Senate, where he worked to cut taxes and expand health care and early education for families. In 2004, he was elected to the U.S. Senate from Illinois with 70 percent of the vote; he focused on lobbying reform, transparency in government, and limiting weapons of mass destruction.

Barack Obama The president poses with his family and pets in front of the White House on Easter Sunday 2015.

> *Change will not come if we wait for some other person or some other time. We are the ones we've been waiting for. We are the change we seek.*
>
> **BARACK OBAMA**

His best-selling book *The Audacity of Hope: Thoughts on Reclaiming the American Dream,* published in 2006, outlined many of the themes on which he based his run for the presidential election in 2008. He defeated Hillary Clinton in the primaries to become the Democratic nominee and defeated John McCain with 52.9 percent of the vote. Obama assumed office in the face of a severe global recession, foreign wars in Afghanistan and Iraq, and a depressed national mood. His first hundred days in office saw the signing of the $787 billion stimulus package to promote short-term economic growth; sizable loans to bail out the automotive and financial industries; expansion of health care insurance for children; and a revamped foreign policy that sought to improve relations with China and Russia, open new negotiations with Iran and Cuba, and withdraw most U.S. troops from Iraq by August 2010.

In March 2010, Obama signed into law the Affordable Care Act, designed to provide low-cost medical insurance to all Americans. It proved to be a controversial and politically divisive law and ultimately was upheld by a 5-to-4 vote of the Supreme Court in 2015. In May 2011, Obama authorized the Navy SEALs action in Pakistan that resulted in the death of al Qaeda leader Osama bin Laden.

The 2012 presidential election resulted in a victory for Obama over Mitt Romney; Obama won with more than 60 percent of the electoral vote. In his second term, he signed a major bipartisan bill that authorized spending cuts and tax increases for the wealthy. Internationally, Obama faced confrontations—and loss in popularity—over the attack on the U.S. mission in Benghazi, Libya, and the subsequent charges of a cover-up and the revelation by German chancellor Angela Merkel that the National Security Agency was wiretapping her cell phone. Turmoil in Syria and Ukraine intensified; Obama authorized the first air strikes against ISIS, the self-proclaimed Islamic State, in August 2014.

In December 2014, he sought to establish diplomatic relations with Cuba for the first time in 50 years; later he lifted sanctions and relaxed travel restrictions, and in March 2016, he and wife Michelle visited Cuba—the first sitting president to do so since Calvin Coolidge in 1928. Toward the end of his second term, he announced the Clean Power Plan aimed at reducing greenhouse gases and issued a series of executive orders related to gun control.

SANDRA DAY O'CONNOR

★ 1930– ★

ASSOCIATE JUSTICE OF THE SUPREME COURT

Nominated by President Ronald Reagan to the Supreme Court in 1981, Sandra Day O'Connor was unanimously approved by the U.S. Senate and became the first woman to serve on the nation's highest court. A 1952 graduate of Stanford University Law School, Texas-born O'Connor served as assistant attorney general of Arizona from 1965 to 1969 and was elected to two terms in the Arizona state senate. In 1974, she was elected to the position of judge on the Maricopa County Superior Court and was later selected to serve on Arizona's court of appeals.

As a justice on the Supreme Court, O'Connor was known as a moderate conservative and also as a moderating voice in the Court's deliberations. She was a believer that the Court's role was to follow the letter of the law, not to pave the way for sweeping social change. She voted in favor of at least one case that upheld the *Roe* v. *Wade* abortion deci-

> *We don't accomplish anything in this world alone . . . and whatever happens is the result of the whole tapestry of one's life and all the weavings of individual threads from one to another that creates something.*
>
> **SANDRA DAY O'CONNOR**

sion of 1973. She was also a key swing vote in the 2000 debate over the presidential election controversy between George W. Bush and Al Gore that paved the way for Bush's victory.

After 24 years, O'Connor retired from the Court in 2006 primarily to care for her husband who was in failing health; he died in 2009. Also in 2006, she was invested as the 23rd chancellor of the College of William and Mary and in 2009 was awarded the Presidential Medal of Freedom by President Barack Obama.

Sandra Day O'Connor She served as the first female justice on the U.S. Supreme Court.

Colin Powell Served as chairman of the Joint Chiefs of Staff and later as secretary of state

COLIN POWELL

★ 1937- ★

MILITARY LEADER,
SECRETARY OF STATE

Colin Powell's career—as he rose quickly through the officer ranks in the U.S. Army—alternated between military assignments at home and around the world and assignments in the political arena. During the Nixon Administration, New York–born Powell held a prestigious White House Fellowship; under Carter, he served as an assistant in the Department of Defense; under Reagan, he worked as national security adviser.

In 1989, President George H. W. Bush appointed Powell, a four-star general, as chairman of the Joint Chiefs of Staff, the first African American to hold that post. In this role he oversaw military actions in Kuwait and Iraq and developed the

"Powell Doctrine" of using overwhelming force to maximize success and minimize casualties. He retired from the Army in 1993 and published a best-selling memoir entitled *My American Journey*. He and his wife, Alma, became active in American Promise, a nonprofit organization focused on encouraging young people.

George W. Bush nominated Powell as secretary of state in 2000, and he was unanimously confirmed—the first African American in that position. Powell initially did not support Bush's plan to invade Iraq, but he eventually agreed to the military action based on intelligence that showed Saddam Hussein was in possession of weapons of mass destruction. In 2004, Powell testified before Congress that the intelligence was "wrong," and he called for a revamping of the intelligence-gathering community. He retired from government in 2005 and continues his work with American Promise.

RONALD REAGAN

★ 1911–2004 ★

ACTOR, GOVERNOR,
40TH U.S. PRESIDENT

Known as the Great Communicator, Ronald Reagan became the 40th president in 1981 at a time of high inflation and a generally despondent national mood. His so-called Reagan Revolution—in the opinion of some—revitalized the nation's self-confidence, increased domestic prosperity, and strengthened the United States' presence abroad. Other Americans felt that his policies failed miserably, further disenfranchising the poor and minorities.

Born in Illinois, Reagan moved to California in 1937 after a successful screen test earned him a contract with Warner Brothers; over the next several years, he starred in 53 films, including

Ronald Reagan The 40th president with his wife, Nancy, in 1980, the year he was elected president

Condoleezza Rice During a meeting in Malaysia, the secretary of state, a classically trained pianist, shows off her skills.

His 1984 presidential victory over Minnesotan Walter Mondale was a landslide. In his second term, Reagan worked to overhaul the tax code, and, internationally, he sought to stabilize relations with Soviet leader Mikhail Gorbachev. Reagan left office with one of the highest approval ratings—63 percent—for a departing president.

He and Nancy retired to Rancho del Cielo, their ranch near Santa Barbara, California. Reagan continued to be active in Republican politics, but in 1994, he announced that he had been diagnosed with Alzheimer's disease. He died from the disease in 2004. Nancy mourned her husband's passing for more than a decade; she died on March 6, 2016.

Knute Rockne, All American and *Kings Row.* As president of the Screen Actors Guild during the period of the Red Scare in the 1950s, Reagan was active in trying to root out Communists. Previously a liberal Democrat, Reagan's political stance became increasingly conservative, and he joined the Republican Party in 1964. In 1966, he was elected governor of California with nearly a million-vote majority and was reelected in 1970. He stabilized the state's finances but faced civil unrest and violent student protests.

An affable and outgoing campaigner, Reagan won the 1980 Republican Party nomination for president and defeated incumbent Jimmy Carter 489 electoral votes to 49. He entered the presidency with the goals of stimulating economic growth, curbing inflation, increasing employment, and revitalizing national defense through a policy of "peace through strength." His controversial

> *Government's first duty is to protect the people, not run their lives.*
>
> **RONALD REAGAN**

economic policy of supply-side economics, dubbed Reaganomics, sought to stimulate the economy through tax cuts and reducing inflation; the 12.5 percent inflation rate during Carter's last year in office was reduced to 3.8 percent by the end of 1982.

Just 69 days into his first term, Reagan was the victim of an assassination attempt by John Hinckley, Jr.; a bullet pierced his lung, barely missing his heart. His spirit and sense of humor during his recovery—he told his wife, Nancy, "Honey, I forgot to duck"—enhanced his approval ratings.

CONDOLEEZZA RICE
★ 1954– ★
POLITICAL SCIENTIST, SECRETARY OF STATE

Born in Birmingham, Alabama, in the segregated South, Condoleezza Rice began a long association with Stanford University when she became a professor of political science there in 1981. Active in political forums, Rice was appointed national security adviser by George W. Bush in 2001; she strongly supported the 2003 war on Iraq. In 2004, Bush nominated her to succeed Colin Powell as secretary of state, the first African-American woman in that role. She stated her agenda in office as "transformational diplomacy," actively supporting democratic, stable, well-governed countries primarily in the Middle East. An accomplished pianist, Rice later returned to Stanford as a professor, and she also works as a consultant and strategic planner.

several science books for children, Ride died of pancreatic cancer after a 17-month battle.

EDWARD SNOWDEN
★ 1983– ★
LEAKER OF TOP-SECRET DOCUMENTS

While working as an analyst at the National Security Agency's offices in Hawaii in 2013, Edward Snowden became concerned by what he perceived to be illegal national and international surveillance programs run by the NSA. Without permission, he copied thousands of top-secret documents, flew to Hong Kong in May, and revealed these documents to two news reporters. On June 14, the U.S. government filed charges against Snowden of violating the Espionage Act. On June 23, he flew to Moscow and was detained in the transit lounge at the Moscow airport for a month. Snowden eventually received asylum in Russia. He is considered by some to be a traitor, by others to be a hero.

Sally Ride In June 1983, space shuttle *Challenger* blasts off with Ride, the first American female astronaut.

SALLY RIDE
★ 1951–2012 ★
ASTRONAUT

In 1978, Sally Ride answered an advertisement about applying to become an astronaut and beat out a thousand other women to enter the astronaut program; she was one of six women picked. Following rigorous training, the California native became the first American woman—and youngest astronaut ever—to fly in space, on the space shuttle *Challenger* on June 18, 1983. She left NASA in 1987 and became the director of the California Space Institute. Author of

STEVEN SPIELBERG
★ 1946– ★
FILM DIRECTOR, PRODUCER

Nominated for an Oscar for his directing seven times, Steven Spielberg is one of the most prolific filmmakers in the recent past, and his films have grossed billions worldwide. His early professional career was in television. As a director on the big screen, Spielberg has explored

Every time I go to a movie, it's magic, no matter what the movie's about.

STEVEN SPIELBERG

many themes. In movies such as *Jaws* (1975) and *Jurassic Park* (1993) he delves into our primal fear of ravenous beasts. A sense of wonder about the unknown permeates movies like *Close Encounters of the Third Kind* (1977) and *E.T.: The Extra-Terrestrial* (1982). History is a key element in *Schindler's List* (1993), *Saving Private Ryan* (1998), and *Bridge of Spies* (2015). And pure swashbuckling adventure flows through the Indiana Jones series.

In 1982, Spielberg founded Amblin, a film company that produced *Back to the*

Steven Spielberg
Director and producer of more than two dozen acclaimed movies

Donald Trump The businessman successfully carried his aggressive style into politics, winning the presidential election in 2016.

Future (1985) and its sequels. In 1994, he was co-founder of DreamWorks, which released dozens of films including Spielberg's *Amistad* (1997), *Munich* (2005), and *War Horse* (2011).

DONALD TRUMP
★ 1946– ★
BUSINESSMAN, 45TH U.S. PRESIDENT

An energetic and assertive child, Donald Trump has maintained those attributes through all phases of his career. After college at the Wharton School of Finance, the New Yorker joined the family real estate business with an initial $1 million gift from his father, and he took control in 1971, renaming it the Trump Organization. He became involved with major real estate deals in Manhattan, especially the Grand Hyatt hotel (1980) and the building known as Trump Tower (1982), a 58-story high-end retail and apartment complex. He became interested in the Atlantic City gambling business and bought an existing property he called Trump Plaza Hotel and Casino in the mid-1980s; he acquired the Taj Mahal in 1990 and expanded his geographic reach to Florida, Los Angeles, and Las Vegas.

Switching his focus from real estate, Trump became executive producer and host of *The Apprentice,* a reality television show that proved successful in part because of his domineering personality. He considered but deferred runs for the presidency in 2000 and 2008, but he declared as a candidate for the 2016 Republican nomination. Early primary wins in 2016 earned him the front-runner position, and he was nominated as the party's candidate at the Republican Convention. His campaign against Democrat Hillary Clinton was divisive and pointedly negative, but in a surprising upset he won the election with an electoral vote majority. Despite the tenor of the campaign, Trump pledged on election night to "be president for all Americans."

News Satire
TELEVISION COMEDY AS SOCIAL COMMENTARY
★★★

A bevy of television comedy shows—*The Daily Show* (anchored from 1999 to 2015 by Jon Stewart), *The Colbert Report, Saturday Night Live, The Simpsons,* and *South Park* among them—as well as a rainbow of stand-up comedians (Tina Fey, Amy Poehler, Chris Rock, Jamie Foxx, Stephen Colbert, and Dave Chappelle, among others) use satire, parody, and irony to hold up a mirror to society and have people confront realities of race, gender, religion, and politics—all done with a laugh. Using comedy as social commentary allows for the exploration of subjects that might otherwise be seen as off-limits or beyond the boundaries of commercial television. *Saturday Night Live,* for instance, has been poking fun at American politics and politicians since 1975. Also part of the goal of shows like *The Daily Show* is to inform as well as satirize, and they have brought news to a generally younger generation that hadn't previously been interested.

Stephen Colbert One of several TV hosts who use satire to poke fun at American society

JAMES WATSON

★ 1928– ★

MOLECULAR BIOLOGIST

Working at England's University of Cambridge Cavendish Laboratory, Chicago-born James Watson and his British colleague Francis Crick discovered the double helix structure of DNA in 1953, thought by many to be the most important scientific discovery of the 20th century. Watson and Crick showed the twisting ladder structure of DNA and how the molecule can duplicate itself. They were awarded the 1962 Nobel Prize in physiology or medicine for their pioneering work. Watson later went on to do research into the causes and treatments of cancer and was associate director of the Human Genome Project in 1988 and director from 1989 to 1992.

VENUS & SERENA WILLIAMS

★ VENUS, 1980– ★

★ SERENA, 1981– ★

PROFESSIONAL TENNIS PLAYERS

Sisters Venus and Serena Williams have dominated women's professional tennis since the mid-1990s. To date, Venus has won 7 Grand Slam singles titles, Serena has won more than 20 Grand Slam singles titles, and together they have won 14 Grand Slam doubles titles. In addition, each has won four Olympic gold medals—one each for a singles championship and playing together three times for doubles championships. Both women are known for their strength and athleticism on the court and off, and for their fierce competitive nature with opponents, including each other. As of 2015, the sisters had faced each other in singles matches 27 times, including eight Grand Slam finals, with Serena winning 16 of them. Both have been ranked number one by the Women's Tennis Association.

They grew up in tough Compton, California, and were strongly encouraged by their father, Richard Williams, to play tennis as a way to pave better lives. Venus turned professional in 1994, and Serena followed suit the next year.

Each has suffered health issues: In 2011, Serena suffered a hematoma and pulmonary embolism, and Venus was diagnosed in 2011 with Sjögren's syndrome, an anti-immune disease that causes fatigue and pain. Both bounced back and have continued to win. Off the court, Venus is a spokesperson for gender equality and has clothing lines and an interior design business, while Serena also has apparel lines and supports educational opportunities for underprivileged youth around the world. In 2015, Serena was listed as #47 on the Forbes list of "World's Highest-Paid Athletes," with earnings of $24.6 million. Serena won her 23rd Grand Slam in January 2017 when she took home the Australian Open trophy, breaking the open-era world record previously held by Steffi Graf.

> *The day I'm not improving will be the day I hang up the racket.*
>
> **VENUS WILLIAMS**

Venus and Serena Williams Outstanding tennis stars, the sisters embrace following a match at Wimbledon in 2015.

E. O. Wilson The scientist explores evolution, social behavior, and the relationship between humans and animals.

E. O. WILSON
★ 1929- ★
BIOLOGIST, NATURALIST

E. O. Wilson, the world's leading expert in myrmecology, the study of ants, is also a bold and comprehensive thinker about evolution and the environment. A childhood accident left Wilson with impaired vision—he could more easily focus on small things rather than large—and this propelled his interest in ants and other social insects. His field research took him to Cuba, Mexico, Australia, New Guinea, Fiji, New Caledonia, and Sri Lanka, where his studies of ants, bees, wasps, and termites led to his theory of sociobiology that explores the basis of social behavior in humans. He believed that social organization in humans—as it is in insects—was a result of evolutionary and inherited traits and tendencies, a controversial theory at the time.

A professor of biology at Harvard for four decades (1956 to 1996), the Alabama native is also the author or co-author of 20 books, two of which— *On Human Nature* (1978) and *The Ants* (1990)—won Pulitzer Prizes. A staunch environmentalist, Wilson explored the relationship between nature and humans in his landmark book *Biophilia: The Human Bond With Other Species,* where he proposes that humanity is deeply connected to our relationship with other animal species and reinforces his belief that "the key to saving life is learning to love it more."

Wilson is considered the father of biodiversity—a term he coined—and he discovered hundreds of new species during his years of research.

> *Nature holds the key to our aesthetic, intellectual, cognitive, and even spiritual satisfaction.*
>
> **E. O. WILSON**

The Business of Sports
AMERICAN ATHLETES MAKE TOP DOLLARS FROM SPONSORS
★ ★ ★

Over the past several decades, American sports has grown into a multibillion-dollar industry, and the basis of the success is building and maintaining the adoration of fans. Without a large—even global—fan base, franchises decline. Savvy sports teams look for ways of deepening the engagement with fans: branded clothing; apps, websites, and instantaneous smartphone updates; building stadiums as entertainment destinations.

Teams increasingly are using analytics and statistics to make personnel as well as on-the-field decisions to enhance the chance of winning and thus retaining fans. Corporate sponsorships have also soared in recent years—not only naming rights for stadiums but also associating corporate products with the team to make the sponsorship connection closer.

In American sports, the Dallas Cowboys (football) and the New York Yankees (baseball) are the wealthiest teams, valued at billions each. In 2015, basketball player LeBron James earned an annual salary of $20.8 million, with an additional $44 million in endorsements. Kevin Durant (basketball), Cam Newton (football), Phil Mickelson (golf), and Tiger Woods (golf) also earn high endorsement dollars.

NBA superstar LeBron James

Oprah Winfrey Media superstar Winfrey, beloved by millions, has dominated the world of entertainment for decades.

OPRAH WINFREY

★ 1954– ★

TALK SHOW HOST, PRODUCER, PHILANTHROPIST

Called the "Queen of All Media," Oprah Winfrey has for decades been a powerful force in television, movies, publishing, and Internet entertainment. Born in rural Mississippi to an unwed mother, Winfrey endured a troubled adolescence; she was sexually abused and lost a premature baby at 14. She settled in Nashville, Tennessee, where she worked in television and radio. In 1976, she moved to Baltimore, Maryland, to become the host of the hit TV talk show *People Are Talking*.

WLS-TV in Chicago recruited Winfrey to host the talk show *AM Chicago*, and she moved the show from last place in the ratings to the top in just months. She gained a national reputation, and Steven Spielberg cast her in his 1985 film *The Color Purple*; she was nominated for best supporting actress. In 1986, she launched *The Oprah Winfrey Show,* an afternoon talk show, to overwhelming success; in the first year she had 10 million viewers and the show grossed $125 million. The show was noted for its forthright discussions about social issues, for in-depth interviews with prominent individuals, and for championing causes such as fighting obesity. She also launched Oprah's Book Club as a segment of the show and introduced her millions of viewers to new and classic books, creating instant best sellers.

In 1999, she co-founded Oxygen Media, a production company aimed at providing cable programming for and about women. The next year she successfully introduced *O: The Oprah Magazine.* In May 2011, she aired the final installment of *The Oprah Winfrey Show* after an incredible 25-year run.

A generous philanthropist, Winfrey has raised more than $80 million for charities, including education for girls in South Africa. She received the first Bob Hope Humanitarian Award in 2002 and the Presidential Medal of Freedom in 2013.

MARK ZUCKERBERG

★ 1984– ★

INTERNET ENTREPRENEUR, PHILANTHROPIST

As a boy, Mark Zuckerberg developed computer games and messaging systems. In high school, he created a music software system called Synapse, a precursor of Pandora. But in college, at Harvard, is where he hit it big—he developed and launched the social networking site Facebook. Three Harvard classmates approached Zuckerberg to help develop a dating site called HarvardConnection. Working with different friends in his sophomore year, Zuckerberg began to think of a broader, more dynamic site where users could upload pictures and information about themselves and communicate with each other. Operating out of his dorm, he launched Facebook, and by the end of 2004 had one million users.

In 2006, two of his HarvardConnection classmates—Cameron and Tyler Winklevoss—sued Zuckerberg for stealing their ideas; he initially denied the charges but eventually settled for $65 million. In the meantime, Facebook continued its wild growth with one billion users by 2012. Also in 2012, Facebook had an initial public offering that raised $16 billion, helping to make Zuckerberg one of the youngest billionaires ever. A generous donor, Zuckerberg and wife Priscilla Chan, with the birth of their first child in 2015, announced they would give 99 percent of their Facebook shares to charity. In September 2016, they pledged $3 billion toward disease prevention.

Mark Zuckerberg The young entrepreneur co-founded and launched the social networking site Facebook.

The American Dream

PROMISE OF HOMEOWNERSHIP FADES WITH MILLENNIAL GENERATION

★ ★ ★

The concept of the American dream flows from the Declaration of Independence, which speaks of the inalienable rights of "life, liberty, and the pursuit of happiness." A key symbolic element of the American dream, along with career and family, has always been owning one's home. Homeownership in the United States reached its highest level at the end of the 1990s, and home prices soared in the early 2000s, building significant wealth for some homeowners. Low interest rates during this period allowed increasing numbers of Americans to purchase homes, and mortgage lenders readily complied by offering subprime loans to individuals who would not normally qualify for the mortgages.

Then, beginning in December 2007, came the Great Recession, which caused widespread unemployment and reduced or frozen salaries; this precipitated a mortgage crisis triggered by mortgage delinquencies and home foreclosures. Home prices plummeted, and many homeowners faced mortgages that were more than the value of their homes. All this in turn caused plunging personal wealth; Americans lost $19.2 trillion in total household wealth during the recession, and some seven million people lost their homes.

Coming out of the recession, a continued decline in homeownership may indicate that the American dream is changing, especially among the millennial generation—those born between the early 1980s and the early 2000s. These younger Americans are experiencing low entry-level wages and high student loans, and they are thus delaying—or perhaps eschewing—the idea of homeownership. Many millennials are choosing to rent, and others are still living with their families.

A street in Greensboro, North Carolina, reflects the impact of the Great Recession, which began in 2007 and negatively impacted homeownership.

America Under Attack

THE DAY THAT CHANGED EVERYTHING

On September 11, 2001, 19 al Qaeda terrorists overpowered the pilots and crews of four commercial airliners; two crashed into the twin towers of the World Trade Center in New York City, leveling the 110-story skyscrapers. A third plowed into the Pentagon near Washington, D.C., causing extensive damage. A fourth—possibly destined for either the White House or Capitol—crashed in a field in Pennsylvania. In total, nearly 3,000 people were killed in these horrifying suicide attacks, including more than 400 police officers and firefighters. Often referred to as 9/11, the events of that day triggered major U.S. initiatives to combat terrorism, including the War on Terror, launched by President George W. Bush. Osama bin Laden, mastermind behind the attacks, remained at large until May 2, 2011, when he was tracked down and killed by U.S. forces in Pakistan.

On September 14, President Bush offers condolences to New York City firefighter Lenard Phelan who lost his brother, Kenneth, also a firefighter, on 9/11.

Found in the rubble, a fire helmet reflects the ravages of the attacks.

Marcy Borders, an American bank clerk who worked at the World Trade Center, survived the attack but was covered with dust from the collapse of the twin towers.

Smoke erupts from the twin towers; two airplanes hijacked by al Qaeda terrorists crashed into them on September 11, 2001. Both buildings soon collapsed.

One World Trade Center now stands where the twin towers fell; the nearby reflecting pool memorial honors the nearly 3,000 victims of the 9/11 attacks.

HEY LOVER BOY –

HOPE YOU HAVE

A WONDERFUL DAY!

I'll be thinking

of you!

Love
Barb

SUMMERFIELD SUITES HOTEL
Orlando-International
8480 International Drive
Orlando, Florida 32819
PH:407/352-2400   FAX:407/352-4631
TOLL FREE: 1-800-833-4353

Found in the buildings' ruins, a poignant love note from a wife to her husband, who was visiting the World Trade Center, evokes the human tragedy of the attacks.

APPENDIX

◇◇◇◇◇◇◇◇◇◇◇◇◇◇◇◇◇◇

★ U.S. Presidents, Vice Presidents & First Ladies ★

YEAR	PRESIDENT	FIRST LADY	VICE PRESIDENT
1789–1797	George Washington	Martha Washington	John Adams
1797–1801	John Adams	Abigail Adams	Thomas Jefferson
1801–1805	Thomas Jefferson	Martha Wayles Skelton Jefferson	Aaron Burr
1805–1809	Thomas Jefferson	Martha Wayles Skelton Jefferson	George Clinton
1809–1812	James Madison	Dolley Madison	George Clinton
1812–1813	James Madison	Dolley Madison	office vacant
1813–1814	James Madison	Dolley Madison	Elbridge Gerry
1814–1817	James Madison	Dolley Madison	office vacant
1817–1825	James Monroe	Elizabeth Kortright Monroe	Daniel D. Tompkins
1825–1829	John Quincy Adams	Louisa Catherine Adams	John C. Calhoun
1829–1832	Andrew Jackson	Rachel Jackson	John C. Calhoun
1833–1837	Andrew Jackson	Rachel Jackson	Martin Van Buren
1837–1841	Martin Van Buren	Hannah Hoes Van Buren	Richard M. Johnson
1841	William Henry Harrison	Anna Tuthill Symmes Harrison	John Tyler
1841–1845	John Tyler	Letitia Christian Tyler & Julia Gardiner Tyler	office vacant
1845–1849	James K. Polk	Sarah Childress Polk	George M. Dallas
1849–1850	Zachary Taylor	Margaret Mackall Smith Taylor	Millard Fillmore
1850–1853	Millard Fillmore	Abigail Powers Fillmore	office vacant
1853	Franklin Pierce	Jane M. Pierce	William R. King
1853–1857	Franklin Pierce	Jane M. Pierce	office vacant
1857–1861	James Buchanan	never married	John C. Breckinridge
1861–1865	Abraham Lincoln	Mary Todd Lincoln	Hannibal Hamlin
1865	Abraham Lincoln	Mary Todd Lincoln	Andrew Johnson
1865–1869	Andrew Johnson	Eliza McCardle Johnson	office vacant
1869–1873	Ulysses S. Grant	Julia Dent Grant	Schuyler Colfax
1873–1875	Ulysses S. Grant	Julia Dent Grant	Henry Wilson
1875–1877	Ulysses S. Grant	Julia Dent Grant	office vacant
1877–1881	Rutherford Birchard Hayes	Lucy Webb Hayes	William A. Wheeler
1881	James A. Garfield	Lucretia Rudolph Garfield	Chester A. Arthur
1881–1885	Chester A. Arthur	Ellen Lewis Herndon Arthur	office vacant
1885	Grover Cleveland	Frances Folsom Cleveland	Thomas A. Hendricks
1885–1889	Grover Cleveland	Frances Folsom Cleveland	office vacant
1889–1893	Benjamin Harrison	Caroline Lavinia Scott Harrison	Levi P. Morton
1893–1897	Grover Cleveland	Frances Folsom Cleveland	Adlai E. Stevenson
1897–1899	William McKinley	Ida Saxton McKinley	Garret A. Hobart
1899–1901	William McKinley	Ida Saxton McKinley	office vacant
1901	William McKinley	Ida Saxton McKinley	Theodore Roosevelt
1901–1905	Theodore Roosevelt	Edith Kermit Carow Roosevelt	office vacant
1905–1909	Theodore Roosevelt	Edith Kermit Carow Roosevelt	Charles W. Fairbanks
1909–1912	William H. Taft	Helen Herron Taft	James S. Sherman
1912–1913	William H. Taft	Helen Herron Taft	office vacant

1913–1921	**Woodrow Wilson**	Ellen Axson Wilson & Edith Bolling Galt Wilson	Thomas R. Marshall
1921–1923	**Warren G. Harding**	Florence Kling Harding	Calvin Coolidge
1923–1925	**Calvin Coolidge**	Grace Goodhue Coolidge	office vacant
1925–1929	**Calvin Coolidge**	Grace Goodhue Coolidge	Charles G. Dawes
1929–1933	**Herbert Hoover**	Lou Henry Hoover	Charles Curtis
1933–1941	**Franklin D. Roosevelt**	Eleanor Roosevelt	John N. Garner
1941–1945	**Franklin D. Roosevelt**	Eleanor Roosevelt	Henry A. Wallace
1945	**Franklin D. Roosevelt**	Eleanor Roosevelt	Harry S. Truman
1945–1949	**Harry S. Truman**	Bess Wallace Truman	office vacant
1949–1953	**Harry S. Truman**	Bess Wallace Truman	Alben W. Barkley
1953–1961	**Dwight D. Eisenhower**	Mamie Doud Eisenhower	Richard M. Nixon
1961–1963	**John F. Kennedy**	Jacqueline Kennedy	Lyndon B. Johnson
1963–1965	**Lyndon B. Johnson**	Lady Bird Johnson	office vacant
1965–1969	**Lyndon B. Johnson**	Lady Bird Johnson	Hubert H. Humphrey
1969–1973	**Richard M. Nixon**	Pat Nixon	Spiro T. Agnew
1973–1974	**Richard M. Nixon**	Pat Nixon	Gerald R. Ford
1974–1977	**Gerald R. Ford**	Betty Ford	Nelson Rockefeller
1977–1981	**Jimmy Carter**	Rosalynn Carter	Walter F. Mondale
1981–1989	**Ronald Reagan**	Nancy Reagan	George H. W. Bush
1989–1993	**George H. W. Bush**	Barbara Bush	Dan Quayle
1993–2001	**Bill Clinton**	Hillary Rodham Clinton	Albert Gore
2001–2009	**George W. Bush**	Laura Bush	Richard Cheney
2009–2017	**Barack Obama**	Michelle Obama	Joseph R. Biden
2017–	**Donald J. Trump**	Melania Trump	Mike Pence

Source: www.loc.gov/rr/print/list/057_chron.html

★ Chief Justices of the United States ★

NAME	STATE APPT. FROM	APPOINTED BY PRESIDENT	JUDICIAL OATH TAKEN	DATE SERVICE TERMINATED
John Jay	New York	Washington	October 19, 1789	June 29, 1795
John Rutledge	South Carolina	Washington	August 12, 1795	December 15, 1795
Oliver Ellsworth	Connecticut	Washington	March 8, 1796	December 15, 1800
John Marshall	Virginia	Adams, John	February 4, 1801	July 6, 1835
Roger Brooke Taney	Maryland	Jackson	March 28, 1836	October 12, 1864
Salmon Portland Chase	Ohio	Lincoln	December 15, 1864	May 7, 1873
Morrison Remick Waite	Ohio	Grant	March 4, 1874	March 23, 1888
Melville Weston Fuller	Illinois	Cleveland	October 8, 1888	July 4, 1910
Edward Douglass White	Louisiana	Taft	December 19, 1910	May 19, 1921
William Howard Taft	Connecticut	Harding	July 11, 1921	February 3, 1930
Charles Evans Hughes	New York	Hoover	February 24, 1930	June 30, 1941
Harlan Fiske Stone	New York	Roosevelt, F.	July 3, 1941	April 22, 1946
Fred Moore Vinson	Kentucky	Truman	June 24, 1946	September 8, 1953
Earl Warren	California	Eisenhower	October 5, 1953	June 23, 1969
Warren Earl Burger	Virginia	Nixon	June 23, 1969	September 26, 1986
William H. Rehnquist	Virginia	Reagan	September 26, 1986	September 3, 2005
John G. Roberts, Jr.	Maryland	Bush, G. W.	September 29, 2005	

Source: www.supremecourt.gov/about/members_text.aspx

Presidential Medal of Freedom Winners

This award, bestowed by the U.S. president, is the highest civilian award in America. It was established in 1963; previously the Medal of Freedom, which had been established by Harry Truman, recognized civilian service, particularly during World War II. The following lists those who were honored during President Barack Obama's tenure.

2017
Joseph Biden

2016
Kareem Abdul-Jabbar
Elouise Cobell
Ellen DeGeneres
Robert De Niro
Richard Garwin
Bill & Melinda Gates
Frank Gehry
Margaret H. Hamilton
Tom Hanks
Grace Hopper
Michael Jordan
Maya Lin
Lorne Michaels
Newt Minow
Eduardo Padrón
Robert Redford
Diana Ross
Vin Scully
Bruce Springsteen
Cicely Tyson

2015
Yogi Berra
Bonnie Carroll
Shirley Chisholm
Emilio Estefan
Gloria Estefan
Billy Frank, Jr.
Lee Hamilton
Katherine G. Johnson
Willie Mays
Barbara Mikulski
Itzhak Perlman

William Ruckelshaus
Stephen Sondheim
Steven Spielberg
Barbra Streisand
James Taylor
Minoru Yasui

2014
Alvin Ailey
Isabel Allende*
Tom Brokaw
James Chaney, Andrew Goodman,
    & Michael Schwerner
Mildred Dresselhaus
John Dingell
Ethel Kennedy
Suzan Harjo
Abner Mikva
Patsy Takemoto Mink
Edward Roybal
Charles Sifford
Robert Solow
Meryl Streep
Marlo Thomas
Stevie Wonder

2013
Ernie Banks
Ben Bradlee
Bill Clinton
Daniel Inouye
Daniel Kahneman
Richard Lugar
Loretta Lynn
Mario Molina
Sally Ride
Bayard Rustin
Arturo Sandoval
Dean Smith
Gloria Steinem
C. T. Vivian
Patricia Wald
Oprah Winfrey

2012
Madeleine Albright
John Doar
Bob Dylan
William Foege
John Glenn

Gordon Hirabayashi
Dolores Huerta
Jan Karski
Juliette Gordon Low
Toni Morrison
Shimon Peres*
John Paul Stevens
Pat Summitt

2011
Robert M. Gates

2010
George H. W. Bush
Angela Merkel*
John Lewis
John H. Adams
Maya Angelou
Warren Buffett
Jasper Johns
Gerda Weissmann Klein*
Dr. Tom Little
Yo-Yo Ma
Sylvia Mendez
Stan Musial
Bill Russell
Jean Kennedy Smith
John J. Sweeney

2009
Nancy Goodman Brinker
Pedro José Greer, Jr.
Stephen Hawking*
Jack Kemp
Edward Kennedy
Billie Jean King
Joseph Lowery
Joe Medicine Crow (High Bird)
Harvey Milk
Sandra Day O'Connor
Sidney Poitier
Chita Rivera
Mary Robinson
Janet Davison Rowley
Desmond Tutu*
Muhammad Yunus

*The award is not limited to U.S. citizens.

Source: www.whitehouse.gov/campaign/medal-of-freedom

NASA and the Race to the Moon

AMERICA'S FIRST ASTRONAUTS

On April 9, 1959, NASA's first administrator, Dr. Keith Glennan, presented the agency's first group of astronauts, known then as the Mercury Seven and now as the Original Seven. The Mercury program made six manned flights from 1961 to 1963. The astronauts were:

Scott Carpenter

L. Gordon Cooper
(also flew in the Gemini program)

John Glenn

Virgil "Gus" Grissom
(also flew in the Gemini program)

Wally Schirra
(also flew in the Gemini and Apollo programs)

Alan Shepard
(also flew in the Apollo program)

Deke Slayton

GEMINI: BRIDGE TO THE MOON

Gemini was NASA's second human spaceflight program and helped NASA prepare for the Apollo moon landings. Ten crews flew missions in 1965 and 1966. In addition to those indicated previously, the astronauts include:

Buzz Aldrin
(also flew in the Apollo program)

Neil Armstrong
(also flew in the Apollo program)

Frank Borman
(also flew in the Apollo program)

Eugene A. Cernan
(also flew in the Apollo program)

Michael Collins
(also flew in the Apollo program)

Charles "Pete" Conrad
(also flew in the Apollo program)

Richard F. Gordon
(also flew in the Apollo program)

James A. Lovell
(also flew in the Apollo program)

James A. McDivitt
(also flew in the Apollo program)

David R. Scott
(also flew in the Apollo program)

Thomas P. Stafford
(also flew in the Apollo program)

Edward H. White II

John W. Young
(also flew in the Apollo program)

THE APOLLO MISSIONS

Apollo was designed to land humans on the moon and bring them home safely. Six of the missions achieved this goal. In addition to those indicated previously, the astronauts include:

William A. Anders

Alan L. Bean

Roger B. Chaffee

R. Walter Cunningham

Charles M. Duke, Jr.

Donn F. Eisele

Ronald E. Evans, Jr.

Fred W. Haise, Jr.

James B. Irwin

T. Kenneth Mattingly

Edgar D. Mitchell

Stuart A. Roosa

Harrison "Jack" Schmitt

Russell "Rusty" Schweickart

John L. "Jack" Swigert

Al Worden

Sources: www.nasa.gov/multimedia/imagegallery /image_feature_157.html, www.nasa.gov/mission_ pages/mercury/missions/program-toc.html, www .nasa.gov/audience/forstudents/5-8/features/nasa -knows/what-was-gemini-program-58.html, nssdc .gsfc.nasa.gov/planetary/chrono_astronaut.html, nssdc.gsfc.nasa.gov/planetary/lunar/apollo.html

Minority Firsts in Political Office

AFRICAN AMERICANS

1836: Alexander Lucius Twilight, first African American elected to public office

1870: Hiram R. Revels, first African-American U.S. senator

1870: Joseph Rainey, first African-American U.S. congressman

1969: Shirley Chisholm, first black U.S. congresswoman

1967: Thurgood Marshall, first African-American Supreme Court justice

1977: Patricia Roberts Harris, first black woman to hold a Cabinet position

1992: Carol Moseley Braun, first black woman U.S. senator

2005: Condoleezza Rice, first African-American female secretary of state

2008: Barack Obama, first African-American president of the United States

Source: www.biography.com/people/groups /african-american-firsts-government-politics

ASIANS

1959: Hiram Fong, first Chinese-American member of Congress and first Asian-American senator

1959: Daniel Inouye, first Japanese American in the House and later the Senate (1963)

1965: Patsy Takemoto Mink, first Asian-American woman elected to the House of Representatives

Sources: www.library.illinois.edu/doc/researchtools /guides/subject/womengov.html, www.senatorfong .com, www.history.com/news/remembering-senator -daniel-inouye-1924-2012

LATINOS

1822: Joseph Marion Hernandez, first Hispanic American to serve in the U.S. Congress

1928: Octaviano Larrazolo, first Hispanic-American U.S. senator, filling an unexpired term

1936: Dennis Chavez, first Hispanic American to serve a full term as U.S. senator

1989: Ileana Ros-Lehtinen, first Hispanic-American woman to serve in the House of Representatives

2010: Susana Martinez, first Hispanic-American woman elected governor of a U.S. state

Sources: www.loc.gov/rr/hispanic/congress/introduction.html, history.house.gov/Historical-Highlights/1800-1850/The-first-Hispanic-American-to-serve-in-Congress/

WOMEN

1887: Susanna Madora Salter, first woman elected mayor of an American town

1916: Jeannette Rankin, first woman to serve in the House of Representatives; first woman elected to national office

1922: Rebecca Latimer Felton, first woman to serve in the Senate (for one day)

1925: Nellie Tayloe Ross, first woman to be sworn in as governor of a U.S. state

1932: Hattie Wyatt Caraway, first woman to be elected to the Senate

1981: Sandra Day O'Connor, first woman to be appointed to the Supreme Court

1997: Madeleine Albright, first woman to serve as secretary of state

2007: Nancy Pelosi, first woman to serve as speaker of the House

Source: www.library.illinois.edu/doc/researchtools/guides/subject/womengov.html

FURTHER RESOURCES

◇◇◇◇◇◇◇◇◇◇◇◇◇◇◇◇◇◇

General

Brinkley, Alan. *American History: A Survey.* McGraw-Hill, 2008.

Miller, James, and John Thompson. *National Geographic Almanac of American History.* National Geographic, 2007.

Treuer, Anton. *National Geographic Atlas of Indian Nations.* National Geographic, 2014.

WEBSITES

americanphilosophy.net

anb.org

avalon.law.yale.edu

britannica.com

docsouth.unc.edu

encyclopediavirginia.org

gilderlehrman.org

memory.loc.gov

millercenter.org/president

nps.gov

oxforddnb.com

pbs.org/wnet/americanmasters

poetryfoundation.org

ushistory.org

Chapter 1

Fischer, David Hackett. *Albion's Seed: Four British Folkways in America.* Oxford University Press, 1989.

WEBSITES

history.org

msa.maryland.gov

pilgrimhall.org

swarthmore.edu

massmoments.org

whitehouse.gov

Chapter 2

Brands, H. W. *The First American: The Life and Times of Benjamin Franklin.* Doubleday, 2000.

Chernow, Ron. *Alexander Hamilton.* Penguin, 2004.

——. *Washington: A Life.* Penguin, 2011.

Ferling, John. *Almost a Miracle: The American Victory in the War of Independence.* Oxford University Press, 2009.

Kostyal, K. M. *Founding Fathers: The Fight for Freedom and the Birth of American Liberty.* National Geographic, 2014.

McCullough, David. *1776.* Simon & Schuster, 2006.

——. *John Adams.* Simon & Schuster, 2002.

Middlekauff, Robert. *The Glorious Cause: The American Revolution, 1763–1789.* Oxford University Press, 2007.

Rakove, Jack. *Declaring Rights: A Brief History With Documents.* Bedford/St. Martin's, 1997.

WEBSITES

libraries.psu.edu

mountvernon.org

monticello.org

Chapter 3

Brands, H. W. *Andrew Jackson: His Life and Times.* Anchor, 2006.

Johnson, Paul E. *The Early American Republic, 1789–1829.* Oxford University Press, 2006.

Kaplan, Fred. *John Quincy Adams: American Visionary.* Harper, 2014.

Petersen, Merrill. *The Great Triumvirate: Webster, Clay, and Calhoun.* Oxford University Press, 1988.

Perdue, Theda, and Michael Green. *The Cherokee Nation and the Trail of Tears.* Penguin, 2008.

WEBSITES

civilwar.org/education/history/
    biographies
www.let.rug.nl/usa/biographies
senate.gov

Chapter 4

Calhoun, Charles W. (ed.). *The Gilded Age: Perspectives on the Origins of Modern America.* Rowan and Littlefield, 2006.

Calloway, Colin. *Our Hearts Fell to the Ground: Plains Indian Views of How the West Was Lost.* Bedford/St. Martin's, 1996.

Donald, David Herbert. *Lincoln.* Simon & Schuster, 2011.

Douglass, Frederick. *Narrative of the Life of Frederick Douglass.* Digireads.com, 2016.

Foote, Shelby. *The Civil War* (multivolume). Vintage.

Goodwin, Doris Kearns. *Team of Rivals: The Political Genius of Abraham Lincoln.* Simon & Schuster, 2006.

Kostyal, K. M. *Abraham Lincoln's Extraordinary Era.* National Geographic, 2009.

McPherson, James. *Battle Cry of Freedom.* Oxford University Press, 2003.

Time Life Civil War Series

WEBSITES

abrahamlincolnonline.org
civilwar.org/education/history
    /biographies

Chapter 5

Brown, Dee. *Bury My Heart at Wounded Knee.* Holt, 1970.

Inventors and Discoverers. National Geographic, 1988.

Josephson, Matthew. *The Robber Barons: The Classic Account of the Influential Capitalists Who Transformed America's Future.* Mariner, 1962.

McCullough, David. *The Wright Brothers.* Simon & Schuster, 2016.

Ritter, Lawrence S. *The Glory of Their Times: The Story of the Early Days of Baseball Told by the Men Who Played It.* Harper Perennial, 2010.

Washington, Booker T. *Up From Slavery: An Autobiography.* Doubleday, 1901.

Chapter 6

Du Bois, W. E. B. *The Souls of Black Folk.* Oxford, 2008.

Egan, Timothy. *The Worst Hard Time: The Untold Story of Those Who Survived the Great American Dust Bowl.* Mariner, 2006.

Miller, James, and John Thompson. *National Geographic Almanac of American History.* National Geographic, 2007.

Rhodes, Richard. *The Making of the Atomic Bomb.* Simon & Schuster, 1986.

Ward, Geoffrey C., and Ken Burns. *The Roosevelts: An Intimate History.* Knopf, 2014.

WEBSITES

pbs.org

Chapter 7

Branch, Taylor. *Pillar of Fire: America in the King Years 1963–65.* Simon & Schuster, 1999.

Goodwin, Doris Kearns. *The Fitzgeralds and the Kennedys.* St. Martin's, 1991.

WEBSITES

millercenter.org
nasa.gov
nobelprize.org
nps.gov

Chapter 8

Anderson, Martin. *Revolution: The Reagan Legacy.* Hoover Institution Press, 1990.

Angelou, Maya. *I Know Why the Caged Bird Sings.* Random House, 1969.

Baker, Peter. *Days of Fire: Bush and Cheney in the White House.* Random House, 2013.

Cannon, Lou. *President Reagan: The Role of a Lifetime.* Public Affairs, 1991.

Diamond, Jared. *Guns, Germs, and Steel: The Fates of Human Societies.* W. W. Norton & Company, 1997.

DiMarco, Damon. *Tower Stories: An Oral History of 9/11.* Santa Monica Press, 2004.

Dwyer, Jim, and Kevin Flynn. *102 Minutes: The Unforgettable Story of the Fight To Survive Inside the Twin Towers.* Times Books, 2005.

Gore, Al. *An Inconvenient Truth: The Planetary Emergency of Global Warming and What We Can Do About It.* Rodale Books, 2006.

Humphreys, Brad R., and Dennis R. Howard (eds.). *The Business of Sports.* 3 vols. Praeger Perspectives, 2008.

Maraniss, David. *Barack Obama: The Story.* Simon & Schuster, 2012.

———. *First in His Class: A Biography of Bill Clinton.* Simon & Schuster, 1995.

Ryan, Johnny. *A History of the Internet and the Digital Future.* Reaktion Books, 2010.

ABOUT THE CONTRIBUTORS

K. M. Kostyal has written nearly 20 adult and children's titles on human history and natural history, prehistory and geologic history, music, world cultures, and wars. Her most recent works for National Geographic include *Founding Fathers: The Fight for Freedom and the Birth of American Liberty, Benjamin Franklin's Wise Words, George Washington's Rules to Live By,* and *Great Migrations,* the companion book to the National Geographic Channel's acclaimed series on animal migrations. Kostyal wrote the introduction and Chapters 1 through 4 and was involved in the general conception of this book. She is currently working on a historical novel based in her native Virginia.

John M. Thompson is the author of two historical novels, *The Reservoir* (2011), which was a finalist for the Library of Virginia's People's Choice Awards, and *Love and Lament* (2013), which was nominated for the David J. Langum, Sr. Prize for American Historical Fiction. His articles have appeared in *Smithsonian,* the *Washington Post, Islands,* and other publications. He has written and contributed to a number of National Geographic books, including *America's Historic Trails* and *Dakotas: Where the West Begins.*

William R. Gray, a book and magazine writer based in Durango, Colorado, was on the staff of the National Geographic Society as a writer, editor, and publishing executive for 33 years beginning in 1968. In 2002, he and his family moved to the Southwest where he resumed his writing career and became a member of the faculty at San Juan College. Published books include *The Pacific Crest Trail, Voyages to Paradise,* and *Legacy of the West.* Gray contributed Chapter 8 of this title.

David Cline is assistant professor of history at Virginia Tech in Blacksburg, Virginia. He is the author of *From Reconciliation to Revolution: The Student Interracial Ministry, Liberal Christianity, and the Civil Rights Movement.* Cline served as expert consultant on this book.

ILLUSTRATIONS CREDITS

Heckscher Collection/BI; 34 (LO), Kean Collection/GI; 35 (UP), © The Trustees of the British Museum/Art Resource, NY; 35 (LO), Governor John Winthrop Performing Apothecary Services in His Home, Thom, Robert (1915–1979)/Private Collection/BI; 36 (UP LE), Tumacacori Mission, 1855, Pratt, Henry Cheever (1803–1880)/Phoenix Art Museum, Arizona, U.S.A./gift of Frances Hover Stanley and Carolanne Smurthwaite, by exchange/BI; 36 (UP RT), Library of Congress, Geography and Map Division; 36 (LO), The Franciscan church at Isleta Pueblo, New Mexico, built 1612/New Mexico, U.S.A./Peter Newark American Pictures/BI; 37 (UP), California Department of Parks & Recreation/Wikimedia Commons; 37 (CTR), Portrait of Bartolomé de Las Casas (Seville, 1484–Madrid, 1566)/De Agostini Picture Library/BI; 37 (LO), Morning light on Mission Santa Barbara in Santa Barbara/AA World Travel Library/BI. **CHAPTER 2:** 38–9, Bettmann/GI; 40, DEA/M. Seemuller/GI; 42 (UP), American Revolution, British Sergeant's Button/Private Collection/Photo © Don Troiani/BI; 42 (LO), Drafting the Declaration of Independence, Chappel, Alonzo (1828–1887)/The Heckscher Museum of Art, Huntington, NY, U.S.A./August Heckscher Collection/BI; 43, Equestrian portrait of George Washington, Peale, Rembrandt (1778–1860)/Private Collection/Photo © Christie's Images/BI; 44 (LE), Sarin Images/Granger, NYC; 44 (RT), National Museum of American History/Smithsonian Institution/BI; 45 (UP), Courtesy Old Sturbridge Village; 45 (LO), Writing the Declaration of Independence in 1776, Ferris, Jean Leon Gerome (1863–1930)/Virginia Historical Society, Richmond, VA, U.S.A./BI; 46 (BOTH), Granger, NYC; 47, Pictorial Press Ltd./Alamy Stock Photo; 48, Richard Allen/Universal History Archive/UIG/BI; 49 (LE), Granger, NYC; 49 (CTR), Proclamation to officers and soldiers of the Continental Army, 20th October 1780/Gilder Lehrman Collection, New York, U.S.A./BI; 49 (RT), © Mary Evans Picture Library/Grosvenor Prints/The Image Works; 50, North Wind Picture Archives/The Image Works; 51 (UP), Michael Ventura/Alamy Stock Photo; 51 (LO), Bettmann/GI; 52 (LE), © The Metropolitan Museum of Art/Art Resource, NY; 52 (RT), Olaudah Equiano alias Gustavus Vassa, a slave, 178/British Library, London, UK/© British Library Board. All Rights Reserved/BI; 53, On to Liberty, 1867, Kaufmann, Theodor (1814–p.1887)/Private Collection/Photo © Christie's Images/BI; 54 (LE), GraphicaArtis/GI; 54 (CTR), Cup showing portrait of Benjamin Franklin, and saucer, 1778/Philadelphia Museum of Art, Pennsylvania, PA, U.S.A./bequest (by exchange) of George D. Widener, 1998/BI; 54 (UP RT), Courtesy, Independence National Historical Park; 54 (CTR RT), Battery of Leyden jars, after 1736, Pieter van Musschenbroek (maker)/courtesy of American Philosophical Society, gift of Joseph Hopkinson, 1836/54 (LO RT), The Library Company of Philadelphia; 55, The Clermont, 1909, Ogden, Henry Alexander (1856–1936)/© Collection of the New-York Historical Society, U.S.A./BI; 56 (LE), Kean Collection/GI; 56 (RT), Nathan Hale, 1890, MacMonnies, Frederick William (1863–1937)/Private Collection/BI; 57 (UP), Portrait of Alexander Hamilton (1757–1804), American politician/De Agostini Picture Library/BI; 57 (LO), AP Images/Julio Cortez; 58 (UP), GI/Tetra images RF; 58 (LO), John Hancock, 1765, Copley, John Singleton (1738–1815)/Museum of Fine Arts, Boston, MA, U.S.A./Carolyn A. and Peter S. Lynch Gallery (Gallery 132)/BI; 59, © The Metropolitan Museum of Art/Art Resource, NY; 60 (UP), The John Jay Freedom Box, 1784/Private Collection/Photo © Christie's Images/BI; 60 (LO LE), John Jay, 1786, Wright of Derby, Joseph (1734–1797)/© Collection of the New-York Historical Society, U.S.A./BI; 60 (LO RT), Thomas Jefferson Foundation; 61 (UP), GraphicaArtis/GI; 61 (LO), Thomas Jefferson Foundation; 62 (LE), John Paul Jones and the Bonhomme Richard in 1779, American School (19th century)/New York Public Library, U.S.A./BI; 62 (RT), Image courtesy of U.S. Naval Academy Museum; 63 (LE), The Star-Spangled Banner, 1926/Private Collection/Photo © GraphicaArtis/BI; 63 (RT), North Wind Picture Archives/Alamy Stock Photo; 64 (LE), Portrait of Gilbert Motier (1757–1834) the Marquis de La Fayette as a Lieutenant General, 1791, Court, Joseph Desire (1797–1865)/Chateau de Versailles, France/BI; 64 (RT), © The Metropolitan Museum of Art/Art Resource, NY; 65, Henry Lee ca 1782 (oil on canvas), Peale, Charles Willson (1741–1827)/Independence Hall, Philadelphia, Pennsylvania, U.S.A./BI; 66 (LE), Lewis & Clark on the Lower Columbia River, 1905, Russell, Charles Marion (1865–1926)/Private Collection/Peter Newark American Pictures/BI; 66 (RT), Missouri History Museum; 67 (LE), Map of the Lewis and Clark American expedition, 1804–1806/Private Collection/Ken Welsh/BI; 67 (RT), National Museum of American History/Smithsonian Institution/BI; 68 (LE), Mrs. James Madison, Alaux, Aline (1813–1856)/© Collection of the New-York Historical Society, U.S.A./BI; 68 (RT), Greensboro Historical Museum; 69, James Madison, 1835, after the original by Gilbert Stuart, Durand, Asher Brown (1796–1886)/© Collection of the New-York Historical Society, U.S.A./BI; 70 (UP), The Charleston Museum; 70 (LO), Scala/Art Resource, NY; 71, Portrait of George Mason, Guillaume, Louis Mathieu Didier (1816–1892)/Virginia Historical Society, Richmond, VA, U.S.A./BI; 72 (UP), Robert W. Nicholson/NGC; 72 (LO), James Monroe Museum; 73 (UP), Gouverneur Morris (1752–1816) 1808, Sully, Thomas (1783–1872)/© Philadelphia History Museum at the Atwater Kent/courtesy of Historical Society of Pennsylvania Collection/BI; 73 (LO), National Portrait Gallery, Smithsonian Institution/Art Resource, NY; 74 (LE), Portrait of Thomas Paine, by George Romney (1734–1802)/De Agostini Picture Library/BI; 74 (RT), Common Sense: Addressed to the Inhabitants of America, new edition by Thomas Paine (1737–1809) printed in Philadelphia, 1776/Private Collection/Photo © Christie's

Images/BI; 75 (UP), James Peale, 1822, Peale, Charles Willson (1741–1827)/Detroit Institute of Arts, U.S.A./BI; 75 (LO), Portrait of Charles Wilson Peale (1741–1827), 1767–69, West, Benjamin (1738–1820)/© Collection of the New-York Historical Society, U.S.A./BI; 76 (UP), Granger, NYC; 76 (LO), Oliver Hazard Perry (1785–1819), ca 1813–14, Peale, Rembrandt (1778–1860)/© Collection of the New-York Historical Society, U.S.A./BI; 77, Richard Nowitz/NGC; 78, Paul Revere warns that the British are coming 1775/Ewing Galloway/UIG/BI; 79 (UP), Benjamin Rush, 1812, Sully, Thomas (1783–1872)/Private Collection/Peter Newark American Pictures/BI; 79 (LO), JT Vintage/Art Resource, NY; 80, Lewis and Clark with Sacagawea, Paxson, Edgar Samuel (1852–1915)/Private Collection/Peter Newark American Pictures/BI; 81 (UP), National Portrait Gallery, Smithsonian Institution/Art Resource, NY; 81 (LO), Universal Images Group/Art Resource, NY; 82, Gilbert Stuart (1755–1828), 1805, Peale, Charles W. (1741–1827) & Peale, Rembrandt (1778–1860)/© Collection of the New-York Historical Society, U.S.A./BI; 83 (UP), John Trumbull. 1793, Trumbull, John (1756–1843)/Detroit Institute of Arts, U.S.A./Founders Society purchase and Dexter M. Ferry Jr. fund/BI; 83 (LO), Field Museum Library/GI; 84 (UP), George Washington at Valley Forge, preliminary sketch, 1854, Matteson, Tompkins Harrison (1813–1884)/Private Collection/Photo © Christie's Images/BI; 84 (LO), National Museum of American History; 85 (UP), Pistol owned by George Washington, from the collections of the New York State Library, Manuscripts and Special Collections, Albany, NY; 85 (LO), Mead Art Museum, Amherst College, MA, USA/bequest of Waldo Hutchins, Jr./BI; 86, Tate, London/Art Resource, NY; 87, The First Continental Congress in 1774, 1911, Deland, Clyde Osmer (1872–1947)/© Philadelphia History Museum at the Atwater Kent/courtesy of Historical Society of Pennsylvania Collection/BI; 88 (UP LE), Martha Washington, 1795, Peale, Charles Willson (1741–1827)/Virginia Historical Society, Richmond, VA, U.S.A./BI; 88 (LO LE), Courtesy of Mount Vernon Ladies' Association; 88 (UP CTR), Courtesy of Mount Vernon Ladies' Association; 88 (LO CTR), National Museum of American History/Smithsonian Institution/BI; 88 (RT), George F. Mobley/NGC; 89 (UP LE), Underwood Archives/GI; 89 (LO LE), Everett Collection/age fotostock; 89 (UP CTR, BOTH), Memento mori engraved watch key, with lock of hair of Martha Wayles Jefferson/Private Collection/Photo © Christie's Images/BI; 89 (LO CTR), The White House/Public Domain; 89 (UP RT), GearedBull/Wikimedia Commons/Public Domain; 89 (LO RT), Portrait of Dolley Madison, 1817, Wood, Joseph (1778–1830)/Virginia Historical Society, Richmond, VA, U.S.A./BI. **CHAPTER 3:** 90–91, The Oregon Trail, 1869, Bierstadt, Albert (1830–1902)/Butler Institute of American Art, Youngstown, OH, U.S.A./gift of Joseph G. Butler III 1946/BI; 92, Spencer Weiner/GI; 94 (LE), Indian Campaign of 1832: Map of the Country/Newberry Library, Chicago, Illinois, U.S.A./BI; 94 (RT), Fototeca Storica Nazionale/GI; 95 (UP), akg-images; 95 (LO), Dr John Doy, with fellow anti-slavery campaigners, 1859/Private Collection/Peter Newark American Pictures/BI; 96, National Portrait Gallery, Smithsonian Institution/Art Resource, NY; 97, Louis Agassiz/Encyclopaedia Britannica/UIG/BI; 98 (LE), Louisiana Heron, from Birds of America, Audubon, John James (1785–1851) (after)/Private Collection/BI; 98 (RT), Paintbox of John James Audubon (1785–1851) (19th century)/Private Collection/Photo © Boltin Picture Library/BI; 99, Henry Ward Beecher (1813–1887) 1874, Baker, George Augustus (1821–1880)/Brooklyn Museum of Art, New York, U.S.A./gift of the American Art Council/BI; 100, Portrait of Black Hawk (1767–1838) by Homer Henderson ca 1870, King, Charles Bird (1785–1862) (after)/© Chicago History Museum, U.S.A./BI; 101 (LE), John Brown/Photo © Gerald Bloncourt/BI; 101 (RT), Universal History Archive/GI; 102 (UP), James Buchanan/Private Collection/© Look and Learn/Barbara Loe Collection/BI; 102 (LO), Adoc-photos/Art Resource, NY; 103 (UP LE), Christopher Houston Carson aka Kit Carson (1809–1868), frontiersman/BI; 103 (LO LE), Courtesy Manitou Auctions; 103 (RT), akg-images; 104 (LE), Stock Montage/GI; 104 (RT), Henry Clay political button, 1845/Private Collection/Photo © Don Troiani/BI; 105 (UP), MPI/GI; 105 (LO), David (Davy) Crockett (1786–1836) with his hunting dogs in 1836/Private Collection/Peter Newark American Pictures/BI; 106 (UP), George Eastman House/GI; 106 (LO), Ralph Waldo Emerson (1803–1882)/Private Collection/Ken Welsh/BI; 107, White House in Washington, May 1821, by Jefferson Vail/De Agostini Picture Library/M. Seemuller/BI; 108 (LE), Millard Fillmore, engraved by Thomas B. Welch (1814–1874)/Private Collection/The Stapleton Collection/BI; 108 (RT), Interim Archives/GI; 109 (UP), Fremont Hoisting the Stars and Stripes on the Loftiest Peak of the Rocky Mountains/Private Collection/© Look and Learn/BI; 109 (LO), National Portrait Gallery, Smithsonian Institution/Art Resource, NY; 110 (UP), Stock Montage/GI; 110 (LO), The Liberator, second illustrated heading, 1838/© Boston Athenaeum, U.S.A./BI; 111 (UP), Poster advertising Goodyear's patent rubber field equipment (19th century)/Private Collection/Photo © Civil War Archive/BI; 111 (LO), William Henry Harrison (1773–1841), Andrews, Eliphalet Frazer (1835–1915)/Private Collection/Peter Newark American Pictures/BI; 112, "Fortyniners" washing gold from the Calaveres River, California, 1858/Private Collection/BI; 113 (UP LE), Election Proclamation by the Governor! (elections before the Civil War), 15th June 1860/Gilder Lehrman Collection, New York, U.S.A./BI; 113 (UP RT), Sam Houston, ca 1851, Flintoff, Thomas (1809–1892)/ Museum of Fine Arts, Houston, Texas, U.S.A./The Bayou Bend Collection, gift of Mr. and Mrs. R. E. Zimmerman/BI; 113 (LO), Nathaniel Hawthorne (1804–1864) 1840, Osgood, Charles (1809–1890)/

© Peabody Essex Museum, Salem, MA, U.S.A./BI; 114 (UP), Library of Congress/GI; 114 (CTR), Hulton Archive/GI; 114 (LO), Culture Club/GI; 115, General Andrew Jackson at the Battle of New Orleans, Chappel, Alonzo (1828–1887)/© Chicago History Museum, U.S.A./BI; 116 (UP), Henry Wadsworth Longfellow (19th century)/Private Collection/© Look and Learn/BI; 116 (LO), Cyrus Hall McCormick (1809–1884)/Private Collection/Peter Newark American Pictures/BI; 117 (UP), Cyrus McCormick's reaping machine of 1831/Universal History Archive/UIG/BI; 117 (LO), Portrait of Osceola (1804–1838), Catlin, George (1796–1872)/Private Collection/BI; 118 (UP), Franklin Pierce/Private Collection/© Look and Learn/Barbara Loe Collection/BI; 118 (LO), U.S. Japan Fleet, Commodore Perry carrying the "Gospel of God" to the Heathens, 1853, Evans, James Guy/© Chicago History Museum, U.S.A./BI; 119 (UP), Pioneer's home in the American wilderness, Palmer, Frances Flora Bond (Fanny)/Private Collection/Peter Newark American Pictures/BI; 119 (CTR), Le Corbeau (The Raven), Manet, Edouard (1832–83)/Hamburger Kunsthalle, Hamburg, Germany/BI; 119 (LO), Poe at work under Catalina's eye, Sheldon, Charles Mills (1866–1928)/Private Collection/© Look and Learn/BI; 120 (LE), Bettmann/GI; 120 (RT), David Frent/GI; 121, From the collection of the Rochester Public Library Local History Division; 122 (UP LE), F&A Archive/Art Resource, NY; 122 (UP RT), Wikimedia Commons/Public Domain; 122 (LO), John Ross, a Cherokee Chief, 1836, illustration from The Indian Tribes of North America, vol.3, by Thomas L. McKenney and James Hall/Private Collection/BI; 123, Se-quo-yah or George Guess, 1828, illustration from The Indian Tribes of North America, vol.1, by Thomas L. McKenney and James Hall/Private Collection/BI; 124 (LE), Universal Images Group/GI; 124 (RT), AP Images/Rick Bowmer; 125 (UP), Wikimedia Commons/Public Domain; 125 (LO LE), Portrait of Suffragist Lucy Stone, 1840–1860/Photo © GraphicaArtis/BI; 125 (LO RT), Yellowstone Park, 1934, Moran, Thomas (1837–1926) (after)/Private Collection/DaTo Images/BI; 126 (UP LE), The Death of Uncle Tom, plate 11 from Uncle Tom's Cabin, engraved by Charles Bour (1814–1881)/© Collection of the New-York Historical Society, U.S.A./BI; 126 (UP RT), Bettmann/GI; 126 (LO), National Portrait Gallery, Smithsonian Institution/Art Resource, NY; 127 (LE), General Zachary Taylor at the Battle of Buena Vista in 1847, Powell, William Henry (1823–1879)/© Chicago History Museum, U.S.A./BI; 127 (RT), Bettmann/GI; 128 (UP), Henry David Thoreau (1817–1862) American writer, 1856/BI; 128 (CTR), The Morgan Library & Museum/Art Resource, NY; 128 (LO), Portrait of Sojourner Truth in 1864/Photo © GraphicaArtis/BI; 129, Underwood Archives/GI; 130 (UP), Discovery of Nat Turner/Private Collection/The Stapleton Collection/BI; 130 (LO), President John Tyler 1863/Universal History Archive/UIG/BI; 131 (UP), Martin van Buren (1782–1862)/Private Collection/Peter Newark American Pictures/BI; 131 (LO), Pair of Cherokee moccasins/Private Collection/Photo © Christie's Images/BI; 132 (UP), Daniel Webster (1782–1852)/Private Collection/Peter Newark American Pictures/BI; 132 (LO), Charles Phelps Cushing/ClassicStock/akg-images; 133 (UP), Mormon pioneers pulling handcarts on the long journey to Salt Lake City in 1856/Private Collection/Peter Newark Western Americana/BI; 133 (LO), Brigham Young/Universal History Archive/UIG/BI; 134 (LE), Secret room for runaway slaves, 2005, Wood, Rob (b. 1946)/Private Collection/Wood Ronsaville Harlin, Inc. U.S.A./BI; 134 (CTR), Louie Psihoyos; 134 (RT), Fugitive slaves fleeing from the Maryland coast to an Underground Railroad depot in Delaware, 1850/Private Collection/Peter Newark American Pictures/BI; 135 (UP), Interim Archives/GI; 135 (LO LE), Thaddeus Stevens (1792–1868)/Private Collection/Peter Newark American Pictures/BI; 135 (LO CTR), The Underground Railroad Aids With a Runaway Slave, Davies, Arthur Bowen (1862–1928)/Private Collection/BI; 135 (LO RT), Chicago History Museum/GI. **CHAPTER 4:** 136–7, "Let Us Have Peace," Ferris, Jean Leon Gerome (1863–1930)/Virginia Historical Society, Richmond, VA, U.S.A./BI; 138, The Hour of Emancipation, 1863, Carlton, William Tolman (1816–1888)/Private Collection/Photo © Christie's Images/BI; 140 (UP), Bettmann/GI; 140 (LO), Fine Art/GI; 141 (UP), Art and Picture Collection, The New York Public Library, Astor, Lenox and Tilden Foundations; 141 (CTR), Portrait of Ulysses S. Grant (1822–1885)/Private Collection/Ken Welsh/BI; 141 (LO), Emancipation Proclamation, by President Abraham Lincoln, 1862/Private Collection/BI; 142, Poster advertising "The Barnum & Bailey Greatest Show on Earth"/Private Collection/Peter Newark American Pictures/BI; 143 (UP), Fine Art/GI; 143 (LO), Clara Barton (1821–1912), ca 1865, Brady, Mathew (1823–1896)/Private Collection/Peter Newark Military Pictures/BI; 144 (LE), George Eastman House/GI; 144 (RT), Isabella Marie Boyd aka Belle Boyd (1844–1900), ca 1865/Photo © PVDE/BI; 145 (LE), Bettmann/GI; 145 (RT), Stock Montage/GI; 146, General Benjamin F. Butler, 1861–65, Brady, Mathew (1823–1896) & studio/Private Collection/The Stapleton Collection/BI; 147 (UP), General Custer's last stand at the Battle of Little Bighorn, June 25, 1876/De Agostini Picture Library/BI; 147 (LO), Portrait of Maj. Gen. George A. Custer, officer of the Federal Army, 1863/Universal History Archive/UIG/BI; 148 (UP), Universal History Archive/GI; 148 (LO), Jefferson Davis, Schwerdt, Christian F. (19th century)/© Chicago History Museum, U.S.A./BI; 149, Hulton Archive/GI; 150 (UP), Bettmann/GI; 150, Amherst College Archives & Special Collections; 151 (UP), Frederick Douglass, 1847–1852, Miller, Samuel J. (1822–1888)/The Art Institute of Chicago, IL, U.S.A./BI; 151 (LO), Moby Dick, McConnell, James Edwin (1903–1995)/Private Collection/© Look and Learn/BI; 152 (UP), Nathan Bedford Forrest—1999, Troiani, Don (b. 1949)/Private Collection/BI; 152 (LO),

Fotosearch/GI; 153 (UP), Alexander Gardner's darkroom on wheels, 1867, Gardner, Alexander (1821–1882)/Private Collection/BI; 153 (LO), Oscar White/Corbis/VCG/GI; 154 (UP), Republican Election Poster, 1888/Private Collection/Peter Newark American Pictures/BI; 154 (LO), Buyenlarge/GI; 155 (UP), MPI/GI; 155 (LO), HIP/Art Resource, NY; 156 (UP), Collis P Huntington/Private Collection/© Look and Learn/Elgar Collection/BI; 156 (LO), Kean Collection/GI; 157 (LE), Eric Blevins, North Carolina Museum of History; 157 (RT), General Robert E. Lee with troops, 1879/Universal History Archive/UIG/BI; 158 (UP), Battle of Kennesaw Mountain, Georgia, 27th June 1864/Private Collection/Peter Newark American Pictures/BI; 158 (CTR), Mathew Brady/Buyenlarge/GI; 158 (LO), Fine Art/GI; 159, PhotoQuest/GI; 160 (LE), The Lincoln Family in 1861, engraved by J. C. Buttre (1821–1893)/© Collection of the New-York Historical Society, U.S.A./BI; 160 (RT), Abraham Lincoln Presidential Library and Museum; 161 (UP), The stage of the Ford Theatre where U.S. president Abraham Lincoln (1809–1865), was assassinated/De Agostini Picture Library/BI; 161 (LO), akg-images/The Image Works; 162 (UP), American Outlaw Billy the Kid, 1875–1880/Photo © GraphicaArtis/BI; 162 (LO), Portrait of General George B. McClellan, 1861–65, Brady, Mathew (1823–1896) & studio/Private Collection/The Stapleton Collection/BI; 163 (UP), Major General George Meade (1815–1872)/Private Collection/Peter Newark Military Pictures/BI; 163 (LO), Medal of the GAR George Meade Post, Philadelphia/Private Collection/Photo © Don Troiani/BI; 164 (UP), Samuel Morse/Photo © CCI/BI; 164 (LO LE), Frontispiece of Moby-Dick by Herman Melville, Schaeffer, Mead (1898–1980)/Private Collection/BI; 164 (LO RT), Apic/GI; 165, Print Collector/GI; 166 (LE), Time & Life Pictures/GI; 166 (RT), Thomas Nast (1840–1902)/American Antiquarian Society, Worcester, MA, U.S.A./BI; 167 (UP), George Steinmetz; 167 (CTR), Bettmann/GI; 167 (LO), General William Tecumseh Sherman on Horseback 1864/Universal History Archive/UIG/BI; 168 (UP), General George Pickett, CSA 1863/Universal History Archive/UIG/BI; 168 (LO), Pickett's Charge, Battle of Gettysburg in 1863, Sainton, Charles Prosper (1861–1914)/Private Collection/BI; 169 (UP), Allan Pinkerton (1819–1884, seated on l), photo by Alexander Gardner/Photo © PVDE/BI; 169 (LO), Red Cloud Chief (1822–1909)/Private Collection/Peter Newark Western Americana/BI; 170 (UP), Sheridan's Ride, pub. L Prang & Co., 1886/Private Collection/The Stapleton Collection/BI; 170 (LO), Bettmann/GI; 171 (UP), Portrait of General William Tecumseh Sherman 1863/Universal History Archive/UIG/BI; 171 (LO), Campaign wagon/Siege Museum, Petersburg, VA, U.S.A./Photo © Civil War Archive/BI; 172 (UP), Lincoln's cabinet, pub. 1865/Private Collection/The Stapleton Collection/BI; 172 (LO), Leland Stanford/Private Collection/Peter Newark American Pictures/BI; 173, Buyenlarge/GI; 174, Holiday Crowd at Grand Central Terminal, New York City, ca 1920/© Royal Geographical Society, London, UK/BI; 175 (UP), Cadets of the American military academy West Point, 1929/© SZ Photo/Scherl/BI; 175 (LO), Walt Whitman, Brady, Mathew (1823–1896)/Private Collection/The Stapleton Collection/BI; 176 (LE), Confederate uniform jacket/Museum of the Confederacy, Richmond, VA, U.S.A./Photo © Civil War Archive/BI; 176 (CTR), Flag: 34 stars American, 1861–63, Forbes, Mrs. John E./© Collection of the New-York Historical Society, U.S.A./BI; 176 (UP RT), Federal officer's kepi/Gettysburg National Military Park Museum, Pennsylvania, U.S.A./Photo © Civil War Archive/BI; 176 (LO RT), Boots of Sergeant Charles Darling/Private Collection/Photo © Civil War Archive/BI; 177 (UP LE), The Battle of Antietam, 1862, Thulstrup, Thure de (1848–1930)/Private Collection/Peter Newark Military Pictures/BI; 177 (UP RT), The American Civil War Museum; 177 (CTR), Library of Congress/Public Domain; 177 (LO LE), Portrait of Thomas J. "Stonewall" Jackson/Private Collection/Peter Newark Military Pictures/BI; 177 (LO CTR), Mark Thiessen/NGC; 177 (LO RT), The American Civil War Museum. **CHAPTER 5:** 178–9, Branger/GI; 180, Bell Collection/NGC; 182 (UP), Stefano Bianchetti/GI; 182 (LO), Science & Society Picture Library/GI; 183 (UP), Galerie Bilderwelt/GI; 183 (LO), AFP/GI; 184 (LE), Portrait of Jane Addams, ca 1901/Private Collection/Prismatic Pictures/BI; 184 (RT), Front cover of Twenty Years at Hull House by Jane Addams, 1910/Newberry Library, Chicago, Illinois, U.S.A./BI; 185 (UP), Bettmann/GI; 185 (LO), Phonograph, by Thomas Alva Edison (1847–1931), U.S.A., 19th century/De Agostini Picture Library/BI; 186 (UP), Paul Thompson/GI; 186 (LO), Susan B. Anthony 1892/Universal History Archive/UIG/BI; 187 (UP), The New-York Historical Society/GI; 187 (LO), Bettmann/GI; 188 (UP), William Radcliffe/GI; 188 (LO), Bell telephone used by Queen Victoria at Osborne House, Isle of Wight, 1877–78/Science Museum, London, UK/BI; 189, Nebraska State Historical Society; 190, Bettmann/GI; 191 (UP), Andrew Carnegie (1835–1919)/Scottish National Portrait Gallery, Edinburgh, Scotland/BI; 191 (LO), Two Seated Women, Cassatt, Mary Stevenson (1844–1926)/Private Collection/BI; 192 (UP), The New-York Historical Society/GI; 192 (LO LE), The Stapleton Collection/Art Resource, NY; 192 (LO RT), Portrait of Colonel William Frederick Cody, also known as Buffalo Bill, Elliott & Fry Photography Studio/Archives Larousse, Paris, France/BI; 193, Wikimedia Commons/Public Domain; 194 (LE), Interim Archives/GI; 194 (RT), Mary Baker Eddy (1821–1910)/Private Collection/Peter Newark American Pictures/BI; 195, Sioux ghost dance, Baraldi, Severino (b. 1930)/Private Collection/© Look and Learn/BI; 196, Thomas Edison in his laboratory, 1906 Byron Company (fl. 1890–1942)/© Museum of the City of New York, U.S.A./BI; 197, Design Pics, Inc/NGC; 198 (UP), Print Collector/GI; 198 (LO LE), Ford Model T/Private Collection/© Look and Learn/

BI; 198 (LO RT), Ford/World History Archive/Universal History Archive/UIG/BI; 199 (UP), Library of Congress/digital version by Science Faction/GI; 199 (LO), Letter from James A Garfield/Private Collection/© Look and Learn/Illustrated Papers Collection/BI; 200 (LE), The U.S. National Archives and Records Administration; 200 (RT), Labor leaders Samuel Gompers, John Burns, and Holmes, 1893–94, Byron Company (fl. 1890–1942)/© Museum of the City of New York, U.S.A./BI; 201 (LE), Baseball World Series Player Award, designed by Gustave Fox Co., 1905/Private Collection/Photo © Christie's Images/BI; 201 (RT), Bettmann/GI; 202 (UP), New York Daily News Archive/GI; 202 (LO), Bettmann/GI; 203 (UP LE), Chicago History Museum/GI; 203 (UP RT), Poster advertising the boxing match between Jack Johnson and Jim Johnson, 1931, Gallice, Emi/Private Collection/BI; 203 (LO), Rykoff Collection/GI; 204 (LE), Courtesy Stacy A. Cordery; 204 (RT), Bettmann/GI; 205 (LE), Apic/GI; 205 (RT), ullstein bild/GI; 206, Library of Congress/GI; 207 (UP), Library of Congress Prints and Photographs Division/Public Domain; 207 (LO), Holt-Anderson Special Collections, University of the Pacific Library, © Muir-Hanna Trust; courtesy of the Oakland Museum of California; 208 (LE), Joseph H. Bailey/NGC; 208 (UP RT), Robert Peary (1856–1920), American Arctic explorer/© Look and Learn/Elgar Collection/BI; 208 (LO RT), Robert E. Peary Collection/NGC; 209 (UP), Bettmann/GI; 209 (LO), Rare Book and Special Collections Division, Library of Congress; 210 (LE), John D. Rockefeller Sr. (1839–1937)/Private Collection/BI; 210 (RT), George Enell/GI; 211 (UP), Courtesy iCollector.com; 211 (LO), Hulton Archive/GI; 212 (UP), GraphicaArtis/GI; 212 (LO), Upton Sinclair (photo)/Universal History Archive/UIG/BI; 213, Chief Spotted Elk, 1899 (oil on canvas), Burbank, Elbridge Ayer (1858–1949)/Butler Institute of American Art, Youngstown, OH, U.S.A./BI; 214 (UP), Archive Photos/GI; 214 (LO), Portrait of Elizabeth Cady Stanton/Universal History Archive/UIG/BI; 215 (LE), Bettmann/GI; 215 (RT), David Frent/GI; 216, Portrait of Nikola Tesla, 1890, by Sarony, Napoleon (1821–1896)/Private Collection/BI; 217 (UP), Photograph of Mark Twain/Private Collection/Ken Welsh/BI; 217 (CTR), Cover of Adventures of Huckleberry Finn by Mark Twain (1835–1910), first American edition, published by Charles L. Webster, 1885/The Stapleton Collection/BI; 217 (LO), The Mississippi in the Time of Peace, pub. by Currier and Ives, New York, 1865 by Palmer, Frances Flora Bond (Fanny)/© Museum of the City of New York, U.S.A./H. T. Peters Collection/BI; 218, MPI/GI; 219 (UP), ullstein bild/GI; 219 (LO), Transcendental Graphics/GI; 220 (UP), Bettmann/GI; 220 (LO), Bettmann/GI; 221 (UP), The Wright Brothers by Tacconi, Ferdinando (1922–2006)/Private Collection/© Look and Learn/BI; 221 (LO), Bettmann/GI; 222 (LE), Library of Congress/GI; 222 (RT), Edwin Levick/GI; 223 (UP), Hawkins/Topical Press Agency/GI; 223 (LO LE), Bettmann/GI; 223 (LO RT), FPG/GI. **CHAPTER 6:** 224–5, Bettmann/GI; 226, APA/GI; 228 (UP), GraphicaArtis/GI; 228 (LO), Transcendental Graphics/GI; 229 (UP), John D. Kisch/Separate Cinema Archive/GI; 229 (LO), Hulton Archive/GI; 230, Chicago History Museum/GI; 231 (UP), Time Life Pictures/GI; 231 (LO), John Springer Collection/GI; 232 (LE), Michael Nicholson/GI; 232 (RT), Donaldson Collection/GI; 233 (UP), Calvin Coolidge/Private Collection/© Look and Learn/Elgar Collection/BI; 233 (LO), Dr. George Washington Carver (1861–1943)/Private Collection/BI; 234, George Rinhart/GI; 235, Science Source/GI; 236 (LE), Mondadori Portfolio/GI; 236 (RT), Cecil B. DeMille's Cleopatra, 1934/Private Collection/Photo © Christie's Images/BI; 237 (LE), Walter Elias Disney (1901–1966)/BI; 237 (RT), GI; 238, Portrait of William Edward Burghardt "W. E. B." Du Bois/Private Collection/Prismatic Pictures/BI; 239 (UP), Science & Society Picture Library/GI; 239 (CTR LE), GI; 239 (CTR RT), Courtesy iCollector.com; 239 (LO), Buffalo Bill Center of the West, gift of Carl Dunrud; 240 (UP), Popperfoto/GI; 240 (LO), Courtesy Terry Heffernan; 241 (UP), Dwight D. Eisenhower as president of Columbia University, on the front cover of Life magazine, 17th April 1950/Private Collection/Peter Newark American Pictures/BI; 241 (LO LE), "I like Ike" election badge/Private Collection/Peter Newark American Pictures/BI; 241 (LO RT), New York Daily News Archive/GI; 242 (LE), Bettmann/GI; 242 (RT), Charles Peterson/GI; 243 (UP LE), Front cover for the first edition of The Great Gatsby by F. Scott Fitzgerald, 1925/Private Collection/Photo © Christie's Images/BI; 243 (UP RT), Portrait of F. Scott Fitzgerald, 1930/Private Collection/© Leemage/BI; 243 (LO), Bettmann/GI; 244 (UP), CBS Photo Archive/GI; 244 (LO), Hulton Archive/GI; 245 (UP), Books/Private Collection/Photo © Christie's Images/BI; 245 (LO), Earl Theisen Collection/GI; 246 (UP), Fred Stein Archive/GI; 246 (LO), PhotoQuest/GI; 247, New York Daily News Archive/GI; 248 (UP), Portrait of Helen Keller smelling a rose/Private Collection/Prismatic Pictures/BI; 248 (LO), Camerique Archive/GI; 249 (UP), Sinclair Lewis, 1935/© SZ Photo/Knorr & Hirth/BI; 249 (LO), Universal History Archive/GI; 250 (UP), Huey P. Long, U.S. senator from Louisiana and former Louisiana governor/Circa Images/BI; 250 (LO LE), Bettmann/GI; 250 (LO RT), ullstein bild/GI; 251, American general Douglas MacArthur on front page of the Illustrated, September 22, 1945/Photo © Tallandier/BI; 252, Bettmann/GI; 253 (UP), Bettmann/GI; 253 (LO), Bettmann/GI; 254 (UP), Edward R. Murrow (1908–1965)/J. T. Vintage/BI; 254 (LO), Front Cover for "The 'Jelly Roll' Blues," by Jelly Roll Morton/Private Collection/Peter Newark American Pictures/BI; 255 (LE), Alfred Eisenstaedt/GI; 255 (RT), 'We can do it!', c.1942, Miller, J. Howard (1918–2004)/Private Collection/Peter Newark American Pictures/BI; 256 (UP), Bettmann/GI; 256 (LO), Dorothy Parker (1893–1967) American poet c. 1945/BI; 257 (UP LE), General George Patton/© SZ Photo/Scherl/BI; 257 (UP RT),

Movie Poster Image Art/GI; 257 (LO), Bettmann/GI; 258 (UP), PhotoQuest/GI; 258 (LO), Bojan Brecelj/GI; 259 (UP), Poster advertising 'Ringling Brothers and Barnum & Bailey Combined Circus," ca 1938/Private Collection/DaTo Images/BI; 259 (LO), Bettmann/GI; 260 (UP), Courtesy of the Franklin D. Roosevelt Presidential Library, Hyde Park, NY; 260 (LO), Eleanor Roosevelt and the Queen, Washington, D.C., 1939/Underwood Archives/UIG/BI; 261 (UP), President Franklin D. Roosevelt, ca 1941/Private Collection/Peter Newark American Pictures/BI; 261 (CTR), Election campaign poster featuring President Franklin D. Roosevelt, 1941/Private Collection/Peter Newark American Pictures/BI; 261 (LO), Courtesy of the Franklin D. Roosevelt Presidential Library, Hyde Park, NY; 262 (UP), Iconic Archive/GI; 262 (CTR), National Museum of American History; 262 (LO), Courtesy of Goldin Auctions; 263, Bettmann/GI; 264 (UP), Margaret Sanger, ca 1930, Underwood & Underwood/Private Collection/BI; 264 (LO), John D. Kisch/Separate Cinema Archive/GI; 265 (UP), Portrait of Ida B. Wells Barnett/Private Collection/Prismatic Pictures/BI; 265 (LO), El Dorado/Photo © Collection CSFF/BI; 266 (UP), Stock Montage/GI; 266 (LO), Frank Lloyd Wright (1867–1959) American architect, 1956/BI; 267 (LE), Richard Nowitz/NGC; 267 (RT), An oak spindle high-back side chair, ca 1900, Wright, Frank Lloyd (1867–1959)/Private Collection/Photo © Christie's Images/BI; 268 (LE), Science & Society Picture Library/GI; 268 (RT), Migrant worker in the American Great Depression, 1939/Universal History Archive/UIG/BI; 269 (UP LE), Camps of the Civilian Conservation Corps, 1933/© SZ Photo/Scherl/BI; 269 (UP RT), Orange pickers' camp in Tulare County, California, 1938/The Stapleton Collection/BI; 269 (LO), Work troop of a work-creation program during the time of the New Deal/© SZ Photo/Scherl/BI. **CHAPTER 7:** 270–71, Neil A. Armstrong/NASA/GI; 272, Francis Miller/GI; 274 (UP), Jack Birns/GI; 274 (LO), GAB Archive/GI; 275, Larry Burrows/GI; 276, Neil A. Armstrong/Space Frontiers/GI; 277 (UP), NASA/GI; 277 (LO), Popperfoto/GI; 278 (UP), Peter Turnley/GI; 278 (LO), Silver Screen Collection/GI; 279, Carl Iwasaki/GI; 280, Derek Berwin/GI; 281 (UP), Hulton Archive/GI; 281 (LO), Alfred Eisenstaedt/GI; 282, James Earl "Jimmy" Carter (b. 1924) ca 1977/Private Collection/Peter Newark American Pictures/BI; 283, Cathy Murphy/GI; 284, Don Hogan Charles/GI; 285 (UP), Steve Pyke/GI; 285 (LO), Hulton Archive/GI; 286 (UP), David Redfern/GI; 286 (LO), Invisible Man by Ralph Ellison (1914–1994), published by Random House, New York, 1952/Private Collection/Photo © Christie's Images/BI; 287 (UP), Bettmann/GI; 287 (LO), David Montgomery/GI; 288, Bettmann/GI; 289 (LE), Feminist Betty Friedan, United States, 1960/Underwood Archives/UIG/BI; 289 (RT), Bettmann/GI; 290 (UP), Billy Graham ad for The Star/Private Collection/© Look and Learn/Elgar Collection/BI; 290 (LO), Billy Graham, 1966, Scott-Stewart, Dick (1948–2002)/Private Collection/BI; 291, MPI/GI; 292, Mikki Ansin/GI; 293, Joseph Scherschel/GI; 294, Bettmann/GI; 295 (UP), Alfred Eisenstaedt/GI; 295 (LO), "President Is Killed," front page of the Chicago Daily News, 22nd November 1963/Private Collection/Peter Newark American Pictures/BI; 296 (LE), Bill Eppridge/GI; 296 (RT), Lawrence Schiller/GI; 297, Robert W. Kelley/GI; 298, Derek Hudson/GI; 299 (LE), Richard Saunders/GI; 299 (RT), Movie Poster Image Art/GI; 300, Bachrach/GI; 301 (UP), Hank Walker/GI; 301 (LO), Ralph Crane/GI; 302 (UP), Bettmann/GI; 302 (LO), Alfred Eisenstaedt/GI; 303, Gene Forte/GI; 304, Jesse Owens at Broad Jumping (b/w photo)/© SZ Photo/Scherl/BI; 305 (UP), William Philpott/GI; 305 (LO), American saxophonist and jazz composer Charlie Parker (1920–1955), 1947/BI; 306 (LE), RB/GI; 306 (RT), Astrid Stawiarz/GI; 307 (UP), Artist Norman Rockwell, Stockbridge, MA, ca 1959/Underwood Archives/UIG/BI; 307 (LO LE), Bettmann/GI; 307 (LO RT), Michael Ochs Archives/GI; 308, Heritage Images/GI; 309 (UP LE), Central Press/GI; 309 (LO LE), National Archives—JFK/GI; 309 (RT), PhotoQuest/GI; 310 (UP), Jean-Regis Roustan/GI; 310 (LO), Paul Sequeira/GI; 311, Yale Joel/GI; 312, Bettmann/GI; 313 (LE), Fototeca Storica Nazionale/GI; 313 (UP RT), Ralph Crane/GI; 313 (LO RT), NASA/GI; 314 (LE), Bettmann/GI; 314 (RT), MPI/GI; 315 (UP), Waring Abbott/GI; 315 (LO), Archivio Cameraphoto Epoche/GI; 316 (LE), Fred W. McDarrah/GI; 316 (RT), Wally McNamee/GI; 317 (UP LE), Underwood Archives/GI; 317 (UP RT), Archive Photos/GI; 317 (LO LE), The Washington Post/GI; 317 (LO RT), Bettmann/GI. **CHAPTER 8:** 318–9, Chip Somodevilla/GI; 320, Bill Ray/GI; 322 (UP), Bloomberg/GI; 322 (LO), AFP/GI; 323, NASA/GI; 325 (UP), Ben A. Pruchnie/GI; 325 (LO), AFP/GI; 326 (UP), Jessica Antola/GI; 326 (LO), Focus On Sport/GI; 327 (UP), Bill Pugliano/GI; 327 (LO), Cynthia Johnson/GI; 328, Stock Montage/GI; 329, Justin Sullivan/GI; 330 (UP), Ted Thai/GI; 330 (LO), ullstein bild/GI; 331 (UP), Robyn Beck/GI; 331 (LO), Bettmann/GI; 332, Lynn Goldsmith/GI; 333 (UP), Fabrice Coffrini/GI; 333 (LO), Dirck Halstead/GI; 334 (UP), John G. Mabanglo/GI; 334 (LO LE), NASA/Public Domain; 334 (LO RT), Future Publishing/GI; 335, Walter Iooss Jr./NBA Photos/GI; 336 (UP), Bob Martin/Allsport/GI; 336 (LO), Darren Hauck/GI; 337, Bob Daemmrich/GI; 338, Photo by Pete Souza/The White House via GI; 339, Marc Hauser Photography Ltd./GI; 340 (UP), © Les Stone/The Image Works; 340 (LO), Harry Langdon/GI; 341, AFP/GI; 342 (UP), Robert Alexander/GI; 342 (LO), Dan MacMedan/GI; 343 (UP), Sarah Rice/GI; 343 (LO), Amy Sussman/GI; 344, Julian Finney/GI; 345 (UP), Boston Globe/GI; 345 (LO), Marc Serota/GI; 346 (UP), Kevin Winter/GI; 346 (LO), Jim Wilson/The New York Times/Redux Pictures; 347, Bloomberg/GI; 348 (UP LE), 8393/GI; 348 (LO LE), Ira Block/NGC; 348 (RT), Stan Honda/AFP/GI; 349 (UP), Robert Giroux/GI; 349 (LO LE), Design Pics, Inc./NGC; 349 (LO RT), Ira Block/NGC.

INDEX

◇◇◇◇◇◇◇◇◇

Boldface indicates illustrations.

ACKNOWLEDGMENTS

Special thanks to the NGP book team for its dedicated work in pulling together this complicated volume: Barbara Payne, project editor; Sanaa Akkach, art director; Matt Propert, illustrations editor; and Michelle Harris, researcher. Appreciation also to Linda Makarov, who helped complete production design.

Since 1888, the National Geographic Society has funded more than 12,000 research, exploration, and preservation projects around the world. National Geographic Partners distributes a portion of the funds it receives from your purchase to National Geographic Society to support programs including the conservation of animals and their habitats.

National Geographic Partners
1145 17th Street NW
Washington, DC 20036-4688 USA

Become a member of National Geographic and activate your benefits today at natgeo.com/jointoday.

For information about special discounts for bulk purchases, please contact National Geographic Books Special Sales: specialsales@natgeo.com
For rights or permissions inquiries, please contact National Geographic Books Subsidiary Rights: bookrights@natgeo.com

Library of Congress Cataloging-in-Publication Data

Names: Kostyal, K. M., 1951- author. | Thompson, John M. (John Milliken), 1959- author. | Gray, William R., 1946- author. | National Geographic Society (U.S.)
Title: Who's who in American history : leaders, visionaries, and icons who shaped our nation.
Description: Washington, D.C. : National Geographic, 2017. | Includes bibliographical references and index.
Identifiers: LCCN 2017011905| ISBN 9781426218347 (hardcover : alk. paper) | ISBN 9781426219047 (deluxe : alk. paper)
Subjects: LCSH: United States--Biography--Encyclopedias. | United States--History--Encyclopedias.
Classification: LCC CT213 .K67 2017 | DDC 920.073--dc23
LC record available at: https://lccn.loc.gov/2017011905

Printed in Hong Kong

17/THK/1

MORE GREAT PEOPLE
MORE GREAT PLACES

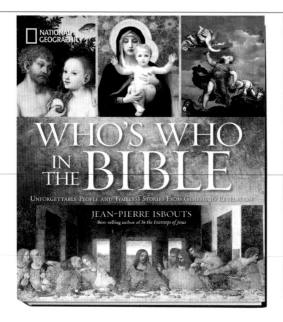

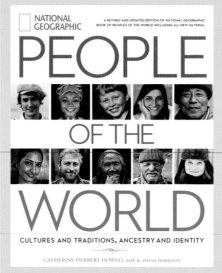

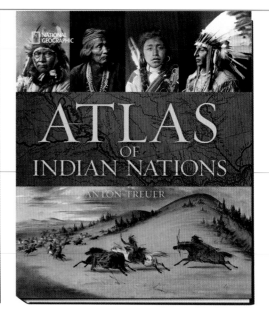